Lives of the Laureates

Lives of the Laureates

Eighteen Nobel Economists

Fourth Edition

Edited by William Breit and Barry T. Hirsch

The MIT Press
Cambridge, Massachusetts
London, England

This book was set in Sabon by Achorn Graphic Services, Inc., and was printed and bound in the United States of America.

Library of Congress Cataloging-in-Publication Data

Lives of the laureates: eighteen Nobel economists—4th ed./William Breit and Barry T. Hirsch, editors.
   p. cm.
Includes bibliographical references.
ISBN 0-262-02562-0 (hc: alk. paper)
1. Economist—Biography. 2. Nobel Prizes—Biography. I. Title: Nobel economists. II. Breit, William. III. Hirsch, Barry T., 1949–

HB76.L58   2004
330′.092′2—dc22
[B]

2003066580

10   9   8   7   6   5   4   3   2   1

Contents

Introduction to the Fourth Edition

This book consists of autobiographical accounts of the careers of eighteen people who have three qualities in common. First, they are all economists. Second, each of them has been awarded the Alfred Nobel Memorial Prize in Economic Science. Third, each traveled to San Antonio, Texas, to deliver his story in person at Trinity University.

The Nobel Prize in Economics was not created by Alfred Nobel himself. In 1901 his will established prizes in physics, chemistry, medicine or physiology, literature, and peace. He wished to reward specific achievements rather than outstanding persons. In the case of the natural sciences, the awards were to be given for "discoveries," "inventions," and "improvements." In 1968 the Central Bank of Sweden, in connection with its tercentenary celebration, initiated a new award, the Central Bank of Sweden Prize in Economic Science in Memory of Alfred Nobel. This prize was to be granted in conformity with the standards that governed the awarding of the original Nobel prizes. According to the rules established by the Central Bank of Sweden, the "Prize shall be awarded annually to a person who has carried out a work in economic science of the eminent significance expressed in the will of Alfred Nobel."[1]

The idea for a series of autobiographical lectures by Nobel laureates in economics was that of the senior editor, who has spent a good part of his academic career studying, teaching, and writing about the lives and ideas of leading contemporary American economists.[2] This abiding interest in the relationship between biography and the creative process led naturally to the thought of providing a forum in which outstanding economists would express in their own words, in any way that seemed congenial, a personal memoir under the general rubric "My Evolution as an Economist." At the very least such a forum would preserve part of the rich record of accomplishment that helped to shape the direction and character of economic science in the post–World War II era. But the larger purpose was to provide important source material for a theory of scientific discovery.

Little is known about the process by which original ideas are germinated and eventually accepted by one's peers. To what extent is the substance of scientific work in social science a reflection of the lives of those who produced it? What is the role of influential teachers and colleagues? To what extent are the problems that these thinkers addressed a result of their own backgrounds and the economic and social problems of their times? What forces were most responsible for leading them to their insights? In short, what is it that enables an individual to discover something that seizes and holds the attention of a large segment of a scientific community? To help answer such questions was the major rationale behind the series.

But whom to invite? It was clear that budgetary and time constraints would limit the number of invitations, and so the roster was restricted in the following ways: (1) only economists who served on the faculties of American universities at the time the Nobel Prize was awarded would be included; and (2) the roster would represent as many different facets of economics in terms of types of contributions, specific areas, methods of analysis, and ideological differences as possible. This meant that only one member of a team of co-recipients of the prize would be invited. In 1983, when the program was being planned, there were twelve winners of the Nobel Prize who met the first criterion, although one was too ill to travel. A difficult winnowing process in accordance with the second criterion narrowed the final list to eight. To our pleasant surprise, only one invitee declined to participate.

The autobiographical lectures that made up the first edition of this volume were presented at Trinity University during the 1984–85 academic year. The success of the project encouraged us to ask then-President Ronald Calgaard to allow the series to continue. An economist himself, President Calgaard quickly agreed. Each October after the Nobel Prize in Economics was awarded in Stockholm, an invitation was to be sent to a newly minted American economics laureate to present an autobiographical lecture.

During the three years immediately following the end of the original series, a trio of Americans was honored with the Alfred Nobel Memorial Prize in Economic Science: Franco Modigliani of MIT in 1985, James M. Buchanan of George Mason University in 1986, and Robert M. Solow of MIT in 1987. Each of them accepted the request to present a lecture in which he would chart the route that led him to the highest accolade a scholar can receive. These lectures were included in the second edition of *Lives of the Laureates,* published in 1990.

Economists at American universities continued to receive the Nobel Prize. The third edition, published in 1995, included Trinity University lectures by William F. Sharpe (co-recipient in 1990), Ronald H. Coase (1991), and Douglass C. North (co-recipient in 1993). This fourth edition of *Lives of the Laureates* includes five new Trinity University lectures: John C. Harsanyi (co-recipient in 1994), Myron S. Scholes (co-recipient in 1997), Gary S. Becker (1992), Robert E. Lucas (1995), and James J. Heckman (co-recipient in 2000).

For most of the laureates, the assignment has been a difficult one. There is an understandable reluctance to give a public talk about one's own intellectual contributions. As one of the invitees put it, "I do not know that I could keep it between the Scylla of false modesty and the Charybdis of boastfulness, and I am afraid I would find the whole business rather stressful." Moreover, most of their work in its professional formulation was technical in nature, closed off to those not trained as economists. Yet each was being asked to make his contribution accessible to a lay audience at a public lecture open to the whole community. This provided greater difficulties for some than for others. Samuelson's and Arrow's scientific contributions are largely in the domain of mathematical economics. Klein and Heckman, among others, make heavy use of statistical techniques and econometrics. All the Nobel economists express themselves in the technical vocabulary of their discipline.

And yet in each instance, as the reader of these pages will discover, each speaker somehow managed to convey the nature and significance of his contributions. (The essays in this book are in the order in which they were presented in the Trinity lecture series.) It is hard to imagine a less painful way of grasping the essentials of Kenneth J. Arrow's "impossibility theorem" than hearing it (or reading about it) in his own words. And is there anywhere a more clearly presented conception of what goes into econometric "model building" than is to be found in Lawrence R. Klein's essay? George J. Stigler's masterful explanation of his "information theory" is made clear and understandable to almost everyone with an interest in this fruitful innovation. Ronald Coase's profound contributions to the theory of the firm and law and economics are made luminously visible. Indeed, each participant achieved the goal of clarity without sacrificing inherently difficult content.

The visit of each of the Nobel laureates was an unqualified success. The audiences were large and appreciative. Some traveled considerable distances to attend. Each economist met with students and faculty informally. At small receptions, at restaurants, over coffee, and at dinners in private homes, students and faculty were able to talk with some of the most highly regarded economists of the twentieth century. Notwithstanding their formidable reputations as scholars and, in some instances, as strong personalities, their lack of arrogance impressed almost everyone who came into contact with them. An important side benefit of the lecture series was the lesson that some of the most illustrious figures of modern economics are human after all.

Looking back over these lectures, one is struck by the many currents within the stream of modern economics. The reader will find that paths cross in unexpected ways; that disparate thinkers were often influenced by the same teachers; that luck as well as perseverance and hard work play a role in the successful creation of scientific knowledge. Equally important, these autobiographical essays reveal psychological truths, perhaps hidden from the subjects themselves, that an especially perceptive reader will discern. Taken as a whole, they provide a comprehensive picture of the diverseness, richness, and profundity that is the hallmark of contemporary economic thought in America.

Apart from an afterword by the editors, this edition of *Lives of the Laureates* ends with James J. Heckman's lecture, delivered in March 2003. The Trinity University series, however, is an ongoing enterprise. Readers who would like to follow subsequent presentations in the series can visit our Web site at <http://www.trinity.edu/nobel>. The site provides a chronology of lectures in the series, plus selected quotations from each laureate's presentation at Trinity University.

Prior to the third edition, two of the laureates in the series had passed from the scene, W. Arthur Lewis, who inaugurated the series in 1984, and George J. Stigler. Both died in 1991. It is sad to record that three additional laureates have died since the previous edition, John C. Harsanyi in 2000, James Tobin in 2002, and Franco Modigliani in 2003. This edition is dedicated to their memory.

Acknowledgments

As scarcely needs saying, an enterprise of this kind requires the cooperation of many people. Our thanks, first and foremost, go to Trinity University. Former President Ronald Calgaard not only provided generous funding but also threw in a large measure of encouragement from the moment the idea for the lecture series was broached. Since 2000, President John Brazil has continued the University's strong support for the series. The precedent initiated by Dr. Calgaard in hosting a dinner at his campus home prior to each lecture has been graciously continued by Dr. Brazil. The dinner is a perfect prologue to each Nobel economist's public lecture.

For this edition, like the previous ones, we owe much to colleagues in the Department of Economics at Trinity University for their enthusiasm and cooperation. Special mention should be made of our colleague Roger Spencer, co-editor of the first three volumes, who helped in establishing the lecture series and in editing the previous editions. It is a pleasure to acknowledge debt to our assistants, Ann Bonin and Rande Spector, for their skillful management of the many tasks and arrangements that accompany such an enterprise.

Throughout all editions of this volume we have appreciated the encouragement and support provided by the MIT Press, in particular senior editor Elizabeth Murry. Meticulous and thoughtful editing by Deborah Cantor-Adams led to a much-improved volume.

Finally, thanks are due to the Nobel economists themselves, who not only accepted the challenge of trying to make their chief contributions intelligible to a lay audience but did so in the demanding context of an autobiographical format. Their insights deepened our perspectives and broadened our understanding of the relationship between autobiography and creativity. For that, and for their kind patience and cooperation at all stages of the project, we are grateful.

William Breit
Barry T. Hirsch

Lives of the Laureates

W. Arthur Lewis

I had never meant to be an economist. My father had wanted me to be a lawyer, but as he died when I was seven he had no vote at the appropriate time. That came when I was awarded the St. Lucia government scholarship in 1932, tenable at any British university. I did not want to be a doctor either, nor a teacher. That put me into a hole, since law, medicine, preaching, and teaching were the only professions open to young blacks in my day. I wanted to be an engineer, but neither the colonial government nor the sugar plantations would hire a black engineer. What to do? My mother, without whom I could not have gone so far, would support whatever I might choose. As I leafed through the University of London prospectus, my eye was caught by something called the Bachelor of Commerce degree, which offered accounting, statistics, business law, business management, economics, a foreign language, and economic history. What was this economics? I had never heard of it before, and nobody in St. Lucia knew what it was—though my sample was small and unrepresentative. No matter. The rest of the degree was very practical and would give me a basis for a job in business or some kind of administrative work. So I settled for this and went off to London for the B.Com. degree in 1933, at the age of eighteen.

At the London School of Economics it turned out that I was good at economics, so when I graduated with a first in 1937 I was given an LSE scholarship to do a Ph.D. in economics. Next year I was appointed for one year as a teaching assistant and the year after that became an assistant lecturer. Years of wondering how I would ever earn a living, and of smiling confidently when friends and relatives pushed the question at me, could now be forgotten. I was going to be an economist.

Though ignorant of economics, I knew what was meant by administration. I had left school in 1929 and had been a junior clerk in the government service for the intervening four years. There I had acquired the clerical skills—to type, make notes, write letters, and file—that helped me as an undergraduate. I became familiar as well with administrative and legal structures, knowledge that would also help me.

Also, of course, I earned some money (three pounds a month) to contribute to the family budget. My mother was unsurpassed in the ways of stretching income, and this, combined with loving care, was what enabled her to bring up five sons, who were all minors when she was widowed. (I was the fourth son.) My mother's story is standard in the life history of achievers. A widow with young children, very little money, an immigrant (my father and she were immigrants from Antigua), the highest integrity, unshakable courage, unlimited faith in God. As a youngster in school, I would hear other boys talking about the superiority of men over women; I used to think that they must be crazy.

I had left school because I had completed the curriculum at the level of the Cambridge School Certificate, which is equivalent to SAT. I had completed at fourteen because when I was six I had had some kind of infection that kept me out of school for three months. My father, a former teacher but at this stage a customs official, said to me, "Don't worry; I will teach you a little every day, so you will not fall behind." This was an understatement. Any intelligent child receiving personal tutoring every day will learn in three months as much as the schoolteacher's class learns in two years. When I returned to school, I was moved up two grades and was still ahead of what was being taught. This was a traumatic experience. It meant that for the rest of my school life I was always in the company of boys two or three years older than myself. They flexed their muscles, but I had nothing to show. They played cricket in the first eleven, whereas I was in the fourth eleven. I acquired an acute inferiority complex with regard to my physique. I learned that acceptance into the group is not a matter of academic performance only: you must meet their criteria as well as your own. I matured faster than I would have done had I stayed in school. I went to England apprehensive that the English eighteen-year-olds would be much better able to handle themselves than I was, only to find that they were not.

Fate had decided that I was to be an economist. What kind of economist I was to be was also settled: an applied economist. This did not mean just that I should apply economics to industrial or other structural problems. It meant that I would approach a problem from its institutional background, recognizing that the solution was as likely to be in the institutional setting as in the economic analysis.

What part of applied economics I would work in was also settled for me, since my assistant lectureship was in the commerce department, under Professor Sir Arnold Plant. He was my mentor, and without his word at crucial points I would have received neither the scholarship nor the assistant lectureship. (This was the school's first black appointment, and there was a little resistance.) He and I had intellectual difficulties, since he was a laissez-faire economist and I was not; but this did not stand in the way of our relationship.

Because Plant was a specialist in the organization of British industry, he put me to lecture in this field and suggested a Ph.D. thesis topic in the field; and so I became an "expert" on British industrial organization. I liked the subject, so it was no hardship to me.

LSE in the 1930s was (as at any other time) a very lively place. Every point of view was represented on the faculty, and as two or three competing courses of lectures were offered on each "hot" topic, those who understood what was going on had marvelous intellectual feasts. The typical high-achieving LSE student was bright, from the effort to keep up with so many conflicting themes, and skeptical, from learning to distinguish so continually between plausibility and truth. We were reputed to make excellent managers but poor parliamentarians.

The school had not quite caught up with Keynesianism, which was taught by the young lecturers but denounced by the big names. On the other hand, the school was in the forefront of the development and worldwide expansion of neoclassical economics, especially with John Hicks, Roy Allen, Nicholas Kaldor, Friedrich Hayek, and Lionel Robbins.

This was where what I was doing fitted in. Most of the writing in this area was concerned with elaborating the theory: turning words into diagrams and diagrams into equations. I was one of a minority engaged in testing the theories against the facts.

I worked in industrial organization from 1937, when I was given a scholarship for the purpose, until 1948, when I went to Manchester and later published *Overhead Costs,* which was essentially an updated version of my Ph.D. thesis.

My interest in overhead costs was the structure of prices in situations where average cost per unit exceeds marginal cost. The Pareto rule was that price should equal marginal cost, but to apply this rule would bankrupt the firm. In practice, such situations oscillate between bankruptcy and monopoly, as in the airline industry today. The general inclination of economists in those cases was to enforce marginal pricing and subsidize firms to the extent of the differences between marginal and average cost. This was hardly practical, as an industry-wide policy. Neither could it be justified, as many taxpayers would be forced to pay for services that they did not use. If one started from the premise that those who use the service should pay for it, the problem reduced to how to spread the fixed costs among the users. Here I started from the railway principle of "charging what the traffic will bear" and linked up with the new price discrimination theory, as elaborated by Joan Robinson.

Another aspect of overhead costs was the time dimension. Demand was not steady, but fluctuated. If the output could not be stored, there would be times of idle capacity, regular or irregular; how was the cost of this to be shared? I demonstrated that the correct approach to this problem was to treat the fixed investment as a producer in joint cost of different outputs at different times, each paying what it could bear, and subject to the sum of payments not exceeding total cost.

The main point of my thesis was, therefore, to examine in the light of these approaches to overhead costs those price systems found in industry other than the simple unit price per unit of output. These included two-part tariffs, time-of-day pricing, quantity discounts, loyalty discounts, and such related systems as trading stamps and tied purchases. My interest also overlapped into the history of the laws relating to pricing. With the spread of price regulation in Britain over the next twenty years my book had a ready-made audience.

This analysis of industrial structure was the background to what I was writing in my spare time, so to speak, which included a small book called the *Principles of Economic Planning,* published in 1949. The Fabian

Society is one hundred years old this year. It is the thinking arm of the British Labour Party, though in fact it is older than the Labour Party and quite independent of it. I went to one of its conferences in 1947 and was roundly abused for a paper I read on the importance of avoiding inflation and on the measures required for that outcome. I in my turn was horrified by the sentiments of the members on this subject and said to the secretary: "You really ought to commission a study on the problems and pitfalls of administering a mixed economy." "Why don't you do it," he said, and after thinking about the subject for a little time I agreed to do so.

Fabian pamphlets usually run from twenty to thirty pages, but this one came out at more than one hundred pages, not because of my long-windedness but because it takes at least that to discuss in detail how to run a mixed economy. The book was not original, but it was timely. It addressed itself exclusively to the problems of Great Britain in the year 1948, but nonetheless was translated into several languages and sold widely all over the world. Its prescriptions for evading inflation were Keynesian and turned on the feasibility of keeping money incomes rising at not more than 3 percent a year. On rereading the book recently for this occasion, the only other point that catches my eye is that governments of mixed economies, coming into power on a wave of popular frustration, always run straight onto the rocks of the balance of payments and have to reverse themselves (for example, France in 1936 and 1981; Britain in 1945; Jamaica in 1976). Somebody should write a manual called something like "The First Two Years," which would map the problems by which the mixed economy is assailed as a new social democratic government moves to implement its program. But that will have to be some other author.

Let me come back to my academic program. I gather that the sponsors of this set of lectures hope to see how one's thinking is tied to one's environment. I am not a very good example. I began by showing you that I became an economist when I really wanted to be an engineer, became a university teacher because there was nothing else for me to do, and became an applied economist because that was my mentor's subject. The next phase of this story continues in the same vein. I am not complaining; fate has been kinder to me than to most other persons. I am merely recording what happened.

I dropped industrial economics in 1945 to teach another subject not of my own choosing, namely a survey of the world economy between the two wars. This came about in the following way. The acting chairman of the economics department in 1945 was Friedrich Hayek. One day he said to me, "We fill up our students with trade cycle theory and explanations of the Great Depression, but the entering class was born in 1927, cannot remember the depression, and has no idea what we are talking about. Why don't you give a course of lectures on what happened between the wars?" "The answer to your question," I said, "is very easy. It is that I myself have no idea what happened between the wars." "Well," said Hayek, "the best way to learn a subject is to teach it." So that was how I came some four years later to publish a small book entitled *Economic Survey 1919–1939,* summarizing what we then thought we knew about the world economy between 1919 and 1939.

Nowadays we would see this as a job for an econometrician, but econometrics had not yet established the despotism over economics that it wields today. Tinbergen had pointed the way, with his model of the British economy before the wars, but indicated only the general direction. Also, the figures for the 1920s were sparse and those for the 1930s only slightly less so. I had hoped to get cues by reading the economics literature of the time, especially the financial weeklies, but they yielded next to nothing. We use language differently today. Economists pepper their sentences with percentages and billions, even in the daily newspaper, and even the lay reader is expected to keep a personal computer in his head that enables him to jump from one measurement to another. Prewar economists spoke of "many" or "a few" or "some" and avoided figures.

Looking back, I feel that I was more successful in treating the Great Depression of the 1930s than the alleged prosperity of the 1920s. The Americans persuaded themselves that the American economy was more prosperous than ever before in the second half of the 1920s, but this is not borne out by the statistics, which reveal only average performance. Dazzled by this misconception, one tended to see prosperity all over the world in the 1920s and to underrate the comparative stagnation of world trade and the effects of that stagnation. Staple industrial products were in surplus supply, especially textiles, steel, ships, and coal, creating for

Britain, Germany, Japan, and India pools of unemployment in industrial centers. The economists of the day saw the troubles mostly in terms of inappropriate exchange rates; we would call this structural unemployment and seek more activist remedies. My book neither asked nor answered why the ten years following the end of World War I would lead into a great depression while the ten years following World War II would lead to unprecedented prosperity. Part of the answer has to be that the world economy was more unstable in the second half of the 1920s than it was in the first half of the 1950s.

Paradoxically, the Great Depression of the 1930s was easier to untangle. The first question to be avoided was, What caused the depression? Our large bundle of trade cycle theories offered a wide range of possible causes, each of which was sufficient, though it might not be necessary. One might as well fight an octopus as proceed along these lines.

My approach was to accept that industrial recessions had occurred from time to time over the preceding century with intervals of four to ten years, and that the problem was not why there was a recession in 1929, but why, having started, it had become so deep. What distinguished the outbreak of this particular sequence? One cannot give an account of the Great Depression in two paragraphs, but one can list the decisive elements. These are seven.

1. In the U.S. economy prosperity coincided with a railway-construction-immigration-housing cycle. Congress having restricted immigration from 1924, the construction boom of the second half of the 1920s was weak, and the abnormal weakness of the first half of the thirties weakened the whole economy.

2. Both domestic and international agricultural prices had been falling since the mid-1920s, capacity having grown faster than demand. Rural consumption was low, and in the United States an abnormal number of rural banks failed.

3. Monetary and fiscal authorities believed that the best way to revive production was to reduce the flow of income and acted accordingly. This action presumably worsened the depression.

4. The industrial slump was as bad in Germany as in the United States. The weakness of the one compounded the weakness of the other.

5. Capitalists everywhere lost confidence and reduced their investment flows. This spiraled. Less investment meant less production, less income, more excess capacity, less investment, and so on.

6. The New York Stock Exchange, which had talked itself into overconfidence in the late twenties, now talked itself down and reflected all the unpleasantness occurring elsewhere.

7. One country after another left the gold standard, imposed exchange controls, and raised tariff levels. International trade fell by 30 percent in volume.

Such a list as this does not show the relative magnitude of these elements, their sequences, or their interrelationships: that is the econometrician's job. It serves only my immediate purpose, which was to show that it was not strange that there was a great depression in 1929, since so many weaknesses came together at that point.

Publication of the book still left two questions unanswered in my mind, on which I would spend a good part of my academic life. The first of these is what determines the terms of trade between industrial and primary products. This question was central to the book, in that the weakness of agricultural prices communicated itself throughout the economy increasingly after 1925, bankrupting farmers, bringing down banks, and forcing countries off the gold standard. But the question was also central to my life, since my home country was subject to violent swings in agricultural prices that played havoc with attempts to manage the economy with some stability.

My subsequent work on the terms of trade started from the observation that there was a constant relationship between an index of world industrial production and an index of world trade in primary products. This relationship said that a 1 percent rise in industrial production was associated with about 0.87 percent rise in world trade in primary products. This relationship extended all the way back to 1873 and all the way forward to 1973, though it did not hold before 1873. In the process I made and published indexes of world industrial production, world trade in manufactures and in primary products, and prices of tropical products and of manufactures back to 1870, in some cases to 1850.

On the theoretical side the short-run determinants of the terms of trade must be demand and supply. One could model and calculate the short-run elasticities for various groups of commodities. The long-run terms for tropical crops, I have suggested (in the model that I will reach in a moment), are determined by the infinite elasticity of supply of tropical produce, and therefore are not affected by changes in demand. Infinite elasticity springs from the fact that agricultural exports are a small part of tropical agriculture output—under 20 percent—and can in the long run (say, over twenty years) be expanded or contracted at constant cost. That cost is very small, since the yield in food cultivation is very small. This analysis has momentous consequences, for it means that the farmers would do better to grow more food than to put resources into more export crops. This controversy is still heated.

Now I come to the second question left over from my book on 1919–1939. As soon as one started to work on the Great Depression, one was faced by the question whether this was a unique event that had never happened before or whether this was merely one of a series. I worked on this subject off and on from 1950 until publishing my book *Growth and Fluctuations 1870–1913* in 1978. This long period results from my nine years of absence from university study and partly from the labor performed in collecting and preparing materials, including the indexes mentioned a moment ago.

To the question of whether the Great Depression was unique, the answer was yes and no. No: the United States had a major recession about once every twenty years. Yes: the Great Depression of 1929 was much greater than any of its predecessors.

The dates of the major recessions were 1872, 1892, 1906, and 1929. (The series, incidentally, continues at 1956 and 1973.) They are called Kuznets depressions because the sequence was first identified by Simon Kuznets. We know a great deal about them, thanks to the work of Abramovitz. They resulted from a long construction cycle, in which, starting from the bottom, frenzied railway building would be resumed, followed by immigration, followed by residential construction. The economy would have about ten years of prosperity followed by ten years incorporating the Kuznets recession. The continuation of this series after World War II, in 1956 and 1973, was unexpected because railway construction had ended and immigration was greatly restricted and noncyclical. Presumably, in the United States as in other countries residential building is big enough to impose a twenty-year cycle on the whole economy.

So much for the twenty-year cycle. It was also alleged that there was a fifty-year cycle, where twenty-five years of relative prosperity would be followed by twenty-five years of relative stagnation. This one was named after Kondratieff, the Russian economist who invented the idea. I worked very hard on this one for my book *Growth and Fluctuations* and did not find evidence of a fifty-year cycle in world industrial production. Agriculture had a turning point in 1899. Agricultural output grew faster from 1873 to 1899 than it did from 1899 to 1920. Agricultural prices rose after 1899, having previously been falling. Real wages slowed down after 1899 because of rising prices. Exports of manufactures grew faster after 1899 partly because of the altered terms of trade. It is not disputed that agricultural output and prices show this change of trend after 1899; but the decisive question is whether world *industrial* production grew faster after 1899, and the answer seems to be no. The long recession that we have had since 1973 has revived Kondratieff, and his literature is growing fast in Europe. This controversy too is heating up.

Let me come back to autobiography. My research career falls into three parts. First I studied industrial structure. Second I tackled the history of the world economy, from the middle of the nineteenth century. And third I worked on problems of economic development. I have told you about the first two and now come to economic development.

My interest in the subject was an offshoot of my anti-imperialism. I can remember my father taking me to a meeting of the local Marcus Garvey association when I was seven years old. So it is not surprising that the first thing I ever published was a Fabian Society pamphlet, called *Labour in the West Indies,* which gave an account of the emergence of the trade union movement in the 1920s and '30s and, more especially, of the violent confrontations between the unions and the government in the 1930s. This was not a propaganda pamphlet. It was based on newspaper research and on conversations with some of the union leaders.

In London, meeting fellow anti-imperialists from all over the world, I launched upon a systematic study of the British colonial empire and its practices—color bars, prohibiting Africans from growing coffee in Kenya so that they were forced into the labor market to work for cash to pay their taxes, and all the rest.

But during the war one felt the atmosphere changing. Talking with many other anti-imperialists, especially British Labour members of Parliament, one got the sense that the powers that be had lost interest in the empire and were going to give it up. I was even invited by the Colonial Office in 1943 to be the secretary of a newly established Economic Advisory Committee. At my suggestion this committee launched on a systematic survey of economic policy in one sector after another, from which I learned, among other things, how much the officials disagreed among themselves as to what should be done.

In 1946 LSE set up a special course for social workers from the colonies, who were brought over for a year, and I was asked to teach them elementary economics. I made it a course on economic policy. I remember stopping a student who was in the middle of a passionate attack on the British governor of his country for some particular policy and saying to him, "But what would you do if you were the minister? Within ten years your country will be independent, and you will be a minister or head of a department. Reciting the evils of the British government will not help you. You will need a positive program of your own. The year you spend at LSE is your opportunity to learn how to face up to difficult problems." My dating was a little premature; it took seventeen years instead of ten for his country to become independent—but otherwise I was right, even to the point of his becoming a department head.

I give you this background because it explains something of the emphasis of my writings. I have always taken it for granted that what matters most to growth is to make the best use of one's own resources, and that the exterior events are secondary. An expert on development should be able to give the minister practical advice. I do not adhere to this austerely. I am interested in historical processes and occasionally excite myself with the philosophy of the international economic order, but what I think about and write about most is domestic policy.

I began to teach development economics systematically when I went to Manchester in 1948 as a full professor. The emphasis was heavily on policy. One must therefore have a good idea of the sociological background and also of the political linkages. There are economists who put too much emphasis on prices, forgetting that it may be easier to solve a problem by changing the institutions wherein it is embedded than by changing prices. There are other, structural economists, who avoid the use of prices as a policy instrument because of adverse effects on the distribution and volatility of income. I am usually somewhere in between. One purpose of the book that I published in 1955, *The Theory of Economic Growth,* was to give shape to the discussion and to ensure that anyone interested in the economics of a problem would find it deployed with all its social ramifications.

My chief contribution to the subject was the two-sector model, advanced the year before. I arrived at this through looking at the distribution of income over a long period. I had read in the works of John and Barbara Hammond that the industrial revolution had not raised urban wages. If this was so, it would explain why the share of profits in the national income would rise, contrary to the expectation of the neoclassical economists that it would be constant. This constancy of real wages I felt to be bound up with another mystery. A number of developing countries had been developing for a long time: Ceylon, for example, for a hundred years. Why was the standard of living of the masses still so low? One could understand this for much-exploited South Africa, but how for fairly enlightened Ceylon?

The answer to both questions came by breaking an intellectual constraint. In all the general equilibrium models taught to me the elasticity of supply of labor was zero, so any increase in investment increases the demand for labor and raises wages. Instead, make the elasticity of supply of labor infinite, and my problems are solved. In this model growth raises profits because all of the benefits of advancing technology accrue to employers and to a small class of well-paid workers that emerges in an urban sea of a low-wage proletariat. In the commodities market an unlimited supply of tropical produce also gives the benefit of advancing technology to the industrial buyers, by the process already described.

This model attracted the attention of economists all over the world, because it applied in so many situations. One had to be careful that it did apply to the particular situation and use it only if it did. It was particularly useful in handling the problem of migration, which rose to significance after the war in most countries of the world, developed or developing, as people moved in vast numbers between the country and the town and from poor to rich countries. It is, for example, the way to approach the effects of mass migration of Mexicans to the United States or Turks to Germany. Add the population explosion, the element of technological unemployment, and the movement of women out of the household into the marketplace, and developing countries find themselves with a supply of urban labor too large for full employment. The wage level of unskilled workers then has upper and lower bounds that function much like an infinite elasticity of supply. Needless to say, absolute infinity is neither needed nor intended. The impact of the model is now greatly reduced. Undergraduates are no longer given models in which the elasticity of supply of labor is always zero, so the possibility that it may sometimes be nearly infinite is no big thing. Actually, several books and articles were written about it over the next few years, but the excitement has died down.

After 1950 I traveled a great deal in the Third World. This became possible because in 1947 I had married Gladys Jacobs, from neighboring Grenada. We are still together. She, too, was brought up on the Protestant ethic. She concentrated on making a home for our two children and me and took my absences on duty in her stride.

My visits were sometimes as an adviser, sometimes attending conferences, and sometimes for teaching. The role of advisers diminished steadily. When one visited a country in, say, 1960, having specialized in the subject over a dozen years and acquired a comparative knowledge of what was being done in different countries, one could almost certainly, when asked for an opinion, say, "In country X they are doing this and in country Y they are trying that." But by 1980 these countries employ numbers of professional economists well trained in economic techniques and policies. They may still be happy to see you, but they know much more than you do about their economic problems.

For my part I learned enormously from what I saw and heard on my travels. For example, I never joined the bandwagon for spending unlimited sums on higher education, partly because Egypt and India made me skeptical as to absorptive capacity and also because a sense of responsibility, during my term as vice-chancellor of the University of the West Indies, made me reluctant to ask the minister of finance for one cent more than

I could justify. So my articles on education used the manpower budgeting approach, instead of the then elite but now discredited marginal productivity approach.

It was in Ghana that I first saw the results of excessive migration into the towns and started writing about it.

It was in Jamaica that I first discovered and wrote about what is now called the "Dutch disease." One industry, itself employing few people but earning a lot of foreign exchange, pays very high wages. This pulls up wages in other industries beyond what they can pay and so causes unemployment.

It was in India that I met the problem of the arid zones and discovered that hundreds of millions of people live on lands that are never going to yield a high standard of living. My book on development planning was based on practical experience in making development plans in the Caribbean and in West Africa.

I learned in many countries just how difficult the political problem is, in many dimensions. The simplest dimension is management: getting things done on time and more or less in the form authorized. Another dimension is the minimization of corruption, which is worse still when it is allied with nepotism and results in appointing incompetent managements. Finally, I observed that most of these countries are not homogeneous: they are divided by religion, language, tribe, or race. My book *Politics in West Africa* highlighted this issue and made proposals. It was hotly attacked at the time, but the analysis is now regarded as obvious.

Development economists can be divided into two categories: the gloomy and the optimistic. The gloomy subgroups do not necessarily agree with each other. Some hold that participation in foreign trade weakens the developing economy by destroying its handicraft industries or by sponsoring the demand for foreign goods. Others are concerned about multinational corporations. Still others believe that the poorest economies cannot get off the ground without financial help, which will not flow in adequate amounts. I have always been in the optimistic category, at first because I took it for granted that anything the Europeans could do we could do; but with the passage of time also because the speed at which developing countries were moving in the 1950s, '60s, and '70s left no room for doubt that most of these economies, though not all, have what it takes.

I make the point to remind you, if reminder be necessary, that the study of economic growth is still in its infancy. Countries rise up and fall, and we are not in a position to predict which ones will do best or worst over the next twenty years. This is equally true of developed and developing countries. Economics is good at explaining what has happened over the past twenty years, but when we turn to predicting the future it tends to be an essay in ideology.

Between 1957 and 1973 I spent nine years out of the library in administrative office: at the United Nations in New York; as economic adviser to the prime minister of Ghana, Dr. Nkrumah; as head of the University of the West Indies; and as president of the Caribbean Development Bank. I learned very little of relevance to the theory of economic development (in contrast with earlier visits to India and to Ghana), but I did learn a lot about administration. I have published ten books and about eighty other pieces. I guess that if I had remained in the university I would have written one more book and a dozen more articles. Set this against what I was doing, which was to build up high-quality institutions, whose high standards would yield fruit of their own and also be an inspiration to others. Sometimes it backfires. At a party in Barbados I met a young accountant and asked why he had not replied to our advertisement. "I wanted to apply," he said, "but one of my friends said don't go to the bank because you'll have to work too hard." "I don't do anything to make them work hard," I said. "No," he said, "but you work very hard yourself and everybody else takes his cue from you."

Looking backward over my life, it has been a queer mixture. I have lived through a period of transition and therefore know what it is like at both ends, even though the transition is not yet completed. I have been subjected to all the usual disabilities—refusal of accommodations, denial of jobs for which I had been recommended, generalized discourtesy, and the rest of it. All the same, some doors that were supposed to be closed opened as I approached them. I have got used to being the first black to do this or that, which gets to be more difficult as the transition opens up new opportunities. Having to be a role model is a bit of a strain, but I try to remember that others are coming after me, and that whether the door will be shut in their faces as they approach will depend to some small extent on how I conduct myself. As I said at the beginning, I had never intended to be an economist. My mother taught us to make the best of what we have, and that is what I have tried to do.

Awarded Nobel Prize in 1979. Lecture presented September 27, 1984.

Dates of Birth and Death

January 23, 1915; June 15, 1991

Academic Degrees

B. Com. University of London, 1937

Ph.D.   University of London, 1940

Academic Affiliations

Lecturer, University of London, 1938–1948

Stanley Jevons Professor of Political Economy, University of Manchester, 1948–1958

Vice Chancellor, University of West Indies, 1959–1963

James Madison Professor of Political Economy, Princeton University, 1963–1991

Selected Books

Overhead Costs, 1949

Principles of Economic Planning, 1949, 1969

The Theory of Economic Growth, 1955

Some Aspects of Economic Development, 1969

The Evolution of the International Economic Order, 1978

Lawrence R. Klein

In studying the development of great economists and trying to understand why economic thinking takes particular directions, it has always seemed fruitful to me to look at the interaction, often one-way, between the prevailing situation of the economy and developing tendencies in economic thought. This has been most noticeable in macroeconomics but is also the case in the whole of economics. A primary example, which is closely tied up with my own development, is the emergence of Keynesian economics to deal with the problems of the 1920s and '30s, especially the Great Depression. Keynes was intensely interested in the problems of the day and tried to develop an economic theory that would deal with these problems. It was long in coming. His career got a large impetus from the Treaty of Versailles, then the problems of the gold standard in England, inflation after World War I, unemployment, and the world collapse after 1929.

For our university catalogue, all professors are being asked to write a sentence or three about why they entered their respective fields. I entered economics because, as a youth of the depression, I wanted intensely to have some understanding of what was going on around me. It was psychologically difficult to grow up during the depression. It was easy to become discouraged about economic life and did not give one, at eighteen or twenty years, the feeling that there were boundless opportunities just waiting for exploitation. The young people of the past two or three decades have had nuclear war to worry about, but they have also had feelings of abundant opportunities if peace could be preserved.

But I was blessed with something else, that just happened. I was carrying around in my head the feeling that mathematics could be used in the analysis of economic problems. I spent most of my undergraduate time in either mathematics or economics classes. I was not a creative mathematician or any kind of a match for *wunderkinder;* I saw that readily enough in math competitions. But I was fascinated by university-level mathematics and had some hunches about applications of mathematics to economics, say, to the expression for demand curves and the estimation of revenues. It was a great surprise for me to go into the U.C. Berkeley library and find journals for a whole budding subject, carried out at an advanced level, handling problems that were far more complicated than anything that I had thought about.

My undergraduate advisers gave me no encouragement to study mathematics along with economics; I went my own way and took the best of Berkeley in the early 1940s—first-class departments in economics, mathematics, and mathematical statistics. Of course, one can go back to high school or, in my case, junior college and find roots; there are some indeed, but my professional beginnings were in the Berkeley that existed just before World War II and the scholarship I won to MIT. There I met the dazzling *wunderkind* Paul Samuelson. When I was browsing in the Berkeley library and came across early issues of *Econometrica,* Samuelson's contributions caught my eye. When I got an opportunity to go to MIT, it was the possibility of working with Samuelson that confirmed all my choices. I was attached to him as a graduate assistant from the outset, and I tried to maximize my contact with him, picking up insights that he scattered on every encounter.

Working with Samuelson, who was at the forefront of interpreting Keynesian theory for teaching and policy application, I was put immediately in the midst of two challenging contests—one to gain acceptance for a way of thinking about macroeconomics and another to gain acceptance for a methodology in economics, namely, the mathematical method. Later, both challenges were to be overcome, but for ten or twenty years opposition was fierce.

Once Samuelson's *Economics* became a widely used text in first courses in the subject, Keynesian economics was firmly embedded. There was no turning back from that achievement. The successive student generations turned more toward the mathematical approach in graduate school, and they taught or did research in this vein. That eventually established the mathematical method, first in the United States, then in Europe, Japan,

India, and other centers. Much of the foundation was built in Europe, and many of the American masters at mathematical economics were immigrants, but Samuelson, Friedman, and others gave it a native-born American flavor, and the approach truly caught on in this country.

The MIT years were, for me, a start in the professional field of economics, and my first position after leaving graduate school was with the Cowles Commission at the University of Chicago. Being just twenty-four years old when I started work there, I was almost in the position of having another chance at graduate school. As in many scientific fields of study, I was essentially a postdoctoral fellow.

A truly exceptional group of people was assembled in Chicago during the late 1940s. I doubt that such a group could ever be put together again in economics. From our closely knit group, four Nobel laureates have emerged, and two others came from the next bunching of Cowles researchers—partly at Chicago and partly at Yale. We worked as a team and focused on a single problem—to put together an econometric model of the American economy (a second attempt after Tinbergen's of the 1930s)—using the best of statistical theory, economic theory, and available data. After about four or five years of intensive research built up around this theme, the team dispersed to new openings in academic life. The effort was kept alive through my own research, and many of the brilliant people of our group went on to do their work in quite different branches of economics—Koopmans in activity analysis, Arrow in general equilibrium theory, Simon in decision analysis, Anderson in statistics, Marschak in the theory of organization, and so on.

In our attempts to bring together econometric methods and Keynesian analysis of the macroeconomy we felt quite confident. In the field of postwar planning we imagined that we had the well-being of the economy right in the palms of our hands. Over the coming decade we accomplished much more by way of model building and using than we ever thought possible in our wildest dreams of postwar America, but it was never good enough. We built systems that evolved from our teamwork at the Cowles Commission, and they have become part of the standard tool kit of economists. They play a very big role, but they do not dominate the policy process. They take a leadership role in forecasting, but they are not the sole survivors in the forecasting derby.

Scientists at Chicago were, secretively, carrying out more significant team research than we economists at the Cowles Commission. Because the director of the Cowles Commission was an old friend (from Europe of the two previous decades) of Leo Szilard, a leader among the scientists, we had a great deal of interaction. Szilard, one of the cleverest people of this century, dabbled in amateur economics. He constructed parlor games of the macroeconomy to demonstrate a scheme of monetary control that he thought would lead the world to a cycle-free existence. He taught us a lot about the strategy of intellectual research and the blending of politics and science. Many of us interacted with him and also with the amazing John von Neumann, who frequently visited Chicago on his way to Los Alamos. In those days, a trip across country involved changing trains in Chicago. Another visitor who had a profound influence on everyone at Cowles was Abraham Wald, the mathematical statistician from Columbia University.

The next phase of my career was to become more internationally minded. These days, some of us travel all over the world every month; European trips are almost routine. But when I left the Cowles Commission in 1947, I set out on an ocean voyage to Europe, after a summer's research activity in Ottawa putting together the first model of the Canadian economy. That project has survived many generations and gave birth to an active professional community in Canada that still functions on an expanded level.

Visits to centers of economic and econometric research throughout Europe were part of my education. I learned a great deal about the world, but was more attracted by the liveliness of the development of our subject in America. Seeing Europe dig out from the postwar rubble was a learning experience, and it opened many professional relationships that remain active. It certainly had a major impact on my own career development.

Before the war Cambridge, England, and London were the centers of economic thinking that shaped the world. Traveling fellows gravitated there for study. America had begun to compete, but from 1946 onward the magnet was the United States. Students came from all over to do their work in America. This was true in many fields and has not changed appreciably in the last forty years.

In that seasoning year abroad I made contact with the true Keynesians, the Cambridge group who worked directly with Keynes. I never met Keynes himself, but I got good insight into the group's thinking from Kahn, Joan Robinson, and Sraffa. I also met Kaldor and Stone on that trip. The interesting thing to me was that my teacher, Paul Samuelson, had inferred all that there was to know about this group without ever having been there. People in Cambridge remarked about this to me.

I had come to Europe for the first time only months ahead of Paul Samuelson and met him on his first stop—Norway—where I was spending most of the year abroad, learning from Frisch. Samuelson had just published *Economics* and was enjoying an early enthusiastic acceptance. He toured Western Europe just as I was completing my year there.

A problem with the interpretation of the Keynesian system was the influence of wealth on savings. In the literature of macroeconomics this became known as the Pigou effect, although Pigou had written about it more in terms of liquid assets rather than total wealth. People had emerged from the war with large holdings of liquid assets (especially government savings bonds), so it was a popular and important subject to investigate.

I had returned from Europe to join the National Bureau of Economic Research under the leadership of Arthur Burns. There I worked on production function estimation, focusing on the railroad sector, but after one year I worked jointly on a project with the Survey Research Center of the University of Michigan and the National Bureau of Economic Research to use the Surveys of Consumer Finance to throw more light on saving behavior, especially with respect to the Pigou effect.

One line of economic research that emerged after World War II was the one I was following in econometrics, particularly macroeconometrics. But survey research flourished during the war, as a tool to help government plan civilian activity in a way that would aid the military effort. One of the primary groups, located in the Department of Agriculture during the war, set up academic ties and formed the Institute for Social Research at the University of Michigan, Ann Arbor. I felt comfortable working with this statistical team. Also the cross-disciplinary attitude intrigued me. I learned a great deal about the interfaces between economics on the one hand and psychology, sociology, and other disciplines on the other.

At the Survey Research Center I learned a great deal about household behavior and techniques for measuring it. The work was based on samples of human populations consisting of a few thousand cases for each study. This initiated me into the realm of large-scale data processing, done by punched cards and electromechanical machines. Electronic computers were in existence but were not yet being used for most economic or social problems.

After I came to Michigan, where I was teaching econometrics on a small scale, but mainly concerned with survey research, I received some money from the Ford Foundation, which suddenly had found it necessary for tax purposes to make large grants of money available to several universities. Few people in the economics department had any ideas about how to spend the sum that was to be allocated to them. I then established the Research Seminar in Quantitative Economics, assembled some research students, and went back to econometric model building —restarting the research begun at the Cowles Commission.

One of those research students was Arthur Goldberger. He and I put together a new model of the U.S. economy called the Klein–Goldberger model. It streamlined the models built at the Cowles Commission, used some of the survey findings, and set about forecasting the economy on a regular basis.

Colin Clark, the intrepid Australian statistical economist, set us up for a great success. In the pages of the influential *Manchester Guardian,* which came my way in the weekly world edition, he observed that the winding down of the Korean War would possibly cause a large-scale recession. He frightened people about the most fearsome economic event of our time—a 1929-style collapse as a result of a cumulative downward spiral.

I looked at our model results for forecasts for 1953–54 and concluded that it did not look like 1929 again. I wrote a paper with Arthur Goldberger for the *Guardian* and was delighted to find that they would publish it, in large display accompanied by an intriguing Low cartoon.

In a piecemeal fashion the statistical work on the Klein–Goldberger model made use of the computer for parts of the computations connected with model estimation. For solution of the model we set aside a day or two of laborious hand calculation with a desktop machine. A large-scale digital computer was installed at Michigan, and we started a project for automatic model solution—simulation, if you like—but it was not quite brought to fruition before I was to leave Ann Arbor.

In the McCarthy era I left Michigan for the peace and academic freedom of Oxford, where I joined the Institute of Statistics and worked on the British Savings Surveys, patterned after the Michigan Surveys. While at Oxford I went back to model building, this time for Great Britain. My friend of twenty-five subsequent years, Professor Sir James Ball, attended my lectures on econometrics at Oxford and worked with me on the Oxford model. Some progress was made in using the computer at Oxford for more of the numerical work, but again it was not for model solution.

In 1958 I returned to America and took up a professorship at Pennsylvania, where I admired the position of the president, provost, and deans on the serious matter of academic freedom. From the beginning of my tenure at Pennsylvania and the Wharton School, I set out again to build a model of the American economy. This time I turned to quarterly data and, encouraged by my survey experience in England and Michigan, I used some *expectations* magnitudes. I started the first generation of a series of Wharton models.

The Wharton models shifted to a quarterly time frame, to emphasize interest in short-run business cycle movements, used more data on survey anticipations, and stated all the accounting identities in current prices. This last change corrected a defect in the specification of the Klein–Goldberger model. The first version of this new model was used for forecasting the American economy, and projections were sent round to economist members of the Kennedy administration, who voiced disbelief in the optimistic forecasts—recovery from the 1960–61 recession. Within a few years I was to turn my attention to a new approach, and I abandoned further work on this first version, but I turned over complete files, consisting of data listings and equations, together with a trained assistant to the Department of Commerce. They had asked me for help in starting a model-building project there. This evolved, with the help of other Pennsylvania Ph.D. products, into what is now the OBE model (Office of Business Economics, Department of Commerce). This model has taken off into its own life and is a distinguished member of the American family of models, but its roots are the first Wharton model.

At this stage I went in two research directions, each of which had a fundamental impact on my own professional development. The Committee on Economic Stability of the Social Science Research Council planned, in 1959, the creation of a new, enlarged, short-run forecasting model. I was one of the principal investigators of that project and played a role in designing a cooperative approach to model building, namely, assignment of a specialist to each sector of the economy. I undertook, together with other members of the steering committee, to fashion it into a consistent whole. In general, we had a model that was composed of the best practice in each department, and it functioned as a whole. But the real advances that emerged from this joint effort were (1) a detailed monetary sector that drew on Federal Reserve talent and was the forerunner of important monetary sectors in many subsequent models, thus repairing a defect of the Klein–Goldberger model; (2) an explicit input-output sector of interindustry flows that was tied consistently with the traditional macro models of final demand and income determination; (3) the preparation of a *databank* for the systematic accounting of all the data used in the system; and (4) automation of the computing for the project with a remarkable breakthrough in the ability to solve large systems of nonlinear dynamic equations. Other features of the research on this joint project have been outstanding and are documented in three project volumes, especially the final one.[1]

After the Social Science Research Council started the cooperative project, it was transferred to the Brookings Institution and became known as the Brookings model. In its cooperative set-up, we consulted many participants on its progress, development, and use. This was particularly striking in the case of computation. We struggled hard with the computer aspects among a group at the University of Pennsylvania (helped a great deal by our innovative young Ph.D. candidates, who prepared many of the first-generation computer programs for econometrics), a group at Brookings, and a group at MIT. I devised a clumsy algorithm at Pennsylvania; a suggestion by E. Kuh at MIT to G. Fromm at Brookings provided the essential link. When they communicated their findings about Gauss iteration methods, we tested them in Philadelphia and immediately switched to what has become a worldwide standard for solving large dynamic systems in economics. From the early days of computer application at Michigan, model simulation had been an obstacle to efficient model application, but once we saw the key principle, we were able to harness the computer for generations to come.

The SSRC–Brookings model was but one line of development, away from the first Wharton model. The second was to develop an entirely new model for a different kind of use—commercial forecasting. I secured a small sum from the Rockefeller Foundation for the construction of the first Wharton model. We then established a research unit at the Wharton School for general quantitative studies in economics, financed by the Ford Foundation and National Science Foundation. But I could see that these sources of support were temporary and would run out during the mid-1960s.

Meanwhile, several major corporations had independently approached me for help in their efforts at econometric model building to assist their economic research departments. I accordingly proposed to five core companies that we build one model for them at the Wharton School and provide forecasts in exchange for support of our research program in econometrics.

Michael Evans joined the Pennsylvania faculty in 1963 and participated in our new forecasting venture with the private sector. He brought with him a separate model that he had developed in his dissertation research at Brown University. At first, we prepared two forecasts, one from his model and one from the original Wharton model. After a short period a combined model was built, fused from the two, and this was the first to be published in a series of Wharton volumes.

The Wharton Econometric Forecasting Unit thrived. From five supporting participants in 1963 it expanded into a separate nonprofit corporation in 1969 (wholly owned by the University of Pennsylvania). It was sold in 1980 to a publishing corporation and was acquired by a French computer company in 1983. Both Data Resources, Inc., and Chase Econometrics took up commercial forecasting after 1969, and an entire new industry was born. It now has many competing firms and does business in the hundreds of millions of dollars.

With the growth of new centers of activity with models and support systems, it was natural to phase out the old Brookings Model Project.

It had served its purpose and was superseded by the expanded commercial modeling systems and some fresh academic ventures.

During the 1960s the computer was finally harnessed for the needs of econometrics; it had first been used for scientific, engineering, and large-scale data processing (such as censuses). During this decade all those complicated calculations that we had contemplated during the development years of econometrics at the Cowles Commission became possible. I spent a great deal of time with student collaborators and IBM researchers working on nonlinear problems associated with maximum likelihood and other methods of statistical estimation, but we also perfected the simulation techniques that grew out of Brookings model research activities. We pioneered two developments that took econometric methods one step further: the presentation of results in standard national accounting form that were readily understood by users of econometric analysis and the use of time sharing. Data banking and perfection of time sharing were carried much further on a "user-friendly" basis for Data Resources, Inc., but the Wharton team had time-sharing facilities before DRI was founded. Computer developments were only started in the 1960s. They flowered in the next decade and became available to a large army of researchers and students throughout the world.

In addition to the standard uses of the computer for data management, statistical inference, applications (mainly simulation), and presentation of results in easy-to-read tables and graphs, many deep research techniques were developed, starting as early as the late 1950s. These were based on stochastic simulations, which involved the disturbance of dynamic model solution by properly drawn random errors. This research was pioneered by Irma Adelman in studying dynamic properties of the Klein–Goldberger model and by Harvey Wagner in constructing Monte Carlo experiments to test statistical techniques in econometrics.[2]

The Wharton team did not use these methods first, but we used them to good advantage to learn a great deal about the cyclical and inference properties of our family of models. Some large-scale stochastic simulations of the Brookings model had already advanced the use of computer-based experimental techniques, and we drew upon this fund of information. In this extended research effort, we learned to understand the various response characteristics of large-scale models—multipliers, sensitivities to parameter shift, and long-term trends of the system. The total computer effort of mechanizing the operation of large-scale models meant that the Wharton team was able to respond quickly and informatively to such major events as President Nixon's new economic policy, the oil embargo, and the fall of the Shah's government in Iran.

During my long stay at Pennsylvania several related efforts were conceived and executed in addition to the build-up of the Wharton models and their various applications to forecasting and macroeconomic analysis. Soon after I arrived, I became involved in a venture with two colleagues in Japan, professors Michio Morishima and Shinichi Ichimura, both of whom I had known in either England or the United States. We collaborated in the founding of a new scholarly journal, the *International Economic Review*. There were two principal objectives: to foster the development of modern (Anglo-American) economics in Japan and to take the burden off *Econometrica*, which had a large backlog of unpublished articles. In looking back at that venture, I would say that it made a contribution to the development of modern economics in Japan, although that might have happened anyway. We probably helped the transformation. We probably did not relieve the pressure on *Econometrica,* except temporarily, and we joined many other new journals in a virtual explosion of article preparation and the opening up of new periodicals. At any rate, the *International Economic Review* still stands as a collegial collaboration between Osaka University and the University of Pennsylvania, of almost twenty-five years' duration, and is now self-sustaining. In the founding years inexpensive Japanese printing, beautiful rice paper, and support from the Kansai Economic Federation made publication of the review possible. Those features are gone, but the review has a healthy existence.

The establishment of the review and other relationships took me to Japan in 1960 and on many subsequent occasions. In this connection, I prepared a model of the Japanese economy with Yoichi Shinkai and participated in a model project at Osaka University. Over the years, many Japanese models have rendered these efforts obsolete, but the research on Japan, together with the previous econometric research on the United Kingdom, directed my interest toward international model building.

In 1966 researchers at the du Pont company in Wilmington asked me to supply three models of developing countries where the company was involved in direct investment. Accordingly, I assembled a research team among the students of the economic research unit of Pennsylvania's economics department and prepared models for Argentina, Brazil, and Mexico. The company, as agreed, made their proprietary use of these models, but the system, complete with databases and equations, were, as agreed in advance, in the public domain. The research scholar for Mexico, Abel Beltrán del Rio, went with me to Monterrey in the summer of 1969. There we obtained a commitment from private companies for research support for elaboration and replicated use of the Mexican model in forecasting, policy, and scenario analysis of the economy. Within Wharton Econometrics we formed DIEMEX (Department de Investigaciones Econometricos de México). From a base of a few private-sector supporters in Monterrey and Mexico City in 1969 this has evolved into a self-sustaining system with some 150 supporters—U.S. companies, Mexican government agencies, international organizations, and others. What interests me most in this success is that the same technologies for model preparation, computer use, presentation of model results, and contributions to decision making in the private and public sectors could be fully transferred from our base in Philadelphia to a developing country. This is a prize case, but similar efforts have worked in many other parts of the world as well.

Starting with Latin America, I was able to foster model-building efforts in many developing countries. There are many models in the Far East, some in Africa, and some in the Middle East. Data deficiency has always been a problem, but that is gradually being overcome, and now practically the entire developing world is being modeled. Some of our best students had gone to various U.N. groups to work on problems of economic development among the emerging countries. I took on a consulting agreement in the mid-1960s with a group in UNCTAD to help them build models of LDCs in order to estimate capital needs for growth.

Parallel with model building for developing countries, a related effort directed at socialist or centrally planned economies was also initiated. The developing country models were deliberately structured to reveal some of the unique characteristics of these areas. They were not simply copies of models in the style of the neoclassical Keynesian synthesis that were being built for each of the industrial democracies (OECD countries); they had unique supply-side features, specialized foreign trade characteristics, distributional aspects, and demographic aspects plainly displayed. I had long been fascinated by the challenging problem of modeling the centrally planned economy, with its controlled markets and plan targets. In the summer of 1970, on the occasion of a lecture in Vienna at the Institute for Advanced Studies, I discussed these problems with economists in Bratislava who had contacted me in the United States. I continued these discussions during that summer in Novosibirsk and Budapest.

Finally, in 1973 I collaborated with my colleagues in Sovietology on a project to model the U.S.S.R. SOVMOD I and succeeding generations grew from that effort. In discussions and formal presentations, this model was put before Soviet economists, and I believe that by now we have a better understanding of that country's economic system. Visiting scholars from Bratislava, Budapest, Łodz, Novosibirsk, Moscow, and Beijing have, over a period of more than ten years, contributed to our appreciation of the fundamental differences in structure between the Western market economy and the Eastern command economy.

The modeling of the pieces—different OECD countries, some LDCs and some CPEs—set the stage for the next step, namely, the modeling of the international system. In a meeting of the SSRC Committee on Economic Stability and Growth in 1967 I suggested that we approach the growing international problem through a cooperative project designed, to some extent, along the lines of the SSRC–Brookings model project. Country representatives would take the place of sector representatives, and we could put together a consistent system of the leading economic centers of the world economy. The SSRC committee had earlier hoped to see such an effort undertaken by the OECD. We held a meeting in London in 1967 under the intriguing title "Is the Business Cycle Obsolete?" We, fortunately, recognized the continuing presence of the cycle, but were not successful in starting research on model building for analysis of the international problem at that conference. We did, however, establish some lasting contacts at that meeting that served us well for later developments.

With a small grant from the Ford Foundation, Bert Hickman, Aaron Gordon, and I assembled a group of international model builders from leading OECD countries in summer 1968 at Stanford, where I was giving some class lectures. We decided to launch a new project to model the international transmission mechanism. Initial support came from the International Monetary Fund, with active participation of Rudolf Rhomberg, and from the National Science Foundation.

This was truly a group endeavor. Many individual model builders from different countries and many specialists in international economics convened at formative meetings, realizing that there was a researchable project but not knowing exactly how to go about it. Through the dynamics of group discussion and person-to-person analysis, we finally decided on some procedures and goals. Out of that effort we spawned project LINK—*The International Linkage of National Economic Models.*[3] More than fifteen years later the project is still functioning and trying to break new ground.

At an early stage we recognized that the developing countries and the socialist countries would play an increasingly important role in the world economy. Although the main interest at the IMF was the analysis of OECD countries, the U.N. supporters of the project continuously pressed for attention to the role of the LDC and CPE areas. The project has grown from a system of thirteen OECD countries, four regions of developing countries, and one region of socialist countries to an enlarged system of seventy-two country/area groups comprising each of the OECD countries, most large developing countries individually, and most large socialist countries individually. That is the most ambitious coordinating task for model building that has ever been undertaken, and we are in the midst of putting all the pieces together now in Philadelphia. Each separate piece exists.

During the fifteen-year period of development we have succeeded in allowing for floating exchange rates, coping with oil price changes, adding country detail, introducing primary commodities, streamlining the enormous computational program, and tackling many policy problems through scenario analysis. Analysis of capital flows, coordination of policies among countries, and methods of optimal control are high on the present research agenda.

The computer, as one can easily see, has played a large role in my involvement with econometric research and application, but that part of the story is not yet finished. Interesting new developments are on the horizon. I am now involved in three research directions: (1) Use of the microcomputer for conventional econometrics. This involves collapsing the size of systems to fit limited, tabletop capacities, but these limitations are steadily disappearing. Some studies, especially of developing countries, are necessarily compact, small enough to fit the present generation of microcomputers. (2) Cooperative computing, whereby conventional computers are linked in a network for simultaneous computation; the LINK system is an ideal trial case. (3) Use of the supercomputer to accommodate the ever-increasing demands of the expanding LINK system, now consisting of more than 15,000 dynamic nonlinear equations.

Just as the Brookings model gave way to improved versions at the various commercial econometric centers, official agencies and some individual university centers, there is a possibility that project LINK could be eclipsed. The Federal Reserve System has their own multicountry model, as does the OECD, Japan's Economic Planning Agency, the Common Market, and Wharton Econometrics. What seemed chancy and questionable in 1968 has become an often duplicated reality for analysis of the world economy.

When I went to Eastern Europe and the U.S.S.R. in 1970, embryonic groups were starting up activity in econometric model building. I helped, where possible, and had many trainees at either the University of Pennsylvania or Wharton Econometrics. The same thing was true of activities in the developing countries. The case of the People's Republic of China is somewhat different. After the renormalization of relationships in 1978, I led a team of economists sponsored by the National Academy of Sciences, in fall 1979, to try to establish scholarly contacts. As a followup to that visit I organized, privately, with the Chinese Academy of Social Sciences, a summer workshop in econometrics in 1980. Also, visiting scholars from China have come to Philadelphia. Progress is limited but promising toward the preparation of a China model, maintained in the PRC, for LINK. We already have our own version of a China model built by Laurence Lau of Stanford University. A repeat visit in 1984 continued in the vein of teaching econometric method and trying to encourage participation in Project LINK. Similar workshops and efforts for LINK-compatible model building were undertaken in Taiwan during 1982 and 1983. Meetings with economists in Manila (Asian Development Bank and Philippine Institute for Development Studies), Bangkok (U.N.

Economic and Social Commission for Asia and the Pacific), and New Delhi (Delhi University) are furthering the effort to have good LINK models for the whole Far East.

This account of forty years' research activity in economics and econometrics has avoided the political or the popular side. In 1976 I served as Jimmy Carter's coordinator of his economic task force. During his administration I tried to be helpful in various White House economic matters. I gave similar assistance to Milton Shapp, the governor of Pennsylvania, and W. Wilson Goode, the mayor of Philadelphia. All these private ventures contributed enormously to my own education. They taught me a bit about handling the media, about public appearances, and about the trade-offs between economic and political considerations. That experience was very interesting and I am glad that I did it, but I feel most comfortable in academia, doing the things I have described in this essay.

As for popularizing, I continue to write a periodic column for the Los Angeles *Times* and have had my stints at *Newsweek, Business Week,* and *Le Nouvel Observateur.* The *Manchester Guardian* in 1954 took my every word and table and published it as is. The same is true in my continuing relationship with the Los Angeles *Times,* but I feel the same way about other popular excursions into the media that I feel about politics. The tradeoffs with what I believe to be good economics are not acceptable, and I feel more comfortable writing in the scholarly domain.

Awarded Nobel Prize in 1980. Lecture presented October 25, 1984.

Date of Birth

September 14, 1920

Academic Degrees

B.A.   University of California, Berkeley, 1942

Ph.D.   Massachusetts Institute of Technology, 1944

Academic Affiliations

Lecturer in Economics, University of Michigan, 1950–1954

Senior Research Officer, Oxford University Institute of Statistics, 1954–1955

Reader in Econometrics, Oxford University Institute of Statistics, 1956–1958

Professor of Economics, University of Pennsylvania, 1958–1964

Visiting Professor, Osaka University, summer 1960

University Professor of Economics, University of Pennsylvania, 1964–1967

Benjamin Franklin Professor, University of Pennsylvania, 1968–1985

Benjamin Franklin Professor, Emeritus, University of Pennsylvania, 1985–present

Distinguished Visiting Professor, City University of New York, 1962–1963, 1982

Visiting Professor, The Hebrew University of Jerusalem, 1964

Visiting Professor, Princeton University, spring 1966

Ford Visiting Professor, University of California, Berkeley, 1968

Visiting Professor, Stanford University, summer 1968

Visiting Professor, Institute for Advanced Studies, Vienna, summer 1970, winter 1974

Visiting Professor, University of Copenhagen, spring 1974

Selected Books

The Keynesian Revolution, 1947, 1966

A Textbook of Econometrics, 1953, 1974

An Econometric Model of the United States, 1929–1952, 1955 (with A. S. Goldberger)

The Brookings Quarterly Econometric Model of the United States, 1965 (with J. Duesenberry, G. Fromm, and E. Kuh)

Econometric Models as Guides for Decision Making, 1981

Kenneth J. Arrow

Studying oneself is not the most comfortable of enterprises. One is caught between the desire to show oneself in the best possible light and the fear of claiming more than one's due. I shall endeavor to follow the precept of that eminent seeker after truth, Sherlock Holmes, on perhaps the only occasion on which he was accused of excessive modesty. "'My dear Watson,' said he, 'I cannot agree with those who rank modesty among the virtues. To the logician all things should be seen exactly as they are, and to underestimate one's self is as much a departure from truth as to exaggerate one's own powers'" ("The Greek Interpreter").

An individual examining himself cannot claim omniscience. I cannot really claim to know all the forces impinging on my life, personal or intellectual. Indeed, as will be seen, there are some elements in the development of my ideas and interests that I cannot now reconstruct. On occasion, on rereading an old scholarly paper of mine, I have realized that my mental recollection was in some degree in error. In effect, the speakers in this series are asked to be historians and biographers of themselves; and like all historians and biographers, they can occasionally make mistakes. Recollection can be taken as reliable when it can be checked against the documentary record. Otherwise, it is imperfectly reliable evidence, though of a kind to which the speaker, such as myself, has unique access.

I have always had an interest in the history of economic thought. In the last few years I have been giving a course in this subject. One question I have been facing is the relative importance of different factors in the development of new ideas. One might suppose, for example, that the personal histories and class backgrounds of economists would be important factors. Yet that does not seem to be the case. Among the great economists of the nineteenth century, David Ricardo was a highly successful businessman, a stock-exchange speculator to be exact, while John Stuart Mill was brought up to be an intellectual by an exacting father. Yet their economic theories were very similar indeed. Of course, access to education is important in intellectual development, and far more so today as economics, like all the natural and social sciences, has become a profession. Further, individual talents and interests may well govern which particular aspects of economics are studied and what techniques are used. But there is no evidence that the personality of an economist plays any significant role in the new concepts that he or she introduces to the subject.

I will therefore be brief in sketching my biography. My family, on both sides, were immigrants who arrived in this country about 1900 and settled in New York. My parents were born abroad but came here as infants, so they were effectively first-generation Americans. My father's family was very poor, my mother's hardworking and moderately successful shopkeepers. Both were very intelligent. My mother completed high school, my father college. My father was unusually successful in business when young, and the first ten years of my life were spent in a household that was comfortable and, more important for me, had many good books. Later, my father lost everything in the Great Depression, and we were very poor for about ten years.

I was early regarded as having unusual intellectual capacity. I was an omnivorous reader, and I added to that a desire to systematize my understanding. As a result, history, for example, was not merely a set of dates and colorful stories; I could understand it as a sequence in which one event flowed out of another. This sense of order crystallized during my high-school and college years into a predominant interest in mathematics and mathematical logic.

My primary and secondary schools were on the whole good. When it came to college, my family's poverty constrained me to attend the City College, which was then a completely free college opportunity that New York City had offered since 1847. I was far from the only able student in the same economic position, so that the quality of the students was high. The faculty, which was generally competent and occasionally better, was stimulated to hold the students to high standards, and I learned a good deal. Fear of unemployment led me to supplement my abstract interests in mathematics and logic with preparation for several alternative practical pursuits, among them high-school teaching, actuarial work, and statistics. It was the study of statistics that turned out to shape my economics career in a decisive way.

By following obscure references in footnotes, I learned about the then rapidly developing field of mathematical statistics, which gave a theoretical foundation to statistical practice and led to profound changes in it. When at college graduation, in 1940, I found there were still no jobs available in high-school teaching, I decided to enter graduate studies in statistics. There were then no separate departments of statistics and few places where mathematical statistics was taught. I enrolled at Columbia University to study with a great statistician, Harold Hotelling. Hotelling had his official position in the department of economics and had written a small number of important papers in economic theory. When I took his course in mathematical economics, I realized I had found my niche.

I received strong moral support from Hotelling and indeed from the whole economics department, somewhat surprisingly, as apart from Hotelling, economic theory was not well regarded by them. The emphasis was almost entirely on empirical and institutional analyses. The department's support was expressed in the most tangible and necessary way—good scholarships. As a result I learned economic theory as I had learned so much else, by reading. In my case at least, I believe this self-education was much better than any lectures I could have attended anywhere. The use of mathematics in economics had had a long history, but it was then still confined to a small group. By reading selectively, I could choose my teachers, and I chose them well.

I was an excellent student, but I was doubtful that I was capable of genuine originality. This concern was concentrated on the choice of topic for a Ph.D. dissertation. There were many possibilities for an acceptable dissertation, but I felt that I had to justify the expectations of my teachers and for that matter of myself by doing something out of the ordinary. This responsibility was crushing rather than inspiring. Four years of military service, though interesting in itself, served further to delay my coming to grips with my aspirations. Finally, a series of abortive research ideas, each of which seemed to be more of a distraction than a help, culminated in my first major accomplishment, known as the theory of social choice.

I will go into some detail about the genesis of this contribution of mine because it displays the interaction between the state of economic thinking in general and my own special talents and background. It differs in one significant way from the other areas of my research, which I will discuss later. The question was essentially a new one, on which there had been virtually no previous analysis. The others had been discussed to some extent in the literature, and my role was to bring new analytic methods or new insights. In social choice theory, I was almost completely the creator of the questions as well as some answers.

It had been argued by the more advanced economic theorists that economic behavior in all contexts was essentially rational choice among a limited set of alternatives. The household chooses among collections of different kinds of goods. The collections available to it are those that it can afford to buy at the prevailing prices and with the income available to it. A firm chooses among alternative ways of producing a given output and also chooses among different output levels. To say that choice is rational was interpreted by these theorists, such as Hotelling, John Hicks, and Paul Samuelson, as meaning that the alternatives can be ranked or ordered by the chooser. From any given range of alternatives, say, the technically feasible production processes or the collections of commodities available to a household within its budget limits, the choosing agent selects the highest-ranking alternative available.

To say that alternatives are ordered in preference has a very definite meaning. First, it means that any two alternatives can be compared. The chooser prefers one or the other or possibly is indifferent between them. Second, and this is somewhat more subtle, there is a consistency in the ordering of alternatives. Let us imagine three alternatives labeled A, B, and C. If A is preferred to B and B to C, we would want to insist that A is preferred to C. This property is referred to as *transitivity*.

Though this formulation of choice had been originated for use in economic analysis, it was clearly applicable to choice in other domains. Hotelling, John von Neumann, Oskar Morgenstern, and Joseph Schumpeter had already suggested some applications to political choice, the choice of candidates for election or of legislative proposals. Voting could be regarded as a method by which individuals' preferences for candidates or legislative proposals could be combined or aggregated to make a social choice.

The question first came to me in an economic context. I had observed that large corporations were not individuals but were supposed (in theory, at least) to reflect the will of their many stockholders. To be sure, they all had a common aim, to maximize profits. But profits depend on the future, and the stockholders might well have different expectations as to future conditions. Suppose the corporation has to choose among alternative directions for investment. Each stockholder orders the different investment policies by the profit he or she expects. But because different stockholders have different expectations, they may well have different orderings of investment policies. My first thought was the obvious one suggested by the formal rules of corporate voting. If there are two investment policies, call them A and B, that one chosen is the one that commands a majority of the shares.

But in almost any real case, there are many more than two possible investment policies. For simplicity, suppose there are three, A, B, and C. The idea that seemed natural to me was to choose the one that would get a majority over each of the other two. To put it another way, since the policy is that of the corporation, we might want to say that the corporation can order all investment policies and choose the best. But since the corporation merely reflects its stockholders, the ordering by the corporation should be constructed from the orderings of the individual stockholders. We might say that the corporation prefers one policy to another if a majority of the shares are voted for the first as against the second.

But now I found an unpleasant surprise. It was perfectly possible that A has a majority against B, and B against C, but that C has a majority against A, not A against C. In other words, majority voting does not always have the property that I have just called transitivity.

To see how this can happen, let me take an election example. Suppose there are three candidates, Adams, Black, and Clark, and three voters. Voter 1 prefers Adams to Black and Black to Clark. We will suppose that each voter has a transitive ordering, so voter 1 will prefer Adams to Clark. Suppose voter 2 prefers Black to Clark and Clark to Adams, and therefore Black to Adams, while voter 3 prefers Clark to Adams and Adams to

Black. Then voters 1 and 3 prefer Adams to Black, so that Adams is chosen over Black by the group. Similarly, Black receives a majority over Clark through voters 1 and 2. Transitivity would require that Adams be chosen over Clark in the election. But in fact voters 2 and 3 prefer Clark to Adams. This intransitivity is sometimes called the paradox of voting. Of course, the intransitivity need not arise; it depends on what the voters' preferences are. The point is that the system of pairwise majority voting cannot be guaranteed to produce an ordering by society as a whole.

The observation struck me as one that must have been made by others, and indeed I wondered if I had heard it somewhere. I still don't know whether I did or not. In any case the effect was rather to cause me to drop the whole matter and study something else.

About a year later my thoughts recurred to the question of voting, without any intention on my part. I realized that under certain special but not totally unnatural conditions on the voters' preferences, the paradox I had found earlier could not occur. This I thought worth writing about. But when I started to do so, I picked up a journal and found the same idea in an article by an English economist, Duncan Black. The result that Black and I had found could have been thought of any time in the last one hundred and fifty years. That two of us came to it at virtually the same time is an occurrence for which I have no explanation.

Priority in discovery is the spur to science, and being anticipated was correspondingly frustrating. I again dropped the study of voting for what I took to be less fascinating but more significant topics, on which I made little progress. But a few months later I was asked a chance question that gave the problem sufficient significance to justify a reawakened interest. The then new theory of games was being applied to military and diplomatic conflict. In this application, nations were being regarded as rational actors. How could this be justified when nations are aggregated of individuals with different preference orderings? My earlier results, I realized, taught me that one could not always derive a preference ordering for a nation from the preference orderings of its citizens by using majority voting to compare one alternative with another.

This left open the possibility that there were other ways of aggregating individual preference orderings to form a social ordering, that is, a way of choosing among alternatives that has the property of transitivity. A few weeks of intensive thought made the answer clear.

Given any method of aggregating individual preference orderings to yield a social choice that satisfies a few very natural conditions, there will always be some individual preference orderings that will cause the social choice to be intransitive, as in the example given.

My studies in logic helped to formulate the question in a clear way, which stripped it of unnecessary complications. But I did not use the concepts of mathematical logic in any deep way.

This result quickly attracted attention. One by-product was that I learned from several correspondents of what previous literature there was. The paradox of majority voting had indeed been discovered before—in fact, by the French author the Marquis du Condorcet in 1785! But there was not a continuous literature. There were some ingenious unpublished proposals for conducting certain elections at Oxford about 1860, based on the possibility of paradox. They were circulated by a mathematician named Charles L. Dodgson. Dodgson also wrote an adventure tale for the daughter of one of his colleagues, Alice Lidell, which he published under a pseudonym, Lewis Carroll. The only significant published paper on social choice had appeared in 1882 in an Australian journal, hardly everyday reading matter. I know few if any interesting research topics that have had such a spotty and intermittent history.

The subsequent record is very different. The literature has exploded. A recent survey, not intended to be complete, listed more than six hundred references. A journal devoted entirely to social choice theory and related issues has been started.

Social choice is a topic in which there was little direct relation to past work, although the connection with parallel developments in the theory of economic choice was important. I would like to discuss two further contributions of mine, which illustrate different relations to current economic theory and to the world of economic reality.

The first of the two is the study of what is known as general equilibrium theory. This is an elaboration of the simple but not easily understood point that in an economic system everything affects everything else. Let me illustrate. The price of oil became very low in the 1930s because of discoveries in Texas and the Persian Gulf area. Homeowners shifted in great numbers from coal to oil for home heating, thereby decreasing the demand for coal and employment in the coal mines. Refineries expanded, so more workers were employed there. There was as well a demand for refinery equipment, a complicated example of chemical processes. This in turn induced demands for skilled chemical engineers and for more steel. Gasoline was cheaper, so that more automobiles were bought and used. Tourist areas accessible by road but not by railroad began to flourish, while railroads decayed. Each of these changes in turn induced other changes, and some of these in turn reacted on the demand for and supply of oil.

The economic lesson of this story is that the demand for any one product depends on the prices of all products, including the prices of labor and capital services, which we usually call wages and profits. Similarly, the supply of any product or of labor or capital depends on the prices of all commodities. What determines what prices will prevail? The usual hypothesis in economics is that of equilibrium. The prices are those that cause supply to equal demand in every market. This hypothesis, like many others in economics and indeed in the natural sciences, is certainly not precisely true. But it is a useful approximation, and those who disregard it completely are much further from the truth than are those who exaggerate the prevalence of equilibrium.

The general equilibrium theory, or perhaps vision, of the economy was first stated in full-fledged form by a French economist, Leon Walras, in 1874. But it was hard to use as a tool of analysis and too difficult for economists with little mathematical training to understand. Only in the 1930s did interest revive, especially through the masterful exposition and development by John Hicks, with whom I had the honor of sharing the Nobel Prize in 1972.

But there was an unresolved analytic issue, recognized by at least some. General equilibrium theory asserts that the prices of all commodities are determined as the solution of a large number of equations, those that state the equality of supply and demand on each market. Did these equations necessarily have a solution at all? If not, the general equilibrium theory could not always be true. Indeed, some work by German economists about 1932 suggested the possibility that the equations need not have a meaningful solution. A Viennese banker named Karl Schlesinger, who had studied economics in the university and continued to follow developments in the subject, recognized that the apparent difficulties rested on a subtle misunderstanding and felt that the existence of general equilibrium could be demonstrated. He hired a young mathematician, Abraham Wald, to work on the problem. Wald came up with a proof of existence under certain conditions not easy to interpret; indeed, in light of later work, they were much too stringent. Even so, the proof was difficult.

The heavy tread of history breaks in on the story. Schlesinger would not believe that Austria could fall to Hitler; when it did, he committed suicide. Wald did succeed in leaving and came to the United States, where he shifted his interests to mathematical statistics. He was one of my teachers at Columbia. I came to learn, I do not know how, of the unsolved or only partially solved problem of the existence of general equilibrium. But when I asked Wald about his work on the question, he merely said that it was a very difficult problem. Coming from him, whose mathematical powers were certainly greater than mine, the statement was discouraging.

As frequently happens in the history of science, however, help came from developments in other fields. The theory of games was in a process of rapid development. One theorem, proved by a mathematician named John Nash, struck me as being parallel in many ways to the existence problem for competitive equlibrium. By borrowing and adapting the mathematical tools used by Nash, I was able to state very generally the conditions under which the equations defining general equilibrium had a solution.

There was more than mathematics involved, though. It was necessary to state the general equilibrium system much more explicitly. As Schlesinger had already shown in part, the exact assumptions that were made needed clarification, and much was learned in the process.

As you may see from this account, the existence proof was based on general theoretical progress in economics and in mathematics, and I was certainly not the only one with access to it. Indeed, while writing up my results, I learned that Gerard Debreu, the Nobel laureate in economic science for 1983, had independently come to essentially the same results. We decided to publish the results jointly. Just before our paper appeared, there was one by a third economist, Lionel McKenzie, along similar though not identical lines.

Multiple discoveries are in fact very common in science and for much the same reason. Developments in related fields with different motivation help one to understand a difficult problem better. Since these developments are public knowledge, many scholars can take advantage of them.

It is pleasant to the ego to be first or among the first with a new discovery. However, in this case at least, the evidence is clear that the development of general equilibrium theory would have gone on quite as it did without me.

I may add that, despite their abstract and mathematical sound, existence theorems in general equlibrium theory have turned out to be very useful. They certainly stimulated many more applications of general equilibrium theory to particular economic problems. They gave a greater understanding of what may be termed "general equilibrium thinking," that is, recognizing that a particular economic change will have remote repercussions that may be more significant than the initial change. More directly, Herbert Scarf showed that the method of proof could be adapted to find a way of actually calculating the solutions to general equilibrium systems. The method has been used to study a variety of policy problems: tariffs, corporate income taxation, changes in welfare measures, and economic development in a number of developing countries.

The third contribution I would like to discuss is drawing the economic implications of differences in information among economic agents. My sustained interest arose from considering a practical problem, the organization of medical care, but the ground had been prepared by my studies in mathematical statistics, some of my earlier theoretical work on the economics of risk bearing, and some developments by others of these topics. My contribution here, unlike the first two examples, has been not so much a specific and well-defined technical accomplishment as a point of view that has served to reorient economic theory.

The general equilibrium theory, like most economic theory up to about 1950, assumed that the economic agents operated under certainty. That is, the households, firms, investors, and so forth knew correctly the consequences of their actions or, in some versions, at least acted as if they did. Thus, producers were assumed to know what outputs they would get for given inputs. Investors would know what prices would prevail in the future for the goods they were planning to sell.

I don't mean to imply that economists were so foolish as not to recognize that the economic world was uncertain or that economic agents didn't realize that this was the case. Indeed, some literature clearly showed that much economic behavior could only be explained by assuming that economic agents were well aware of uncertainty; for example, investors held diversified portfolios and bought insurance. However, a general formulation that would permit integration with standard economic theory and in particular with general equilibrium theory was lacking. I was able to work out such a formulation, which introduced the concept of contingent contracts, contracts for delivery of goods or money contingent on the occurrence of any possible state of affairs. In effect, I postulated the existence of insurance against all conceivable risks. My rather sketchy paper was greatly enriched and extended by Gerard Debreu. The idea was simplicity itself and yet novel.

It has become a standard tool of analysis, in this case rather more than I intended. I considered the theory of contingent contracts as a sketch of an ideal system to which the methods of risk bearing and risk shifting in the real world were to be compared. It was clear enough empirically that the world did not have nearly as many possibilities for trading risks as my model would have predicted. I did not, however, have at first a particularly good explanation for the discrepancy.

A considerable insight came a few years later. I was asked by the Ford Foundation to take a theorist's view of the economics of medical care. I first surveyed the empirical literature on the subject. My theoretical perspective suggested that there was inadequate insurance against the very large financial risks. Indeed, insurance coverage, both governmental and private, has expanded greatly since then. But I soon realized that there were obstacles to the achievement of full insurance. Insurance against health expenditures creates an incentive to spend more freely than is desirable.

Was there a general theoretical principle behind this? The concept of insurance against uncertainties did not fully reflect the actual situation, namely, that different individuals may have different uncertainties. The person insured knows more about his or her state of health than the insurer. The fact that individuals have informational differences is a key element in any economic system, not just in health insurance.

To take a very different example, consider tenant farming. If the landlord hired someone to work his or her farm, the farm worker would have limited incentives to work to full capacity, since the worker's income is assured. The owner could indeed direct the worker if fully informed about what the worker was doing. But his information can be obtained only by costly supervision. In its absence, the two parties will have different information, and production will be inefficient. The other extreme alternative is to rent the farm at a fixed fee. Then indeed incentives to the worker (or, in this case, tenant) are very strong. But farming is a risky business, and poor farmers at least may not be able to bear the uncertainty. Hence, the compromise of sharecropping arose. It dulls incentives, but not completely, and it shares risks, but not completely. Similarly, most health insurance policies have a coinsurance feature, so that risks are partially shared, while the patient still has some incentive to economize.

The theme may be stated without elaboration. Informational differences pervade the economy and have given rise to both inefficiencies and contractual arrangements and informal understandings to protect the less informed. My own contributions here were conceptual rather than technical, and the present theory is the result of many hands.

I have tried to present, as clearly as I can, the genesis of some of my researches. They have all been related to the present state of thinking by others. The field of science, indeed, the whole world of human society, is a cooperative one. At each moment, we are competing, whether for academic honors or business success. But the background, and what makes society an engine of progress, is a whole set of successes and even failures from which we all have learned.

Awarded Nobel Prize in 1972. Lecture presented November 5, 1984.

Date of Birth

August 23, 1921

Academic Degrees

B.S.   City College, New York, 1940

M.A.   Columbia University, 1941

Ph.D.   Columbia University, 1951

Academic Affiliations

Assistant Professor of Economics, University of Chicago, 1948–1949

Acting Assistant Professor of Economics and Statistics, Stanford University, 1949–1950

Associate Professor of Economics and Statistics, Stanford University, 1950–1953

Executive Head, Department of Economics, Stanford University, 1953–1956

Professor of Economics, Statistics, and Operations Research, Stanford University, 1953–1968

Visiting Professor of Economics, Massachusetts Institute of Technology, fall 1966

Fellow, Churchill College (Cambridge), 1963–1964, 1970, 1973

Professor of Economics, Harvard University, 1968–1974

James Bryant Conant University Professor, Harvard University, 1974–1979

Joan Kenney Professor of Economics and Professor of Operations Research, Stanford University, 1979–1991

Joan Kenney Professor of Economics and Professor of Operations Research, Emeritus, Stanford University, 1991–present

Selected Books

Social Choice and Individual Values, 1951, 1963

Studies in the Mathematical Theory of Inventory and Production, 1958 (with S. Karlin and H. Scarf)

Public Investment, the Rate of Return, and Optimal Fiscal Policy, 1970 (with M. Kurz)

Essays in the Theory of Risk-Bearing, 1971

The Limits of Organization, 1974

Collected Papers of Kenneth J. Arrow, Volumes 1–6, 1983–1985

Paul A. Samuelson

Economics in My Time

The last five or six decades have seen American economics come of age and then become the dominant center of world political economy. When I began the study of economics back in 1932 on the University of Chicago Midway, economics was literary economics. A few original spirits—such as Harold Hotelling, Ragnar Frisch, and R. G. D. Allen—used mathematical symbols; but, if their experiences were like my early ones, learned journals rationed pretty severely acceptance of anything involving the calculus. Such esoteric animals as matrices were never seen in the social science zoos. At most a few chaste determinants were admitted to our Augean stables.

Do I seem to be describing Eden, a paradise to which many would like to return in revulsion against the symbolic pus-pimples that disfigure not only the pages of *Econometrica* but also the *Economic Journal* and the *American Economic Review*?

Don't believe it. Like Tobacco Road, the old economics was strewn with rusty monstrosities of logic inherited from the past, its soil generated few stalks of vigorous new science, and the correspondence between the terrain of the real world and the maps of the economics textbook and treatises was neither smooth nor even one-to-one.

The Great Takeoff
Yes, 1932 was a great time to be born as an economist. The sleeping beauty of political economy was waiting for the enlivening kiss of new methods, new paradigms, new hired hands, and new problems. Science

is a parasite: the greater the patient population the better the advance in physiology and pathology; and out of pathology arises therapy. The year 1932 was the trough of the Great Depression, and from its rotten soil was belatedly begot the new subject that today we call macroeconomics.

Do I refer to the Keynesian revolution? Of course I do. But people are wrong to associate with that name the particular policies and ideologies found fifty years ago in the writings of John Maynard Keynes, Alvin Hansen, Joan Robinson, Abba Lerner, and Michael Kalecki. The New Classical School, through the quills of Robert Lucas, Tom Sargent, and Robert Barro, reverse those Keynesian doctrines 180 degrees. Nevertheless, the present-day equations found in monetarism, eclectic mainstream Keynesianism, or rational expectationism are a galaxy removed from what were in Walras and Marshall—or in Frank Knight and Jacob Viner, my great neoclassical teachers in Chicago. The macromethodology innovated by Keynes' 1936 *General Theory* constitutes both the 1985 swords that slash at Keynesianism and the shields that defend mainstream macroeconomics.

So far I have been talking about the internal logic and development of economics as a science. It has been an inside-the-seminar-room survey of the subject, where of course the observations of the economic world have been brought into that seminar room. As a result of outside influences the period from 1932 to 1975 was a favorable one for economists like me, in that it was an epoch of tremendous university expansion and job opportunity. If one can borrow from the vulgar terminology of economic science fiction, my generation of economic activity was buoyed along by the great wave of a Kondratieff expansion.

The New Deal and welfare state created a vast new market for economists in government. Then came the war, which was carried on by armaments, cannon fodder, and economists: when the business cycle was put into hibernation by the wartime command economy, whenever problems of quantitative resource allocation ran out, economists could chance their arm on the new science of operations research, a game at which only the rare brilliant physicist could beat the run-of-the-mill economists.

Then came the postwar boom in education. Where there had been in 1935 only a few strong centers for economic research—Harvard, Chicago, Columbia, and a few others—now everywhere in the land there grew up excellent graduate departments. No longer did one wait to be made a full professor at forty-five; the typical new Shangri-La in the firmament of postwar economics was created by an activist department chairman, given the go-ahead signal by his administration to go out and hire hotshot stars at twice his own salary. Like beardless colonels in the wartime air corps, thirty-year-old full professors deigned to grace prestigious academic chairs.

Pax Americanus

The sheer number of American economists gave them unfair advantage over economists abroad. In addition, Hitler gave us even before the war the cream of the continental crop. Just as Chicago is the biggest Polish city after Warsaw, and New York the greatest Swedish city after Stockholm, America obtained practically the whole of the Austrian school in economics. Along with such names as Einstein, von Neumann, and Fermi go such American economist names as Koopmans, Leontief, Schumpeter, Marschak, Haberler, Kuznets, and many others. Later, as strength draws to itself strength, there began to appear in the American lineup the names of Hurwicz, Debreu, Theil, Bhagwati, Coase, Fischer, and many others.

Again and again I have seen in recent decades the tremendous stimulus that top postdoctoral scholars from abroad have received from a year's sojourn in the States, hopping on the grand tour from Cambridge to Stanford. They go back home fired up to change the old world. For half a decade their reprints keep coming. Then, almost in accordance with some second law of thermodynamics, the Schumpeterian burst subsides.

Evidently science itself is not subject to the law of constant returns to scale. The book of Matthew applies: To him who hath shall be given. Unfair? you say. Well, as Jack Kennedy observed: Who said life is fair?

Life at the Top

I have seen economists grow in public esteem and in pecuniary demand. Surveys have shown that the highest-paid scientists, physical and biological scientists as well as economists, are not to be found in private industry but rather in the university—perhaps in-and-out of the universities would put it more accurately. I don't know scholars who have agents. But some do have lecture bureaus. And being a public member on corporate boards has become a new way of life.

It is a heady experience to advise the Prince on a sabbatical tour of duty in Washington. Newspaper columnists from academia, serendipitously, acquire the omniscience they need for the job.

"And gladly teach" used to refer to the lecture hall and seminar table, but now includes telling congressional committees there is no free lunch and telling TV audiences to buy cheap and sell dear.

Trees do not grow to the sky. Every Kondratieff wave has its inflection point. The 1932–1965 expansion in economists' prestige and self-esteem has been followed by some leaner years. We have become more humble and, as Churchill said, we have much to be humble about. Economists have not been able to agree on a good cure for stagflation. That disillusions noneconomists. And, to tell the truth, it punctures our own self-complacency. We shop around for new paradigms the way alchemists prospect for new philosophers' stone. Just because a National Bureau paper is silly does not mean it is uninteresting. Just because it is profound does not mean that it is admired.

Mea Culpa

So far I have been talking about economics. The title of this series, "My Evolution as an Economist," suggests that I should be talking about *me*. Mr. Dooley said that Theodore Roosevelt was going to write a book about the Spanish–American War called *Me and Cuba*. It would begin with Teddy's tribute, "My black sergeant was the bravest man I ever knew. He followed me up San Juan Hill."

I can claim that in talking about modern economics I am talking about me. My finger has been in every pie. I once claimed to be the last generalist in economics, writing about and teaching such diverse subjects as international trade and econometrics, economic theory and business cycles, demography and labor economics, finance and monopolistic competition, history of doctrines and locational economics. Kilroy, having been there, must share the guilt. (Goethe wrote that there was no crime he ever heard of that he didn't feel capable of committing. Bob Solow's reaction was that Goethe flattered himself. And perhaps what I called "crime" is a mistranslation of what Goethe meant only as "error.")

Here is my worst error. Do you remember the infamous wrong prediction by economists that after World War II there would be mass unemployment? I was not part of the multi-agency team that produced the official 1945 forecast of doomsday. But, if you look at the yellowing files of the *New Republic,* you will find a well-written article by this humble servant that involves a large squared forecasting error on the downward side. My friend and mentor, Alvin Hansen, who believed in a postwar restocking boom, could have taught me better. And so could Sumner Slichter and a host of Keynesians and non-Keynesians.

I reproach myself for a gross error. But I would reproach myself more if I had persisted in an error after observations revealed it clearly to be that. I made a deal of money in the late 1940s on the bull side, ignoring Satchel Paige's advice to Lot's wife, "Never look back." Rather I would advocate Samuelson's Law: "Always look back. You may learn something from your residuals. Usually one's forecasts are not so good as one remembers them; the difference may be instructive." The dictum "If you must forecast, forecast often," is neither a joke nor a confession of impotence. It is a recognition of the primacy of brute fact over pretty theory. That part of the future that cannot be related to the present's past is precisely what science cannot hope to capture. Fortunately, there is plenty of work for science to do, plenty of scientific tasks not yet done.

Other Testimonies

I shall not shirk talking more specifically about my own development as a scholar and scientist. But, as I do not believe in the kind of elegant variation that follows "he said," by "he averred," and then by "vouchsafed the speaker," I shall not try to duplicate some earlier autobiographical writings. Peppered through many of the technical articles in the four volumes of my *Collected Scientific Papers* are various personal reminiscences. But the richest vein of this kind of ore will be found in, first, my 1968 presidential address before the World Congress of the International Economic Association. It is cunningly entitled "The Way of an Economist," ambivalent words denoting both the economic road traveled and the personal style of the Siegfried traversing that road. Similarly, today in speaking of "Economics in My Time," I also mean economics in my own peculiar rhythms and style.

A second source is my "Economics in a Golden Age: A Personal Memoir," which appeared in the Daedalus book Gerald Holton edited, *The Twentieth Century Sciences: Studies in the Biography of Ideas* (New York: W. W. Norton, 1972).

A third source, one whose title was imposed on me, is *My Lifetime Philosophy*. This appeared in the series for students of *The American Economist* 27 (1983): 5–12, and in the fifth volume of *Collected Scientific Papers of Paul A. Samuelson* (2000).

The Scientist Delineated

Here briefly, in the third person for objectivity, is the superficial outline of my scientific career.

PAS has already been incredibly lucky throughout his lifetime, overpaid and underworked. A bright youngster, favored by admiring parents, he shone at school until the high-school years when he became an underachiever. The calendar lies in naming May 15, 1915, as his time of birth. Truly he was born on the morning of January 2, 1932, at the University of Chicago.

He was made for academic life. An A student at Chicago and an A+ one at Harvard, PAS wandered by chance into economics. Economics turned out to be made for him as the Darwinian genes from generations of commercial ancestors encountered their teleological destiny.

Every honor he aspired to came his way, and came early. He got the undergraduate social science medal his undergraduate year. Just when commencement loomed near, the Social Science Research Council created a new experimental fellowship program in economics, whose first award supported him handsomely at Harvard. Having drawn from Chicago giants like Knight, Viner, Henry Schultz, Henry Simons, Paul Douglas, John U. Nef, and Lloyd Mints, he levitated to Harvard Yard to learn from Joseph Schumpeter, Wassily Leontief, Edwin Bidwell Wilson, Gottfried Haberler, Edward Chamberlin, and Alvin Hansen. Before his SSRC fellowship gave out, he overcame the opposition of the Society of Fellows to economics and rode on the shoulders of Vilfredo Pareto into the sacred circle of Junior Fellows. The philosopher Willard van Orman Quine, the mathematician Garrett Birkhoff, the double-Nobel physicist John Bardeen, the chemists Bright Wilson and Robert Woodward, the polymath

Harry T. Levine were his companions in arms in the Society of Fellows. There he hit his stride and began to turn out articles faster than the journals could absorb such quasi-mathematical stuff.

It is not true that PAS began life as a physicist or mathematician. Well into his undergraduate course he discerned that mathematics was to revolutionize modern economics. Proceeding to learn mathematics, PAS still remembers how a Lagrange multiplier first swam into his ken and how, with a wild surmise, it gave him independent discovery of the Edgeworth-Stackelberg asymmetric solution for duopoly—an insight that has kept him immune to the false charms of Nash–Cournot purported solutions.

His *Foundations of Economic Analysis*, written mostly as a Junior Fellow but usable later for the Ph.D. union card, won the David A. Wells Prize at Harvard. Later, in 1947, it helped him receive the first John Bates Clark Medal of the American Economic Association, awarded for scholarly promise before the age of forty. Its quality was thrice blessed: later still it contributed to his 1970 Nobel Prize in economics, the second time that fabricated (or "forged") honor was awarded and the first time to an American.

Hegira down the River

If PAS was born as a child his freshman year at Chicago, he was born a second time as a man that October 1940 day he succumbed to a call from MIT. MIT's force met no detectable Harvard resistance, so the movable object moved. It was the best thing that could have happened to PAS. A boy must always remain a boy in his father's house. On his own acres a man can build his own mansion and after 1941 PAS, along with magnificent colleagues, was able to help build up what became recognized as a leading world center for economics. Living well is the best revenge, Hemingway's crowd used to say; but, in sober truth, the example of MIT's Norbert Wiener, who in his days of fame still brooded over his ejection from Harvard Yard, led PAS ever to cherish his Harvard connections and labor for the greater glory of Cambridge and Middlesex County.

Peer recognition came early and often: from the American Academy of Arts and Sciences, the National Academy, the American Philosophical Society, and the British Academy. Just as it is the first million that is the hardest, one honor leads to another. After the first dozen honorary degrees, all it takes is longevity to double the number. The first such degree—from Chicago, alma mater and basilica of a church he no longer believed in—PAS found most touching. When Harvard honored a prophet in his own country, he also liked that.

Vice-presidencies and presidencies in professional societies came his way: the Econometric Society, the American Economic Association, the International Economic Association. As yet there is no Galaxy Political Economy Club.

A scholar at a new place for economic study like MIT receives plenty of offers from all over the world. PAS revealed a preference to be an immovable object, and when made an institute professor in 1966, with magnificent research opportunities and optional teaching duties, he in effect returned to the womb of a perpetual junior fellowship. Having arrived in paradise, he stayed there.

But not without excursions to the outside. Many a tutorial he gave to congressional committees. Often when he became a consultant to a federal agency, that precipitated its demise. The U.S. Treasury and the Federal Reserve Board did, however, survive his academic counsels. Murmuring that the United States is too precious to be turned over exclusively to big-picture thinkers like John Kenneth Galbraith and Walt Whitman Rostow, PAS gave economic tutorial to Adlai Stevenson and Averell Harriman; and worked his way as adviser to Senator J. F. Kennedy, candidate Kennedy, and president-elect Kennedy. Moses-like PAS did not pass into the promised land beyond the Potomac, but as an *eminence grise* he had the fun of backing the poker hands of such magnificent Joshuas as Walter Heller, James Tobin, and Kermit Gordon at the Kennedy Council of Economic Advisers.

What can the good fairies give the man who has everything? George Stigler, referring to Samuelson's 1947 *Foundations* and his newly published 1948 best-selling textbook *Economics,* introduced him with the words, "Samuelson, having achieved fame, now seeks fortune." Soon the smoke of burning mortgage could be sniffed in Belmont, Massachusetts. More than this, J. K. Galbraith's prophesy in a *Fortune* review, that a new generation would receive its economics from *Economics,* turned out to be right on the mark. PAS was heard to mutter complacently, "Let those who will write the nation's laws if I can write its textbooks." Being denounced by William Buckley for blaspheming God and man at Yale, the textbook took on a new aura of respectability and sales soared all over the world.

A quarter of a century ago the author of *Economics* commented on the new layer of fame that accrues to a scholar who writes a best-seller, stating modestly,

Writing a beginning textbook is hard work. But its rewards have been tremendous—and I do not mean simply pecuniary rewards. Contact with hundreds of thousands of minds of a whole generation is an experience like no other that a scholar will ever meet. And writing down what we economists know about economics has been truly an exciting experience. I can only hope that some of this excitement will rub off on the reader.

By Joy Possessed

Stop! Enough is enough. Of such *Who's Who* boilerplate, enough is too much. What has been described above could be said of many a successful go-getter. A West Pointer who hated soldiering might settle for a Faustian bargain in which promotions and blue ribbons compensate for a wasted life.

The reward that has counted for me in scholarship and science is the marvelous hunt through enchanted forests. I began to write articles for publication before I was twenty-one. I have never stopped. I hope never to stop. When Harry Johnson died, he had eighteen papers in proof. That is dying with your boots on! (Even for Harry, who never did things by halves or held down to the golden mean, eighteen was overdoing it.)

My mind is ever toying with economic ideas and relationships. Great novelists and poets have reported occasional abandonment by their muse. The well runs dry, permanently or on occasion. Mine has been a better luck. As I have written elsewhere, there is a vast inventory of topics and problems floating in the back of my mind. More perhaps than I shall ever have occasion to write up for publication. A result that I notice in statistical mechanics may someday help resolve a problem in finance.

Like a gravid spouse I achieve the release of publication. Have I published too much? Others must form their judgment on this. Speaking for myself, in my heart of hearts I have regretted almost no chapter, article, note, or footnote my quill has penned. And I have rued many an excision forced on me by editors of only finite patience or self-imposed for reasons of space and aesthetic measure.

Perhaps this betrays the lack of taste that marks the gourmand and not the gourmet? I hope not. I certainly sympathize with the view expressed in the following conversation of the classicist-poet A. E. Housman. A friend asked him why he was not including in a collection of his writings on Latin a certain item: "Don't you think it good?" "I think it good," Housman replied, "but not good enough for me." And not infrequently when I read some scholar's latest work, I have asked of Robert Solow what G. H. Hardy asked of J. E. Littlewood: "Why would a man who could write such an article do so?"

The able scholar with writer's block elevates by the mere passage of time the standards each future work must hurdle. It is easy to write a letter every day, but when you have not done so for five years, there is really nothing to report.

Repeatedly I have denied the great-man or great-work notion of science. Every drop helps, the old farmer said, as he spat into the pond. One does the best one can on the most pressing problem that presents. And, if after you have done so, your next moves are down a trajectory of diminishing returns, then still it is optimal to follow the rule of doing the best that there is to do. Besides, at any time a Schumpeterian innovation or Darwinian mutation may occur to you, plucking the violin string of increasing return.

Between Mozart and Brahms, I'm for Mozart. I am thankful for the precious gold pieces Pierro Sraffa left us. But economics would be the better if he had also blessed us all with some dozens of rubies and pearls. And, as I remember his eloquent but sad eyes, one wonders whether he would not have been the happier man if—as William James puts it—he had been born with a bottle of champagne to his credit. Maynard Keynes, who suffered from no writer's cramp, when asked at the end of his life what he'd have done different if he had it all over to do, replied, "I'd have drunk more champagne."

Earlier I confessed to having always been overpaid and underworked. Even good friends might agree with the first of these adjectives, but several will protest at the second, perhaps protesting, "Come off it, you work all the time, weekends and during vacations and, if legend holds, often during the reveries of the midnight hours." True enough. It is precisely my point though that working out economic analysis is play, not work. I am notorious for shirking tasks I hate to do. I minimize administrative duties, displaying an incompetence in their performance that chokes off additional assignments. Like Dennis Robertson, I always wash the forks last in the realization that should an atomic holocaust be imminent there may never be a need to do them.

If I am required to fill out an elaborate questionnaire, that liability is likely to stimulate me to write a new model in the theory of trade or in population genetics. Anything to put off the evil day of duty.

Remembered Kisses

Novels about painters, musicians, poets, or scientists notoriously fail to convey what they do in the working hours of the week. Come to think of it, novels about allegedly great business tycoons similarly fail to capture what it is precisely that they do.

Therefore, speaking to an audience of economists, I should be more specific and describe some particular acts of scientific gestation. How did I first notice the problem? When did a breakthrough occur? What were the steps of development? And how, in retrospect, was the pattern of knowledge affected by the research?

But where to begin? I toyed with the experiment of describing the big ledger that, for a year like 1983, served as a partial diary of research doodlings. Thus, the January 1 entry might be jottings on how to devise a numerical example of a linear programming system that violates a crude version of the Le Chatelier principle in economics. This never got published. Yet. It refers back to work done in 1949, and indeed in 1937, when I was a student at E. B. Wilson's knee—or perhaps shoulder. One might then trace in the daybook a return on January 2 and 3 to the problem, and perhaps discern how it modulates into a related problem.

Suffice it to say that, in the course of a year, there will be a half a hundred such finger exercises. But it would be misleading to believe that my 1983 research is well described, or even sampled, by the chance items that happen to get jotted down in one bedside journal. Therefore, I had better reserve for another and longer day detailed discussion of how some familiar result was conceived and came into being. (The impatient reader can be referred for a sample to my 1982 contribution to the Jørgen Gelting Festschrift, which I entitled "A Chapter in the History of Ramsey's Optimal Feasible Taxation and Optimal Public Utility Prices.")

Chasing the Bitch Goddess of Success

Let me close with a few remarks on the motivations and rewards of scientists. Scientists are as avaricious and competitive as Smithian businessmen. The coin they seek is not apples, nuts, and yachts; nor is it the coin itself, or power as that term is ordinarily used. Scholars seek fame. The fame they seek, as I noted in my 1961 American Economic Association presidential address, is fame with their peers—the other scientists whom they respect and whose respect they strive for. The sociologist Robert K. Merton has documented what I call this dirty little secret in his book *The Sociology of Science*.

I am no exception. Abraham Lincoln's law partner and biographer William Herndon observed that there was always a little clock of ambition ticking in the bosom of honest and whimsical Abe. No celebrity as a *Newsweek* columnist, no millions of clever-begotten speculative gains, no power as the Svengali or Rasputin to the prince and president could count as a pennyweight in my balance of worth against the prospect of recognition for having contributed to the empire of science.

Once I asked my friend the statistician Harold Freeman, "Harold, if the Devil came to you with the bargain that, in exchange for your immortal soul, he'd give you a brilliant theorem, would you do it?" "No," he replied, "but I would for an inequality." I like that answer. The day I proved that no one could be more than 60,000 standard deviations dumber than the mean, that Samuelson inequality made my day. The fact that subsequent writers have both generalized beyond it and discovered antecedents of it in earlier writings has not altered my pleasure in it. For that is the way of science, and sufficient to the day is the increment to the house of science that day brings.

Being precocious, I got an early start. Unconsciously and consciously, I was a young man in a hurry because I felt that the limited life span of my male ancestors tolled the knell for me. My father died young when I was twenty-three. I was supposed to resemble him, and the effect on me was especially traumatic. What I was to do I would have to do early, is what I thought. Actually, modern science granted me respite. Heredity, always, is modifiable by environment. Whatever the reason, I have been granted bouncing good health, a factor given too little weight in allocating merit to scientists and in explaining their achievements. A respected friend of mine, sometimes unfairly marked down as an under-achiever, has been subject all his life to debilitating migraines. I say he is the meritorious one for having, as the Bible says, used his pound so judiciously.

There is another aspect to early, full (even overfull) recognition. It re-laxes you. Why fret about priorities when, in the time you might spend in recriminations and turf claiming, you can dip your hook into the wa-ters and be pulling out other pretty fish?

I long ago enunciated the doctrine that scholars work for their self-esteem, in the sense of what they all agree to judge meritorious. However, once your need for glory in the eyes of others has been somewhat ap-peased, you become free to work for your own approval. The job you will think well done is the one that brings true bliss. Perhaps part of this involves the faith that what one craftsman will like, so will eventually the rest.

There was never a time when I didn't strive to please myself. There have been those who thought that my fooling around with thermodynam-ics was an attempt to inflate the scientific validity of economics; even perhaps to snow the hoi polloi of economists who naturally can't judge intricacies of physics. Actually, such methodological excursions, if any-thing, put a tax on reputation rather than enhancing it. So what? Taxes are the price we pay for civilization. Such work is fun. And I perceive it adds to the depth and breadth of human knowledge.

At a deeper level one works not just to gain fame and esteem with colleagues. Not just to please oneself and enjoy the fun of the chase. At a deeper level the antagonist of Dr. A. B. Physiologist is not some rival physician at Göttingen or Oxford. The opponent is cancer. So at bottom is it with the economist. There is an objective reality out there that we

are trying to understand, hard as that task may be. If ever a person becomes sick to death of faculty intrigue and professional infighting, if ever
one sees democracy and civilization crumbling around one, always one
can retreat to that objective study of reality. The complex numbers do
not dissemble and even for toothache there is no better anodyne than five
fast rounds with the puzzler of the business cycle or the intricacies of the
theory of control.

I mean this literally and can illustrate what I mean by a true story. The
late Voss Neisser, a refugee economist who graced the New School for
Social Research, once told me what a relief it was in those grim days of
Hitler's march toward power to grapple with the problem of the determining of Walrasian competitive equilibrium. I understood perfectly
and agreed completely.

Someone asked me whether I enjoyed getting the Nobel Prize. I thought
before answering. "Yes," I replied, "few things in life bring undiluted
pleasure, but this one actually did." The honor was a pleasant surprise
and came early, but not so early as to worry even me. Friends whose
opinions I valued were pleased. If there were contrary opinions, I was
too obtuse to be aware of them. My family enjoyed the Stockholm
hoopla. Some colleagues in science have looked back with pain at the
public interviews and turmoil that took them out of their laboratories. I
bore up well and discovered that it takes only a few days of dependence
upon one's own chauffeur to develop an addiction.

Indian Summer

Sociologists of science study how the Nobel award affects a scholar. Do
the laureates go into an era of depressed fertility? Do they write fewer
or more joint papers, and more often list their names first or list them
last? Does citing of them accelerate? What is the propensity to change
fields—for a physicist to tackle the problem of the brain, for a chemist
to become an expert on peace or the minimum wage?

To me it was a case where my cup runneth over—almost. The last
vestiges of guilt disappeared when I chose to go off the main turnpike of
my discipline of economics: to explore R. A. Fisher's notion of survival
value, or Clerk Maxwell's image of a Demon who cheats the second law
of thermodynamics of its certainty. I still monitor business trends and

the latest fads like a hawk. I still write articles in the many different provinces of political economy. But the last generalist no longer feels it necessary to keep on top of—I mean try to keep on top of—all the literatures of economics.

As I veer toward the traditional three score and ten, how do I feel about it? Goethe, who like Wagner and Verdi had a great long run, wrote that the difference between age and youth was that in youth, when you called on it, it was always there in response. By contrast, only on the best good days could the octogenarian attain the peak performance. To myself, I am sixty-nine going on twenty-five. All the days seem as good as ever. But, as the lyricist says and reason insists, the stock of what's left of the good times must shrink as you reach September.

Awarded Nobel Prize in 1970. Lecture presented February 6, 1985.

Date of Birth

May 15, 1915

Academic Degrees

B.A.   University of Chicago, 1935

M.A.   Harvard University, 1936

Ph.D.   Harvard University, 1941

Academic Affiliations

Assistant Professor of Economics, Massachusetts Institute of Technology, 1940

Associate Professor of Economics, Massachusetts Institute of Technology, 1944

Professor of International Economic Relations, Fletcher School of Law and Diplomacy, Tufts University, 1945

Professor of Economics, Massachusetts Institute of Technology, 1947

Institute Professor, Massachusetts Institute of Technology, 1966–1986

Institute Professor, Emeritus, Massachusetts Institute of Technology, 1986–present

Vernon F. Taylor Visiting Distinguished Professor, Trinity University, 1989

Selected Books

Foundations of Economic Analysis, 1947, 1983

Economics, 1948, 2001 (17th ed., with W. Nordhaus)

Linear Programming and Economic Analysis, 1958, 1987 (with R. Dorfman and R. M. Solow)

The Collected Scientific Papers of Paul A. Samuelson, Vols. 1–5, 1966–2000

Milton Friedman

The topic assigned to me was "My Evolution as an Economist." I am sure, however, that some questions about the Nobel Prize hold greater interest for at least some of you than my evolution as an economist—in particular, how to get a Nobel Prize in economics. So, as an empirical scientist, I decided to investigate statistically what an economist has to do to get a Nobel Prize.

As most of you may know, the economics award is relatively recent. It was established by the Central Bank of Sweden in 1968 to commemorate its three-hundredth anniversary. So far, twenty-two people have received the Nobel award in economics. Not one of them has been female—so, to judge only from the past, the most important thing to do if you want to be a Nobel laureate is to be male. I hasten to add that the absence of females is not, I believe, attributable to male chauvinist bias on the part of the Swedish Nobel Committee. I believe that the economics profession as a whole would have been nearly unanimous that, during the period in question, only one female candidate met the relevant standards—the English economist Joan Robinson, who has since died. The failure of the Nobel Committee to award her a prize may well have reflected bias but not sex bias. The economists here will understand what I am talking about.

A second requirement is to be a U.S. citizen. Twelve of the twenty-two recipients of the Nobel Prize were from the United States, four from the United Kingdom, two from Sweden, and one each from four other countries. This generalization is less clear-cut than the first because the population of the United States is more than three times as large as Britain, but the number of Nobel recipients only three times as large. So on a per-capita basis, Britain has a better record than we have.

A third generalization is, at least to me, the most interesting statistical result. Of the twelve Americans who have won the Nobel Prize in economics, nine either studied or taught at the University of Chicago. So the next lesson is to go to the University of Chicago. And I may say, in addition to those nine, one other, Friedrich Hayek, also taught at the University of Chicago for ten years. However, I have classified him as an Austrian rather than an American in my compilation. Beyond that, the statistics won't go, and that's all the advice I can give to potential Nobel laureates.

The most memorable feature of receiving a Nobel award is the week in Sweden in early December during which the formal ceremonies are held. It seemed to my wife and me when we were there that all of Sweden spends that week doing nothing but paying attention to the Nobel ceremonies. One party or affair succeeds another. The week culminates in a feast and a dance at which each laureate is required to give a toast lasting not more than three minutes to an already tipsy audience. I thought you might like to hear part of the toast that I gave in 1976. I will leave out the pleasantries that began it and ended it and give just the central part:

My science is a latecomer, the Prize in Economic Sciences in Memory of Alfred Nobel having been established only in 1968 by the Central Bank of Sweden to celebrate its tercentenary. That circumstance does, I admit, leave me with something of a conflict of interest. As some of you may know, my monetary studies have led me to the conclusion that central banks could profitably be replaced by computers geared to provide a steady rate of growth in the quantity of money. Fortunately, for me personally, and for a select group of fellow economists, that conclusion has had no practical impact—else there would have been no Central Bank of Sweden to have established the award I am honored to receive. Should I draw the moral that sometimes to fail is to succeed? Whether I do or not, I suspect some economists may.

Delighted as I am with the award, I must confess that the past eight weeks [this was in December 1976] have impressed on me that not only is there no free lunch, there is no free prize. It is a tribute to the worldwide repute of the Nobel awards that the announcement of an award converts its recipient into an instant expert on all and sundry, and unleashes hordes of ravenous newsmen and photographers from journals and TV stations around the world. I myself have been asked my opinion on everything from a cure for the common cold to the market value of a letter signed by John F. Kennedy. Needless to say, the attention is flattering but also corrupting. Somehow, we badly need an antidote for both the inflated attention granted a Nobel laureate in areas outside his competence and the inflated ego each of us is in so much danger of acquiring. My own field suggests an obvious antidote: competition through the establishment of many more such awards. But a product that has been so successful is not easy to displace. Hence, I suspect that our inflated egos are safe for a good long time to come.

To turn to the suggested autobiographical subject matter, as I have thought back over my own life experience and that of others, I have been enormously impressed by the role that pure chance plays in determining our life history. I was reminded of some famous lines of Robert Frost:

Two roads diverged in a yellow wood,
And sorry I could not travel both
I took the one less traveled by,
And that has made all the difference.

As I recalled my own experience and development, I was impressed by the series of lucky accidents that determined the road I traveled. The first, and surely the most important, was the lucky accident that I was born in the United States. Both my parents were born in Carpatho-Ruthenia, which when they emigrated to the United States was part of Austro-Hungary, later, part of Czechoslovakia, currently, part of the Soviet Union. Both came to the United States as teenagers; they met and married in this country. If they had stayed at home, had nonetheless married one another, and had the same children, I would today be a citizen of the Soviet Union and not of the United States. That was surely pure accident, as it is for most residents of the United States, who like myself are the descendants of people who came to this country as immigrants one or two or three generations ago. As with my parents, most of them brought little with them except their hands and their mouths.

The second major lucky accident was a high-school teacher I had as a sophomore. His field was political science—or civics, as it was called then—but he had a great love for geometry. The course I took from him in Euclidean geometry instilled in me a love and respect for and interest in mathematics that has remained with me ever since. I shall never forget his using the proof of the Pythagorean theorem (the theorem that the sum of the squares of the two sides of a right triangle equals the square of the hypotenuse) as an occasion to quote the last lines of Keats's *Ode on a Grecian Urn,* "Beauty is truth, truth beauty—that is all/Ye know on earth,/and all ye need to know."

A third event, or rather series of chance events, occurred during my college career. As Bill Breit told you, I went to Rutgers University, which today is a mega-university, a mammoth state university. In 1928, when I entered Rutgers, it was a small private college, though the process of converting it to a state university was already in its early stages, in the form of a system of competitive scholarships, tenable at Rutgers and funded by the state of New Jersey. I managed to win one of those scholarships, which relieved me of having to pay tuition to go to college.

My parents, like so many immigrants of that time, were very poor. We never had a family income that by today's standards would have put us above the poverty level. In addition, my father died when I was a senior in high school. However, thanks to the state scholarship plus the usual combination of such jobs as waiting on tables, clerking in stores, and working in the summer, I was well able to pay my own way through college—and indeed ended up with a small nest egg that helped meet the expenses of my first year of graduate study.

Because of my interest in math, I planned to major in mathematics. I was very innocent and the only occupation I knew of that used mathematics was being an insurance actuary, so that was my intended career. The actuarial profession is a highly specialized profession, which has an association that conducts a series of examinations that a budding actuary must pass to become a fellow and to become established in the profession. As an undergraduate, I took some of those exams. I passed a couple and failed a couple—the only exams I can remember ever failing.

By accident, I also took some courses in economics, and that is where the Goddess of Chance entered the picture, because the Rutgers economics faculty included two extraordinary teachers who had a major impact on my life. One was Arthur F. Burns, who many years later became chairman of the Federal Reserve System and is currently our ambassador to West Germany. When I first studied under him, more than fifty years ago, Arthur was in the process of writing his doctoral dissertation. Then, and in my later contacts with him, he instilled a passion for scientific integrity and for accuracy and care that has had a major effect on my scientific work. The other teacher who changed my life was Homer Jones, who was teaching at Rutgers to earn a living while working on a doctoral degree at the University of Chicago. Both are still among my closest friends a half-century later.

Homer later went on to become a vice-president in charge of research at the Federal Reserve Bank of St. Louis. In that capacity he has had a major influence on the spread of interest and knowledge about money in the United States. The publications of the Federal Reserve Bank of St. Louis are unquestionably cited more frequently in the scientific literature than those of any of the other eleven Federal Reserve banks; that is entirely attributable to Homer.

If not for my good fortune in encountering those two extraordinary people, my life would have been radically different, which brings me to the fourth accident. When I finished college I still didn't know whether I wanted to continue in mathematics or economics. Like all youngsters who need financial assistance, I applied to a number of universities for fellowships or scholarships. In the 1930s the kind of assistance a student could get was much less generous than it is these days—it was a different world altogether. I was lucky enough to receive two offers of tuition scholarships, one in applied mathematics from Brown University and one in economics from the University of Chicago. The offer from Chicago undoubtedly came because Homer Jones intervened on my behalf with Frank Knight, who was his teacher at Chicago.

It was close to a toss of a coin that determined which offer I accepted. If I had gone to Brown, I would have become an applied mathematician. Having chosen Chicago, I became an economist. As Frost said, "Two roads diverged in a yellow wood." I cannot say I took the less traveled one, but the one I took determined the whole course of my life.

The reason I chose as I did was not only, perhaps not even primarily, the intellectual appeal of economics. Neither was it simply the influence of Homer and Arthur, though that was important. It was at least as much the times. I graduated from college in 1932, when the United States was at the bottom of the deepest depression in its history before or since. The dominant problem of the time was economics. How to get out of the depression? How to reduce unemployment? What explained the paradox of great need on the one hand and unused resources on the other? Under the circumstances, becoming an economist seemed more relevant to the burning issues of the day than becoming an applied mathematician or an actuary.

The first quarter I was at Chicago, the fall of 1932, one course, with Jacob Viner, who was a great teacher, had a major effect on both my professional and personal life. Professionally, Viner's course in theory opened up a new world. He made me realize that economic theory was a coherent, logical whole that held together, that it didn't consist simply of a set of disjointed propositions. That course was unquestionably the greatest intellectual experience of my life.

In addition, it so happened that a fellow classmate was a beautiful young lady by the name of Rose Director. Because Viner seated people alphabetically, she sat next to me, and that too has shaped my whole life. We were married some years later and some forty-seven years later are still in that happy state. Again, consider the role of pure chance. Rose grew up in Portland, Oregon. I grew up in a small town in New Jersey. We met in an economics classroom in Chicago. Hardly something that could have been planned by anybody.

Other faculty members at Chicago included Frank Knight, Henry Simons, Lloyd Mints, Paul Douglas, and Henry Schultz. Economists will recognize their names; the rest of you will not. They were an extraordinarily talented and varied group of eminent economists. The graduate students were equally outstanding there—indeed one of them in addition to Rose is in this audience, Kenneth Boulding. I formed the view at that time, and have never seen reason to alter it since, that students don't learn from professors but from fellow students. The real function of a professor is to provide topics for bull sessions.

To continue with my own experience, Henry Schultz, who taught statistics and mathematical economics at Chicago, was a close friend of Harold Hotelling, a mathematical economist and statistician at Columbia, and recommended me to him. As a result, I was awarded a fellowship to Columbia. So after spending one year at Chicago I went to Columbia the next year.

Harold Hotelling gave me the same kind of feeling for mathematical statistics that Viner had for economic theory. In addition, Wesley C. Mitchell introduced me to both the institutional approach to economic theory and the various attempts to explain the business cycle, and John

Maurice Clark, to his own inimitable combination of pure theory and social and institutional detail. At Columbia, too, the graduate students were a remarkably able group, some of whom have remained lifelong friends.

As a result of my experience, I concluded that, at least in the mid-thirties, the ideal combination for a budding economist was a year of study at Chicago, which emphasized theory, and a year of study at Columbia, which emphasized institutional influences and empirical work.

The following year I returned to Chicago as a research assistant for Henry Schultz, and once again chance was good to me. Two fellow graduate students happened to be George Stigler and W. Allen Wallis.

George Stigler is also a Nobel laureate and a fellow lecturer in this series. He still teaches at the University of Chicago. George was and is a delight and a treasure as a friend and an intellectual influence. No economist has either a more lively and original mind or a better writing style. His writings are almost unique in the economic literature for their combination of economic content, humor, and literary quality. Few economists have germinated so many new ideas and so profoundly influenced the course of economic research. Allen Wallis went on to be dean of the business school at the University of Chicago, then chancellor of the University of Rochester, and is currently undersecretary of state for economic affairs. Allen and George remain among Rose's and my closest friends and both have had a continuing influence on my own professional work.

The combination of influences stemming from Chicago and Columbia—the one heavy on theory, the other heavy on statistical and empirical evidence—has shaped my scientific work, essentially all of which has been characterized by a mixture of theory and fact—of theory and attempts to test the implications of the theory. I refer to "scientific work" to distinguish it from Rose's and my writings for the general public: *Capitalism and Freedom, Free to Choose,* and *Tyranny of the Status Quo.*

My doctoral dissertation grew out of a study I worked on under Simon Kuznets, another American Nobel laureate. Simon was then at the National Bureau of Economic Research. He hired me to work with him on a project growing out of data on professional incomes that he had collected in the course of constructing the initial Department of Commerce estimates of national income. The end result was a book Simon and I collaborated on entitled *Income from Independent Professional Practice.* The core of the book is the use of the economic theory of distribution to explain and interpret the data on the incomes of various professions. The book was finished just before World War II, but was not published until after the war because of a controversy about one of its findings. That finding had to do with the effect of the monopolistic position of the American Medical Association on the incomes of physicians—not exactly a topic that has lost interest over the subsequent forty-odd years. Similarly, a later book, *The Theory of the Consumption Function,* had the same characteristics of combining theory and empirical evidence, and that is also true of the various books I've written alone or in collaboration with Anna J. Schwartz on money.

Another major influence on my scientific work was the experience during World War II. The first two years of that war—1941–1943—I spent at the U.S. Treasury as an economist in the division dealing with taxes. Indeed, Rose has never forgiven me for the part I played in devising and developing withholding at source for the income tax. There is no doubt that it would not have been possible to collect the amount of taxes imposed during World War II without withholding taxes at source. But it is also true that the existence of withholding has made it possible for taxes to be higher after the war than they otherwise could have been. So I have a good deal of sympathy with the view that, however necessary withholding may have been for wartime purposes, its existence has had some negative effects in the postwar period. Those two years in Washington gave me a liberal education in how policy is and is not made in Washington—a most valuable experience. Fortunately, I escaped before I caught Potomac Fever, a deadly disease for someone whose primary interest is scientific.

The second two years of the war—1943–1945—I spent as a mathematical statistician at the Statistical Research Group of the Division of War Research of Columbia University. It had been set up to provide statistical assistance to the military services and to other groups engaged in war research. It was a subsidiary of the wartime-created Office of Scientific Research and Development. Harold Hotelling was its intellectual sponsor and Allen Wallis its executive director. That experience exposed me to physical scientists from a wide range of fields with whom I would otherwise never have had much contact. It also required me to apply statistical techniques to noneconomic data. Surprisingly, perhaps, it turned out that social scientists were often more useful than physical scientists in doing operational research that involved interpreting the results of battlefield experience. The reason is simple: social scientists are used to working with bad data and the wartime data were all very bad. Physical scientists are used to working with accurate data generated by controlled experiments. Many of them were at a loss as how to handle the data generated by experience in the field.

One episode from that period has contributed greatly to my long-term skepticism about economic forecasts and especially about econometric forecasts based on complex multiple regressions. One project for which we provided statistical assistance was the development of high-temperature alloys for use as the lining of jet engines and as blades of turbo superchargers—alloys mostly made of chrome, nickel, and other metals. The efficiency of jet engines and of gas turbines depends critically on the temperature at which they can operate. Raising the temperature a bit increases substantially the efficiency of the turbine, turbo supercharger, or jet engine. Experimentation was being carried on at MIT, Battelle Laboratory in Pittsburgh, and elsewhere. Our group advised on the statistical design of experiments and analyzed much of the resulting data. At one point in the course of doing so, I computed a multiple regression from a substantial body of data relating the strength of an alloy at various temperatures to its composition. My hope was that I could use the equations that I fitted to the data to determine the composition that would give the best result. On paper, my results were splendid. The equations fitted very well and they suggested that a hitherto untried alloy would be far stronger than any existing alloy. The crucial test was to hang a heavy weight on a specimen of the alloy, put it in an oven heated to a high and stable temperature, and measure how long it took for it to break. The best of the alloys at that time were breaking at about ten or twenty hours; my equations predicted that the new alloys would last some two hundred hours. Really astounding results!

A great advantage of the physical sciences over economics is that is possible to test such a prediction promptly. It is not necessary to wait ten years until experience generates new evidence, as is necessary with economic forecasts. So I phoned the metallurgist we were working with at MIT and asked him to cook up a couple of alloys according to my specifications and test them. In order to keep track of them, we had to name them. I had enough confidence in my equations to call them F1 and F2 but not enough to tell the metallurgist what breaking time the equations predicted. That caution proved wise, because the first one of those alloys broke in about two hours and the second one in about three. Ever since, I've been very skeptical of the economic forecasts that people like myself and others make by using multiple regression equations.

In my final comments, let me shift to a different aspect of the Nobel Prize in economics. As some of you may know, the establishment of a Nobel Prize in economics has been criticized on the grounds that economics is not a science. One of the severest critics has been Gunnar Myrdal, the Swedish economist who was awarded the Nobel Prize jointly with Friedrich Hayek. That was an alloy of a very peculiar kind—left and right. Myrdal accepted the prize, but subsequently he had second thoughts and wrote a series of articles condemning the prize and expressing regret that he had accepted it. Economics, he said, is not a science in the same sense as physics or chemistry or biology.

I believe that Myrdal is wrong. It is important to distinguish between the scientific work that economists do and the other things that economists do. Economists are members of a community as well as scientists. We do not spend 100 percent of our lives on our purely scientific work, and neither, of course, do physicists or chemists. In principle, I believe that economics has a scientific component no different in character from the scientific component of physics or chemistry or any of the other physical sciences. True, as those who believe otherwise often stress, the physicist can conduct controlled experiments and the economist cannot. But that is hardly sufficient ground to deny the scientific character of economics. Meteorology is a recognized science in which controlled experiments are seldom possible, and there are many other scientific fields that are equally limited. Economists may seldom be able to conduct controlled experiments—although some are possible and have been done—but uncontrolled experience often throws up data that are the equivalent of a controlled experiment. To give you a simple example, it would be hard to devise a better controlled experiment for comparing different economic systems than the experience provided by East Germany and West Germany: two nations that formerly were one, occupied by people of the same background, the same culture, and the same genetic inheritance, torn apart by the accident of war. On one side of the Berlin Wall is a relatively free economic system; on the other side, a collectivist society. Similar controlled experiments are provided by Red China and Taiwan or Hong Kong, and by North and South Korea.

No so-called controlled experiment is truly completely controlled. Two situations can differ in an infinite number of ways. It is impossible to control for all of them. Hence, I do not believe that there is any difference in principle between so-called controlled experiments and so-called uncontrolled experience or between the possibility of doing scientific work in economics and in physics. In physics no less than in economics, it is important to distinguish between what people do in their scientific capacity and what they do as citizens. Consider the argument that is now raging about Star Wars, the strategic defense initiative. Some physicists issue manifestos opposing Star Wars; other physicists issue manifestos supporting Star Wars. Clearly, those manifestos do not reflect simply agreed scientific knowledge, but in large measure reflect the personal values, judgments about political events, and so on of the physicists. Their scientific competence or contribution should not be judged by such statements. It should be judged by their scientific work. The same thing, I believe, is true of economists.

To return to my own experience, I have been active in public policy. I have tried to influence public policy. I have spoken and written about issues of policy. In doing so, however, I have not been acting in my scientific capacity but in my capacity as a citizen, an informed one, I hope. I believe that what I know as an economist helps me to form better judgments about some issues than I could without that knowledge. But fundamentally, my scientific work should not be judged by my activities in public policy.

In introducing me, Bill Breit referred to my wanting to be judged by my peers. The episode he referred to occurred in a parking lot in Detroit. The morning on which it was announced that I had been awarded the Nobel Prize, I had agreed to go to Michigan to barnstorm on behalf of a proposed amendment to the state constitution requiring a balanced budget and limiting spending. I had to leave Chicago very early. In Detroit I was picked up at the airport by some of the people running the Michigan campaign and taken to the Detroit Press Club, for a press conference before we started our day of barnstorming. When we got to the parking lot of the press club, we were astonished to see how many reporters and TV people were there, and I remarked that I was amazed that the attempt to get an amendment was receiving so much attention. As I stepped out of the car, a reporter stuck a microphone in my face and said, "What do you think about getting the prize?" I said, "What prize?" He said, "The Nobel Prize." Naturally, I expressed my pleasure at the information. The reporter then said, "Do you regard this as the pinnacle of your career?" or something to that effect, and I said no. I said I was more interested in what my fellow economists would say about my work fifty years from now than about what seven Swedes might say about my work now.

When I was barnstorming that state, I wasn't doing it as a scientist; I was doing it as a citizen deeply concerned about a public issue. Similarly, when I engage in activities to promote a federal constitutional amendment to balance the budget and limit spending, I'm doing so as a citizen.

The public has the impression that economists never agree. They have the impression that if three economists are in a room they will get at least four opinions. That is false. If scientific issues are separated from policy and value issues, there is widespread agreement among economists whatever their political views. Over and over again I have been in a group that includes both economists and practitioners of other disciplines. Let a discussion start about almost anything and, in ten minutes or so, you will find all the economists on the same side against all the rest—whether the economists are on the left or on the right or in the middle.

I have great doubts about whether Nobel Prizes as a whole do any good, but I believe that such doubts apply equally to Nobel Prizes in physics as to Nobel Prizes in economics.

I have wandered over much terrain and I am not sure that I have explained my evolution as an economist. Let me only say in closing that my life as an economist has been the source of much pleasure and satisfaction. It's a fascinating discipline. What makes it most fascinating is that its fundamental principles are so simple that they can be written on one page, that anybody can understand them, and yet that very few do.

Awarded Nobel Prize in 1976. Lecture presented March 21, 1985.

Date of Birth

July 31, 1912

Academic Degrees

B.A.   Rutgers University, 1932

M.A.   University of Chicago, 1933

Ph.D. Columbia University, 1946

Academic Affiliations

Part-time Lecturer, Columbia University, 1937–1940

Visiting Professor of Economics, University of Wisconsin, 1940–1941

Associate Professor of Economics and Business Administration, University of Minnesota, 1945–1946

Associate Professor of Economics, 1946–1948, Professor of Economics 1948–1963, Paul Snowden Russell Distinguished Service Professor of Economics 1963–1982, University of Chicago

Visiting Fulbright Lecturer, Cambridge University, 1953–1954

Wesley Clair Mitchell Visiting Research Professor, Columbia University, 1964–1965

Visiting Professor, UCLA, winter quarter, 1967

Visiting Professor, University of Hawaii, winter quarter, 1972

Senior Research Fellow, Hoover Institute (Stanford), 1977–present

Selected Books

Essays in Positive Economics, 1953

A Theory of the Consumption Function, 1957

Capitalism and Freedom, 1962, 2002

Price Theory: A Provisional Text, 1962, 1976

A Monetary History of the United States, 1867–1960, 1963 (with Anna J. Schwartz)

George J. Stigler

It is a good rule that a scientist has only one chance to become successful in influencing his science, and that is when he influences his contemporaries. If he is not heeded by his contemporaries, he has lost his chance: brilliant work that is exhumed by a later generation may make the neglected scientist famous, but it will not have made him important. Gossen was a genius, but nothing in the development of utility theory is different for his having lived. Cournot was a genius, and perhaps a bit of his work rubbed off on Edgeworth and later writers on oligopoly, but the theory of the subject dates from the 1880s, not from when he published it in 1838.

Contemporary fame does not ensure lasting fame—the leaders of what prove to be scientific fads recede from even the histories of the science. Today a young economist will not know that a stagnation thesis concerning the American economy was widely discussed in the late 1930s, and Alvin Hansen's name will never regain its onetime prominence. Even Edward Chamberlin's theory of monopolistic competition, it is now clear, failed to initiate a fundamentally new direction of economic theorizing.

So scientific creativity—successful, lasting creativity—must be recognized at the time or it becomes a personal rather than a social achievement. This series of lectures is presented by economists who have met at least the requirement that their work has been recognized by contemporaries. A later age will separate the fundamental from the faddish contributions.

The conditions for creativity in economics have changed in one absolutely basic respect in the last hundred years or so. Until as late as the 1870s or 1880s it was possible for an amateur to become an influential economist; today it is almost inconceivable that major contributions could come from a noneconomist. The knowledge of economics possessed by Adam Smith, or David Ricardo, or even Leon Walras and Francis Edgeworth, was self-taught: they had not received formal training in the subject. In more or less modern times the only influential noneconomists I can name are Ramsey, Hotelling, and von Neumann; of course, each was a highly trained mathematician, and all date back forty or more years.

So to understand the conditions under which modern work in economics has emerged, one must look at the conditions of training and work of the modern scholar. Those conditions are no substitute for creativity, but they have become an indispensable condition for creativity to be exercised. I turn, therefore, to a semi-autobiographical sketch of my own life in economics, with primary attention to how the conditions of training and work influence the problems and methods of economic research.

Some Autobiography

I grew up in Seattle, attended schools there through a BBA degree at the University of Washington, proceeded to an MBA on the downtown Chicago campus of Northwestern University, spent one more year dodging unemployment at the University of Washington, and then went to the University of Chicago to get a Ph.D. That breathless sentence covers twenty-two years, on which I shall elaborate a bit. My father and mother migrated to the United States from Bavaria and Hungary, respectively. My father, whose skills as a brewer were devalued by Prohibition, went into the business of buying, repairing, and reselling residential property in Seattle during its depressed 1920s as well as the 1930s. I was a fully relaxed student before college days, a voracious and promiscuous reader but not a strong scholar.

At the University of Washington I did very well in classes, but usually chose the wrong classes. Lacking good judgment as well as guidance from my parents, whose formal education had been modest, I took innumerable "applied" business courses and a good deal of political science, but nothing in mathematics or the physical sciences. I was unknowingly providing proof of a proposition I have come to believe: that undergraduate training is to graduate training perhaps as 1 is to 8 in the acquisition of a research-level mastery of a field. Washington had some respectable economists but none who was at the first level.

Northwestern University began to open my eyes. I took, again, too many applied courses, this time chiefly in urban land economics. I studied with one able and stimulating economist, Coleman Woodbury, and he did as much as anyone to arouse my interest in scholarship as a career. But the University of Chicago was receiving pretty close to a tabula rasa in 1933, when I enrolled. Not that I knew it: twenty-two is not an age of humility.

There I met and got to know three economists I still consider to be outstanding: Frank Knight and Henry Simons, and a year later, on his return from the U.S. Treasury, Jacob Viner.

Knight was both a great and an absurd teacher. The absurdity was documented by his utterly disorganized teaching, with constant change of subject and yet insistent repetition of arguments. In the course on the history of economics he was interested mostly in the seamy side of religious history, but got great relish out of emphasizing the perversities and blunders of Ricardo and other historic figures in economics. His greatness is attested best by the fact that almost all of the students were much influenced by him. He communicated beyond any possible confusion the message that intellectual inquiry was a sacred calling, excruciatingly difficult for even the best of schol-ars to pursue with complete fidelity to truth and evidence.

Henry Simons was Frank Knight's disciple, but his example was enough to teach us that a disciple may have an independent mind, an ambivalent attitude toward some of his master's beliefs, and a wholly different goal in life. Simons believed that in the 1930s the world was at a crisis of historic magnitude: the survival of freedom and the economic viability of the Western world were at stake. With a wider perspective, Knight believed that the history of man was a history of social folly; the then-current crises were grave, but had equally grave precedents and would be handled as badly as they had been previously. Simons believed with all his heart that the crisis of the 1930s had to be handled well or the basic values of civilization would be lost, and he dedicated his life to that task.

One thing that Knight and Simons both succeeded in teaching me, and in fact overtaught, was that great reputation and high office deserve little respect in scientific work. We were told to listen to the argument and look at the evidence, but ignore the position, degrees, and age of the speaker. This studied irreverence toward authority had a special slant: contemporary ideas were to be treated even more skeptically than those of earlier periods. I didn't realize this distinction at the time because it was implicit rather than explicit. We were taught by example that Ricardo's errors and Marshall's foibles deserved more careful and thorough attention than the nonsense or froth of the day. One can make a case for the greater respect for earlier economists on the basis of the fact that their work had stood the test of time, but that case was not made explicitly.

When Viner returned to Chicago the next year we met a very different type of scholar: immensely erudite, rigorous and systematic in his instruction. Viner was the founder of the Chicago tradition of detailed training in neoclassical microeconomics, including training in its application to real problems. Viner filled the class of Economics 301 with a respect bordering on terror. I still recall the time when he asked a student to list the factors determining the elasticity of demand for a commodity. The student began well enough but soon put the conditions of supply in the list of determinants of demand elasticity. Viner calmly said, "Mr. X, you do not belong in this class." This remark produced a suitable tension in the rest of us. Yet outside the classroom he was kind and helpful, and my appreciation of him has risen steadily over time.

Among the very able people I met in Chicago were several students, and of course we knew each other in a way one could not know the professors. My special friends were Milton Friedman and Allen Wallis. It did not take long to recognize Milton's talents: he was logical, perceptive, quick to understand one's arguments—and quick to find their weaknesses. Friedman has surely exercised one of the major intellectual influences upon me throughout my life.

Allen Wallis was so competent and systematic that we soon predicted, to his annoyance, that he would become a university president. A year later Paul Samuelson appeared as a senior in some of our graduate classes, and we had no difficulty in recognizing his quality. The give-and-take among us students (a group that included Kenneth Boulding and Sune

Carlson) was the first experience I had of constant exchanges in a circle of first-class minds, and I acquired a lifelong taste for it.

I wrote my dissertation in the history of economic thought under Knight. He was the soul of kindness and generosity in dealing with me, then and forever after, but in retrospect there was a fly in the ointment. He was so strong-minded and so critical a student of the literature that it was a good many years before I could read the economic classes through my eyes instead of his. I have never brought myself to read through my doctoral dissertation, *Production and Distribution Theories: The Formative Period,* because I knew I would be embarrassed by both its Knightian excesses and its immaturity.

So when I left Chicago in 1936 to begin teaching at Iowa State College, I had acquired a light smattering of mathematics, a partial command of price theory, a fondness for intellectual history, and an irreverence toward prevailing ideas bordering on congenital skepticism. In retrospect a most modest intellectual arsenal.

Iowa and Minnesota and Later

At times I found myself in the midst of a group of vigorous young economists, who were being brought together by Theodore W. Schultz. I still remember my first class, in economic principles. I had prepared the first few weeks of the course in outline, so I entered the class with confidence. Forty minutes later I had covered all the material in my outline, and there remained ten minutes, not to mention ten and a half weeks, still to go! I wish I could state that eventually I encountered the problem so often reported by colleagues, of never being able to cover all the material, but I never reached this utopia of knowledge or loquacity.

I spent most of my spare time at Ames finishing my doctoral thesis, and I received my Ph.D. in the spring of the second year. I had a number of excellent colleagues and students at Ames, but before I was well settled in, Frederic Garver invited me to come to Minnesota, and I accepted.

My closest colleagues at Minnesota were Garver, Francis Boddy, and Arthur Marget. Alvin Hansen had just gone to Harvard and indeed it was largely his classes, but not his rank or salary, that I had inherited. It was rumored that my main rival had been Oskar Morgenstern; if that was true, I have fantasized that if he had been chosen I might have become the junior author of the theory of games!

By 1942 the outbreak of war led to a general retrenchment of academic life, and I took a sustained leave of absence from Minnesota, first to the National Bureau of Economic Research. I was hired to study the service industries as part of a program of studies of the trend of the output, employment, and productivity in the American economy. I and my associates collected an awful lot of numbers and published some monographs on such exotic fields as domestic science, education, trade, and (later) scientific personnel. These works were mostly quantitative, with mildly analytical skeletons, as when I made the first productivity measures relating output to an index of *all* inputs.

At the bureau I got to know Arthur Burns, Solomon Fabricant, and Geoffrey Moore. From them, and even more from Milton Friedman, I became persuaded of the importance of empirical evidence in the appraisal of economic theories; that is a theme to which I will return later. From the bureau I went to the Statistical Research Group at Columbia University, where statistical analysis was being used on military problems. The director was Allen Wallis, and the senior figures included Harold Hotelling, Milton Friedman, Jacob Wolfowitz, and, among other statisticians, L. J. Savage and Abraham Wald. I learned a little statistics there, and I did not seriously delay our nation's victory.

Near the end of the war I returned to Minnesota, and a year later Milton Friedman joined us. The reunion, alas, was brief, for a year later Friedman went to Chicago, and I to Brown. (I may mention that in 1946 I was offered a Chicago professorship, but managed to alienate the president, Ernest Colwell, in an interview and was vetoed. Thereby I probably hastened Friedman's return to Chicago by a year, and can claim some credit for helping found the new Chicago school.) And a year after that, I went to Columbia University, where Albert Hart, William Vickrey, and I taught the graduate theory course. I also assumed the teaching of industrial organization and the history of economics. Columbia then, as now, had a strong department, which included Arthur F. Burns, Carl Shoup, Ragnar Nurkse, and others. And that speedy journey brings me back to Chicago in 1958.

Back to Chicago

I was returning to an economics community in a stage of high prosperity. Friedman was an ascendant figure in world economics: his *Consumption Function* had revolutionized the statistical analysis of economic data, and his work on monetarism constituted the major attack on the ruling Keynesian doctrine. Modern labor economics was being fashioned by Gregg Lewis and by a recent Chicago Ph.D. already at Columbia, Gary Becker, and his colleague Jacob Mincer. Theodore Schultz was well into his work on the economics of education as well as continuing his influential work on economic growth. Arnold Harberger was making fundamental studies in public finance and developing a major role through both his work and his students in economic development.

My main work was to be in industrial organization. I already had Reuben Kessel and Lester Telser as colleagues, and to my great delight Ronald Coase joined us three years later. The main influence on me, however, was Aaron Director, with whom I had formed a close friendship at the first meeting of the Mt. Pelerin Society in 1946. Aaron was and is a paragon of all collegial virtues. He has a strong, independent mind and he has thought deeply on many questions, dissecting widely accepted and comfortable ideas to reveal their essential superficiality and frequent inconsistencies. He was in the law school, teaching primarily the antitrust course with Edward H. Levi, so his primary work was in antitrust economics.

I cannot recount the number of times in which Director's always courteous questioning led me either to change my views or to seek evidence to reinforce their relevance and weight. If we had been in Greece, I'm sure I would have called him Socrates. His questioning of McGee had already led to John's famous article on predatory pricing, his questioning of Telser soon contributed to Lester's famous article on resale price maintenance, and his questioning of Ward Bowman and Meyer Burstein and George Hilton led to their articles on price discrimination and the metering of demand. Concluding that Director would never write, later I was provoked to present one of his ideas with the title, "Director's Law of Income Redistribution."

A Digression on Research and Originality

There is good reason for believing that economics is a social science in quite another sense from the indisputable one that it concerns itself with mankind in social relationships. It appears also to be a social science in the literal sense that it is a science in which it is difficult to do creative work if one is not in a congenial intellectual environment.

Consider the fact that two of the premier nations of Western Europe, France and Germany, have made on the whole rather minor contributions to the evolution of modern economic analysis. They are nations with long histories of preeminence in mathematics and with great periods in physics, chemistry, and astronomy. Therefore we cannot ascribe their minor roles in economics to lack of powerful scientific capacities. Nor can we easily believe that these nations were sufficiently different in their social or economic or political systems from that of Great Britain so that they should have less reason to be interested in political economy.

Consider again the fact that economics has been characterized by periods of intense scientific progress and controversy, periods that have often lasted for several generations. Cambridge University was the scene of such activity, almost without a break, from 1890 to 1940, and Vienna has a similar history beginning twenty years earlier and also ending in the thirties. Or consider Chicago, which has been the home of similarly intense activity in economics from the 1930s to the present. These periods of sustained scientific enterprise must have some elements of a chain reaction. Indeed, the very notion of a Cambridge or Austrian or Chicago school implies the existence of more than one gifted person with a temporary coterie of disciples.

I will be told, most properly, that von Thünen and Gossen or Cournot were hardly minor economic theorists, just to cite examples from the Germany and France that I have said made rather minor contributions to economics. They were theorists of great creativity, but, as I argued earlier, they did not have any influence upon their contemporaries. The main reason, at least in the case of the two Germans, must have been their intellectual isolation. That isolation allowed von Thünen to spend prodigious energies on the attempt to discover the formula for a God-given fair wage, a will-of-the-wisp that he asked to have engraved on his tombstone ($\sqrt{ap}$). Gossen's book gets its ferocious difficulty not from the inherent complexity of his analysis but from its cryptic, crabbed, unmotivated exposition. Able colleagues would have helped to harness these geniuses. Cournot's book was in one respect similar: despite its splendid lucidity, it was written in a language of mathematics that no important contemporary economist was prepared to speak.

If scientific work is a social activity, discovery is surely not. The discovery of a new theory or a new dimension of an existing theory is an act of creativity that is most imperfectly understood, at least by me. We have little understanding of why Jevons and Gossen discovered marginal utility theory, rather than John Stuart Mill and Senior—certainly the latter two possessed the ingredients and the ability. I have given the explanation for the *adoption* of the utility theory by the profession that it only became useful as economics became a formalized study of academicians in the latter part of the nineteenth century.[1] Even if this is correct it does not explain how a young assayer in the mint in Sydney, Australia, or an unsuccessful minor civil servant in Germany came upon the idea.

Something can perhaps be said about the sources of new ideas in economics. I believe that we can usually divide new economic ideas into two classes: those that arise out of the critical examination of the ideas of other economists, and those that seek directly to explain some body of empirical phenomena. The classes are not sharply exclusive because the ideas of other economists are presumably directed ultimately to the explanation of real phenomena and therefore are a conduit to those phenomena. Nevertheless, the classification has some value, I believe.

Consider two greats of the late Victorian period, Walras and Marshall. Walras sought to construct a consistent theoretical structure to describe the nature of an enterprise economy. Almost nothing in that elegant structure was calculated to explain any observable behavior, except only the phenomenon of negatively sloping demand curves—and even that was not demonstrated.

Marshall, on the other hand, was concerned to explain the role of time in the formation of prices and the allocation of resources, and this is the central contribution of his *Principles*. He also made many improvements on predecessors' theories, a striking example being the identification of those elements of land (namely, its spatial relations and annuity of weather) that really constitute Ricardo's original and indestructible properties of the soil. Nevertheless, his eyes were mainly on economic phenomena to be explained, not on predecessors to be corrected.

It is worth pursuing Marshall's two kinds of work a step further. The influence of time was illustrated by a host of persuasive everyday examples, and this was proof enough to make market and short- and long-run normal prices a part of the standard theory of economics. The redefinition of land was elegant, for it isolated the proper empirical content of Ricardian land, but it had no effect upon subsequent economics. I attribute this, at least proximately, to Marshall's failure to show that this concept of land had interesting empirical or policy implications.

On my reckoning, the immediate stimulation to advances in economics has overwhelmingly been the attempt to improve on other economists' work. This was the primary source of stimulation for Ricardo, Mill, Edgeworth, Pigou, and most modern economists. Grappling directly with real phenomena is less popular, as well it might be, for the phenomena appear disorderly and poorly enumerated. Yet in addition to Marshall I would put much of the work of Smith, Keynes, and Friedman in this tradition.

For quite a few thousand years most new or unfamiliar ideas must have been wrong: if they were not, the task of being a well-educated scholar would be quite overwhelming. Many "new" ideas are not new at all, only unfamiliar, and most new or unfamiliar ideas are mistaken or infertile.

This raises the question of how a science adopts a new idea, which returns us to the social element in scientific work. Even the new ideas that are eventually judged by many to be good ideas are not often easily absorbed by a discipline. New ideas look at new things or look at familiar things in a new perspective, and their fertility and usefulness are not self-evident. They carry no label or halo that certifies their value, and the claims of their inventors are no different from the claims of the inventors of poor ideas.

A successful innovator therefore finds his work only half done when he has developed a new idea. Indeed the fraction is probably less than half, since the criticisms and misunderstandings his idea encounters will force him to work further on it. He will have to show how it can be developed further, how it is applicable in interesting ways, and how its weaknesses can be patched up. He will be much assisted in all this work if he can enlist a few fervent disciples. Not only may they help in developing the theory, but they can engage in a variety of controversies, which are the best of ways in which to publicize the idea.

If the discoverer lacks the energy or position to pursue the new idea, it is likely to lie fallow. A host of creative ideas—not only those of Cournot and Gossen but some of those of successful economists like Edgeworth and Pareto—required decades to become subjects of active investigation. In passing, I may remark that I have usually moved on to another subject fairly soon after working on one, and as I read the history of science that is a failing.

My Work

Much the most important contribution I have made to economics is information theory. It could have originated in the attempt to generalize economic theories that usually assumed that economic actors had complete knowledge of their markets and technology. But it did not: my discomfort was with a theory that did not account for the fact that almost every product or service will have a distribution of prices, not a unique price, at a given time.

My own observations, partly of price data in antitrust areas, confirmed the existence of a variety of prices of a reasonably homogeneous good. The most obvious available explanation, product differentiation of Chamberlin's sort, seemed inappropriate to markets in automobiles of a given model at retail, bituminous coal, and the like. The apparent near-homogeneity of the products aside, there appeared to be no interesting empirical predictions derivable from monopolistic competition theory as to the extent of price dispersion, its changes over time, and the factors that led to the dispersion.

It occurred to me that it was the expensiveness of knowledge that sustained price differences. Search is never free and often expensive. To visit eight or ten automobile dealers in my search for a given automobile could cost a day plus transportation costs. To visit a second supermarket could require twenty minutes, and the average value of twenty minutes to an American adult is perhaps three dollars.

From the theory of search for the lowest price by a buyer or the highest price by a seller, we can deduce many corollaries. Clearly, the price dispersion relative to the average price will be less the more the buyer spends on it, because the costs of search do not go up as fast as the value of the commodity purchased. The dispersion of prices of automobiles relative to their average price will be lower than that of prices of microwave ovens. Again, knowledge decays gradually with the passage of time, so we expect goods bought frequently to have less price dispersion than infrequently purchased goods of equal value. The amount of search varies with the length of time one lives in a community, so tourists on average pay more for things than natives do.

I applied the theory to the labor markets and it shed light on a variety of the observed wage patterns. Information has other dimensions besides price, so I made a wholly different application of information to the problem of colluding oligopolists, where the central problem is to detect departures from the collusive agreement. Here I invoked observable quantities, not unobservable genuine transaction prices, to detect surreptitious competitive behavior. I also made an attempt to view the functions of advertising in this light, in contrast to the tradition of economists' hostility to advertising.

I must confess that I did not imagine the variety of informational problems in economics that would emerge in the next two decades. For a time it seemed essential to have the phrase "asymmetrical information" in the title of every journal article. Yet the subject is far from exhausted, and I have recently returned to the problem of political information.

I was not led to the economics of information by the previous literature; indeed that previous literature was virtually nonexistent. Only later did I realize that a suggestive treatment resided in Charles Babbage's discussion of what he called the verification of prices.

My work in the theory of economic regulation has a different but related intellectual history. Starting in the early 1960s, I made a series of studies of the actual effects of several public regulatory policies: state utility commission regulation of electric utility rates; SEC regulation of new stock issues; and the antitrust laws. I made these studies because I was skeptical of the prevailing practice in economics of treating the prescriptions of law as actual practice. My findings were often surprising: the regulation of electric utilities did not help residential users; the regulation of new stock issues did not help the widows and orphans who bought these issues.

Only slowly, I should say inexcusably slowly, did I come to the most obvious of questions: why do we get public regulation? I attempted to answer the question by looking at costs and benefits to the various parties. This approach was highly incompatible with the ruling approach in political science. There the introduction of a regulatory policy simply represented the response of the legislature to an aroused public demand for protection of the public interest. The demand of the public, in turn, was due to the existence and growth of some social evil, perhaps called to public attention by vigorous reformers. This "public interest" theory did very poorly in explaining protective tariffs or the farm program and had nothing to say about the dates at which policies were initiated: why was the social security system begun in the 1930s rather than the 1890s or the 1950s?

My work on regulation was much more closely related to that of others than was my work on information. Anthony Downs, James Buchanan, and Gordon Tullock had made large beginnings in the application of economic logic to politics, and my style of approach differed primarily in its strong empirical orientation.

These are examples of my theoretical work directed to the explanation of observed phenomena, with little or no relationship to the work of other economists. It is instructive to look also at a problem I worked on that emerged directly from the literature.

The determination of the efficient sizes of business enterprises is an interesting example. Economists sought to establish the most efficient size of enterprise in any industry by one of three methods: (1) a direct comparison of observed costs of enterprises of different sizes; (2) a direct comparison of rates of return on investment of enterprises of different sizes; and (3) an estimation of cost functions on the basis of technological information. Each of these methods encounters severe problems, always of data and often of logic.

I sought an answer by resorting to a sort of Darwinian approach, which had already been employed in a related manner by Alchian. My argument was essentially this: if I wish to know whether a tiger or a panther is the stronger animal, I put them in the same cage and return after a few hours. Similarly, by seeing the sizes to which firms competing in an industry were tending, I could deduce the efficient sizes—a method called the survivor technique.

The method seems obvious and, I later found, had antecedents as illustrious as John Stuart Mill, but for a considerable time the method encountered substantial opposition. The National Bureau of Economic Research, where it was written, did not wish to publish it, perhaps because it was too controversial.

There is no reliable way to discover something new: if there were, it would infallibly be discovered. It seems evident to me that Friedman's splendid theory of consumption function arose out of puzzles displayed by observable data, and Arrow's splendid impossibility theorem arose out of profound thought about the process of social decision making.

Conclusion

I should warn you, although I confess I should have done so at the outset rather than at the conclusion of this lecture, that I am a strong supporter of the view that a knowledge of the life of a scholar is more often a source of misunderstanding than of enlightenment about his work. Obviously, my arguments for this view have not been convincing, or Professor Breit would not have organized this lecture series.

The reason that this biographical approach—it bears the oppressive name of prosopography—is misleading is that its devotees usually pick out of a scholar's life some circumstance or event that they find explains a given theory. To give you real and absurd examples, one historian said life on a small island led Malthus to fear overpopulation; another said John Stuart Mill could not be original because he wrote his *Principles* in less than two years.

I am not prepared to say that one's work is independent of one's life. Possibly if I had gone to Harvard instead of Chicago, I would have been a believer in monopolistic competition, a student of input-output tables, or a member of the Mason school of industrial organization. But I do not attach high probabilities to these possibilities. I am no longer a faithful follower, although I am still an admirer, of Frank Knight and Henry Simons: each person has a mind-style of his own, and eventually it asserts itself. This does not mean that we are immune to our environment, but it does argue for me that environmental influences will be subtle.

I not only believe this to be true but also I hope that it is true: the prospects for scientific progress would be bleak if we could train our students to become truly faithful disciples. If you understand my scientific work better for having heard me, I shall be both pleased and envious.

Awarded Nobel Prize in 1982. Lecture presented April 17, 1985.

Dates of Birth and Death

January 17, 1911; December 1, 1991

Academic Degrees

B.B.A.   University of Washington, 1931

M.B.A.   Northwestern University, 1932

Ph.D.   University of Chicago, 1938

Academic Affiliations

Assistant Professor, Iowa State, 1936–1938

Assistant, Associate, and Full Professor, University of Minnesota, 1938–1946

Professor, Brown University, 1946–1947

Professor, Columbia University, 1947–1958

Charles R. Walgreen Distinguished Service Professor of American Institutions, University of Chicago, 1958–1981

Director, Center for the Study of the Economy and the State, University of Chicago, 1981–1991

Selected Books

Production and Distribution Theories, 1941, 1994

The Theory of Price, 1946, 1987

Essays in the History of Economics, 1965

The Organization of Industry, 1968, 1983

The Citizen and the State: Essays on Regulation, 1975

James Tobin

Beginning with Keynes at Harvard

Rare is the child, I suspect, who wants to grow up to be an economist, or a professor. I grew up in a university town and went to a university-run high school, where most of my friends were faculty kids. I was so unfailing an A student that it was boring even to me. But I don't recall thinking of an academic career. I liked journalism, my father's occupation; I had put out "newspapers" of my own from age six. I thought of law; I loved to argue, and beginning in my teens I was fascinated by politics. I guess I knew that there was economics at the university, but I didn't know what the subject really was. Of course, economic issues were always coming up in classes on history and government—civics, in those days. I expected economics to be among the social science courses I would someday take in college, probably part of the pre-law curriculum.

I grew up happily assuming I would go to college in my hometown, to the University of Illinois. One month before I was scheduled to enroll as a freshman, I was offered and accepted a Conant Prize Fellowship at Harvard. I should explain how this happened. My father, a learned man, a voracious reader, the biggest customer of the Champaign Public Library, discovered in the *New York Times* that Harvard was offering two of these new fellowships in each of five midwestern states. President Conant wanted to broaden the geographical and social base of Harvard College. Having nothing to lose, I accepted my father's suggestion that I apply. University High School, it turned out, had without even trying prepared me superbly for the obligatory College Board exams. Uni High graduates only thirty to thirty-five persons a year, but it has three Nobels to its credit and, once I had broken the ice, many national scholarships.

Thus James Bryant Conant, Louis Michael Tobin, and University High School changed my life and career. Illinois was and is a great university. But I doubt that it would have led me into economics. For several reasons, Harvard did.

Harvard was the leading academic center of economics in North America at the time; only Columbia and Chicago were close competitors. Both its senior and junior faculty were outstanding. Two of the previous lecturers in this series were active and influential members of the community when I was a student, Wassily Leontief on the faculty and Paul Samuelson as a Junior Fellow, a graduate student free of formal academic requirements. Of the senior faculty of the 1930s, Joseph Schumpeter would have been a sure bet for a Nobel, Alvin Hansen, Edward Chamberlin, and Gottfried Haberler likely choices. Haberler, still active, remains a possibility. Naturally, Harvard attracted remarkably talented graduate students. That able undergraduates might go on to scholarly careers was taken for granted.

When I arrived at Harvard, I knew I would want to major—at Harvard the word is *concentrate*—in one of the social sciences or possibly in mathematics. By the end of freshman year I was leaning to economics. But I hadn't yet taken any. In those days even Ec A, the introductory course, was considered too hard for freshmen. As a sophomore all of eighteen years old, I began Ec A in a section taught by Spencer Pollard, an advanced graduate student specializing in labor economics and writing a dissertation on John L. Lewis and the United Mine Workers.

Pollard was also my tutor. A Harvard undergraduate, besides taking four courses, met regularly, usually singly, with a tutor in his field of concentration, generally a faculty member or graduate student associated with the student's residential house. Tutorial was not graded. It was modeled, like the house system itself, on Oxford and Cambridge. Pollard suggested that we devote our sessions to "this new book from England." He had recently been over there and judged from the stir the book was creating even before publication that it was important. The book was *The General Theory of Employment, Interest and Money* by John Maynard Keynes, published in 1936.

Pollard was no respecter of academic conventions; that I was only an Ec A student meant nothing to him. I was too young, and too ready to assume that teacher knows best, to know that I knew too little to read the book. So I read it, and Pollard and I talked about it as we went through it. Cutting my teeth on *The General Theory*, I was hooked on economics.

Like many other economists of my vintage, I was attracted to the field for two reasons. One was that economic theory is a fascinating intellectual challenge, on the order of mathematics or chess. I liked analytics and logical argument. I thought algebra was the most eye-opening school experience between the three Rs and college.

The other reason was the obvious relevance of economics to understanding and perhaps overcoming the Great Depression and all the frightening political developments associated with it throughout the world. I did not personally suffer deprivations during the depression. But my parents made me very conscious of the political and economic problems of the times. My father was a well-informed and thoughtful political liberal. My mother was a social worker, recalled to her career by the emergency; she was dealing with cases of unemployment and poverty every day.

The second motivation, I observe, gave our generation of economists different interests and priorities from subsequent cohorts dominated by those attracted to the subject more exclusively by the appeal of its puzzles to their quantitative aptitudes and interests.

Thanks to Keynes, economics offered me the best of both worlds. I was fascinated by his theoretical duel with the orthodox classical economists. Keynes's uprising against encrusted error was an appealing crusade for youth. The truth would make us free, and fully employed too. I was already an ardent and uncritical New Dealer, much concerned about the depression, unemployment, and poverty. According to Keynesian theory, Roosevelt's devaluation of the dollar and deficit spending were sound economics after all.

By sheer application, unconstrained by the need to unlearn anything, I came to know Keynes's new book sooner and better than many of my elders at Harvard. Keynes was the founder of what later came to be known as macroeconomics, what his young associate Joan Robinson called at the time "the theory of output as a whole," a phrase I found strikingly apt. The contrast was with the theory of output and price in particular markets or sectors. This—what we now call "micro"—was the main stuff of the theory course we economics concentrators took after Ec A. I liked the methodology of the new subject, modeling the whole economy by a system of simultaneous equations; by now I had calculus to add to my algebra. J. R. Hicks and others showed, more clearly than Keynes himself, how the essentials of *The General Theory,* and it differences from classical theory, could be expressed and analyzed in such models.

Harvard was becoming the beachhead for the Keynesian invasion of the new world. The senior faculty was mostly hostile. A group of them had not long before published a book quite critical of Roosevelt's recovery program. Seymour Harris, an early convert to Keynes, was an exception, especially important to undergraduates like myself, in whom he took a paternal interest. Harris was an academic entrepreneur. He opened the pages of the *Review of Economics and Statistics,* of which he was editor, and the halls of Dunster House, of which he was senior tutor, to lively debates on economic theory and policy.

The younger faculty and the graduate student teaching fellows were enthusiastic about Keynes's book. Their reasons were similar to my own but better informed. A popular tract by seven of them, *An Economic Program for American Democracy,* preached the new gospel with a left-wing slant.

Most important of all was the arrival of Alvin Hansen to fill the new Littauer chair in political economy. Hansen, aged fifty, came to Harvard from the University of Minnesota the same year I was beginning economics. He had previously been critical of Keynes and had indeed published a lukewarm review of *The General Theory.* He changed his mind 180 degrees, a rare event for scholars of any age, especially if their previous views are in print. Hansen became the leading apostle of Keynesian theory and policy in America. His fiscal policy seminar was the focus of research, theoretical and applied, in Keynesian economics. Visitors from the Washington firing lines mixed with local students and faculty; I had the feeling that history was being made in that room. For undergraduates the immediate payoff was that Hansen taught us macroeconomics, though under the course rubric Money and Banking. Hansen was a true hero to me, and in later years he was to be a real friend also.

I wrote my senior honors thesis on what I perceived to be the central theoretical issue between Keynes and the classical economists he was attacking. The orthodox position was that prices move to clear markets, rising to eliminate excesses of demand over supply and falling to eliminate excess supplies. Applied to the labor market, this meant that reductions of wages would get rid of unemployment. Excess supply of labor could not be a permanent equilibrium. Unless wage cuts are prevented by law or by monopolistic trade unions, competition for jobs will lower wages and in turn restore or create jobs for the unemployed. This was just an application of the central thesis of orthodox economics, the Invisible Hand proposition of Adam Smith. Individual agents are selfish and myopic. They respond in their own interest to the market signals locally available to them. Their actions miraculously turn out for the best for the society as a whole. Competition brings this miracle about.

Keynes's heresy was to deny that this mechanism could be counted on to eliminate involuntary unemployment. He didn't say just that the mechanism was slow and needed help from government policy. He said it might not work at all. Instead, the economy would be stuck in an underemployment equilibrium. Orthodox economists thought they could prove that free competitive markets allocate resources efficiently. In saying that willing and productive workers can't get jobs, Keynes was indicting the market system for a massive failure. After all, there is no greater inefficiency than to leave productive resources idle.

My honors thesis found fault with Keynes's logic. That may seem surprising. But I didn't think Keynes needed to insist on so sweeping a theoretical victory on his opponents' home court. His practical message was just as important whether unemployment was an incident of prolonged disequilibrium or of equilibrium. My first professional publication (1941) was an article in the *Quarterly Journal of Economics* based on my senior thesis; the *QJE* is, of course, edited and published at Harvard. The issue is very much alive today. It has also remained an interest of mine, a subject on which I have published several other papers, including my 1971 presidential address to the American Economic Association (1972).

Tools of the Trade, Theoretical and Statistical

By graduation time in 1939 I had forgotten about law and drifted into the natural decision, to become a professional economist. Harvard has a way of keeping its own: my fellowship was extended and I went on to graduate school. The transition was easy; I had taken courses with graduate students while I was a senior. Now I needed to pick up some tools of the trade. One was formal mathematical economic theory, and another was statistics and econometrics. Harvard was just beginning to catch up to the state of these two arts.

I see in retrospect that our professors left most of our education to us. They expected us to teach ourselves and learn from each other, and we did. They treated us as adult partners in scholarly endeavor, not as apprentices. I am afraid our graduate programs today try too hard to convey a definite and vast body of material and to test how well students master what we know. I wrote my undergraduate thesis under the nominal supervision of my senior-year tutor, Professor Edward Chamberlin. He said he knew nothing about my subject and left me on my own. Our tutorial sessions were nonetheless interesting; we argued about Catholic agrarianism, his vision of economic utopia. The faculty adviser for my doctoral dissertation in 1946–47 was, by my choice, Professor Schumpeter, one of the truly great economists, indeed social scientists, of the century. He had no use for Keynes and little for my topic, the consumption function. He read what I wrote and made helpful suggestions, but mostly he kept hands off. When I saw him, we talked of many other things, to my lasting benefit.

The theory we were taught was largely in the Anglo-American tradition, in which mathematical argument was subordinated to verbal and graphical exposition and relegated to footnotes. The great book was *Principles of Economics* by Alfred Marshall, Keynes's own mentor in the other Cambridge. Markets were analyzed mostly one at a time—*partial* equilibrium analysis. Little rigorous attempt was made to describe a *general* equilibrium of the system as a whole, with many commodities, many consumers and producers, many markets interconnected with each other.

Mathematical models of general equilibrium were a stronger tradition in continental Europe, to which the French-Swiss economist Leon Walras had made the seminal contribution in 1870. Though F. Y. Edgeworth at Oxford and Irving Fisher at Yale had written in the same vein, they had not greatly influenced the main line of English-language economics from Adam Smith to David Ricardo to John Stuart Mill to Marshall. But in the late 1930s and 1940s the mathematical general equilibrium approach was coming into vogue, thanks to J. R. Hicks and R. G. D. Allen in Britain and Wassily Leontief and Paul Samuelson at Harvard. Joseph Schumpeter fostered this development, believing that Walras had provided economics its "magna charta," even though his own theory of the dynamics of capitalism was wholly different.

I liked the general equilibrium approach; that was one of the great appeals of macroeconomics. But those models of output as a whole were small enough and specific enough to understand and manipulate. I have never been an aficionado of formal mathematical general equilibrium theory, which is so pure and general as to be virtually devoid of interesting operational conclusions. Moreover, I have come to think that its elegance gives many economic theorists today an exaggerated presumptive faith that free competitive markets work for the best. I did use the approach in some articles in the late 1940s on the theory of rationing, all but one of them in collaboration with Hendrik Houthakker.

In statistics and econometrics Harvard was further behind the times. The professors who taught economic statistics were idiosyncratic in the methods they used and quite suspicious of methods based in mathematical statistical theory. Until the 1950s Harvard was pretty much untouched by the developments in Europe led by Ragnar Frisch and Jan Tinbergen or those in the United States at the Cowles Commission. Students like me, who were interested in formal statistical theory, took refuge in the mathematics department. For econometrics we squeezed as much as possible from a seminar on statistical demand functions offered by a European visitor, Hans Staehle. We also discovered that regressions, though scorned by professors Crum and Frickey, were alive and well under the aegis of Professor John D. Black's program in agricultural economics. In the basement of Littauer Center we could use his electromechanical or manual Marchands and Monroes.

I did just that for my second published paper (1942), originally written for Edward S. Mason's seminar in spring semester 1941, on how to use statistical forecasts in defense planning; my example was estimation of civilian demands for steel. The paper was one reason Mason recommended me for a job in Washington with the civilian supply division of the nascent Office of Price Administration and Civilian Supply. So I left Harvard in May 1941, having completed all the requirements for the Ph.D. except the dissertation. I would not return until February 1946. After nine months of helping to ration scarce materials, I went in the Navy and served as a line officer on a destroyer until Christmas 1945.

Statistics and econometrics were important in my research after the war. In my doctoral dissertation (1947) on the determinants of household consumption and saving, I tried to marry "cross-section" data from family budget surveys with aggregate time series, the better to estimate effects of income, wealth, and other variables. In a later study of food demand (1950), I refined the method. This, along with my empirical and theoretical work on rationing, took place in England in 1949–50, at Richard Stone's Department of Applied Economics in Cambridge. I hoped that cross-section observations could resolve the ambiguities of statistical inference based on time series alone. Later my interest in cross-section and panel data led me to the work of the Michigan Survey Research Center, where I spent a fruitful semester with George Katona, James Morgan, and Lawrence Klein in 1953.

My work on data of this type led me to propose a new statistical method, which became known as Tobit analysis (1958). Probit analysis, which originated in biology, estimates how the probabilities of positive or negative responses to treatment depend on observed characteristics of the organism and the treatment. In economic applications, Yes responses often vary in intensity; for example, most families in a sample would report No when asked if they bought a car last year, while those who answer Yes spent varying amounts of money on a car. My technique would use both Yes-No and quantitative information in seeking the determinants of car purchases.

The label Tobit was perhaps more appropriate than Arthur Goldberger thought when he introduced it in his textbook. Perhaps not. My main claim to fame, a discovery enjoyed by generations of my students, is that, thinly disguised as a midshipman named Tobit, I make a fleeting appearance in Herman Wouk's novel *The Caine Mutiny*. Wouk and I attended the same quick Naval Reserve officers' training school at Columbia in spring 1942, and so did Willy, the hero of the novel.

Innovative and seminal work in mathematical economics and econometrics took place at the Cowles Commission for Research in Economics in the years 1944–54. The commission was then affiliated with the University of Chicago. Its research output over that period is one of the most fruitful achievements in the history of organized scientific inquiry. The leaders were Jacob Marschak and Tjalling Koopmans; Koopmans was awarded a Nobel Prize for his contributions to the theory of resource allocation, including linear programming, during this period. The remarkable teams Marschak and Koopmans assembled included two of the previous speakers in this series at Trinity, Arrow and Klein, and two other Nobel laureates, Simon and Debreu.

When I was a graduate student at Harvard after the war, I stood in awe of the Cowles Commission and of Marschak and Koopmans. I came to know them at meetings of the Econometric Society. For the December 1947 meeting in Chicago I was asked to be a discussant of a paper by Marschak. I didn't get the paper until a few days before the meeting, indeed a day or so before Christmas. I worked hard on the paper— neglecting my wife, Betty, pregnant with our first child, and holiday festivities with our families. I was able to report some important flaws in Marschak's model and to offer some constructive suggestions. One thing led to another. I was asked to join the commission, and in 1954 I was asked to become its research director, to succeed Koopmans as he had succeeded Marschak.

The offer was flattering, challenging, and tempting. But I was very happy at Yale, and Betty and I had come to like New Haven very much as a place to live and raise a family. It turned out that we could have our cake and eat it too. Koopmans was quite interested in relocating the commission, because of difficulties in attracting staff to Chicago at that time and problems in the relation between the commission and the university. He gave me not the slightest inkling of this interest until I had definitely declined the offer. The founder and financial angel of the commission, Alfred Cowles, was a Yale graduate; he hoped his creation could find permanent hospitality from his alma mater.

In 1955 the commission moved to Yale, renamed the Cowles Foundation for Research in Economics at Yale University. I became its research director after all. Cowles Foundation Discussion Paper 1 (1955) was a precursor of the Tobit analysis mentioned above. The coming of Cowles was an important factor in the rise of economics at Yale to front-rank stature. I broadened the scope of the foundation's research to include macroeconomics. I was particularly eager to make room for the interests and talents of a young Yale assistant professor, Arthur Okun, who was working on macroeconomic forecasting and policy analysis.

Developing Keynesian Macroeconomics; Synthesizing It with the Neoclassical Tradition

My main program of research and writing after the war continued my early interests in Keynes and macroeconomics. I sought to improve the theoretical foundations of macro models, to fit them into the main corpus of neoclassical economics, and to clarify the roles of monetary and fiscal policies. In this endeavor I shared the objectives of many other economists, notably Abba Lerner, Paul Samuelson, Franco Modigliani, Robert Solow, J. R. Hicks, and James Meade. A new mainstream, synthesizing the Keynesian revolution and the classical economics against which it was revolting, was in the making. I am proud that Paul Samuelson called me a "partner in [this] crime."

The building blocks of the Keynesian structure were four in number: the relation of wages and employment; the propensity to consume; liquidity preference and the demand for money; the inducement to invest. I have already referred to my work on the first. I turn now to the other three.

Keynes's "psychological law" of consumption and saving stated that saving would be an ever-larger proportion of income as per capita real incomes became greater. National income data between the two world wars appeared to confirm his law. Statistical equations, fit to those data, extrapolated to much higher incomes, foretold trouble after the Second World War. Investment would have to be a much larger fraction of national income than ever before to absorb the high saving and avoid recession and unemployment. The extrapolation was wrong. Incomes rose as expected, but consumption was no smaller a proportion than before. This forecasting error triggered an agonizing reappraisal of the consumption function, with fruitful results.

My doctoral dissertation (1947) was on this subject. I thought Keynes's law should be interpreted to refer to the relation of lifetime consumption to lifetime income, not to a relation between those variables year by year. The same considerations implied that wealth, not just current income, determines consumption in the short run. As so often happens, this idea was in the air. Milton Friedman's permanent income theory and Franco Modigliani's life-cycle model were elegant explanations of saving behavior in this spirit. They showed how cyclical data could look "Keynesian" even though saving would be roughly proportional to income in the long run. I have written a number of papers on this subject over the years.

The episode is, I believe, an example of how economic knowledge advances when striking real-world events and issues pose puzzles we have to try to understand and resolve. The most important decisions a scholar makes are what problems to work on. Choosing them just by looking for gaps in the literature is often not very productive and at worst divorces the literature itself from problems that provide more important and productive lines of inquiry. The best economists have taken their subjects from the world around them.

The bulk of my work in the 1950s and 1960s was on the monetary side of macroeconomics. I had several objectives.

First, I wanted to establish a firm foundation for the sensitivity of money demand or money velocity to interest rates. Why was this important? The quantity theory of money, later called monetarism, asserted that there was no such sensitivity, that the velocity of money was constant except for random shocks and for slow, secular changes in public habits, banking institutions, and financial technology. The implication was that fiscal stimulus, such as government spending or tax reduction, could not affect aggregate spending on goods and services unless accompanied by money creation. The same implication applied to autonomous changes in private investment. In this sense Milton Friedman and other monetarists were saying not just that money matters, with which I agreed, but also that money is all that matters, with which I disagreed.

In an empirical paper in 1947 I let the data speak for themselves, loudly in favor of Keynes's liquidity preference curve. But I was not satisfied with Keynes's explanation of liquidity preference. He said people preferred liquid cash because they expected interest rates to rise to "normal" prosperity levels of the past, causing capital losses on holdings of bonds. As William

Fellner, later to be my colleague at Yale, pointed out in a friendly debate with me in journal pages, Keynes could hardly call "equilibrium" a situation in which interest rates are persistently lower than investors' expectations of them. Fellner was espousing a principle of model building later called "rational expectations," and I agreed with him.

I found and offered two more tenable sources of the interest sensitivity of demand for money. One (1956) was based on an inventory theory of the management of transactions balances. As I learned too late, I had been mostly anticipated by William Baumol, but the model is commonly cited with both names. The second paper (1958) gave a new rationalization of Keynes's "speculative motive": simply, aversion to risk. People may prefer liquidity, and prefer it more the lower the interest rate on noncash assets, not because they expect capital losses on average but because they fear them more than they value the equally probable capital gains.

I had been working for some time on portfolio choices balancing such risks against expected returns, and the liquidity preference paper was an exposition and application of that work. Harry Markowitz had already set forth a similar model of portfolio choice, and our paths also converged geographically when he spent a year at Yale in 1955–56. My interest was in macroeconomic implications, his more in advising rational investors.

When my prize was announced in Stockholm in 1981, the first reports that reached this country mentioned portfolio theory. This caught the interest of the reporters who faced me at a hastily arranged press conference at Yale. They wanted to know what it was, so I did my best to explain it in lay language, after which they said "Oh no, please explain it in lay language." That's when I referred to the benefits of diversification: "You know, don't put all your eggs in one basket." And that is why headlines throughout the world said "Yale economist wins Nobel for 'Don't put all your eggs . . . ,'" and why a friend of mine sent me a cartoon he had clipped, which followed that headline with a sketch of next year's winner in medicine explaining how his award was for "An apple a day keeps the doctor away."

The fact that one of the available assets in the model of my paper was riskless turned out to have interesting consequences. I felt somewhat uneasy and apologetic that I was pairing the safe asset with just one risky asset to represent everything else. This aggregation followed Keynes, who also used "*the* interest rate" to refer to the common yield on all non-money assets and debts. I proved that my results would apply even if any number of risky assets were available, each with different return and risk. The choice of a risky portfolio, the relative weights of the various risky assets within it, would be independent of the decision how much to put into risky assets relative to the safe asset, money. This "separation theorem" was the key to the capital asset pricing model developed by Lintner and Sharpe, beloved by finance teachers and students, and exploited by the investment managers and counselors who compute and report the "betas" of various securities.

The debate about fiscal and monetary policy, as related to the interest-sensitivity of demand for money, went on for a long time, too much of it a duel between Milton Friedman and me. In a Vermont ski line a young attendant checking season passes read mine and said in a French-Canadian accent, "Tobeen, James Tobeen, not ze economiste! Not ze enemy of Professeur Friedman!" He was an economics student in Quebec; it made his day. He let me pass to the lift. This debate, I would say, ended for practical purposes when Friedman shifted ground, saying that no important issue of monetary policy or theory depended on interest-sensitivity of money demand. The ground he shifted to was the basic issue between Keynes and the classics, the contention that the economy is always in a supply-constrained equilibrium whether neither monetary nor fiscal policy can enhance real output.

Second, I proposed to put money into the theory of long-run growth. In the 1950s one phase of the synthesis of Keynesian and neoclassical economics was the development of a growth theory along neoclassical lines. Some, not all, Keynesians were ready to agree that in the long run employment is full, saving limits investment, and "supply creates its own demand." The short run was the Keynesian domain, where labor and capital may be underemployed, investment governs saving, and demand induces its own supply. Roy Harrod had started modern growth theory in 1939, followed by Evsey Domar in the 1940s and Trevor Swan, Robert Solow, Edmund Phelps, and many others in the 1950s and 1960s.

I was involved too. My 1955 piece, "A Dynamic Aggregative Model," may be my favorite; it was the most fun to write. It differed from the other growth literature by explicitly introducing monetary government debt as a store of value, a vehicle of saving alternative to real capital, and by generating a business cycle that interrupted the growth process. In three subsequent papers (1965, 1968, and 1985) I showed that the stock of capital in a growing economy is positively related to the rates of monetary growth and inflation.

Third, in a long series of papers I developed, together with William Brainard and other colleagues at Yale, a general model of asset markets and integrated it into a full macroeconomic model. In a sense we generalized Hicks's famous IS/LM formalization of Keynes by allowing for a richer menu of assets. As I already indicated, I had been uncomfortable with that unique "*the* interest rate" in Keynes and with the simple dichotomy of money versus everything else, usually described as money versus bonds. I thought nominal assets versus real capital was at least as important a way of splitting wealth, if it must be split in only two parts, and this is what I did in the growth models cited above.

Portfolio theory suggested that assets should be regarded as imperfect substitutes for each other, with their differences in expected yields reflecting their marginal risks. Our approach also suggested that there is no sharp dividing line between assets that are money and those that are not. The "Yale approach" to monetary and financial theory has been widely used in empirical flow-of-funds studies and in modeling international capital movements.

Our approach also explicitly recognizes the stock-flow dynamics of saving, investment, and asset accumulation, as in my 1981 Nobel lecture. These dynamics were explicitly ignored in Keynes, who defined the short run as a period in which the change in the stock of capital due to the flow of new investment is insignificant. Stock-flow dynamics are also ignored in IS/LM models. But flows do add to stocks. Investment builds the capital stock, government deficits enlarge the stocks of government bonds and possibly of money, trade surpluses increase the net assets of the nation vis-à-vis the rest of the world, and so on. Without these effects, macro stories about policies and other events are incomplete.

The bottom line of monetary policy is its effect on capital investment, in business plant and equipment, residences, inventories, and consumer durable goods. The effect is not well represented by the market interest rates usually cited, or by quantities of money or credit. Our approach to monetary economics and macroeconomics led us naturally to a different measure, closer to investment decisions. This has become known as "Tobin's q." It is the ratio of the market valuations of capital assets to their replacement costs, for example, the prices of existing houses relative to the costs of building comparable new ones. For corporate businesses, the market valuations are made in the securities markets. It is common sense that the incentive to make new capital investments is high when the securities giving title to their future earnings can be sold for more than the investments cost, i.e., when q exceeds one. We see the reverse in takeovers of companies whose qs are less than one; it is cheaper to buy their productive assets by acquiring their shares than to construct comparable facilities from scratch. That is why in our models q is the link from the central bank and the financial markets to the real economy.

Policy and Public Service

As must be clear from my narrative, I have always been intensely interested in economic policy. Much of my theoretical and empirical research has been devoted to analyzing and discerning the effects of monetary and fiscal policies. In the 1950s I began writing occasional articles on current economic issues for general readership, some of them in the *New Republic*, the *Yale Review, Challenge*, the *New York Times*.

Some of my friends in Massachusetts were advising Senator Kennedy. They told him and his staff about me. In summer 1960 Ted Sorenson came to see me and arranged for the Kennedy campaign to employ me to write some memoranda and position papers on economic growth. Sorenson signed me up despite the fact that I had felt it necessary to tell him I favored Stevenson for the nomination. I didn't notice any effects of my memos during the campaign, but I was told that they were used by the Kennedy team at the party platform deliberations, mainly to oppose the exaggerated "spend to grow" views of Leon Keyserling and some union economists.

My message at the time was that we needed a tight budget, one that would yield a surplus at full employment, and a very easy monetary policy, one that would get interest rates low enough to channel the government's surplus into productive capital investment. The point was to have full employment, but by a mix of policies that promoted growth in the economy's capacity to produce. Incidentally, my message is similar today.

After the 1960 election I served on a transition task force on the domestic economy chaired by Paul Samuelson. One day in early January 1961 I was summoned from lunch at the faculty club to take a phone call from the president-elect. He asked me to serve as a member of his Council of Economic Advisers. JT: "I'm afraid you've got the wrong guy, Mr. President. I'm an ivory-tower economist." JFK: "That's the best kind. I'll be an ivory-tower president." JT: "That's the best kind." I took a day or two to talk to Betty and to my colleagues and then said Yes. I served for twenty months.

Walter Heller was the chairman of the council, and Kermit Gordon was the other member. We had a fantastic staff, including Art Okun, Bob Solow, Ken Arrow, and a younger generation whose names would also be recognized as leaders in our profession today. We were all congenial, intellectually and personally, and we functioned by consensus without hierarchy or bureaucracy. We were optimistic, confident that our economics could improve policy and do good in the world. It was the opportunity that had motivated me to embrace economics a quarter century before.

The January 1962 *Economic Report* is the manifesto of our economics, applied to the United States and world economic conditions of the day. The press called it "the new economics," but it was essentially the blend of Keynesian and neoclassical economics we had been developing and elaborating for the previous ten years. The report was a collective effort, written mainly by Heller, Gordon, Solow, Okun, and Tobin. It doesn't appear on my personal bibliography, but I am proud of it as a work of professional economics as well as a public document. The January 1982 *Report* is the comparable document of Reaganomics, likewise the effort of professional economists to articulate a radically new approach to federal economic policy. It is interesting to compare the two; we have nothing to fear.

The Kennedy council was effective and influential because the president and his immediate White House staff took academics seriously, took ideas seriously, took us seriously. JFK was innocent of economics on inauguration day. But he was an interested, curious, keen, and able student. He read what we wrote, listened to what we said, and learned a lot.

Our central macroeconomic objective was to lower unemployment, 7 percent in January 1961, to 4 percent, our tentative estimate of the inflation-safe unemployment rate. That goal was achieved by the end of 1965, with negligible increase in the rate of inflation and with a big increase in capital investment. The sweet success turned sour in the late 1960s, when contrary to the advice of his council and other Keynesian advisers President Johnson failed to raise taxes to pay for the escalating costs of the war in Vietnam. Critics looking back on the 1960s accuse the Kennedy–Johnson economists of naïve belief in a Phillips trade-off and of policies explicitly designed to purchase lower unemployment with higher inflation. The criticism is not justified. The council did not propose to push unemployment below what came to be known as the "natural rate." Moreover, beginning in 1961 the council and the administration adopted wage and price policies designed to achieve an inflation-free recovery—"guideposts for noninflationary price and wage behavior" were espoused in the report.

I returned to Yale in September 1962. I loved the job at the council, but I knew my principal vocation was university teaching and research. Fifteen-hour days and seven-day weeks were a hardship for me, my wife, and our four young children. I remained active as a consultant to the council, particularly on international monetary issues that had concerned me as a member. Moreover, I was now more visible outside my profession, so I wrote and spoke more frequently on issues and controversies of the day. But I knew that alumni of Washington often have difficulty getting back into mainline professional scholarship. I determined to accomplish that re-entry, and I believe I did.

Kennedy and Johnson added the war on poverty to their agenda. Walter Heller and the council were very much involved. I became quite interested in the economic disadvantages of blacks and in the inadequacies, inefficiencies, and perverse incentives—penalties for work and marriage—of federal and state welfare programs. I wrote major papers on these matters in 1965 and 1968. This was not macroeconomics, but one implication of the Keynesian-neoclassical synthesis was that

welfare and redistributional policies could be, within broad limits, chosen independently of macroeconomic goals. Nothing in our view of the
functioning of capitalist democracies says either that prosperity requires
hard-hearted welfare policies and small governments or that it requires
redistribution in favor of workers and the poor.

I favored a negative income tax. So did Milton Friedman—although
his version seemed to me too small to fill much of the poverty gap, and
he refused to join a national nonpartisan statement of economists fa-
voring the approach. I helped to design a negative income tax plan for
George McGovern in 1972. Unfortunately, he and his staff botched its
presentation in the heat of the California primary; I am sure most people
to this day think McGovern was advocating a kooky budget-breaking
handout. After the election Nixon proposed a family assistance plan
pretty much the same as the McGovern scheme he had ridiculed during
the campaign.

I have lived long enough to see the revolution to which I was an eager
recruit fifty years ago become in its turn a mainstream orthodoxy and
then the target of counterrevolutionary attack. The tides of political opinion and professional fashion have turned against me. Many of my young
colleagues in the profession are as enthusiastic exponents of the new classical macroeconomics as I and my contemporaries were crusaders against
old classical macroeconomics in the 1930s. Many of the issues are the
same, but the environment is quite different from the Great Depression.
The contesting factions are better equipped—our profession has certainly
improved its mathematical, analytical, and statistical tools. I do not despair over the present divisions of opinion in economics. Our subject has
always thrived and advanced through controversy, and I expect a new
synthesis will evolve, maybe even in my lifetime. I haven't abandoned the
field of battle myself. I hope I learn from the new, but I still think and
say that Keynesian ideas about how the economy works and what policies
can make it work better are relevant today—not just as Keynes wrote
them, of course, but as they have been modified, developed, and refined
over the last half-century.

Awarded Nobel Prize in 1981. Lecture presented April 30, 1985.

Dates of Birth and Death

March 5, 1918; March 11, 2002

Academic Degrees

A.B.   Harvard University, 1939

M.A.   Harvard University, 1940

Ph.D. Harvard University, 1947

Academic Affiliations

Junior Fellow, Harvard University, 1946–1950

Associate Professor of Economics, Yale University, 1950–1955

Professor of Economics, Yale University, 1955–1957

Sterling Professor of Economics, Yale University, 1957–1988

Sterling Professor of Economics, Emeritus, Yale University, 1988–2002

Selected Books

The American Business Creed, 1956 (with S. E. Harris et al.)

National Economic Policy, 1966

Essays in Economics, Vols. 1–4, 1971–1982

The New Economics One Decade Older, 1974

Franco Modigliani

Ruminations on My Professional Life

It's been a lot of fun for me to prepare this talk because it has forced me
to go over my history and pick up a number of things I had forgotten
and see connections I did not see before. I was somewhat taken aback
and overawed by the title, "My Evolution as an Economist." It sounded
as if I had to start from my invertebrate state and then move up to higher
states. I then suddenly realized or remembered a very important thing:
economics is a very old profession. In fact I think it is the oldest profession
in the world. I know this claim is disputed by others. There is a story, I
think authentic, of an argument about this among an engineer, an economist, and a surgeon. The problem was that each claimed that his profession was the oldest. The surgeon spoke first and said, "Remember at the
beginning when God took a rib out of Adam and made Eve? Who do
you think did that? Obviously, a surgeon." The engineer, however, was
undaunted by all this and said, "Just a moment. You remember that God
made the world before that. He separated the land from the sea. Who
do you think did that except an engineer?" "Just a moment," protested
the economist, "Before God made the world, what was there? Chaos.
Who do you think was responsible for that?"

So tonight I am going to tell you about my contribution to chaos. One
thing I want to stress, because I want you to consider it as I move through
my story, is the very important question regarding an award like the Nobel Prize: How much is deserved and how much is luck? After I received
the award many people wrote to me asking for a prescription for getting
a Nobel Prize. How many books do you need and how many hours do

you work? I have always answered that you need many books and you must work many hours, but most important: manage to have lots of luck. I have had a lot of luck. And as you may have already gathered, perhaps the first piece of luck in my life was to marry my wife, Serena. It was luck in the sense that I was a fresh, brash kid at that time—very, very, young. It was hard to recognize what could come out of this, but she helped me come through. I am sure that she decided to prove that the brash kid she married really was a good investment, and I hope that she feels she has succeeded.

Let me now try to deal with the history of my development. I was born in Rome, Italy, in 1918 and spent my youth there under Fascism. My family consisted of my father, a leading Rome pediatrician; my mother, a dedicated volunteer social worker; and my older brother. I had a happy childhood protected by the love of my family, though I was supposedly very hardheaded. Otherwise there was nothing very notable in my early career. I was a middling student until I reached senior high school. I had the good fortune of attending one of Italy's outstanding high schools, a school in Rome that produced many popes, bishops, and cardinals. I didn't get to become one of them, but nonetheless the air was full of those great minds. I decided to try to skip the last year of high school and somewhat to my surprise succeeded, thus entering university at seventeen, two years ahead of normal schedule. But I did not know yet want I wanted to do. For awhile it was thought that I should study medicine because my father was a physician. Unfortunately he died when I was quite young, and there was an expectation in the family that I should follow in his footsteps. I went to the registration window to sign up for medicine, but then I closed my eyes and thought of blood! I got pale just thinking about blood and decided that under those conditions I had better keep away from medicine. So what to do then? I didn't have any other special interests, so I did what was fashionable at the time: I enrolled in the Faculty of Law, which at that time opened up many possible careers. The curriculum in law was really very easy, and I had a lot of time on my hands (there wasn't very much to do except when you were cramming for exams, and I didn't go to the lectures because they weren't particularly interesting). Casting about for something to do, I happened to get into some economic activities. I knew some German and was asked to translate from German into Italian some articles for one of the trade associations. Thus I began to be exposed to the economic problems that were in the German literature. At that time there was a lot about price controls.

There was then in Italy an essay competition among university students on various subjects. There was one in engineering, one in music, one in literature, and one in economics. The economic topic for that year was price controls because they had been imposed on Italy during the Ethiopian War (1935). I thought I was an expert, having translated at least twenty articles on price controls from German, and I decided to participate in the contest, albeit without high expectations. But to my great surprise I came out first. The commission told me that obviously I had some facility for economics. So I decided, why not? From then on I began to think of myself as a possible economist. That was around 1936, and at that time economics was one of the subjects in the Faculty of Law. What was taught in fact was the theory and institutions of the "corporate state" and bore little relation to modern economics. But on the good advice of some competent economists in Italy I began to study the economic literature. I studied Marshall and other classics, but could not get hold of Keynes. Although Keynes's *General Theory* already existed, I could not find it in Italian or even in English.

A year after I began my training in economics, we left Italy, as the political situation was deteriorating. The Fascist regime, under the pressure of its Nazi ally, passed a set of laws discriminating against Jews, making an academic career impossible. My then future father-in-law, Giulio Calabi, who had already experienced difficulties with the regime, decided to leave Italy immediately for France where he had many connections, especially with the great publishing house of Hachette. I was more than happy to take advantage of his offer to join the family. I tried to continue my study of economics in France. Again I was not very successful, because the French university was even worse than the Italian. People did go to class in large numbers but, as far as I could tell, their only purpose was to make noises of various kinds—very effectively so that you could not hear what was going on. Why they attended I still don't understand. I went to study in the library (the Bibliothèque St. Geneviève), and again made some progress with my studies. Then as the clouds were gathering in Europe, the Calabi family decided to come to the United States, more as tourists than as permanent residents.

Serena and I were married in May 1939, after which I traveled to Italy to defend my thesis and thus complete my degree—just in time to depart for the United States in August 1939.

We arrived in September 1939, just as war broke out. So when we landed, we knew we were to be here for a long time. I then cast around for something to do. It was now a matter of finding a job in order to live, and I began to work selling Italian and other foreign books. But I also looked around to see what I could do to continue my study of economics. And here again I was lucky and obtained a scholarship at the New School for Social Research, a great center for European scholars. There were many notable names in various disciplines, but a man who was particularly important to me was Jacob Marschak, recently arrived from England. Jacob Marschak was at once a great economist, a magnificent teacher, and an exceptional and warm human being. He took me in hand and persuaded me first of all that if I wanted to get anywhere as an economist, I had to study mathematics. I had had no training at all in math and in fact had a certain aversion to it. He persuaded me to carry out a certain amount of study of mathematics and statistics, which played a very important role as I tried to develop my own papers. The time was 1939. The *General Theory* of Keynes was the center of discussion, together with the work of Schumpeter on business cycles. We had seminars devoted to them and they were very exciting. Of course at that time we were coming out of the depression. Keynes gave you the feeling that the mysterious disease that produced the depression was something that could be understood and avoided in the future. So there was a lot of excitement associated with that study. In addition Marschak invited me to participate in a seminar that was held in New York, organized by Oskar Lange, the famous economist from Poland. The participants included, in addition to Lange and Marschak, such powerful economists as Tjalling Koopmans and Abraham Wald. It was a very exciting experience. Unfortunately in 1941 Marschak left the New School to go to the University of Chicago at the invitation of Oskar Lange, who was there permanently. But by that time I was well on my way, and furthermore, as Marschak left, another outstanding economist, Abba Lerner, came to the New School. I began to have some serious discussions with Abba Lerner, because although I respected him, I thought that he was oversimplifying

the message of the *General Theory*. He accepted one aspect of the Keynesian theory that I think is not its essence, namely, the notion that rigid
wages and a special feature of the demand for money—the so-called liquidity preference—could result in a "liquidity trap," where the economy
is fundamentally an unstable system that will get buffeted by all shocks.
There is no stable equilibrium to which it returns. I think Abba Lerner
held very strongly to this view, and this led him to the idea that the only
way to stabilize the economy is through fiscal policy. Running surpluses
and deficits is the only way to compensate for shocks. I thought this was
a much too simple view of Keynes. From my perspective this represented
a limiting case of Keynes but not the normal run of things, and I began to
work on the article that was to appear in 1944 under the title, "Liquidity
Preference and the Theory of Interest and Money."

While I was working on the article, I began my first teaching job at
the New Jersey College for Women, an institution within commuting distance of New York. I was able to get this offer because Pearl Harbor had
been attacked and people were moving from colleges to Washington. As
a result, an opening arose there for a term. I have fun these days telling
our younger faculty what my teaching load was at that time: four courses
per term, including two sections of economics, one section of statistics,
and one section of economic history. On top of that I was teaching a
course at the New School for Social Research. From the New Jersey College for Women I went to Bard College, which was then a part of Columbia University. It is there that I completed my 1944 article on liquidity
preference, which was to attract a good deal of attention.

I had excellent students. Some of them are good economists and many
have become personal friends with whom I still have contact. The com-
panionship and friendship that often develops between professors and
students is a characteristic of American higher education that is lacking
in Italian universities, which are far more impersonal. Several of these
students helped me improve my English (which was still a little rusty in
1942) and were helpful in editing my article.

It turned out that the referee for my 1944 article was Leonid Hurwicz,
a very young economist with a great future who was to become a close
friend when we were together at the University of Illinois. Its publication,
while I was still relatively young, contributed greatly to my recognition as

an economist and to my unexpected election to fellow of the Econometric Society in 1949. The main theme of the paper was that, except for the questionable assumption of absolute wage rigidity, the Keynesian system did allow in general for a self-restoring full employment equilibrium along classical lines. But there were some special circumstances under which this mechanism breaks down, and perhaps that is what happened in the Great Depression. These special circumstances should not have been regarded as the rule but as a limiting case. In particular the main stabilization device should be monetary policy, not fiscal policy. That was the theme of this paper.

My career at Bard College ended when I was called up for service in the armed forces. I had been left out for awhile because I had a pre–Pearl Harbor child—a very valuable item at that time! However, on the verge of my induction the draft board told me that they were able to find other nonfathers, and I was released. Not long afterward the war ended, and I was offered the opportunity of returning to the New School.

I was there in two capacities: as a researcher at the Institute of World Affairs and as a teacher of mathematical economics at the New School itself. My research project at the institute was to build, together with Hans Neisser, a large-scale (for the time) econometric model of the world economy showing the linkages between countries. At a time when the most powerful computational device was an electric calculator, this was a rather ambitious scheme. But at least we succeeded in putting together a structure that was later used as a guide and a source of ideas for similar projects.

The other thing that happened during this period was that I began to be very much concerned with the study of saving, which was to be a central theme throughout my life. Why was I concerned? Because there was an idea that had its origin in some of the Keynesian writings that people were saving too much. If people save too much, the consequence might be a serious depression. The Keynesian followers argued that saving depends on income and that the proportion of income saved grows with income: if you are richer you save a larger fraction of your income. Because income was expected to rise in the postwar period, there was the implication that the saving rate would get larger and larger, and there were great doubts as to whether there would be enough investment opportunities to absorb the saving.

I didn't believe that the saving rate would tend to grow and grow. It just didn't sound right to me. I thought that this was one of the fads of the time, and I began to work on this problem and pursue the idea that the saving rate has a cyclical characteristic but not a rising trend. My findings suggested that saving is determined more by a person's income relative to his accustomed level than by his absolute income in a given period. This idea happened to be pursued at the same time by James Duesenberry at Harvard. The resulting theory is now known as the Duesenberry–Modigliani hypothesis.

It was approximately at this time that I suddenly received an invitation from Harvard. At that time Harvard had the best economics department in the country—it was Harvard and then nothing and then nothing and then nothing, and then came Columbia and Chicago. So this invitation was not something that I could ignore, and I went to Harvard with some curiosity. I had a great day because the first thing that happened is that I was received by the head of the department who, although I did not know it at the time, had a reputation for not being very sympathetic to foreigners. He had been ordered by the faculty to offer me a job, so he did, but then he went on to say, "Now look, Modigliani, if you've got any sense, you will never accept this job, because you know we have people like James Duesenberry, Sidney Alexander, Richard Goodwin, and others—you will never make it. So why don't you go back to the New School and be a big fish in a small pond. Don't try to be a big fish in this pond." I had been uncertain about accepting the offer because it would have meant taking a cut in salary. Thus I was able to say, "Well fine, I think you have a very good idea," and so I said "No." After finishing my interview, I had meetings with various members of the faculty. I had lunch with Joseph Schumpeter and Gottfried Haberler, and they asked, "Well, how did it go?" and I told them. "Oh, you fool," they replied. "You should never listen to what Professor Burbank says. You should have accepted." But by that time I had made up my mind that if such a person was the head of the department, Harvard did not appeal to me. So I went back to the New School. Within a year I was offered the Political Economy Fellowship at the University of Chicago. This was a fairly prestigious and high-paying scholarship, something like $3,000 a year—a big salary at that time and enough to live on with the family.

So I accepted the offer, took leave, and went there. But I had hardly arrived when I was approached by Howard Bowen, the dean of the College of Commerce at the University of Illinois, and asked to join the University of Illinois on a project entitled "Expectations and Business Fluctuations." The salary was excellent, and the university was prestigious and had some very good people. I accepted. Rejecting the Harvard offer turned out to be a blessing in disguise. I had a much faster career at Illinois and a much higher salary than my colleagues at Harvard. Also I had a chance to get to know the Middle West, which was very important for me, having been born in Europe.

The purpose of the expectations and business fluctuations project was to explain the role of expectations in business planning in order to answer the question: Can expectations independently be a source of instability in an economy? It was in the course of the project that I acquired some basic ideas that would play an important role in many of my later contributions. Let me mention them briefly. First was the idea that a lot of production scheduling in the firm was controlled by the notion of smoothing production in the face of seasonal fluctuations in sales. If you can produce at an even rate, you will have lower costs than if you fluctuate. If you try to hire and fire people or if you keep them idle and pay them overtime, it is more costly than producing evenly. Production does not depend on current sales, it depends on the expectation for the current cycle. It will be seen in a moment why that is relevant to other things. Second, I found that this particular way of looking at production planning has some interesting implications for what expectations are worth forming and what information is needed to make decisions. An interesting implication is that, with few exceptions, the only information that is useful for production scheduling is that which pertains to the rest of this season, and you couldn't care less what's going to happen thereafter—within broad limits. Thus the whole notion of irrelevant expectations, that is, expectations not relevant for current behavior, was one of the interesting ideas that emerged from the project.

The third interesting idea developed from the study of actual business forecasts is that failure to adjust for seasonal factors can be a source of major forecasting errors. Yet many executives do not appear to really understand seasonal adjustments, falling back on the very inaccurate device of four quarter changes.

In addition to this research project I had other significant experiences while at Illinois. I ran into a brilliant and delightful young man by the name of Richard Brumberg, a first-year graduate student. He became a very close friend of the entire family. I had been asked by Kenneth Kurihara to write a paper for a book to be called *Post-Keynesian Economics,* and I invited Brumberg to work with me on the paper. We hadn't decided on a topic until we went to a conference on saving at the University of Minnesota and were both very unhappy with the papers given. On the trip back by car to the University of Illinois we hatched an idea that looked like a possible improvement: the hypothesis that came to be called the life cycle theory of saving.

While still at Illinois, I was invited to become an associate of the Cowles Commission, a Chicago-based organization connected with the Econometric Society. This connection put me in contact with another group of outstanding people that included Tjalling Koopmans, Jacob Marschak, Kenneth Arrow, Carl Christ, Herman Charnoff, and Herbert Simon.

The University of Illinois experience terminated with a dramatic fight in which essentially the McCarthy forces were trying to push out the dean, Howard Bowen, as well as the people he had brought in. He had attracted an excellent cast of people, but they were not from the "black earth" of Illinois. They came from the East Coast, they came from the West Coast, they were Keynesians—they had to be eliminated, particularly because they bothered the old guard who felt passé, inferior to this new group. So the old guard was able to orchestrate a very famous fight in which the main figure was a trustee, Red Grange; I think some of you have heard of this name. To me he was completely unknown, but everybody knew the great football player Red Grange (the Galloping Ghost), and Red Grange led the fight against Bowen. Bowen resigned as did most of the people who came with him. I still had to complete the project so I stayed on for a year, but I began to look around. When I received an invitation from the Carnegie Institute of Technology, now Carnegie Mellon, I wisely accepted and spent eight precious years there, from 1952 to 1960.

During my stay at Carnegie Mellon I matured into the economist I am today. How did that happen? Well, Carnegie at that time was a very exciting place. The key figure of course was Herbert Simon, a genius and a great colleague. But around him there were some other fine scholars like Charles Holt, Merton Miller, William Cooper, Richard Cyert, and James March—all outstanding people. We also had great students such as Jack Muth. He has become one of the heroes of the present time as the man who laid the foundations for the so-called rational expectations hypothesis, which is what young economists live by. All this provided an exciting atmosphere.

In this environment there were two kinds of activities. There were, first of all, important innovations in terms of teaching in a business school. Essentially Carnegie Mellon introduced the quantitative, discipline-oriented approach to business administration. And that was an exciting thing to be doing at that time. Second, there were research projects. For example, Simon, Holt, Muth, and I worked on a book about production scheduling, which again focused on the question of short-run decision making with respect to the scheduling of how much to produce, how many to hire, and how much to hold in inventories. In this book we developed a mathematical model embodying my idea about smoothing out seasonal fluctuations in sales. It has been influential in the production areas and has been used extensively in courses in production both here and abroad. This was a very good example of teamwork—that is, each of us was able to provide a new push when the others were at the end of their ropes.

The second important thing that happened is that together with Richard Brumberg I was able to complete a first contribution on the life cycle hypothesis that dealt with individual behavior and a second part that dealt with aggregate behavior. This hypothesis explained saving patterns in much the same way as I had earlier explained the production pattern of firms: People consume at a relatively constant rate determined by their lifetime earnings. Therefore when their income is highest, they save a great deal, but when it is low, such as during their youth and in their later retirement years, they actually "dissave." This is similar to Milton Friedman's permanent income hypothesis, but differs in that Friedman assumes an infinite time horizon for consumption and saving decisions whereas my hypothesis depends on life being finite and differentiated—dependency, maturity, retirement. In essence a person's lifetime pattern of wealth accumulation can be described as a hump. Wealth is low during one's youth but grows as one begins to earn. It reaches a peak during one's middle years before retirement and declines after retirement. There may be some bequest element. That is, we allowed for the fact that some portion of wealth may be bequeathed. Our estimates now suggest that maybe one-fifth of wealth is the result of bequest, but the remaining four-fifths—or something between 75 percent and 80 percent—is of this hump type.

Hump wealth has one important implication that Richard and I discovered to our great delight. When you aggregate, that is, when you look not at the individual family but at the economy as a whole, it turns out that the aggregate wealth of a country (the aggregate saving) can be different in different countries in which each individual behaves identically over his life cycle. That is, imagine that in every country each person over his life cycle has identical behavior. Yet one country can have no saving and another country can save a lot. Why? Because, if you think of the implication of hump wealth, you will see that the main determinant of national saving is not income—which should not affect the path of wealth relative to income—but growth; the faster the country grows, the higher the saving income. The less you grow, the less you save. If you don't grow at all, aggregate ratio saving is zero. This macro implication and a number of corollaries that follow from it are significant because they give an entirely different view of the saving process. People tend to say that the Japanese save a lot because they are thrifty and we save little because we aren't thrifty. If my model is correct, it says that's nonsense. We are equally thrifty. They are growing at 8 percent per year and we are growing at 3 percent per year, and that is why we normally save 12 percent and they save well over 20 percent of their income.

It turns out that there is a lot of evidence to support the life cycle hypothesis (or LCH) point of view. LCH does not imply that individual thriftiness is entirely immaterial. Rather it suggests that one can reduce the rate of saving to two elements: the shape of the path of wealth over life and how fast the economy grows. For a given path saving depends only on growth. However, the shape of the path has an influence. So it could be that the Japanese are inclined to postpone their consumption. If that were the case, they would have a bigger hump. Incidentally, there is some evidence that that is true. In Japan housing is enormously expensive, and there were until very recently very few facilities for the financing of housing—mortgages were very rare and extremely expensive. So people were forced to save a lot when they were young in order to be able to acquire a house. And that means they had to postpone higher consumption until after they had purchased a house.

There were several other contributions that were completed during this period at Carnegie Mellon. First, I took another crack at the working of the monetary mechanism in the economy, which I had handled in my 1944 article. I allowed for various developments that had happened in the meantime. This was 1963, and it represented a fairly definitive form of my view of how money works in the economy. In addition it was around 1957 that Merton Miller and I produced our two papers, the so-called Modigliani–Miller theorems, which have come to be known as Mo-Mi and Mi-Mo.

Mo-Mi is the proposition that the financial structure (debt-equity ratio) of a firm in a perfect capital market has no effect on its market valuation. This paper has since become quite well known, and it has been assigned to students in business and finance all over the world. And I regret that this is the case because students who read this paper usually come out hating me. They think it's a terrible paper, a very hard one to understand—and they are right. The reason is that this paper was never meant for students. The paper was meant to upset my colleagues in finance by arguing that the core issue that received most attention in corporation finance, namely finding out what exactly is the optimum capital structure, was not really an issue. It didn't make any difference. To be sure, it might make a difference if there were taxes. If so, you would have to approach the problem precisely in that way and ask what is the effect of taxes and why do they make a difference.

Aside from the specific message about capital structure, the main methodological contribution—which I think is the reason the paper has become so important in the area of finance—was in changing the method of attack regarding the choice of financial structure and investment policy: The focus should be on the maximization of the market value of the firm debt plus equity rather than on the traditional, but not operational, maximization of profits. This contribution was much more general than the specific one about the fact that leverage doesn't count.

The second paper had to do with dividend policy. If you have a perfect capital market and no taxes, it makes no difference whether you pay a lot of dividends or very little; the market value of the firm would be unaffected. This once again went against the grain of the time. The profession spent a lot of time deciding whether you could fool the investors, seen as outsiders rather than owners of the firm, by giving them a little more of this or a little more of that. We essentially show that this is all irrelevant.

I produced two other articles at Carnegie Mellon. These were out of my mainstream, but have had considerable influence. One is an article written in 1958 while on leave at Harvard, on oligopoly theory, which developed a very simple way of understanding pricing behavior under conditions of oligopoly. The other one was even more unorthodox. It is called "The Forecastability of Social Events." Written with one of my colleagues, Emile Grunberg, the paper deals with the belief that economists can't forecast accurately because people respond to the forecasts and therefore behave differently, invalidating the forecast. This article said that accurate forecasts are perfectly possible even when agents react to them. When you make a forecast, you must simply take into account the effect of the forecast on behavior. Under some very general mathematical conditions (continuity) it can be shown that forecasting is, in principle, possible. The implied message to our colleagues was therefore: don't kid yourself, don't make excuses. If we can't forecast it's because of our ignorance, not because agents react.

An important aspect of my life at this time is that I reestablished relations with Italy. Until 1945 we had considered going back to Italy. But as we watched what was going on there, we decided that we had had enough and were going to become U.S. citizens and make this our home. For awhile I more or less cut off relations, but in the mid-50s I reestablished contact and began to be interested in issues of economic policy in Italy.

In 1955 I spent a year as a Fulbright lecturer at the Universities of Rome and Palermo. I had completely forgotten how profoundly different the Italian and the American systems of higher education were. The

Italian system was a three-caste structure, with the few and mostly old full professors occupying the upper caste, close to God; a group of hopeful, sometimes servile assistants constituted the second layer; and the students were at the bottom of the heap. I will always remember an episode that occurred during my stay at the University of Rome when Professor Papi, then rector of the university and a symbol of the system, invited me to speak at his faculty seminar but introduced me (then thirty-eight) as a promising young star! I thanked him but remarked that in the United States I was regarded as a bit passé!

In 1960 we left Carnegie Mellon and went to Northwestern for just a year. After this year we moved permanently to MIT. Let me divide the MIT period into two parts: the period up to 1974—corresponding to the first oil crisis—and the period since.

The decade from 1960 to 1970 was what you might call the golden era of Keynesianism. It should be understood of course that when I speak of Keynesianism I speak of wise Keynesians. I speak of Solow and Samuelson and Tobin and Heller and others of their ilk. I don't speak of the many aberrations that always exist. In the mid-1960s I was asked by the Federal Reserve Board to build a model of the American economy that could be used for forecasting and policy analysis. That model was built in collaboration with Albert Ando along basically Keynesian lines, but our type of Keynesian lines in which money is very important. In fact we discovered that money was even more important than was thought because of the interaction between my consumption function and monetary policy. Because my consumption function shows that consumption depends on income and wealth, and because interest rates affect that wealth, here is one more channel through which monetary policy can have an effect on income. Furthermore we showed that in terms of our estimates this was faster than the traditional channel through investment, which involves considerable lags.

In terms of intellectual history I think it is important to acknowledge that there were two points on which we had to change our initial course. The first is that we started out with a model of the determinant of the price level that in the traditional Keynesian literature was referred to as the Phillips curve. This formulation allowed for the possibility of a long-run trade-off between inflation and unemployment. That mechanism was shown to be invalid by Ned Phelps and Milton Friedman, particularly in Friedman's presidential address to the American Economic Association during which he introduced the "vertical" Phillips curve. We readily accepted that, and by the late 1960s we had revised our model so that it included a vertical Phillips curve, for which we found plenty of support. The vertical Phillips curve essentially says that you cannot push unemployment below some critical level through inflation; if you try to have too much employment, you will get accelerating inflating, which will eventually have to be stopped by accepting a lot of unemployment.

As for the second change, when we started the model, inflation was not yet a problem. But by the late 1960s, however, it had become serious. We had to allow for various effects of inflation on the economy, beginning with such a simple thing as the concept of the real interest rate, the rate of interest adjusted for the effect of inflation. The model is still used at the Federal Reserve together with other devices.

The other contributions of that period included, first of all, a fair amount of work pursuing the implications of the life cycle model. One that has become very important of late relates to the economic effects of deficit financing, or more broadly, the public debt. Using the life cycle framework, one can show that these deficits or debts have an effect on the well-being of future generations because they displace productive capital. When the government borrows, it absorbs a certain amount of saving, reducing what's available for investment, or equivalently, for increasing the stock of capital. That is the fundamental mechanism by which a deficit is deleterious. It was recognized that the deficit need not displace investment dollar per dollar because of the fact that life, though finite, extends beyond the time of the deficit. People therefore should recognize that if the deficit is increased now, they will have to pay additional taxes over the rest of their lives, and that should be reflected in their current behavior by some increase in saving. But still much of the deficit should displace private investment.

Then there were several attempts at testing the life cycle model empirically. One of these attempts consisted of gathering evidence that the debt displaces private productive capital. Another one was a comparative study across countries testing whether differential saving behavior could be explained in terms of rates of growth and population structure. These were found to be the main determinants of saving, accounting for a great deal of the observed differences. Finally with my colleague Jacques Drèze there was an extension of the life cycle to a world of uncertainty, which has since given rise to a substantial body of literature, including the combination of life cycle with the theory of portfolio.

There is a third line of contributions (inspired by emerging economic problems), where I was led to pursue some current issues of economic policy. The major issue in the fifties and sixties, a golden period during which all the world was developing in a remarkable fashion, was the emerging stresses on the international payments system, a product of the Bretton Woods agreement. The problem revolved around the inadequate and unsatisfactory mechanisms for creating liquidity to finance world trade—basically through U.S. deficit on current and capital accounts. In a paper with Peter Kenen I suggested that the problem could be resolved through a mechanism for the creation of a new means for international payments called the Medium for International Transactions, which abbreviated into MIT. That was, I hope, a worthwhile contribution to the history of the international means of payment!

The suggestion was not followed, and the problem grew worse as the creation of liquidity by the United States got out of control. In 1971 a second suggestion was advanced, in collaboration with my former student Hossein Askari, to avoid the impending crisis. It involved ratifying the inconvertibility of the dollar but at the same time endowing the rest of the world with the power to control the U.S. deficit through unilateral control of exchange rates. Furthermore countries were to be given an option of protecting their dollar reserves through an exchange guarantee. But whatever its merits, the proposal came too late to prevent a run on the dollar. As the United States had neither the will nor the gold to convert its dollar liabilities into gold, the so-called Bretton Woods system came to an end.

It was also during this period that I agreed to write a regular front-page column for Italy's most prestigious newspaper, *Il Corriere della Sera,* a commitment that I fulfilled fairly faithfully for about five years beginning in late 1972. The most memorable episode in my journalistic career occurred in 1975. The Association of Manufacturers accepted the union's demands for a novel type of escalator clause, which gave for each one percentage increase in the cost of living the same number of liras (rather than the same percentage increase) to all workers, including white-collar workers. The agreement meant that higher-paid workers would not keep up with inflation, whereas lower-paid workers would achieve higher real wages. I warned my former compatriots of the dire consequences that contract would have for the country in terms of inflation, undermining incentive, etc., but I initially found little support. Even my fellow economists kept strangely silent. It was several years before the country, including the workers, understood the damage wrought by that form of indexation and nearly ten years until it was abandoned altogether.

This brings me to the last period: 1974 to date. The essay about which I am keenest in this period was my presidential address to the American Economic Association, of which I had become president in 1976. It was called "The Monetarist Controversy, or Should We Forsake Stabilization Policies?" This was essentially a head-on collision with the monetarists, who had become very powerful for a variety of reasons. The theme of this essay is that the differences between monetarists and nonmonetarists are not about the working of the economy or the potency of monetary versus fiscal policy; they are instead basically philosophical and political. The monetarists do not want to give the government the power to use discretion because they believe that the government is incapable of using it well. Due to their stupidity or bad faith the monetary authority could not be trusted with any discretionary power in deciding on the appropriate expansion of the money supply. It must be left instead to a mechanical rule. You can trust a computer to compute 3 percent but not the chairman and the board of the Federal Reserve to change that number as circumstances dictate. My argument was to show that this was the only important difference. In addition I pointed to evidence that a fixed rule is not adequate to stabilize the economy, that there is room for stabilization. Finally I showed that in fact stabilization policy tended to work. That was the fundamental message. This issue has reemerged lately, and I'll come back to it briefly.

Other things that happened during this period were further extensions of the life cycle hypothesis. In particular, one interesting application was a study of the effect of transitory tax cuts. In our history we have had a few cases in which taxes were reduced or increased with the announcement that the original tax rates would be reinstated within a year or two.

That's what we call a transitory tax cut. The life cycle hypothesis implies that such tax cuts are rather powerless to affect consumption. Since people know that the tax cut is only for a short time, the difference that it makes to their life resources is small. So if they are rational, their consumption will not change much. But if you make a tax change that is "permanent," then of course you will know that you are going to be poorer hereafter, and that will affect consumption. There is evidence, especially from the 1969 temporary tax increase, that in fact transitory tax changes are not very effective in terms of affecting consumption.

Finally there was a series of tests on the then-fashionable idea that the national debt makes no difference to the economy. This idea is associated with the name of Robert Barro, who happens to be one of my students. But despite this circumstance I completely disagree with his theory even though it can be viewed as an extension of the life cycle model. As I indicated before, the original life cycle model asserts the opposite. Mr. Barro's contrary result rests on the assumption of perfect rationality and infinite life. In this case if the government cuts your taxes, incurring a corresponding deficit, and you are rational, you would save the additional after-tax income because you would realize that otherwise you would consume more now at the expense of less consumption thereafter, when additional taxes would be levied to service and retire the debt. Numerous tests carried out for the United States, Italy, and a cross section of other countries all decisively reject the Barro hypothesis.

Another new approach is the rational expectations paradigm, whose foundation happens to rest on my earlier analysis of the forecastability of social events. That is, they have in common the notion that a warranted forecast must be based on all relevant information available for the economy and must take fully into account the effect of the expectation on the event forecasted. This approach has led to the conclusion that policy is altogether powerless in systematically affecting the real economy. The economy goes its own way no matter what you do. However, I happen to disagree wholly with their formulations, not in principle but in every application I have seen. In particular, the ineffectiveness of policy is derived from two highly questionable assumptions: (1) that the economy is unaffected by policy even in the shortest run, as long as agents believe it, and (2) that the agents believe it.

I reject both hypotheses, the first because of slow adjustments in the economy that can be offset by policy, and the second because in my view agents can be expected to use a variety of models, including extrapolation of past experience, and in any event few could be expected to believe that policy is instantly neutral, because it is not. Empirical evidence fully supports my rejection of monetarists' attempts to build their models on their assumptions. Indeed such models have produced much poorer forecasts than those obtained by models like the MPS.

I have tried to make a number of contributions to other current policy issues. I've done a certain amount of work on the effects of inflation. There are two schools here. One school thinks that inflation is catastrophic, and the other thinks that inflation makes no difference at all. Economists, for example, frequently take the position that money has no real effect on the economy and therefore that inflation has none. However, a great deal of work shows that inflation has a lot of effects, some of which are connected with the fact that agents (not unlike many economists!) do not understand the consequences of inflation. I've used that argument in particular to explain a phenomenon that is very puzzling. Why is it that in inflation the stock market typically goes down instead of rising in parallel with inflation? One would think it would rise because equities are a real asset. But, systematically, it goes down.

In the late 1970s the stock market was very low, and I wrote an article explaining the very low market in terms of irrational behavior generated by inflation. I argued that the public does not understand the difference between real and nominal interest rates and that in computing profits the interest rate component must be corrected for inflation. As a result, I said, if the stock market had been rationally valued, it would have been twice as high as it was. The stock market was then at approximately 800, and I predicted that it would double if and when inflation abated. Inflation did abate to 2 to 3 percent and the market did double. The problem was that it then trebled. Actually I had anticipated this possibility, relying on the experience of the World War I period culminating in 1929. Specifically I suggested that, in the process of returning to normal, there would be a lot of capital gain that would be misinterpreted as a maintainable addition to profits. As a result there would be a tendency for stock prices to be bid up beyond the level warranted by fundamentals. Well, I believe that is going on right now. The market is now overshooting. That is, when one takes into account the change in profits and the change in interest rates, one finds that the market is really overshooting rational valuation. Since the market can continue to behave irrationally, it may very well go even higher, but at some point the bubble may be expected to burst [as it finally did a few months later in October 1987].

As I contemplate my contributions, I find one unifying thread: a propensity to swim against the current by challenging the self-evident orthodoxies of the moment, be it that the classics are altogether outdated, or that the rich must save a larger fraction of their income than the poor, or that debt financing is cheaper because the interest rate on high-quality debt is lower than the return on equity.

I would love to be able to continue to play that role. But I don't want to think too much about where I am going. I just like to let things come and be ready to jump in where there is excitement.

Awarded Nobel Prize in 1985. Lecture presented March 24, 1987.

Dates of Birth and Death

June 18, 1918; September 25, 2003

Academic Degrees

D (Jurisprudence) University of Rome, 1939

D (Social Science) New School for Social Research, 1944

Academic Affiliations

Instructor, Bard College, 1942–1944

Assistant Professor of Economics, New School for Social Research, 1943–1944, 1946–1948

Associate Professor of Economics, University of Illinois, 1949–1950

Professor of Economics, University of Illinois, 1950–1952

Professor of Economics and Industrial Administration, Carnegie Institute of Technology, 1952–1960

Professor of Economics, Northwestern University, 1960–1962

Professor of Economics and Finance, Massachusetts Institute of Technology, 1962–1970

Institute Professor, Massachusetts Institute of Technology, 1970–1988

Institute Professor, Emeritus, Massachusetts Institute of Technology, 1988–2003

Selected Books

National Incomes and International Trade, 1953 (with H. Neisser)

Planning Production, Inventories and Work Forces, 1960 (with others)

The Collected Papers of Franco Modigliani, Vols. 1–5, 1980–1989

James M. Buchanan

Born-Again Economist

I have been tempted to expand my title to "Born-Again Economist, with a Prophet but No God." Both parts of this expanded title are descriptive. I was specifically asked to discuss my evolution as an economist, an assignment that I cannot fulfill. I am not a "natural economist" as some of my colleagues are, and I did not "evolve" into an economist.[1] Instead I sprang full blown upon intellectual conversion, after I "saw the light." I shall review this experience below, and I shall defend the implied definition and classification of who qualifies as an economist.

The second part of my expanded title is related to the first. It is my own play on the University of Chicago saying of the 1940s that "there is no god, but Frank Knight is his prophet." I was indeed converted by Frank Knight, but he almost single-mindedly conveyed the message that there exists no god whose pronouncements deserve elevation to the sacrosanct, whether god within or without the scientific academy. Everything, everyone, anywhere, anytime—all is open to challenge and criticism. There is a moral obligation to reach one's own conclusions, even if this sometimes means exposing the prophet whom you have elevated to intellectual guruship.

In an earlier autobiographical essay, "Better Than Plowing,"[2] I identified two persons who were dominant intellectual influences on my own methodology, selection of subject matter, attitude toward scholarship, positive analysis, and normative position. One of these, Knut Wicksell, influenced me exclusively through his ideas. I used the occasion of my Nobel Prize lecture to trace the relationship between Wicksell's precursory foundations and later developments in the theory of public choice, notably its constitutional economics component with which I have been most closely associated. By comparison and contrast this paper offers me the opportunity, even if indirectly, to explore more fully the influence of the second person identified, Frank H. Knight, an influence that was exerted both through his ideas and through a personal friendship that extended over a full quarter century.

The paper is organized as follows. In the following section I try as best I can to describe my state of mind, intellectually and emotionally, before I enrolled in the University of Chicago in 1946. Then I offer a retrospective description of my Chicago experience, with an emphasis on my exposure to the teachings of Frank Knight along with a subconscious conversion to a catallactic methodological perspective on the discipline. The next section briefly traces the catallactic roots of my contributions to public choice theory. After that I discuss the remembered events and persons who were important in giving me the self-confidence that was surely necessary for any career success. Frank Knight was important but by no means unique in this evolution (and in this respect the word "evolution" can be properly applied). I then discuss the influence of Knight's principle of the "relatively absolute absolute" upon my own stance, as moral philosopher, as constitutionalist, and as economic analyst. Finally, I defend my use of the title of my earlier autobiographical essay, "Better Than Plowing," which has been questioned by colleagues and critics. Here I try to examine the motivations that, consciously or unconsciously, may have driven me throughout the course of a long academic career. Why did I do what I did? It may be helpful to explore, even if briefly, this most subjective of questions.

Pre-Chicago: Standards without Coherence

From 1940 I called myself an "economist," as my military records will indicate. I did so because after graduating from Middle Tennessee State Teachers College in June 1940, I was awarded a graduate fellowship in economics at the University of Tennessee for the academic year 1940–41, and I earned a master's degree in 1941. By the academic counters, I took courses labeled "economics," and I made good grades. But as

I have noted, however, I learned little or no economics in my preferred definition during that Knoxville year. I surveyed the workings and structures of the institutions of Roosevelt's New Deal; I came to understand central banking theory and policy; I learned something about taxation and budgeting processes; I learned a bit of elementary statistics, especially in practice. But neither in these courses nor in my prior undergraduate experience did I have proper exposure to the central principle of market organization. I remained blissfully ignorant of the coordinating properties of a decentralized market process, an ignorance that made me vulnerable to quasi-Marxist arguments and explanations about economic history and economic reality but also guaranteed that my mind was an open slate when I finally gained the exposure in question.

During the Knoxville year I did learn to appreciate the dedication of the research scholar though my association with Charles P. White, whose course in research methods was the intellectual high point. White instilled in me the moral standards of the research process. My experience with him, as both graduate student and research assistant, gave me something that seems so often absent in the training of the economists of the postwar decades, whose technology so often outdistances their norms for behavior.

By subject matter, by terminology, and with a bit of technique I left Knoxville as an "economist," but I lacked the coherence of vision of the economic process that I should now make the sine qua non of anyone who proposes to use this label. I have often wondered whether or not I was relatively alone in my ignorance, or whether something akin to my experience has been shared by others who purport to pass as professional economists without the foggiest notion of what they are about.

Chicago, 1946

I enrolled in the University of Chicago for the winter quarter, 1946. I had chosen the University of Chicago without much knowledge about its faculty in economics. I was influenced almost exclusively by an undergraduate teacher in political science, C. C. Sims, who had earned a doctorate at Chicago in the late 1930s. Sims impressed on me the intellectual ferment of the university, the importance of ideas, and the genuine life of the mind that was present at the institution. His near-idyllic sketch appealed to me, and I made the plunge into serious study for the first time in my life. In retrospect I could not have made a better selection. Sims was precisely on target in conveying the intellectual excitement of the University of Chicago, an excitement that remains, to this day, unmatched anywhere else in the world.

During the first quarter I took courses with Frank Knight, T. W. Schultz, and Simeon Leland. I was among the very first group of graduate students to return to the academy after discharge from military service during World War II. We swelled the ranks of the graduate classes at Chicago and elsewhere.

Within a few short weeks, perhaps by mid-February 1946, I had undergone a conversion in my understanding of how an economy operates. For the first time I was able to think in terms of the ordering principle of a market economy. The stylized model for the working of the competitive structure gave me the benchmark for constructive criticism of the economy to be observed. For the first time I was indeed an economist.

I attribute this conversion directly to Frank Knight's teachings, which perhaps raises more new questions than it answers. Knight was not a systematic instructor. More important, he remained ambiguous in his own interpretation of what economics is all about. He was never able to shed the allocating-maximizing paradigm, which tends to distract attention from the coordination paradigm that I have long deemed central to the discipline.[3] But Knight's economics was a curious amalgam of these partially conflicting visions. And for me the organizational emphasis was sufficient to relegate the allocative thrust to a place of secondary relevance. In this respect I was fortunate in my ignorance. Had I received "better" pre-Chicago training in economics, as widely interpreted, I would have scarcely been able to elevate the coordination principle to the central place it has occupied in my thinking throughout my research career. Like so many of my peers, aside from the few who were exposed early to Austrian theory, I might have remained basically an allocationist.

There are subtle but important differences between the allocationist-maximization and the catallactic-coordination paradigm in terms of the implications for normative evaluation of institutions. In particular the evaluation of the market order may depend critically on which of these partially conflicting paradigms remains dominant in one's stylized vision. To the allocationist the market is efficient *if it works*. His test of the market becomes the comparison with the abstract ideal defined in his logic. To the catallactist the market coordinates the separate activities of self-seeking persons *without the necessity of detailed political direction*. The test of the market is the comparison with its institutional alternative, politicized decision making.

There is of course no necessary implication of the differing paradigms for identifying the normative stance of practicing economists. Many modern economists remain firm supporters of the market order while at the same time remaining within the maximizing paradigm. I submit here, however, that there are relatively few economists whose vision is dominated by the catallactic perspective on market order who are predominantly critics of such an order. Once the relevant comparison becomes that between the workings of the market, however imperfect this may seem, and the workings of its political alternative, there must indeed be very strong offsetting sources of evaluation present.

The apparent digression of the preceding paragraphs is important for my narrative and for an understanding of how my conversion by Frank Knight influenced my research career after Chicago. Those of us who entered graduate school in the immediate postwar years were all socialists of one sort or another. Some of us were what I have elsewhere called "libertarian socialists," who placed a high residual value on individual liberty but simply did not understand the principle of market coordination. We were always libertarians first, socialists second. And we tended to be grossly naive in our thinking about political alternatives. To us, the idealized attractions of populist democracy seemed preferable to those of the establishment-controlled economy. It was this sort of young socialist in particular who was especially ready for immediate conversion upon exposure to teachings that transmitted the principle of market coordination.[4]

An understanding of this principle enabled us to concentrate our long-held anti-establishment evaluative norms on politics and governance and open up the prospect that economic interaction, at least in the limit, need not embody the exercise of man's power over man. By our libertarian standards, politics had always been deemed to fail. Now by these same standards market may, just may, not involve exploitation.

An important element in Knight's economics was his emphasis on the organizational structure of markets, and it was this emphasis that elevated the coordination principle to center stage despite his continued obeisance to economizing-maximizing. Once attention is drawn to a structure, to process, and away from resources, goods, and services, many of the technical trappings of orthodox economic theory fall away. Here Knight's approach became institutional, in the proper meaning of this term.

It is useful at this point to recall that Frank Knight's career shared a temporal dimensionality with the seminal American institutionalists Clarence Ayres, John R. Commons, and Thorstein Veblen. He treated their technical economics with derision, but he shared with them an interest in the structure of social and economic interaction. Knight did not extend his institutional inquiry much beyond the seminal work on human wants that exposed some of the shallow presuppositions of economic orthodoxy. He did not, save in a few passing references, examine the structure of politics, considered the only alternative to markets.

Public Choice and the Catallactic Paradigm

Public choice is the inclusive term that describes the extension of analysis to the political alternatives to markets. It seems highly unlikely that this extension could have been effectively made by economists who viewed the market merely as an allocative mechanism, quite independently of its political role in reducing the range and scope of politicized activity. I can of course speak here only of my own experience, but it seems doubtful if I could have even recognized the Wicksellian message had not Knight's preparatory teachings of the coordination principle paved the way.

The point may be illustrated by the related, but yet quite distinct, strands of modern inquiry summarized under the two rubrics "social choice" and "public choice." I have elsewhere identified the two central elements in public choice theory as (1) the conceptualization of politics as exchange, and (2) the model of Homo economicus.[5] The second of these elements is shared with social choice theory, which seeks to ground social choices on the values of utility-maximizing individuals. Where social choice theory and public choice theory differ—and dramatically— lies in the first element noted. Social choice theory does not conceptualize politics as complex exchange; rather politics is implicitly or explicitly modeled in the age-old conception that there must exist some unique and hence discoverable "best" result. This element in social choice theory, from Arrow on, stems directly for the allocative paradigm in orthodox economics, and the maximization of the social welfare function becomes little more than the extension of the standard efficiency calculus to the aggregative economy.

By contrast, the extension of the catallactic paradigm—the emphasis on the theory of exchange rather than allocation—to politics immediately calls attention to the institutional structure of political decision making. Without Frank Knight as teacher and as role model, would Knut Wicksell's great work have been discovered by the fledgling economist that I was in 1948? I have strong reasons for doubt on this score.

The Evolution of Confidence

When I reflect on my own experiences over a tolerably long academic career, I come back again and again to identifiable events and persons that built up or bolstered my confidence, that made me, always an outsider, feel potentially competent among my academic peers. The first such event came with the release of academic grade records at the end of my second year at Middle Tennessee State Teachers College in 1938. My name led all the rest. For the first time I realized that despite my rural origins, my day-student status, and my graduation from a tiny struggling high school, I could compete with the town students, the live-in students, and with all those whose earlier education was acknowledged to be superior to mine.

A second such event occurred in January 1942, when I finished a three-month stint as a midshipman and was commissioned an ensign in the United States Naval Reserve. Again, despite my Tennessee heritage and my mediocre academic experience at both Middle Tennessee and the University of Tennessee, I ranked sixth or seventh in a midshipman class of some six hundred college and university graduates from across the land. The Tennessee country boy could indeed hold his own.

After a successful, interesting, exciting, and easy four years on active military duty in the Pacific theater of war, which I spent for the most part on the staff of Admiral Nimitz at Pearl Harbor and at Guam, my confidence was once again put to the test when I entered graduate school at the University of Chicago in January 1946. Here the test was of a totally different dimension. I knew that I could compete successfully in terms of the ordinary criteria—academic grades, degrees, and honors. I do not recall ever entertaining the slightest doubt about my ability to finish doctoral requirements. What I did not know was whether I could go beyond these criteria and enter the narrowed ranks of producing scholars who could generate ideas worthy of the serious attention of their disciplinary peers.

At this point Frank H. Knight again enters my narrative. Had my Chicago exposure been limited to the likes of Jacob Viner and Milton Friedman, both of whom were also my teachers there, I doubt that I should have ever emerged from the familiarly large ranks of Ph.D.'s with no or few publications. Jacob Viner, the classically erudite scholar whose self-appointed task in life seemed to be that of destroying confidence in students, and Milton Friedman, whose dominating intellectual brilliance in argument and analysis relegated the student to the role of fourth-best imitation—these were not the persons who encouraged students to believe that they too might eventually have ideas worthy of merit.

Frank Knight was dramatically different. In the classroom he came across as a man engaged always in a search for ideas. He puzzled over principles, from the commonsensical to the esoteric, and he stood continuously dismayed at the arrogance of those who spouted forth the learned wisdom. Knight gave those of us who bothered to listen the abiding notion that all is up for intellectual grabs, that much of what paraded as truth was highly questionable, and that the hallmark of a scholar was his courage in cutting through the intellectual haze. The willingness to deny all gods, to hold nothing sacrosanct—these were the qualities of mind and character that best describe Frank Knight. And gods, as I use the term here, include the authorities in one's own discipline as well as those who claim domain over other dimensions of truth. Those of us who were so often confused in so many things were bolstered by this Knightian stance before all gods. Only gradually, and much later, did we come to realize that in these qualities it was Frank Knight, not his peers, who attained the rank of genius.

As he was the first to acknowledge, Frank Knight was not a clever or brilliant thinker. He was an inveterate puzzler; but his thought process probed depths that the scholars about him could not realize even to exist. To Knight, things were never so simple as they seemed, and he remained at base tolerant in the extreme because he sensed the elements of truth in all principles.

There were many graduate students, both in my own cohort and before and after my time, who could not take in or relate to the Knightian stance before the gods. To these "outsiders" Knight seemed a bumbling and confused teacher, whose writings mirrored his thought and whose primary attribute appeared to be intellectual incoherence. To a few of us, what seemed confusion to others came across as profundity, actual or potential, and despite the chasm that we acknowledged to exist between his mind and ours, Knight left us with the awful realization that if we did not have the simple courage to work out our own answers, we were vulnerable to victimization by false gods.

My own understanding, appreciation, and admiration for Frank Knight were aided and abetted by the development, early on, of a close personal relationship. Some three or four weeks after enrollment in his course I visited Knight's jumbled office. What was expected to be a five-minute talk stretched over two hours, to be matched several times during my two and a half years at Chicago, and beyond. He took an interest in me because we shared several dimensions of experience. Both of us were country boys, reared in agricultural poverty, well aware of the basic drudgery of rural existence but also appreciative of the independence of a life on the land. Knight left his native Illinois in his teens for rudimentary college instruction in my home state of Tennessee, and he enrolled in graduate studies at the University of Tennessee where I too had first commenced graduate work. These common threads of experience established for me a relationship that I shared with no other professor. We shared other interests, including an appreciation of the gloomy poetry of Thomas Hardy and the fun of the clever off-color joke.

Of course I was a one-way beneficiary of this relationship. Knight was the advisor who told me not to waste my time taking formal courses in philosophy, who corrected my dissertation grammar in great detail, and who became the role model that has never been replaced or even slightly dislodged over a long academic career. In trying to assess my own development, I find it impossible to imagine what I might have been and become without exposure to Frank Knight.

Let me return to confidence, lest I digress too much. Both T. W. Schultz and Earl J. Hamilton deserve inclusion in this narrative account. Schultz encouraged students by his expressed willingness to locate potential merit in arguments that must have often approached the absurd. I was never a formal student of Earl Hamilton. I did not enroll in his economic history courses at Chicago. Nonetheless during my last year at Chicago, 1948, Hamilton sought me out and took a direct personal interest in my prospects. As with Knight, the sharing of common experience in rural poverty created a personal bond, supplemented in this case by a passion for baseball, reflected by trips to both Cubs and White Sox home games. Hamilton enjoyed giving advice to those he singled out for possible achievement, and with me two separate imperatives stand out in recall: the potential payoff to hard work and the value of mastery of foreign languages.

Perhaps Earl J. Hamilton's most important influence on my career came after 1948, during his tenure as editor of the *Journal of Political Economy*. First of all he forced me to follow up on his recommendation about language skills by sending me French, German, and Italian books for review. Second, he handled my early article submissions with tolerance, understanding, and encouragement rather than with brutal or carping rejections that might have proved fatal to further effort. Hamilton was indeed a tough editor, and every article that I finally published during his tenure was laboriously transformed and dramatically pared down through a process of multiple revisions and resubmissions. Without Hamilton as an editor who cared, my writing style would never have attained the economy it possesses, and my willingness to venture into subject matter beyond the boundaries of the orthodox might have been squelched early. With Earl J. Hamilton as editor, by the mid-1950s I had several solid papers on the record—a number sufficient to enable me to accept the occasional rejection slip with equanimity rather than despair.

I noted earlier how Friedman's analytic brilliance exerted a negating effect on those he instructed. An event occurred early in my post-Chicago years that tended to erase this negative influence by placing Milton

Friedman too among the ranks of those who take intellectual tumbles. A relatively obscure scholar, Cecil G. Phipps, of the University of Florida, located and exposed a logical error in one of Friedman's papers,[6] an error that Friedman graciously acknowledged.[7] To this day I have never told Milton how this simple event contributed so massively to my self-confidence.

The Relatively Absolute Absolute

I have already discussed how Frank Knight's willingness to challenge all authority—intellectual, moral, or scientific—indirectly established confidence in those for whom he served as role model. Any account of such an influence would be seriously incomplete, and indeed erroneous, if the philosophical stance suggested is one of relativism-cum-nihilism against the claim of any and all authority. It is at precisely this point that Frank Knight directly taught me the philosophical principle that has served me so well over so many years and in so many applications. This principle is that of the *relatively absolute absolute,* which allows for a philosophical way station between the extremes of absolutism on the one hand and relativism on the other, both of which are to be rejected.

Acceptance of this principle necessarily requires that there exist a continuing tension between the forces that dictate adherence to and acceptance of authority and those very qualities that define freedom of thought and inquiry. Knight's expressed willingness to challenge all authority was embedded within a wisdom that also recognized the relevance of tradition in ideas, manners, and institutions. This wisdom dictates that for most purposes and most of the time prudent behavior consists of acting as if the authority that exists does indeed possess legitimacy. The principle of the relatively absolute absolute requires that we adhere to and accept the standards of established or conventional authority in our ordinary behavior, whether this be personal, scientific, or political, while at the same time and at still another (and "higher") level of consciousness we call all such standards into question, even to the extent of proposing change.

In relation to my own work this principle of the relatively absolute absolute is perhaps best exemplified in the critically important distinction between the postconstitutional and the constitutional levels of political interaction. More generally, the distinction is that between choosing among strategies of play in a game that is defined by a set of rules and choosing among alternative sets of rules. To the chooser of strategies under defined rules, the rules themselves are to be treated as relatively absolute absolutes, as constraints that are a part of the existential reality but at the same time may be subject to evaluation, modification, and change. In this extension and application of the Knightian principle to the political constitution—and particularly by way of analogy with the choices of strategies and rules of ordinary games—I was stimulated and encouraged by my colleague at the University of Virginia, Rutledge Vining, who had also been strongly influenced by the teachings of Frank Knight.

Why "Better Than Plowing"?

As noted, in 1986 I wrote an autobiographical essay called "Better Than Plowing," a title I borrowed directly from Frank Knight, who used it to describe his own attitude toward a career in the academy. To me the title seemed also descriptive, and it does, I think, convey my sense of comparative evaluation between "employment" in the academy and in the economy beyond. This title also suggests, even if somewhat vaguely, the sheer luck of those of us who served in the academy during the years of the baby-boom educational explosion, luck that was translated into rents of magnitudes beyond imaginable dreams.

To my surprise constructive critics have challenged the appropriateness of the "Better Than Plowing" title for my more general autobiographical essay. To these critics this title seems too casual, too much a throwaway phrase, too flippant a description of a research career that, objectively and externally considered, seems to have embodied central purpose or intent. This unexpected invitation to write a second autobiographical essay provides me with an opportunity to respond to these critics and at the same time to offer additional insights into my development as an economist.

The many books and papers that I have written and published between 1949 and 1987 make up an objective reality that is "there" for all to read and to interpret as they choose. These words and pages exist in some space analogous to the Popperian third world. There is a surprising coherence in this record that I can recognize as well or better than any interpretative critical biographer. As Robert Tollison and I have suggested in our analysis of autobiography,[8] the autobiographer possesses a record over and beyond that which is potentially available to any biographer. The person whose acts created the objective record lives with the subject record itself. And such a person, as autobiographer, would be immoral if he relied on the objective record to impute to his life's work a purpose-oriented coherence that had never emerged into consciousness.

I recognize of course that my own research-publication record may be interpreted as the output of a methodological and normative individualist whose underlying purpose has always been to further philosophical support for individual liberty. In subjective recall, however, this motivational thrust has never informed my conscious work effort. I have throughout my career and with only a few exceptions sought to clarify ambiguities and confusions and clear up neglected pockets of analysis in the received arguments of fellow economists, social scientists, and philosophers. To the extent that conscious motivation has entered these efforts, it has always been the sheer enjoyment of working out ideas, of creating the reality that is reflected finally in the finished manuscript. Proof of my normative disinterest lies in my failure to be interested in what happens once a manuscript is a finished draft—a failure that accounts for my sometimes inattention to choice of publisher, to promotional details, and to the potential for either earnings or influence.

I look on myself as being much closer in spirit to the artist who creates on canvas or stone than to the scientist who discovers only that which he accepts to exist independently of his actions. And I should reject, and categorically, any affinity with the preacher who writes or speaks for the express and only purpose of persuading others to accept his prechosen set of values.

In all of this, once again, Frank Knight has served as my role model. His famous criticism of Pigou's road case is exemplary.[9] By introducing property rights, Knight enabled others to see the whole Pigovian analysis in a new light. Something was indeed created in the process. I like to think that perhaps some of my own works on public debt, opportunity cost, earmarked taxes, clubs, ordinary politics, and constitutional rules may have effected comparable shifts in perspective. The fact that these efforts have been commonly characterized by a reductionist thrust embodying an individualist methodology is explained, very simply, by my inability to look at the world through other than an individualist window.

It is as if the artist who has only red paints produces pictures that are only red of hue. Such an artist does not choose to paint red pictures and then, instrumentally, purchase red paints. Instead the artist uses the instruments at hand to do what he can and must do, while enjoying himself immensely in the process. The fact that others are able to secure new insights with the aid of his creations and that this in turn provides artist with a bit of bread—this gratuitous result enables the artist, too, to entitle his autobiographical essay "Better Than Plowing."

Awarded Nobel Prize in 1986. Lecture presented October 28, 1987.

Date of Birth

October 3, 1919

Academic Degrees

B.A.   Middle Tennessee State College, 1940

M.S.   University of Tennessee, 1941

Ph.D. University of Chicago, 1948

Academic Affiliations

Associate Professor, University of Tennessee, 1948–1950

Professor, University of Tennessee, 1950–1951

Professor, Department of Economics, Florida State University, 1954–1956

Professor, James Wilson Department of Economics, University of Virginia, 1956–1962

Paul G. McIntire Professor of Economics, University of Virginia, 1962–1968

Professor of Economics, University of California, Los Angeles, 1968–1969

University Distinguished Professor, Virginia Polytechnic Institute and State University, 1969–1983

Holbert L. Harris University Professor, George Mason University, 1983–present

Selected Books

Fiscal Theory and Political Economy, 1960

The Calculus of Consent, 1962 (with G. Tullock)

The Limits of Liberty, 1975

The Power to Tax, 1980 (with G. Brennan)

The Reason of Rules, 1985 (with G. Brennan)

Liberty, Market, and State, 1985

Economics: Between Predictive Science and Moral Philosophy, 1987

Explorations into Constitutional Economics, 1989

The Collected Works of James M. Buchanan, Vols. 1–20, 1999–2002

Robert M. Solow

To be honest, I should warn you that I am going to tell you as little about myself as I can get away with in a lecture about "My Evolution as an Economist." My reason is not that I have anything to hide. I wish I had more to hide; that would at least suggest an exciting life. My problem is that I think the "cult of personality" is slowly swamping our culture. You can see it at its most dangerous in presidential elections, where eyebrows seem to be more important than ideas. I tend to blame that on television, which is a better medium for eyebrows than for economic theory. But that sort of technological determinism won't quite do: it leaves us with the task of explaining the psychologization of almost everything, the success of pop books on character, the fact that seven out of ten nonfiction best sellers are biographies, the importance attached to the "personal relationship" between Mr. Reagan and Mrs. Thatcher. Something pretty deep is going on there. (I don't mean between Mr. Reagan and Mrs. Thatcher!) Fortunately, academic economists seem to have a big comparative disadvantage when it comes to personal interest. I wouldn't have anything to say to Barbara Walters even if she had anything to say to me.

Anyway, what I have called the cult of personality has to be a sign of cultural decay. ("Just lie back and tell us when you first had that feeling, Professor Solow.") I don't mean to twist and turn in order to avoid biographical details, but I would rather concentrate on social and intellectual currents of slightly broader significance.

Shortly after the death of John von Neumann some thirty-odd years ago Robert Strotz, who was then editor of *Econometrica,* asked me to write a memorial article about him. Von Neumann and Frank Ramsey must be the two noneconomists who have, in their spare moments, had the greatest influence on what professional economists actually do. (On the merits, Harold Hotelling certainly belongs in their class; but he is much closer to having been, or having become, a part-time professional economist.) I never wrote the article, but I did think about it for a while. A puzzle presented itself: How did von Neumann become interested in economics anyway? I asked a number of people who might have known, but none could give me a useful answer. Then I sent a note to Karl Menger (the grandson of the Menger who was a cofounder of the Austrian school of economics) because he had run a mathematical seminar in Vienna that was attended occasionally by von Neumann, Abraham Wald, and some economists. Menger gave me a wonderful answer to my question. He said that everyone in Austria-Hungary was interested in economics.

Well, I grew up in the 1930s—graduated from high school in January 1940, in fact. I can certainly say that everyone in Brooklyn in the 1930s was interested in economics. And not only in economics: intelligent high school students of my day were conscious not only of the Great Depression but also of the rise of Fascism and Nazism, events that were certainly not independent of the worldwide depression. It was an obvious fact of life to us that our society was malfunctioning politically and economically and that nobody really knew how to explain it or what to do about it.

This is important for the subject at hand. I think it throws some light on the current state and recent evolution of economics. I said that I graduated from high school in 1940. I was a couple of years younger than my classmates; but anyone who was eighteen in 1940 is sixty-six now. Soon there will be no more active economists who remember the 1930s clearly. The generation of economists that was moved to study economics by the feeling that we desperately needed to understand the depression will soon have retired. Most of today's younger and middle-aged macroeconomists think of "the business cycle" as a low-variance, moderately auto-correlated, stationary, stochastic process taking place around a generally satisfactory trend. That is an altogether different frame of mind from the one with which I grew up in the profession.

Now maybe they have the right idea. I don't want to sound like an old codger who goes around all the time bundled up in fear that the Blizzard of '88 may happen again tomorrow. The underlying intellectual problem is more complicated than that. I don't think for a minute that a major depression is a probabilistically frequent event. But I am not sure that it is useful to model it as a probabilistically rare event either. I rather doubt that the probabilistic way of thinking about major depressions sends the right signals—or receives them—in the first place. I think that a lot of my contemporaries regard the possibility of deep recession mainly as an indicator that there are mechanisms latent in an industrial capitalist economy that can cause it to stall for an uncomfortably long time away from any satisfactory equilibrium. The trigger may be a mixture of endogenous and exogenous events. One of the jobs of macroeconomics, perhaps its main job, is to understand what those mechanisms are and what defensive policies they call for. That is surely not the only way of sizing up or thinking about macroeconomics. But it strikes me as a mistake for contemporary macroeconomics to assume away any such possibility.

I arrived at Harvard College in September 1940. Economics A was one of my four freshman courses. I had no idea then of becoming an economist; I probably didn't know there was such a thing as a professional economist, or what one did. My recollection is that I had some notion of studying biology; I certainly took a two-semester course in biology that first year and got an A, but it was pretty clear that biology was not for me. So I opted for a sort of general social science major, and for the next year or two I took courses in sociology, anthropology, and psychology as well as economics.

Undergraduate students of economics at Harvard College in 1940–1942 did not learn any coherent way of thinking about the Depression from which the United States was just emerging. The fact that real GNP rose by 8 percent between 1939 and 1940 and another 18 percent between 1940 and 1941 and that the unemployment rate fell by 7.3 percentage points between 1939 and 1941 under the stimulus of war production, both for export and for use at home, might have offered some hint. (We didn't know what the real GNP was, you realize; the data came later. But industrial production, which was measured, rose by 15 and 18 percent in 1940 and 1941, respectively.) Our textbooks and courses offered us no sense of a systematic understanding of the dramatic events taking place all around us. The memoirs of political figures of the time make it clear that they had no clue either.

It wasn't all dull, of course. I heard Sumner Slichter and John Dunlop lecture about labor economics, and Paul Sweezy about Marxian economics, and I learned things from all of them that I still remember.

Two of the three books that really formed my generation of economists after the war had already been published: *The General Theory of Employment, Interest and Money* in 1936 and Hicks's *Value and Capital* in 1939. (The third, Samuelson's *Foundations of Economic Analysis,* appeared in 1947.) The galaxy of star graduate students of the time—Samuelson, Metzler, Musgrave, Tobin, Alexander, et al.—were no doubt clued in to these ideas that would come to dominate economics for a while. None of it percolated to undergraduates so soon. The ideas were too new and Harvard economics was too sclerotic at the time. The point is that I had no feeling that economic analysis could penetrate to the heart of what was going on in the world. I certainly hadn't made up my mind to major in economics or to become an economist. What I did instead was to volunteer for the army. It seemed more constructive than what I was doing.

Three years later I came back and, almost without thinking about it, signed up to finish my undergraduate degree as an economics major. The timing was such that I had to make a decision in a hurry. No doubt I acted as if I were maximizing an infinite discounted sum of one-period utilities, but you couldn't prove it by me. To me it felt as if I were saying to myself: "What the hell."

At that time, September 1945, Harvard still had an effective "tutorial system." Every junior and senior—I was still a junior—was assigned a member of the faculty as a "tutor" to be seen for an hour once a week. The tutor would assign things to read, occasionally ask the tutee to write a short paper, and then the two would discuss the week's work. My tutor was Wassily Leontief. Maybe it was just dumb luck. Maybe the powers that be took note of the fact that I had been an A student. Maybe it was just the opposite; maybe being tutored by a foreigner—and a theorist at that—was like being stuck in a ghetto. In any case it was a turning point for me. From Leontief I learned that economics was not a hodgepodge but a subject with a disciplined theoretical and empirical structure. Over the next few years he taught me the details of some of that structure. I would have to say that it was Leontief who turned me into an economist.

He did one other thing for me that will now seem quaint, but it is worth mentioning for just that reason. In those days you could do an undergraduate degree in economics at Harvard, and probably a Ph.D. as well, without knowing or using a bit of calculus. (Everyone had to read the text of *Value and Capital* [or at least part I] but not the mathematical appendix, elementary as that is by today's standards.) I had been a good math student in high school; it might have been my best subject. But it never occurred to me to do any more at the college level, certainly not in connection with economics. It was probably forbidden for Professor Leontief to recruit students to the study of mathematics and mathematical economic theory, nor did he do so. What he did do was to begin some of our weekly sessions by saying: "You should read thus and such an article . . . but no, you can't. You don't know any mathematics. Well, try this one instead." I may be slow-witted, but I'm not *stupid*. I wanted to read the good stuff. So pretty soon I signed up for the calculus sequence and went on in mathematics until I had learned a little more than I needed to know for everyday work. That is probably less than any good graduate student with an interest in theory knows today. It is amazing that it was such a big deal in those days. People got hot under the collar about it.

What I did not learn from Professor Leontief—and in fact did not learn at all during the years 1945 to 1949 while finishing my undergraduate degree and taking courses and examinations for the Ph.D.—was macroeconomics. That is an anachronistic turn of phrase anyway. There were no courses in macroeconomics in the catalog. There were courses on "business cycles;" mine was taught by Gottfried Haberler, and a very good course it was. *Prosperity and Depression* sticks to the ribs. I recommend it to anyone. When I began to teach at MIT in 1950, one of the first economics courses I taught was called "Business Cycles." It first acquired the label "Macroeconomics" a decade later, I would guess.

By macroeconomics I mean the study of complete aggregative models of the economy. Back then it was almost a code word for Keynesian economics, what he called "the theory of output as a whole." Trivial historical accident was at work in shaping my education. My contemporaries, some of them, learned about macroeconomics from Alvin Hansen. The locus was the graduate course in money and banking that he taught jointly with John H. Williams. As luck would have it, I enrolled in "Money and Banking" right after the war, probably in 1945 or 1946. Hansen was on leave; the entire two-semester course was taught by Williams. Moreover, because of the flood of returning veterans the graduate and undergraduate versions of "Money and Banking" were combined. (We used to say that the only difference was that the undergraduates were graded to a higher standard.) So I was never called upon to take the specifically graduate-level course.

John Williams was a famous skeptic about Keynes, about macroeconomics, in fact about everything. Skepticism is a very good thing in an economist, and perhaps his lesson stuck with me. In the particular case of macroeconomic theory, however, I never really learned what it was I was supposed to be skeptical *of*. Caught up as I was in learning economic theory in the Leontief manner, I never had as much contact with Alvin Hansen as I should have. I was never formally enrolled in the famous fiscal policy seminar, though I occasionally attended a session and my wife was a regular member.

There is a temptation to exaggerate this picture. I learned something about macroeconomics from slightly older and more advanced colleagues like John Duesenberry and Thomas Schelling. From Richard Goodwin, then an assistant professor, I learned not only the technique of building dynamic macroeconomic models but a whole attitude toward them that still strikes me as right. It emphasizes keeping them simple and focused, answering a simple question with a strong model. The art is in concentrating the subtlety in the right place.

And of course I could read. But graduate students then—and now?—had time to read only what they were expected to read. It is probably fair to say that I finished my coursework at Harvard in 1949 and passed my exam, still not having acquired what I thought economics was supposed to provide: a working understanding, not exactly of the business cycle but of the moving level of economic activity, its equilibrium or self-perpetuating properties, and its disequilibrium properties. It is hard to describe because the vocabulary that later came to seem suitable—that of Keynesian economics, not necessarily the "economics of Keynes"—is now unfashionable, and the vocabulary that is now fashionable seems designed to suppress the very curiosity that I am trying to describe.

I have gone on about this nevertheless because I think that the difference between the attitude I am reporting and the attitude that gives rise to today's "equilibrium business cycle theory" has to do with a sense of the precariousness of aggregate economic performance. It may be the experience of the 1930s and the dissolution of the 1930s in the Second World War that lies at the bottom of this difference in approach. But the difference is not simply to be dismissed as an anachronistic fear that 1932 might come around again. That is hardly the point. The point, to repeat my earlier remark, is rather the feeling that such extreme events suggest the existence of mechanisms that macroeconomic theory ought to be able to talk about.

Anyway, I had plenty to do. I spent all of 1949–50 and part of 1950–51, when I started teaching at MIT, producing a Ph.D. thesis that tried to model the dynamics of the size distribution of incomes, mostly wage and salary incomes, as the outcome of a random process into and out of employment with accompanying transitions from one wage level to another. It was entirely my own idea. There is a story behind that choice too.

The Harvard of my time taught statistics scandalously badly. I would hardly have known what I was missing if Sidney Alexander, filling in for a couple of weeks as lecturer in the graduate course in economic statistics, had not lifted the curtain and let the class peek at the real thing. Also, Frederick Mosteller arrived at Harvard in the Department of Social Relations and taught a one-semester introductory course in mathematical statistics and then took me in for a reading course. My recollection is that he taught me not so much technique as understanding. On his advice I grabbed the chance offered by a dissertation fellowship from the Social Science Research Council to work on my thesis while taking courses in mathematical statistics at Columbia University. So I learned the details of statistical theory from Abraham Wald (in his last year of teaching before his death in an airplane crash in India), Jacob Wolfowitz, and T. W. Anderson.

When I began teaching at MIT in September 1950 it was as an assistant professor of statistics in the Department of Economics and Social Science. In the glow of what I had learned from Mosteller and the Columbia department, I think I tended to spend my life working on probability models in economics. I already had a head start on my Ph.D. thesis. (It won the David A. Wells Prize at Harvard, good for five hundred 1951 dollars and publication in book form as soon as I submitted the manuscript. I never did so. The Harvard endowment is today several thousand dollars richer because I thought that the job could be better done but never found time to do it.) Anyone who gets his kicks out of making comprehensible models that are applicable to real life can hardly help noticing that the theory of probability rates pretty high on the scales of intrinsic interest and practical success. But that was not the way it worked out.

Along with statistics and econometrics courses, I taught, as I mentioned earlier, the graduate course on business cycles. Then of course I had to figure out for myself what it was that I wanted students to know. We often say among ourselves that the best way to learn a subject is to teach it. There is some truth in that, but one wants to be clear about what the kernel of truth is. You don't have to teach a subject to master its mechanical and technical details. Books will do quite nicely for that. The experience of teaching does, if you take it seriously, require you to figure out how to explain the subject at hand clearly; and that is already a higher level of understanding than the first. But there is a higher level yet. The second or third time you teach a course you may realize that you have a feeling for the topic's shape, its organizing principles, its message, its relation to the rest of economics and to real economic life. So it was; I began by teaching about business cycle theories—Pigou, Robertson, Haberler, Kalecki, Metzler, Hansen, Samuelson, Hicks, that sort of thing—and I ended up teaching macroeconomics (and growth).

It would be satisfying to say that I educated myself. But that would be at most half true. My new colleagues at MIT—Paul Samuelson, of course, but also Robert Bishop and Cary Brown—had been part of the transitional generation. They had been among the first to feel the shock waves when J. M. Keynes invented macroeconomics. (Make no mistake: that is what he did. I have elsewhere quoted A. C. Pigou, who must have known, on this subject. "Nobody before [Keynes], so far as I know, had brought all the relevant factors, real and monetary at once, together in a single formal scheme, through which their interplay could be coherently investigated." That is exactly what I am talking about.)

Macroeconomics in that spirit is what I had been missing. I found it in the conversation of my colleagues in the MIT de- partment and pretty quickly and easily made it part of my own mental furniture. Strangely enough, for an American, I was at that time more familiar with the writings of the Swedish economists than with Keynes or the immediate English Keynesians. Somewhere in graduate school I had read Lindahl, Myrdal, Ohlin, Lundberg, and most especially Wicksell. Those books are still on my shelves. It was probably Haberler who introduced me to the modern Stockholm school (and the GI Bill that paid for the books). Wicksell I found for myself, and he has always been a favorite for several reasons. The one that matters here is that he, among the great nineteenth-century economists, came closest to the spirit of macroeconomics. In *Interest and Prices* and again in the note on "Åkerman's problem" one gets the feeling that he is verging on Pigou's definition. If only Wicksell had been able to put the two together!

Elsewhere I have described how I came to work on the theory of economic growth in the 1950s, and I do not want to repeat that story now. What I did not sufficiently emphasize in my Nobel lecture—it became clear to me only in the course of thinking through what I have just been saying—is the extent to which involvement in growth theory can be seen as (and really was) an integral part of my education in macroeconomics. Harrod-Domar theory was addressed to serious issues about the path of a capitalist economy. I was led to modify the model just to make it yield a path that could more plausibly claim to look like what one actually saw in historical time series. But this is just part of the general macroeconomic problem of representing a complete, closed, aggregative model. That my version of growth theory had capital-theoretic overtones was probably a residue from Wicksell.

The next evolutionary step was probably my stint at the Council of Economic Advisers during the Kennedy administration. Day-to-day economic policy had never been my specialty. I had been shocked to hear Paul Samuelson say at lunch one day that he thought the fundamental function of economic theory was to permit the writing of good financial journalism. I had to mature a little before I realized how close to true that was. But I was an onlooker during the campaign of 1960; no one asked me to serve on one of Kennedy's task forces or transition teams. So I was taken by surprise to get a late-night call from the three members of the council—Walter Heller, James Tobin, and Kermit Gordon—asking me to take leave and join the staff. The bait held out to me, the boy growth-theorist, was that I could be the council's ivory-tower economist and spend my time thinking about longer-term policy rather than the daily hurly-burly.

I believed it and I am sure they believed it. But it took me about two days in the old Executive Office Building to realize that all the action, and I mean intellectual action, was in meeting each day's excitement as it arose. It arose right away. The outgoing council had of course prepared the January 1961 *Economic Report*. The new council had to prepare a "mini-report" as the basis for its testimony before the Joint Economic Committee on March 6. Everyone pitched in of course, but the main authors of that statement were the three council members, Arthur Okun, and I (and Joseph Pechman, who was not on the staff but, as a longtime friend of Heller's, served as our old Washington hand). It was a six-week crash course in practical macroeconomics. I do not mean that phrase as a euphemism for sloppy macroeconomics. What I cherish about that experience was the conscious effort to use macroeconomic theory to interpret the world and, in a small way, to change it.

Tobin and I (alas, Gordon, Okun, and Heller are all dead) have just republished the 1961 statement and the January 1962 *Economic Report*, which was clearly intended as a kind of declaration of principle. (The volume also contains the January 1982 *Report*, introduced by the members of the first Reagan council. They can speak for themselves.) To many contemporary readers the 1962 *Report* will seem like a compendium of everything that was wrong with (Keynesian) macroeconomics before the "new classical" counterrevolution, a kind of "before" picture in a before-and-after advertisement. It goes without saying that neither Tobin nor I (nor Okun, if only he were still with us) would wish to write exactly the same things if we were writing the *Report* now, knowing what we have learned in the past quarter century. In fact it is not my purpose to defend the viewpoint of the *Report* even where I think it deserves defense. It is offered as a fair example of what people like me believed in 1961.

First of all—and perhaps here I am being defensive—there is no way we can be said to have neglected the supply side of the economy. There is a whole chapter on the importance of supply factors and supply-side incentives. We were, after all, the people who gave you the investment tax credit in the Revenue Act of 1962. How could the boy growth-theorist have neglected the supply side? What we did do was to give a reasoned argument that the U.S. economy was then, and had been for some time, operating with excess supply, involuntary unemployment, and underutilized capacity. We insisted on a sharp distinction between increases in real output that could be had just by stimulation of demand—what we called "closing the gap between actual and potential output"—and further increases in real output, which would require movement on the supply side. (It is worth remarking, especially now, that way back then Tobin and I were proposing that the right fiscal policy target was a federal budget surplus at full employment, maintained by monetary ease. Our goal was a higher rate of domestic investment and national saving, and we doubted that enough private saving was achievable. So much for the notion that "Keynesians" had some allergic fear of saving.)

A certain sort of contemporary economist would simply dismiss the very possibility of persistent excess aggregate supply. Is it not the hallmark of the well-trained economist to *know* that "markets clear"? Is there any coherent alternative? I have to admit that the 1962 *Economic Report* offers no sustained rebuttal of that view. It was, after all, written for the general public, not for other economists. So I have to reconstruct what we would have said had anybody put the question.

There are two possible answers. One is in a way Keynes's own: An economy can be in aggregative "equilibrium" with widespread involuntary unemployment and underutilized capacity. The equilibrium cannot be Walrasian, with all markets clearing, but it can be equilibrium all the same, in the relevant sense that there is no internal pressure for the situation to change. Keynes was not so precise, nor did he ever make good his claim to have demonstrated the theoretical soundness of this idea; but that is what he claimed. I think we would not have taken that line. The alternative answer could have gone something like this. There are dozens of nitty-gritty reasons why nominally quoted prices and wages should be imperfectly flexible. A list of them would be just a list, not a theory. It hardly needs to be added that miscellaneous nominal rigidities imply that real quantities and relative prices will often be in the wrong place and perhaps moving in the wrong direction. In consequence the economy's approach to market-clearing equilibrium after any disturbance may be intolerably slow and costly. Even if there were but One Equilibrium and It were Pareto-efficient, there would still be a large payoff to corrective policy, whether automatic or discretionary.

In the 1960s we would have taken that second line. It is the one that true believers have labeled "American Keynesianism," thus presumably classifying it with Wonder Bread and "Wheel of Fortune." Of course it had quintessential early expression in the famous articles by John Hicks and Franco Modigliani, not exactly backwoods Americans, but never mind that. The 1962 *Report* did not make such arguments, for the reason I have already stated, but I am sure that it is what was in Tobin's mind, and Okun's, and mine. The usual shorthand presumption was that the nominal wage is the sticky price; and that is enough to get the standard American-Keynesian results. But that was just a formality, an up-front way of establishing the model's credentials. If pressed, we would cheerfully have produced a variety of rigidities and imperfections and noted that they only strengthened the case.

A few years later I wrote a paper with Joseph Stiglitz, then just out of graduate school, that formalized the view of the world I have just been ascribing to "the old folks." We took it for granted that nominal wages and prices both adjusted slowly to excess demand or supply. Thus neither market had to clear in the short run, and the "short-side principle" applied in both. We were able to show how such an economy might have quite perverse dynamics and might even get itself trapped in situations a little like unemployment equilibrium, though not quite. Our model was quite clearly a precursor of the Benassy–Drèze–Malinvaud "fixed-price temporary equilibrium" models that came to light five or ten years later (and have received less attention in the United States than they deserve). Our paper fell with a dull thud. This fate may have come about because we did not even discuss the "spillovers" from quantity-rationed markets to others that form much of the stuff of the French fixed-price models and give them their claim to be modeling "effective demand." We were not much interested in such microeconomic underpinnings; we were trying to show how a model economy could sometimes be demand-limited and sometimes supply-limited. Our intended goal was a contribution to the "neoclassical synthesis" or, more picturesquely, "Bastard Keynesianism."

The funny thing is that I now think that Keynes had the right instinct. It is a better move to look for alternative, non-Walrasian equilibrium concepts as a foundation for macroeconomic analysis of modern industrial capitalism. It is better partly because of the hold that equilibrium analysis has on economists; and more significantly it is better because it corresponds at least as well to our intuitions and observations of economic life. Keynes could not make good on his claim to have produced a consistent notion of "unemployment equilibrium" because he lacked the analytical tools to do the job. Those came into economics only much later.

Nowadays there is a body of macroeconomic theory that goes under the name "New Keynesian Economics" and pursues the task of showing how information symmetries, transactions costs, and similar facts of life can lead to the possibility of equilibria—self-sustaining situations—with "wrong" levels of employment and output. Usually, then, it can be shown that simple fiscal and monetary policies can improve the situation. (It is true, but hardly news, that inappropriate policies can make things worse. That is why baseball teams fire their managers.)

To my eye the New Keynesian Economics is a mixed bag. Its aims are right and its techniques are nice. But sometimes the particular facts of life it chooses to emphasize seem too farfetched or insignificant to bear the weight that is placed on them. It comes, maybe, from a kind of yearning for respectability and the well-founded belief that respectability comes from staying close to the traditional simplifying assumptions of economics. That is not wholly bad. It is certainly better than wholesale "new paradigm"-mongering. But there are times when common sense leads away from the tradition, and then I would choose common sense every time. If I am right that the main question in macroeconomics is why, after the inevitable real shocks, the economy can stay so far from full employment for so long, then transactions costs and information asymmetries seem too tangential to be the main answer.

In those days the Phillips curve was the particular way we coped with the idea of imperfectly flexible wages. Paul Samuelson and I wrote a paper in 1960 that may have coined the phrase "Phillips curve" and certainly helped to domesticate it in the United States. That is one of the things I would do differently now, but I want to say explicitly how.

About six months ago at a conference in Helsinki, Michael Parkin described that paper as "unfortunate." He didn't mean that it was unlucky in love; he meant that it had misled many people into the untrue belief that there was a stable trade-off between inflation and unemployment, along which policy could move and place the economy. I reacted defensively and pointed out that a careful reading of the paper would disclose that we had stated just about every qualification that one would now wish to attach to the Phillips curve idea. In particular we had remarked explicitly that any attempt to exploit the inflation-unemployment trade-off in policy terms, by buying low unemployment at the expense of permanently higher inflation, could easily have the effect of causing the Phillips curve to shift adversely, canceling the hoped-for gain. We even mentioned changing expectations as the route by which that could happen. It's true—we did.

After the conference Assar Lindbeck observed to me that I had dodged the issue. Yes, the formal qualifications were there; but the tone of the paper was certainly optimistic about the possibility of choosing, by standard policy means, a point on the Phillips curve. I had to admit the justice of that observation. The eclectic American Keynesians of the 1960s were not sufficiently alert to the force of inflationary expectations. They expected more from the Phillips curve than it could deliver in practice.

That raises the question: What do I believe now? What I do not believe is the notion of a reasonably stable "natural rate of unemployment." That idea asserts the existence of a knowable, at worst slowly changing, unemployment rate (or rate of utilization more broadly defined) with the crucial property that maintaining a lower unemployment rate entails ever-accelerating inflation and maintaining a higher unemployment rate entails eventually ever-accelerating deflation. There was a time when I think I was the only respectable(?) economist who rejected this so-called long-run vertical Phillips curve, but I am glad to see that I am now acquiring some allies. From the very beginning I found both the theoretical and empirical foundations of the natural rate hypothesis to be flimsy.

On the theoretical side, Milton Friedman had defined the "natural rate" as the unemployment rate "ground out by the Walrasian equations of general equilibrium." But surely not very many of those who accepted the natural rate hypothesis realized that it made sense only if they took Walrasian general equilibrium to be a valid description of the real everyday economy. Other theoretical foundations were just as farfetched. On the empirical side, econometric estimates of the natural rate were usually based on weak empirical relationships, any of which was susceptible to several interpretations. It is no great caricature to say that believers would assert, say, that the unemployment rate in Great Britain, some 9 to 10 percent, was below the natural rate. How do you know? Because inflation is accelerating. Why is inflation accelerating? Because unemployment is below the natural rate.

My preferred hypothesis is that there is no such thing as the natural rate, not in the sense of a well-defined number with the accelerationist property. Of course at any given time you can imagine puffing up aggregate demand so much that inflation accelerates. (Maybe, just maybe, you can imagine a level of demand so low that wages and prices fell faster and faster. I'd rather see than be one.) But what that critical level is depends on history, institutions, attitudes, and beliefs, including beliefs about the natural rate. If there are many equilibria for the economy, there are probably many possible "natural" rates.

You may have noticed that I have been very selective, even fragmentary, in telling you about my evolution as an economist. For instance, I have skipped completely over the famous Two-Cambridge controversy. That is because I regard that episode as a living counterexample to the proposition that where there is smoke there is fire. It was all smoke and no fire. If I were to tell you about it, I would soon drift into psychologizing, and that is the disease of which it purports to be the cure. You may also have noticed that I seem to have no intention of carrying the story much past the 1960s, except for the odd implicit comment about the course of recent economic research. That too is deliberate. It is hard to be cool about current ideas and controversies, and it is unfair to be hot about them.

That leaves me with the problem of getting off the stage in a dignified way, like the terrified pianist in *Beyond the Fringe,* who cannot seem to play the sort of notes that signify "The End." So I will just finish by telling you one or two things that I have learned about myself and about contemporary economics, more particularly things that I have learned or realized in the process of thinking about what to say in this lecture.

First of all, I have the feeling it is a mistake to think of economics as a Science, with a capital *S*. I also find it temperamentally uncongenial, and that may even be the source of my feeling. Theoretical physicists nowadays think they are on the verge of what they call, only partially self-mockingly, "The Theory of Everything." There is no Economic Theory of Everything, and attempts to construct one seem to merge toward a Theory of Nothing. If you think I am making a sly comment about some tendencies in contemporary macroeconomics, you are right.

That is perfectly consistent with a strong belief that economics should try very hard to be scientific with a small *s*. By that I mean only that we should think logically and respect fact. I will have more to say about "fact" in a minute.

I once heard Paul Streeten say that the world is divided into two kinds of people: those who think the world is divided into two kinds of people and those who do not. Economic theorists (and even some applied economists) seem to be divided into two classes of people, System Builders and Puzzle Solvers. What I have just been saying expresses a prejudice in favor of Puzzle Solvers. Puzzles are things that need explaining. They can arise from the pursuit of theory: paradoxes to be resolved, examples to be discovered (e.g., the optimal excise tax), questions in the form, "Is it possible that X?" Puzzles can just as well arise from observation: the corn-hog cycle, the "constancy" of distributive shares, the regularities that led to Okun's law. The closest I ever came to system building in the theory of economic growth was actually an attempt to solve a puzzle: How to reconcile the intrinsic instability in Harrod–Domar theory with the failure of economic history to look that way? We can certainly afford some true system builders, and they are certainly highly decorative; my hunch is that the system is too complex and too embedded in the noneconomic ever to be built by our methods.

Now I want to say something about fact. The austere view is that "facts" are just time series of prices and quantities. The rest is hypothesis testing. I have seen a lot of those tests. They are almost never convincing, primarily because one senses that they have very low power against lots of alternatives. There are too many ways to explain a bunch of time series.

And sure enough, the next issue of the journal will contain an article exhibiting quite different functional forms, slightly different models. My hunch is that we can make progress only by enlarging the class of eligible facts to include, say, the opinions and casual generalizations of experts and market participants, attitudinal surveys, institutional regularities, even our own judgments of plausibility. My preferred image is the vacuum cleaner, not the microscope.

I am not, repeat not, saying that common sense or the opinion of the "practical man" is always right. The theories held by practical men are very often wrong or empty. What I am saying is that the economist cannot dispense with keeping his or her eyes open, looking around, and forming judgments about what makes sense and what is simply farfetched. Those cannot be uncritical judgments, but judgments to be defended by appeal to observation and to logic.

Enough of the Dismal Science. A friend of mine once presented me with a Columbia University Economics Department T-shirt. It shows a helicopter-drop of money—a favorite abstraction of monetary theorists—falling on an island—the favorite abstraction of economists—and the slogan is "Not half as dismal as you think." With that thought, I leave you.

Awarded Nobel Prize in 1987. Lecture presented October 13, 1988.

Date of Birth

August 23, 1924

Academic Degrees

B.A   Harvard College, 1947

M.A. Harvard University, 1949

Ph.D. Harvard University, 1951

Academic Affiliations

Assistant Professor of Statistics, Massachusetts Institute of Technology, 1950–1954

Associate Professor of Statistics, Massachusetts Institute of Technology, 1954–1958

Professor of Economics, Massachusetts Institute of Technology, 1958–1973

Institute Professor, Massachusetts Institute of Technology, 1973–1995

Institute Professor, Emeritus, Massachusetts Institute of Technology, 1995–present

Selected Books

Linear Programming and Economic Analysis, 1958, 1987 (with R. Dorfman and P. A. Samuelson)

Capital Theory and the Rate of Return, 1963

Growth Theory: An Exposition, 1970, 2000

A Critical Essay on Modern Macroeconomic Theory, 1995 (with F. Hahn)

Monopolistic Competition and Macroeconomic Theory, 1998

William F. Sharpe

Introduction

What an honor. What an opportunity. What a challenge. What a temptation.

To speak about oneself before a captive audience is a rare opportunity indeed. The possibilities for self-aggrandizement boggle the mind. Why not abandon all pretense of false modesty? At the very least, seize the chance to propagandize for causes held dear—academic, political, personal.

Had I not read the contributions of my predecessors I might have succumbed to these temptations. However, not one of the others did. And I shall try very hard to resist any siren songs to the contrary.

The Invitation

When invited to give this lecture, I happily accepted. Surely speaking about one's evolution as an economist would be both easy and pleasant. But afterwards I read the written versions of the previous lectures. Not surprisingly, I found that my colleagues had been eloquent, erudite, sagacious, humorous, and both deep and broad in their coverage. How to follow in such footsteps? I considered feigning illness. The possibility of employing a ghost writer crossed my mind. But ultimately, I did neither. Here, for better or worse, are my comments on the subject at hand.

The Prize

First, the prize and the citation.

The Royal Swedish Academy awarded the 1990 Prize in Economic Sciences in Memory of Alfred Nobel to Harry Markowitz, Merton Miller, and myself "for their pioneering work in the theory of financial economics." I wish to emphasize the latter, for with this award, the field of *Financial Economics* completed *its* evolution to achieve the status of a field in both *Economics* and *Finance*.

A field of inquiry is much more important than anyone who practices it. Hence I will precede the personal chronology with some remarks on my field.

Financial Economics

One defines a subject at one's peril. This is especially true if the subject is one's own. But let me try.

In his speech at the prize ceremony Professor Assar Lindbeck of the Royal Swedish Academy of Sciences focused on financial markets, and the use thereof, by firms. Certainly the characteristics of financial instruments and their proper uses are central. From a more theoretical viewpoint, one can focus on the nexus between the *present* and the *future*. A financial instrument typically represents a property right to receive future cash flows. Such cash flows will, of course, come in the future—hence the *economics of time* must be understood. In many cases the flows are uncertain, hence the need for an approach to the *economics of uncertainty*. In addition, cash flows in the far future may depend on actions taken (or not taken) in the near future. This gives rise to the need for a theory of the *economics of options* (broadly construed). Finally, one needs information to estimate likely future outcomes, hence the requirement for an understanding of the *economics of information*.

I define financial economics so that it embraces all four of these important, difficult, and fascinating aspects of economics. While some may dispute the attempted appropriation of so much territory in the name of a group of *nouveax-arrivistes,* I believe that I am not alone in regarding this as appropriate.

Financial economics can be found in both economics departments and in finance departments of business schools. It also pervades practice. In economics departments, *positive* aspects tend to be emphasized; in the finance departments and in practice, *normative* applications. Positive theory attempts to describe the world; normative to offer prescriptions for action. The dichotomy is, however, far from complete. Positive theories assume various types of stylized normative behavior, and normative theories require a *gestalt,* which is usually based on positive theory.

The central question for positive financial economics is *valuation*—what is the value today of a set of future prospective cash flows? The central question for normative financial economics is the appropriate *use* of financial instruments in a world in which values are set wholly or partially in accord with the principles of positive financial economics.

Finance

Business school finance departments often break their offerings into three categories. The study of *investments* deals primarily with the *purchase* of financial instruments by individuals, pension funds, and the like. *Corporate finance,* to a major extent, deals with the *issue* of financial instruments by corporations. The third category, *financial institutions,* concerns organizations for which both the purchase and issuance of financial instruments are key.

To oversimplify, one can think of three different prototypical balance sheets. For investments, visualize financial instruments on the left and the net worth (or utility) of an individual or organization on the right. For corporate finance, visualize bricks and mortar, turret lathes, and the like on the left and financial instruments on the right. For financial institutions, visualize financial instruments on both sides.

Some business schools now begin their finance curriculum with a core course in financial economics, followed by required and/or elective courses in these three major areas of application. I had a small hand in bringing the Stanford curriculum to a rough approximation of this model. However, such a structure is still relatively unusual. In most business schools, financial economics is simply part of the first course in each of the applied areas. But it is inevitably an important part.

It was not always thus. Let me engage in some self-plagiarism by quoting from the 1978 edition of my textbook, *Investments:*

In recent years the field of finance has truly undergone a revolution. Not too many years ago, investment textbooks were primarily devoted to . . . the mysteries of accounting, some of the details of the operations of major industries, and various rules of thumb for selecting "good" or "bad" securities. Institutional details . . . were presented, along with historical data, but the reader was provided with no framework for understanding such phenomena. A theory of the formation of prices in capital markets was lacking.[1]

Needless to say, I went on to suggest that such a theory was at hand and that the student who used my book could use it to illuminate the dark corners of finance. I was even bold enough to say that ". . . empirical analysis has shown that it [the theory] describes the behavior of major capital markets quite well." This view now appears to have been somewhat too optimistic. Again I quote, this time from the 1985 edition of the book:

Recent empirical work has cast some doubt on this comforting view of the world. Early statistical tests have been found to be relatively weak, suggesting that they may have been unable to identify important disparities between theory and reality. Moreover, systematic "anomalies" have been found, calling into question at least some aspects of the standard theories.[2]

This being said, however, theories of financial economics have not been discredited. Rather, they have become more comprehensive. In so doing they may have lost some of their simplicity and intuitiveness. But today only the foolhardy would venture into the world of finance without a solid understanding of financial economics. It is indeed here to stay.

Economics

Financial economics has had less impact on economics departments than on finance departments. Nonetheless, the synergy between the fields is great. And economists have had a profound influence on the development of financial economics. Again I beg indulgence for a quotation from my own writings. This from the Preface to a 1982 book entitled, *Financial Economics, Essays in Honor of Paul Cootner.*

In 1950 the intersection of the fields of finance and economics was small indeed. Academic work in finance relied more often on rules of thumb and anecdotal evidence than on theory and adequate empirical studies.

Economists showed only fleeting interest in financial institutions, speculation, and the host of other aspects of uncertainty that comprise much of the domain of the field of finance.

Three decades later the situation is radically different. There is now a rich body of theory relevant to problems in finance; and extensive empirical tests have been conducted to see how well the theoretical constructs accord with reality. . . .

Many of those who helped bring about the changes in finance were trained as economists. They approached finance problems with the attitudes and the standard tools of the economist. When they found the paradigms of traditional economics inadequate for the subject at hand, they invented new approaches. But, throughout, their style was that of the economist. As a result, we now have a domain increasingly referred to as *financial economics*.[3]

Paul Cootner, a close friend and colleague who died at far too young an age, was (as I said at the time) one of the first and one of the best financial economists. But there were, of course, many others. And almost all of those in the vanguard of the field were trained as economists, including Harry Markowitz, Merton Miller, and myself. Interestingly, five of those who contributed articles in honor of Paul Cootner are now laureates in Economics, and four (Paul Samuelson, Bob Solow, George Stigler, and myself) were participants in this lecture series.

In pronouncing the name of this field one should thus put equal emphasis on both the first and the second words.

Professional Practice

I suspect that no other field taught in business schools has had such an impact on its associated profession as has financial economics. Professional investors routinely speak of expected values; standard deviations; correlations; R-squared, beta, delta, and gamma values; convexity; binomial processes, and the like. Concepts that seemed abstract if not abstruse only a decade or two ago are now part of the everyday life of large numbers of traders throughout the world.

Financial economics has also influenced financial institutions. It spawned the index fund—a strategy designed to replicate the performance of a segment of the overall market with great precision and low cost. It provided the impetus for the huge market in derivative securities such as traded options, index futures, index options, swaps, and so on. Each of these formerly exotic instruments provides an efficient way for individuals and institutions to better control risk while pursuing specific objectives. Financial economics provides the structure for both the valuation and efficient use of such instruments.

A phrase of which I am particularly fond is this: *practical theory*. Financial economics contains an incredibly rich set of examples of such theories, and Wall Street, LaSalle Street, and Main Street have been quick to adopt them.

For a fascinating view of how this came about I strongly recommend Peter Bernstein's recently published *Capital Ideas: The Improbable Origins of Modern Wall Street*,[4] which documents the influence of a number of people, including six past Nobel Laureates, on investment practice.

Personal Evolution

I turn now to more personal reflections.

Whether one calls the development of financial economics a revolution (as I was wont to do in my youth) or evolution (in accordance with my charter here), it has been my great privilege to be both an observer of and a participant in the birth and maturation of this important field of inquiry. My own development was only a bit of a sideshow. But it may provide a better understanding of the larger canvas.

If there is a common thread in what follows it is the importance of luck. To be sure, good genes and hard work are necessary conditions for the attainment of this podium in this circumstance. But they are by no means sufficient. At many points in my decision tree, fortune decreed that I should take the branch on this path rather than another. To get here one must have the good luck to draw a great many favorable random numbers.

Undergraduate Work

My parents were both educators—my father a college president and my mother an elementary school principal. Due to disruptions caused by the Second World War, each had to return to graduate school in mid-life. More than most, I learned at an early age to appreciate the joys of learning.

After completing my secondary education in the (then) excellent public schools in California I enrolled at the University of California at Berkeley—intending to become the medical doctor that my mother wanted me to be. A lab course or two convinced me that such was not my métier. I then transferred to UCLA, determined to major in business administration. In the first semester of my sophomore year I took required courses in accounting and microeconomics. The former was, in reality, bookkeeping— and mindless bookkeeping at that. I loathed it. But microeconomics had everything: rigor, relevance, structure, and logic. I found its allure irresistible. The next semester I changed my major to economics and never turned back.

Thus my first stroke of luck. I sometimes break out in a cold sweat thinking about what might have happened had I taken a modern accounting course and an institutional economics course.

I more or less supported myself while completing my education, through a succession of jobs including night work in a gas station, a swing shift posting transactions for a large company, grading papers for seven courses at once, various summer jobs,\a\teaching assistantship, and ultimately, a position as an economist.

As an undergraduate economics major I took an additional business course—one on investments. It was very traditional, very confusing, and very frustrating. Try as I might, I could find no unifying principle, no underlying structure. I was convinced that studying investments was not for me.

But again, luck was on my side. In my senior year I was able to work as a research assistant for J. Fred Weston, a professor in the business school and a major figure in the field of corporate finance. Fred introduced me to the early work in the then-nascent field of financial economics. I wasn't hooked yet, but I was certainly intrigued.

After graduation I interviewed for jobs in banking. Here my grades proved an impediment. The interviewer would typically look over my records, congratulate me, then ask why I hadn't considered graduate school. After a few such cases I tried grabbing the form, turning it over to the section on activities, offices held, fraternities, etc. then handing it back. Despite such attempts to show that I was a reasonably well-adjusted human being, nothing interesting came my way, and so I proceeded to a master's degree in economics at UCLA.

The Master's Degree

It was during this year that I irrevocably crossed the line to become an economist. Much of the credit (or blame) for this goes to Armen Alchian, who taught the graduate microeconomics sequence at UCLA. While personally gentle and traditional, Armen was (and is) clearly an eccentric economic theorist. He started the course by asserting that 95% of the material in economics journals was wrong or irrelevant—an assertion that I sometimes regard as not unduly pessimistic. He then proceeded to discuss the economics of the illegal market for buying babies. At one point he spent five of six lectures wrestling (somewhat unsuccessfully) with the meaning of *profit*. Indeed, most of his classes had the characteristics of a wrestling match. We witnessed a brilliant mind grappling (usually very successfully) with the most difficult concepts in economics in thoroughly creative and innovative ways. There could be no better training for a fledgling theorist and no higher standard. After two semesters with Armen Alchian, I was hooked. I wanted to be a microeconomist.

After obtaining the M.A., I fulfilled part of my ROTC obligation by serving as a Second Lieutenant in the Army Quartermaster Corps. I must admit that I rather enjoyed being outdoors much of the time and being (for once in my life) in reasonable physical condition.

The Rand Corporation

By indenturing myself to seven and a half years of reserve duty with two weeks of summer camp each year, I managed to limit my active duty to six months. Then through the good offices of Armen Alchian I was able to obtain a position at the Rand Corporation as a junior economist.

The Rand of 1956 was a truly unique organization. Funded almost entirely by the Air Force, it had contracted simply to do research that it considered worthwhile for its main client, along with a goodly dose of other work that would serve the public good. Employees were free to work any hours they chose, within wide limits. Office doors were open, intellectual discussions on the most wide-ranging topics were de rigueur, and everyone was expected to spend one day per week on research of strictly personal interest.

Those were heady days. Some of the key work in systems analysis, operations research, computer science, and applied economics was being done at Rand. One of our first computers was designed by John von Neumann. George Dantzig was working on linear programming. Some of the most illustrious academics served as consultants. Everyone was on a first-name basis. If ever there was a place for one interested in practical theory, the Rand Corporation in the 1950s was it.

Now, of course, the idea of working in a classified facility for the military establishment would prove an anathema for liberals (in the American political sense of the term), such as myself and most of the others at Rand. But those were simpler times. We truly believed that by improving the efficiency of the defense establishment we could help prevent war. There seemed to be no ambiguity and no moral dilemma.

At Rand I worked on problems involving optimization and trade-offs. We built many models, engaged in both data collection and empirical analysis, then brought all the pieces together using every bit of the then-available computer capacity at hand.

Rand pioneered in many aspects of computer science, leading me to become a "computer nerd" before the term came into common use. Time has in no way diminished my enthusiasm in this regard as my wife and my colleagues will attest.

Doctoral Work

Although Rand provided an extremely hospitable environment, I felt that ultimately I wanted to teach. Since personal economics precluded returning to full-time study, I thought my best choice would be to take the three education courses that, with my M.A. degree, would procure a credential for teaching in what were then termed junior colleges. I took only one of these—a night course on audio-visual education. It was, to be charitable, vacuous. The nadir came when the instructor showed a slide of a painstakingly constructed prize-winning bulletin board featuring the calendar for October. Another student pointed out that the bulletin board showed 30 days, not 31. The instructor was surprised but not embarrassed. While I would be the last to deny the importance of form, it seemed to me in this case it had totally triumphed over substance.

Rather than take the risk of having to endure another course of this calibre, I arranged to take the courses in the Economics Ph.D. program at UCLA while still working full-time at Rand. In addition to fields in microeconomics, monetary economics, economic history, and the development of economic thought, I managed to exploit a little-known provision in the department rules that allowed me to take a field in finance under Fred Weston. It was in this connection that I learned of the pioneering work of Harry Markowitz, which in large part began the development of financial economics.

After completing my courses and examinations, I set out to write what I hoped to be the definitive dissertation on transfer prices—the internal "shadow prices" that large firms sometimes use to provide incentives for divisions to operate efficiently. My interest in the subject had been piqued by some of the problems under investigation at Rand and by key work on the subject by Jack Hirshleifer, then at the University of Chicago. As it turned out, Jack moved to UCLA when I was approximately three months into the project. At Armen Alchian's suggestion, Jack read my work to date. To put it simply, he didn't consider it promising and strongly suggested that I find another topic.

To this day, I consider Jack one of my greatest benefactors.

Bent but not broken, I talked with Fred Weston. He suggested I talk with Harry Markowitz (who had recently joined Rand) about possible ideas for a dissertation. I did, and he suggsted some. Armen Alchian was more than happy to have me work under Harry, even though Harry could not even appear as a member of my committee.

In 1952 Markowitz had shown that the investor's choice of a portfolio could be treated as a problem subject to mathematical and statistical formulation. Two key aspects of an investment strategy are its *expected return* and its *risk*. The former can be represented by the *mean* of a probability distribution of future return and the latter by the *variance* (or its square root, the *standard deviation*) of the distribution. An *efficient strategy* is one that provides the maximum expected return for given risk. Harry showed how to formulate the problem of finding all efficient strategies, given estimates of security expected returns, risks and correlations, and how to solve such problems using a quadratic programming algorithm that he had developed. His focus was strictly normative—he was concerned with the proper use of forecasts, not their properties.

My dissertation dealt with three related subjects. First, I explored the implications of a suggestion in Harry's 1958 book that one might characterize the "return-generating process" with what is today termed a *one-factor model*. In general, factor models identify one or more key influences, attempt to measure the sensitivity of each security to each of the specified factors, and assume that all other sources of risk are idiosyncratic—that is, unrelated across securities. In the dissertation I derived and experimented with computational schemes that would be efficient if only one such factor were posited. In later work I extended this to cover more realistic cases involving multiple factors.

Second, I worked with a practicing investment manager to attempt to apply the theory and the one-factor model using subjective judgments about future returns. This set of experiments was only partially successful. Curiously, the optimal portfolios kept producing large holdings of a relatively unknown company then called Haloid Xerox. Its price soon doubled several times over, perhaps justifying combining the manager's foresight with the discipline of the procedure. But I took from this experience the lesson that econometric methods are best suited to risk estimation, with judgment applied, if at all, to return estimation.

Third, and most important (as it has turned out), I asked the question that microeconomists are trained to ask. If everyone were to behave optimally (here, follow the prescriptions of Markowitz's portfolio theory), what prices will securities command once the capital market has reached *equilibrium*? To make the problem tractable I assumed that all investors made the same predictions and that returns were generated by the one-factor model. The conclusion was both startling and provocative. Security prices will adjust until there is a simple linear relationship between expected return and sensitivity to changes in the factor in question. Following the conventions of regression analysis, I used the symbol *beta* for the latter. Thus the result could be succinctly stated: securities with higher betas will have higher expected returns. Only the portion of risk due to the influence of the common factor will be rewarded in the long run. No compensation is needed nor available for the remainder (which I termed "nonsystematic risk"), since it can be reduced to a small amount by sensible diversification.

Thus was the capital asset pricing model born.

The University of Washington

Before completing my dissertation I had the opportunity to spend a day in Seattle. Uncharacteristically, the sun was shining and the waters were filled with sailboats. Since sailing was and is one of my passions, I applied for a position at the University of Washington. One was forthcoming, and I moved to Seattle.

At the time, the U.W. Business School was in the early stages of its transition from a traditional, nonrigorous, institutionally oriented program to the rigorous discipline-based academic school that it is now. This led to some frustrations but provided great opportunities. Teaching loads were heavy but those willing to try new courses were encouraged to do so. Continuing in the eclectic tradition of Rand, I taught courses in statistics, operations research, computer science and microeconomics, in addition to offerings in corporate finance and investments. It is certainly true that the best way to learn something is to attempt to teach it to others. At Washington I (at least) learned a great deal.

I also managed to complete a substantial amount of research. Most importantly, I derived the remaining essential elements of the capital asset pricing model in my first year there.

While the equilibrium results I had obtained in the dissertation were satisfying, they appeared to rely heavily on the strong assumption that only one factor was responsible for correlations among security returns. My instincts told me that it should be possible to generalize the model so that such an assumption would not be needed. After several false starts I found that in an efficient market of the type posited, the key relationship between expected returns and beta values would hold *no matter what the process generating security returns*. I proceeded to write the results, under the title "Capital Asset Prices: A Theory of Market Equilibrium under Conditions of Risk." Publication was delayed for over two years due to initial rejection by a referee and a change in the editorship of the *Journal of Finance*. In the meantime I presented my results and exchanged work with others in the rapidly developing field that we now call financial economics. One way or another we found each other and managed to convene at various conferences. The process of academic communication is somewhat mysterious, even to those who participate in it. But it is remarkably effective.

While at Washington but with funding from Rand, I combined two of my interests to produce a book called *The Economics of Computers*. I also took a year's leave to return to Rand to work on several nonmilitary projects, including one investigating the possible use of time-varying fees to better allocate landing rights and air space at the three major New York airports.

Irvine

After several productive years at Washington I succumbed to an appeal to my entrepreneurial instincts and joined the School of Social Sciences at the University of California's new Irvine campus. The plan was to establish an economics department devoted primarily to the "economics of uncertainty." Unfortunately, life at a publicly supported campus in Orange County at the height of the antiwar movement was not one conducive to scholarly reflection. Everyone from the Chancellor on down had to be pressed into service to insure that the University remained free to investigate ideas of all kinds, be they from the left or the right.

While at Irvine I consulted with Merrill Lynch in New York, helping implement early practical applications of some of the concepts that I and others had developed. I also managed to complete another book, *Portfolio Theory and Capital Markets*, summarizing much of the work that had been done to date.

After a year it became clear to a number of us that our hopes to create innovative and high-quality new departments at Irvine would, at the very least, require a great deal of patience. Many found greener pastures, I among them.

Stanford

In 1970 I moved to my current home—the Stanford Graduate School of Business. At the time Stanford was already prominent in finance and eager to incorporate more of the recent economics-based work in both the curriculum and the research program. Accordingly, Alan Kraus, Bob Litzenberger, and I set up the first formal Ph.D. sequence in finance and taught it as a team. In the process, we began to see the outlines of what we now call financial economics. My knowledge of the area also grew phenomenally, thanks to Alan and Bob.

In the 1970s, the Stanford Business School was rushing to achieve the "balanced excellence" in both research and teaching that it had set as a goal. To build on a finance faculty that already included Alan Kraus, Bob Litzenberger, Alex Robicheck, Ezra Solomon, and Jim Van Horne, we hired Paul Cootner, John Cox, Sandy Grossman, and Myron Scholes. In the economics department, Joe Stiglitz was working in the area, and we were all using Ken Arrow's monumental contributions to the field. We also set up a joint seminar series with U.C.–Berkeley, which brought us into contact with the likes of Hayne Leland, Barr Rosenberg, and Mark Rubenstein. There could have been no better place for one with my interests.

At Stanford I taught finance and microeconomics at both the M.B.A. and Ph.D. level. Paul Cootner and I set up the Ph.D. sequence in microeconomics, from which I learned a great deal. However, I soon realized that I would rather concentrate my energy on financial economics, per se.

My biggest undertaking in these years was the writing of the previously quoted *Investments* textbook. It seemed to me that there was a need for a text in this area based solidly on financial economic theory. I postponed the project for two or three years since I realized that I would have to learn much about institutional details and industry practice if the book were to be sufficient for the purpose. Eventually I succumbed. The task proved to be formidable, but was a remarkable learning experience (to use a cliché).

In writing the text I found it necessary to not only document current theory but also to provide substantial amounts of new theory. The book thus became both the motivating force for my research and, in many cases, the venue for its publication.

Two examples of this stand out in my mind. One was an intuitive yet practical algorithm for solving a restricted class of portfolio optimization problems. Although simply a variant of a general class of approaches to nonlinear optimization, its rules can be stated in familiar economic terms such as utility maximization, choices based on marginal utilities, etc. The technique has proven quite useful and enjoys rather wide commercial application.

The second example concerned the valuation of options. The basis for the important Black–Scholes option valuation formula was, for me, hard to understand and virtually impossible to explain, since it was grounded in the difficult mathematics of continuous processes. Surely, I thought, there must be a discrete-time, discrete-state counterpart. Happily, there was. Moreover, numeric experiments showed that values obtained with the resultant *binomial process* converged quite rapidly to those of the continuous form as the number of discrete steps increased. I presented this approach in 1978 in my textbook. John Cox, Steve Ross, and Mark Rubenstein built on this foundation and showed that a wide variety of valuation problems could best be formulated in analogous ways. Such models, which we now realize to be special cases of the Arrow–Debreu state-preference paradigm, are also widely used by practitioners.

Wells Fargo

In the 1970s and 1980s I worked closely with an extremely innovative group at the Wells Fargo Bank in San Francisco to bring some of the lessons of financial economics to the world of money management. Under the leadership of Bill Fouse and Jim Vertin, Wells Fargo pioneered in the creation of index funds, passive portfolios tailored to meet investor objectives, estimation of beta values and expected returns using forecasts of future cash flows, estimation of risk, and more. Today Wells Fargo and Bill Fouse's Mellon Capital Management group manage over $125 billion using procedures based on financial economics.

Commerce

In 1986 I ventured more directly into the world of commerce. My wife Kathy (who served as administrator) and I established a firm devoted to research and consulting on problems faced by the administrators of large, multiply managed pension, endowment and foundation funds. Our goals were to apply existing theory, develop new theory, and conduct empirical analyses to deal with issues associated with the *asset allocation* decision, taking into account the objectives of each fund. In all our work we assumed that markets were efficient—that is, we wished to help *tailor* a fund's investments to meet its needs, rather than try to "beat the market."

Working with a talented group of colleagues and a highly sophisticated and supportive group of clients, we accomplished much in this connection. Of the several new techniques that we developed, the one that we termed *style analysis* has proven particularly useful.

By far the largest part of the month-to-month variation of the return provided by, say, a mutual fund is attributable to the *types* of securities held, rather than the specific securities chosen within each type. For example, using a set of twelve *asset classes* to represent security types, we found that 80 to 90% of the variance in monthly returns for a typical U.S. mutual fund was due to "asset allocation." Given this, it is crucial that one be able to determine a fund's allocation across such major asset classes, which we termed its *style*.

Rather remarkably, we found that in many cases this can be accomplished quite well by comparing the monthly returns provided by the fund over past years with those that could have been obtained from index funds representing each of the major asset classes. The required procedure (quadratic programming) is simple in concept, although somewhat complex in practice.

Style analysis allows an external analyst to estimate a manager's exposures to key sectors of the market. The investor can thus align his or her holdings of funds much more efficiently than would be possible without this information. A fund's *performance* can also be separated into that due to its *style* and the remainder, which may be considered due to *selection*. This type of *performance attribution* makes possible far more precise answers to questions concerning market efficiency, the extent to which past performance can predict future performance, etc.

The firm's clients were not alone in welcoming this type of analysis. Our papers and lectures on the subject have been warmly received and several other firms are preparing to offer similar services. If imitation is the sincerest form of flattery, we have been well-flattered.

Further Research

Throughout my career I have tried to keep one foot in the academic world and one in the world of affairs. There is much to learn from each, and each needs the other. This is, of course, a difficult balancing act. At Sharpe Associates, I placed substantial emphasis on practice. After several years it seemed appropriate to stand back somewhat to allow more reflection, deeper research, and preparation of the proverbial book or two. Hence a decision to concentrate more on research and teaching.

It seems to me that my comparative advantage lies in the development, application and communication of *practical theory*. I expect to continue to focus on financial economics, with special attention to investment applications, with somewhat greater emphasis on the integration of existing ideas than the development of new ones (as befits one my age).

Conclusion

Academic practice dictates that one should end a paper or lecture with a set of conclusions. I shall not do so. This is due in part to a belief that I lack the necessary perspective and unbiasedness. I also fear that the result might sound too much like an obituary—which I hope would prove premature.

I will, however, say this. It has been exciting and satisfying almost beyond belief to have played a role, however small, in the evolution of a field of inquiry as important and lasting as that of financial economics. Happily, there is far more to come, so that many generations of financial economists can look forward to the same sorts of thrills that I have been fortunate to experience.

Awarded Nobel Prize in 1990. Lecture presented February 19, 1992.

Date of Birth
June 16, 1934

Academic Degrees
A.B. University of California, Los Angeles, 1955
M.A. University of California, Los Angeles, 1956
Ph.D. University of California, Los Angeles, 1961

Academic Affiliations

Assistant Professor, University of Washington, 1961–1963

Associate Professor, University of Washington, 1963–1967

Professor, University of Washington, 1967–1968

Professor, University of California, Irvine, 1968–1970

Professor, Stanford University, 1970–1973

Timken Professor of Finance, Stanford University, 1973–1989

Timken Professor Emeritus of Finance, Stanford University, 1989–1992

Professor of Finance, Stanford University, 1993–1999

Professor of Finance, Emeritus, Stanford University, 1999–present

Selected Books

Portfolio Theory and Capital Markets, 1970, 2000

Investments, 1978, 1999 (6th ed., with G. Alexander and J. Bailey)

Asset Allocation Tools, 1987

Fundamentals of Investments, 1989, 2001 (with G. Alexander and J. Bailey)

Ronald H. Coase

After accepting Professor Breit's invitation to give a lecture in the series, "Lives of the Laureates," I read the book containing the previous lectures and found that the subject of my lecture was to be "My Evolution as an Economist." This led me to consider in what ways my ideas can be said to have evolved. The notion of an evolution in someone's ideas suggests a move from the simpler and cruder to something more complicated and more refined, brought about by a thought process which gradually improves the analysis. Lars Werin, speaking for the Royal Swedish Academy of Sciences, in introducing me at the Nobel Prize award ceremony, after referring to my article, "The Nature of the Firm," published in 1937, in which I explained, as I thought, why firms exist, said that I "gradually added blocks to [my] theoretical construction and had eventually—in the early 1960s—set forth the principles for answering all the questions," that is, the *principles* for answering all the questions relating to the institutional structure of the economic system. His statement about the final result is, I believe, substantially correct. But if his words are interpreted to mean that I started with a relatively simple theory and gradually, purposefully added building blocks until I had accumulated all that were needed to construct a theory of the institutional structure, it would give a misleading view of the development of my ideas. I never had a clear goal until quite recently. I came to realize where I had been going only after I arrived. The emergence of my ideas at each stage was not part of some grand scheme. In the end I found myself with a collection of blocks which, by some miracle, fit together to form, not a complete theory, but, as Lars Werin indicated, the foundation for such a theory.

The development of my ideas seems to me to have been more like a biological evolution in which the changes are brought about by chance events. How all this happened will be the subject of this lecture. It will, I think, throw some light on what Professor Breit calls the major rationale for this lecture series, learning about "the process by which original ideas are germinated and eventually accepted by one's peers." But if the occasion for the emergence of my ideas was provided by chance events, my response to them was no doubt influenced by the spirit of the age. Virginia Woolf has asserted that "on or about December 1910 human character changed" leading to "a change in religion, conduct, politics and literature."[1] If it is true that this date marks a turning point in human affairs, one would hardly expect that my approach in economics would be exactly the same as that of those who preceded me.

As you will by now have guessed, I was born in December, 1910. To be precise, I was born on December 29th at 3:25 P.M. The place was Willesden, a suburb of London. I was to be the only child of my parents. My father was a telegraphist in the post office where my mother had also been employed until her marriage. Although both my parents had left school at the age of 12, they were completely literate. However, they had no understanding of, or interest in, academic scholarship. My interests were always academic. But I grew up with no idea of what scholarship involved, had no guidance in my reading, and was unable to distinguish the charlatan from the serious scholar. But in two respects I am greatly indebted to my parents. They may not have shared my interests but they always supported me in what I wanted to do. And my mother taught me to be honest and truthful. Frank Knight has said: "The basic principle of science—truth or objectivity—is essentially a moral principle."[2] My endeavors to follow my mother's precepts have, I believe, been important in my work. My aim has always been to understand the working of the economic system, to get to the truth, rather than to support some position. And in criticizing others, I have always tried to understand what their position was and not to misrepresent it. I have never been interested in cheap victories.

When young I had a weakness in my legs which led to my wearing irons. I went to the local school for physical defectives. It was run by the same department of the council that ran the school for mental defectives, and I suspect that there may have been an overlap in the curriculum. I have no clear recollection of what I was taught there. All I can now remember is having been taught, at one stage, basket-weaving, a useful skill that I am afraid I failed to master.

I missed taking the entrance examination for the local secondary school at the usual age of 11 (perhaps because I was at the school for physical defectives). But, through the efforts of my parents, I was allowed to take the examination at the age of 12, as a result of which I was awarded a scholarship to go to the local secondary school, the Kilburn Grammar School. The teaching there was good, and I received a solid education in the usual school subjects. I passed the matriculation examination in 1927, with distinction in history and chemistry. It was then possible to spend the next two years at the Kilburn Grammar School studying for the intermediate examination of the University of London. This covered the subjects that would have been taken during the first year at the University. I had to decide what degree to take. My inclination had been to take a degree in history but I found that to do this, at least for the degree I wanted to take, it was necessary to know Latin, and having arrived at Kilburn Grammar School one year later than usual, boys of my age who had chosen to study Latin had already done so for a year. I had therefore been assigned to the science side of the school. This meant that I would not be able to take a degree in history. So I turned to the other subject in which I had secured distinction and started to study for a science degree, specializing in chemistry. However, I found I did not like mathematics, essential for a science degree, and decided to switch to the only other degree for which it was possible to study at the Kilburn Grammar School, one in commerce. Thinking back over this episode, I have concluded that the reason I disliked mathematics was that we learned formulas and mathematical operations without understanding the sense of what we were doing. Had I come across Silvanus Thompson's *Calculus Made Easy,* which explained the sense of these mathematical operations, or if the teaching at the Kilburn Grammar School had adopted a similar approach, it is very likely that I would have continued with my science degree. It is good that I did not as I would have made a mediocre mathematician and would never have become a first rate scientist. As it was, I studied at school for the intermediate examination of the Bachelor of

Commerce of the University of London (apart from accounting, not taught at the Kilburn Grammar School and which I studied by means of a correspondence course). Although I had only a rudimentary knowledge of the subjects, I managed to pass the examinations. And in 1929, at the age of eighteen, I went to the London School of Economics (LSE) to continue my studies for a B.Com. I passed part I of the final examination in 1930. For part II, I decided to take the Industry Group, supposedly intended for those who wanted to be works managers, but what universities say about their courses is not always to be taken seriously. However, although I could not have known this, I had made a fateful decision, one that would change my whole life.

Arnold Plant was appointed Professor of Commerce (with special reference to business administration) at the London School of Economics in 1930, having held a similar position at the University of Cape Town in South Africa. He took charge of the Industry Group. I therefore studied for the Industry Group in the very year that Plant took it over. In 1931, some five months before I completed my studies, I attended Plant's seminar. It was a revelation. He introduced me to Adam Smith's "invisible hand." You should remember that I had not taken a course in economics at LSE although some of the courses had economic content. The result was that my notions on economics were extremely wooly. What Plant did was to make me aware that producers compete, with the result that they supply what consumers value most. He explained that the economic system was coordinated by the pricing system. I was a socialist at the time, and all this was news to me. I passed the B.Com., part II, final examination in 1931. However, as I had taken the first year of university work while still at the Kilburn Grammar School and three years of residence at LSE were required before a degree could be granted, I had to decide what to do during this third year. The course that I had found most interesting in my studies for part II was industrial law, and my tentative decision was to use this third year to study for the B.Sc. (economics) degree, specializing in industrial law. Had I done so, I would undoubtedly have ended up as a lawyer. But this was not to be. No doubt as a result of Plant's influence, I was awarded a Sir Ernest Cassel Traveling Scholarship by the University of London for the year 1931–32. I was to work under the direction of Plant, and the year would be counted as a year's residence at LSE. This is how it happened that I took the road that would lead to my becoming an economist and *not* a basket-weaver, a historian, a chemist, a works manager, or a lawyer. "There is a divinity that shapes our ends, rough hew them though we may."

When I had completed my studies for the B.Com. degree, I knew a little about accounting, statistics, and law. Although I had never taken a course in economics at LSE, I had also picked up a little economics. Acting on hints in Plant's seminar, I had discussed economic problems with my friend Ronald Fowler, who was also taking the Industry Group. And LSE was a relatively small institution at that time. I knew students who were economics specialists and had discussions with them, particularly with Vera Smith (later Vera Lutz), Abba Lerner, and Victor Edelberg. That I had come to economics without any formal training was to prove a great advantage. I had never been trained what to think and therefore what not to think, and this gave me a lot of freedom in dealing with economic questions.

I proposed to use my Cassel Traveling Scholarship to go to the United States and to study vertical and lateral integration in industry. Plant had discussed in his lectures the various ways in which industries were organized, but we seemed to lack any theory that would explain why there were these differences. I set out to find this theory. There were two other problems that seemed in my mind to be connected to my main project. Plant had spoken in his seminar about the economic system being coordinated by the pricing system and had been critical of government schemes for the rationalization of industry—particularly those for coordinating the various means of transport. And yet, in his lectures on business administration, Plant spoke of management as coordinating the factors of production used in a firm. How could these two views be reconciled? Why did we need management if all the coordination necessary was already provided by the market? What was essentially the same puzzle presented itself to me in another form. The Russian Revolution had taken place in 1917. But we knew very little about how a communist system would operate. How could we? The first five-year plan was not adopted until 1928. Lenin had said that under communism the economic system would be run as one big factory. Some western economists were arguing that this could not be done. Yet there were factories in the western world and some of them were very large. Why couldn't the Russian economy be run as one big factory?

These were the puzzles with which I went to the United States. I visited universities but in the main I carried out my project by visiting businesses and industrial plants. I talked with everyone I met and read trade periodicals and the reports of the Federal Trade Commission. At the end of the year there was much about the organization of industry that I felt I did not understand. But I believed that I had solved part of the puzzle. Economists talked about the economic system as being coordinated by the pricing mechanism (or the market) but had ignored the fact that using the market involved costs. From this it followed that means of coordination other than through use of the market could not be ruled out as inefficient—it all depended on what they cost as compared with the cost of using the market. I realized that this way of looking at things could affect one's views on centralized planning. But, and this was what really mattered to me, it also meant that we could understand why there were firms in which the employment of the factors of production was coordinated by the management of the firm while at the same time there was also coordination conducted through the market. Whether a transaction would be organized within a firm or whether it would be carried out on the market depended on a comparison of the costs of organizing such a transaction within the firm with the costs of a market transaction that would accomplish the same result. All this is very simple and obvious. But it took me a year to realize it—and many economists seem unaware of it (or its significance) to this day.

It was an extraordinary piece of luck that the last year of my studies for the B.Com. coincided with Arnold Plant's first year at LSE. It was another piece of luck that the next year I was able to secure a Cassel Traveling Scholarship. This was followed by a piece of luck even more extraordinary. I came on to the labor market in 1932, the worst year of the Great Depression. Unemployment was rife among LSE graduates. And yet I secured employment. It came about this way: in 1931, with the financial support of George Bonar, a prominent member of the jute industry, there had been established, with the advice of Sir William Beveridge and others at LSE, a School of Economics and Commerce in Dundee, to be administered by the Dundee Educational Authority. The purpose of the school was to train students for business. The senior appointments were made in 1931. The junior appointments were made in 1932, just when I needed a job. It is easy to see in retrospect that my qualifications, meager though they were, would have seemed more appropriate for this position than those of most graduates in economics. I was appointed an assistant lecturer at the Dundee School of Economics and Commerce in October, 1932. If the Dundee School had not been established in 1931, I don't know what I would have done. As it was, everything fell into place. I was to be an economist and could evolve.

My duties involved lecturing in three courses all of which started in October. How I did it I can't now imagine. Duncan Black, the other assistant lecturer, has described how I arrived in Dundee with my head full of my ideas on the firm. Fortunately, one of the courses was on "The Organization of the Business Unit." In a letter to my friend Ronald Fowler that has been preserved, I described the contents of my first lecture in that course. It was essentially the argument that was later to be published as "The Nature of the Firm" (one of the two articles cited by the Royal Swedish Academy of Sciences in 1991 as justification for the award of the Nobel Prize). I could never have imagined in 1932 that these ideas would come to be regarded as so significant. Of course, I liked the lecture. In my letter to Fowler, after describing the contents of the lecture, I expressed my great satisfaction with it: "As it was a new approach (I think) to this subject, I was quite pleased with myself. One thing I can say is that I made it all up myself." As I said in my Nobel Prize lecture, "I was then twenty-one and the sun never ceased to shine."

At Dundee I began to read the literature of economics—Adam Smith, Babbage, Jevons, Wicksteed, Knight. Writing of my days at Dundee, Duncan Black, in notes prepared for Kenneth Elzinga in connection with the article he was writing about me for the *International Encyclopedia of the Social Sciences,* commented that at this early date my attitude was "surprisingly definite." "He wanted an Economics that would both deal with the real world and do so in an exact manner. Most economists are content to achieve one or the other of these objectives and to my mind the distinguishing mark of Coase's work in Economics is that, in a fair measure, it achieves both objectives." Whether I succeeded or not, Black does describe what my aim in economics was, and is. I ascribe it to the fact that I started not with an academic study of economics but with an education in commerce and that when I began to study economics it was with a view to using it to understand what happened in the real world.

However, I was not immune to what was happening in the economics world. In 1933 Chamberlin's *Theory of Monopolistic Competition* and Joan Robinson's *Economics of Imperfect Competition* were published. These books created a great stir in economics, and I was swept up along with the others. While still at Dundee I wrote an article in which I used the analysis developed by Joan Robinson to examine the problems discussed by Chamberlin. This article was published in 1935. More illustrative of my general attitude was the work I did on expectations at that time.

While at Dundee I spent my vacations at LSE. Much of my time was taken up with discussions on economics with Ronald Fowler, who had been appointed an assistant lecturer at LSE. One question that interested us was the belief, held by many economists, that producers, in deciding on output, assumed that existing prices and costs would continue in the future. It had been shown that if producers acted in this way, it would result in fluctuations in prices and output (termed the "cobweb theorem" by Kaldor). An example of the cobweb theorem was thought to be provided by the pig-cycle in Britain. We undertook a statistical investigation that showed, as we thought, that pig producers in Britain did not assume that existing prices would continue unchanged in the future. When prices were unusually high they expected them to fall, and when they were unusually low they expected them to rise. As my correspondence shows, I intended to use the techniques we had developed in this study to investigate the formation of producer expectations in other areas—and Fowler had a similar intention. What I then had was a strong interest in measuring the concepts which were usually only treated theoretically by economists. In this I was greatly influenced by the work of Henry Schultz of the University of Chicago in deriving statistical demand schedules. Apart from my work on expectations I also started an investigation of the cost of capital and how it varied with the size of the issue, and the size and industry of the firm. None of this work was completed. Fowler did however complete a study of the elasticity of substitution between scrap and pig iron in the production of steel which was published in the *Quarterly Journal of Economics* in 1937.

At this time my own expectation was that my future research would be to engage in similar quantitative investigations. But this did not happen. It is easy to see why. In 1934 I was appointed an assistant lecturer in the University of Liverpool with the duty of lecturing on banking and finance, subjects on which I knew next to nothing. More important was that in 1935 I was appointed an assistant lecturer in economics at LSE. Here my duties were to lecture on the theory of monopoly (taking over a course that had previously been given by John Hicks who had gone to Cambridge), to assist Plant in the Department of Business Administration (the DBA) and to give the course on the economics of public utilities (previously given by Batson, who had gone to South Africa). The lectures on the theory of monopoly created no particular difficulty for me. We had Joan Robinson's book, and I had written on the theory of duopoly. In 1937, I published an article, "Notes on the Theory of Monopoly," which contained some of the ideas that came from these lectures. My work in the Department of Business Administration was more humdrum. I prepared some cases in the manner of the Harvard Business School and assisted in the teaching.

Ronald Edwards, whose field was accounting, had joined the DBA, and Fowler and I collaborated with him in the work of the Accounting Research Association. Among other things, we investigated how far the figures in the published accounts could be used for economic research. We showed that they could be so used, once the basis for the figures was understood, by publishing a study of the British iron and steel industry using the material in published balance sheets. I also published in *The Accountant* a series of articles on cost accounting, articles which have since been reprinted and much referred to, largely I think because they contain the only systematic account of the opportunity cost concept as it was taught at LSE in the 1930s. My main research activity was, however, in connection with my course on public utilities. I soon found that very little was known about public utilities in Britain, and I made a series of historical studies of the water, gas, and electricity supply industries, and particularly of the post office and broadcasting. Another publication should be noted. In 1934 while still at Dundee, I had written the draft of an article entitled "The Nature of the Firm," a systematic exposition of the ideas in my 1932 lecture. At LSE I revised this draft and submitted it to *Economica,* in which it was published in 1937. It created little inter-est. I have recounted how, on the day it was published, on the way to lunch the two professors of commerce congratulated me but never re-ferred to the article again. Lionel Robbins, in whose department I was, never referred to the article ever. It was not an instant success.

In September, 1939, war was declared. What I have just described is the work on which I was engaged in the seven years from 1932 to 1939. In 1940 I was appointed head of the Statistical Division of the Forestry Commission (responsible at that time for timber production in the United Kingdom), and in 1941 I moved to the Central Statistical Office, one of the Offices of the War Cabinet. I ended up responsible for munitions statistics, those relating to guns, tanks, and ammunition. I did not return to LSE until 1946. My six years in government service played little part in my evolution as an economist, except perhaps to confirm my prejudices.

On my return to LSE I became responsible for the course on the princi-ples of economics, a conventional exposition of mainstream economics. In 1946 I published an article, "Monopoly Pricing with Interrelated Costs and Demands," based on material in my prewar monopoly course. An-other article published the same year, "The Marginal Cost Controversy," should also be mentioned because it illustrates the way in which my ap-proach to economic policy differed from that of most of my contemporar-ies. Towards the end of the war, the economists in the Economics Section of the Offices of the War Cabinet began to consider the problems of post-war Britain. James Meade and John Fleming, in the Economics Section, wrote a paper on the pricing policies of state enterprises in which they advocated marginal cost pricing. Keynes, who was an advisor to the Trea-sury, saw the paper, was enthusiastic about it, and reprinted it in the *Economic Journal,* of which he was editor. I also saw the paper as did Tom Wilson (also in the Economics Section), and we did not like it. I published a short critical note in the *Economic Journal,* and after the war I wrote "The Marginal Cost Controversy." I was already familiar with the case for marginal cost pricing before I saw the Meade–Fleming piece. Abba Lerner had been an enthusiastic advocate and an able expositor of marginal cost pricing at LSE, and it was undoubtedly pondering over Lerner's argument that gave me my view. I maintained that a general policy of marginal cost pricing would lead to waste on a massive scale.

It would also bring about a redistribution of income and would lead to taxation that would introduce elsewhere divergencies between price and marginal cost that had not previously existed. Tom Wilson pointed out that the policy would lead to a substitution of state enterprise for private enterprise and of centralized for decentralized operations. What had happened is that, through concentrating on getting the right marginal adjustments, economists (for at that time belief in marginal cost pricing was the dominant view among academic economists) had completely ignored the effects their policy would have in other ways. They fiddled while Rome burned. I have called their way of proceeding "blackboard economics" since what they described could happen only on a blackboard. In the meantime at LSE I had been promoted to become a "reader in economics, with special reference to public utilities." My main research activity was the continuation of my historical studies of British public utilities. In 1950 I published a book, *British Broadcasting: A Study in Monopoly.*

In 1951 I migrated to the United States. What prompted me to take this step was a combination of a lack of faith in the future of socialist Britain, a liking for life in America (I had spent part of 1948 there studying the working of a commercial broadcasting system), and an admiration for American economics. Among the older economists it was Frank Knight that I most admired; among my contemporaries it was George Stigler. And I have already mentioned the influence of Henry Schultz. My first appointment in America was at the University of Buffalo, due to the presence there of John Sumner, a specialist on public utilities, who had visited LSE before the war. In 1958 I joined the faculty of the University of Virginia and in 1964 the faculty of the University of Chicago.

On coming to the United States I decided to make a study of the political economy of broadcasting, based on experience in Britain, Canada, and the United States. This was essentially a continuation of the kind of research I had been conducting at LSE. I collected a great deal of material for this project. I spent the year 1958–59 at the Center for Advanced Study in the Behavioral Sciences at Stanford. While there I wrote an article on "The Federal Communications Commission" which was published in the *Journal of Law and Economics.* This was to have far-reaching consequences.

In that article I examined the work of the Federal Communications Commission (the FCC) in allocating the use of the radio frequency spectrum. I suggested that this should be done by selling the right to use a frequency. The use of pricing for the allocation of resources was hardly a novel idea for an economist (and in any case the suggestion had already been advanced for the radio frequency spectrum by Leo Herzel). What was unusual in my paper was that I went on to discuss the nature of the rights that would be acquired. The main problem in the case of the radio frequency spectrum concerned interference between signals transmitted on the same or adjacent frequencies. I argued that if rights were well-defined and transferable, it did not matter what the initial rights were—they would be transferred and combined so as to bring about the optimal result. As I put it: "The ultimate result (which maximizes the value of production) is independent of the legal [position]."[3] This simple and, as I thought, obvious proposition, was disputed by the economists at the University of Chicago with whom I was in touch. It was even suggested that I should delete this passage from the article. However, I held my ground and later, after the article was published, a meeting was held at the home of Aaron Director at which I was able to convince the Chicago economists that I was right. I was then asked to write up my ideas for publication in the *Journal of Law and Economics*.

I took on this task with enthusiasm. I was a great admirer of what the *Journal of Law and Economics*, under the editorship of Aaron Director, had been accomplishing. In it were being published articles that examined actual business practices, the effects of different property rights systems, and the working of regulatory systems. I considered it essential if economics (and particularly that part called industrial organization) was to make progress, that articles such as these should be published, but they were articles that, at that time, would have found difficulty in being published in the normal economic journals. My article on the FCC was an example. However, I wanted to go beyond the passage in the FCC article to which objections had been made and to deal more generally with what may be termed the rationale of a property rights system. I had discussed the case of *Sturges v. Bridgman* in the FCC article, but I wanted to examine other nuisance cases (something I could do because of the familiarity I had acquired with the Law Reports in my student days at LSE). Also, I had long thought (again from my student days) that although Pigou's *Economics of Welfare* was a great book for the problems it tackled, Pigou was not very sure-footed in his economic analysis. I had made two passing references to Pigou in the FCC article but did not discuss his views since that article was wholly devoted to the problem of the allocation of the use of the radio frequency spectrum. However, my discussions at Chicago had made clear to me the strength of the hold that Pigou's approach had on the economics profession, and this led me to want to deal with it directly. I also wanted to discuss the influence of positive transaction costs on the analysis, something that I had only alluded to in a footnote in the FCC article. These were the various objectives or themes that I wanted to weave together and which I think I managed to do in "The Problem of Social Cost."

This article received considerable attention almost immediately. Articles were written attacking and defending it. It became one of the most cited articles in the economics literature. It contained ideas that I had long held at the back of my mind but had never articulated. It is a curious aspect of this story that had these Chicago economists not objected to the passage in the FCC article, "The Problem of Social Cost" would probably never have been written and these ideas would have remained in the back of my mind.

I wrote the article in the Summer of 1960 at LSE, where I had access to the Law Reports. I argued that Pigou had been looking at the problem of what is termed "externality" in the wrong way. It is a reciprocal problem, and it was Pigou's failure to recognize this (or at any rate to incorporate it in the analysis) that had prevented him (and the economics profession which had followed him) from developing the appropriate analysis. It was also true that Pigou's policy recommendations were unnecessary in a regime of zero transaction costs (which was implicitly his assumption) since in this case negotiations between the parties would bring about the optimal result. However, transaction costs are not zero and real world situations cannot be studied without introducing positive transaction costs. Once this was done, it became impossible to say what the appropriate policy recommendation should be without knowing what the transaction costs were and the factual situation of each case under consideration. What should be done could only be learned as a result of empirical studies. What I did in "The Problem of Social Cost" was to provide not a solution, but an approach. As I said in that article: "Satisfactory views on policy can only come from a patient study of how, in practice, the market, firms, and governments handle the problem of harmful effects. . . . It is my belief that economists and policymakers generally have tended to overestimate the advantages which come from governmental regulation. But this belief, even if justified, does not do more than suggest that governmental regulation should be curtailed. It does not tell us where the boundary line should be drawn. This, it seems to me, has to come from a detailed investigation of the actual results of handling the problem in different ways."[4]

A year or two after the appearance of "The Problem of Social Cost" I received an invitation to join the faculty of the University of Chicago. What attracted me to the position at Chicago was that part of my duties would be to edit the *Journal of Law and Economics*. I have already spoken of my admiration for the *Journal* and the articles it contained. I wanted to continue this work, and I went to Chicago to do it. I greatly enjoyed editing the *Journal*. Using the resources of the law and economics program at the University of Chicago Law School and the opportunity of publication in the *Journal*, I encouraged economists and lawyers (at Chicago and elsewhere) to undertake empirical studies of the kind advocated in "The Problem of Social Cost." As a result, many splendid articles were published. This was a very happy period for me. Every article was an event. In the 1970s and '80s, articles of a similar character began to appear in other journals, and there were many citations to the "Nature of the Firm" as well as to "The Problem of Social Cost." I felt the time had come to bring together my essays on the institutional structure of production and in 1988 published *The Firm, the Market and the Law*, which reprinted my chief articles on this topic. It included an introductory essay which explained my central message.

The next event to be noted as affecting the evolution of my ideas occurred in 1987 when Oliver Williamson and Sidney Winters organized a conference at Yale to celebrate the fiftieth anniversary of the publication of "The Nature of the Firm." This was probably the best conference that I have ever attended. The papers by eight distinguished economists were not designed to praise nor to bury "The Nature of the Firm" but to examine the issues it had raised and to extend, and—where they found error—to correct, what I had said. I contributed three lectures on the origin, meaning, and influence of the article. Attendance at this conference and preparation of my lectures had a great effect on my thinking. Writing "The Problem of Social Cost" and my later discussions with Steven Cheung in the 1960s had made me aware of the pervasive influence of transaction costs on the working of the economy, but I had not examined the problem in a systematic way. When Williamson, in his paper, ascribed the limited use of the thesis of "The Nature of the Firm" to the fact that it had not been made "operational," I had no doubt that he was essentially correct. What he had in mind was that the concept of transaction costs had not been incorporated into a general theory which could be checked and developed by empirical studies. However, this would be no easy task. The incorporation of transaction costs in an economic theory which assumed they were zero would involve a complete change in its structure. Even if we confined ourselves to the thesis of "The Nature of the Firm," narrowly conceived, there were formidable obstacles to making it "operational." Whether the coordination of the factors of production needed to produce a given result will be undertaken administratively within a firm or by means of pricing on the market depends on the relative costs of carrying out the coordination in these different ways, and whether it will be profitable depends on their absolute height. But what are the factors that determine these relative and absolute costs? Discovering them will not be at all easy. But there is an even more difficult problem. The analysis cannot be confined to what happens within a single firm. The costs of coordination within a firm and the level of transaction costs that it faces are affected by its ability to purchase inputs from other firms, and their ability to supply these inputs depends in part on their costs of coordination and the level of transaction costs that they face, which are similarly affected by what these are in still other firms. What we are dealing with is a complex interrelated structure.

The Yale conference rekindled my interest in the issues raised by "The Nature of the Firm" and led me to decide, once my existing commitments were out of the way, to devote myself to helping in the construction of a theory that would enable us to analyze the determinants of the institutional structure of production. For now I was not alone. As the papers at the conference had demonstrated, important work was being undertaken, aimed at the clarification and improvement of the theory while many empirical studies of high quality were being conducted which were providing data on the basis of which further advances could be expected to be made. We were beginning to see what needed to be explained and I felt confident that, although it would take many years of dedicated work by many economists to achieve this goal, we would ultimately be able to construct a comprehensive theory of the institutional structure of production. Although it is obvious that I will be able to travel only part of the way, I decided at Yale that this is what I should do in my few remaining years.

And then, in 1991, I was awarded the Alfred Nobel Memorial Prize in Economics. The two articles cited as justification for the award were "The Nature of the Firm," published over 50 years before and "The Problem of Social Cost," published 30 years before. The first article had been received with indifference, the second provoked controversy. Neither had commanded the assent of the economics profession and if, of which I am not sure, there is now general recognition of the importance of my work, it must have come very recently. Lars Werin at the awards ceremony in Stockholm, after saying that I had "remarkably improved our understanding of the way the economic system functions," added "although it took some time for the rest of us to realize it."

This lecture clearly provides grist to Professor Breit's mill in his quest to understand "the process by which original ideas are germinated and eventually accepted by one's peers." But what has my tale to contribute? It has often been remarked that original ideas commonly come from those who are young and/or have newly entered a field. This certainly fits my case. In 1932, when, in a lecture in Dundee, I introduced the concept of transaction costs into economic analysis, I was 21, and, if economics was my field, I had only just entered it. However, at first sight, it is not easy to understand why the inclusion of transaction costs in economic analysis was an "original" idea. The puzzle I took with me to America was there for all to see, and my solution was simple and obvious. The explanation for this failure to include transaction costs in the analysis is not that other economists were not smart enough but that, in their work, they did not concern themselves with the problems of the institutional structure of the economy and so never encountered my puzzle. This situation came about, as Demsetz has explained, because economists since Adam Smith have taken as a major task to formalize his view that an economic system could be coordinated by the pricing system. What has been produced is a theory of the working of an economic system of extreme decentralization. It has been a towering intellectual achievement and has enduring value, but it is an economics with blinkers and has had the unfortunate effect of diverting attention from some very important features of the economic system. This explains, among other things, why, when it first appeared, "The Nature of the Firm" excited so little interest.

But why did "The Problem of Social Cost" attract so much attention so soon? I have recounted the somewhat peculiar circumstances that led to its writing. This had the result that, when it appeared, it had the strong support of a powerful group of economists at the University of Chicago and especially of George Stigler. My argument that the allocation of resources in a regime of zero transaction costs would be independent of the legal position regarding liability was formalized by Stigler and named by him the "Coase Theorem." This attracted attention to my article, and many papers were published attacking and defending the "theorem." The fact that the "Coase Theorem" dealt with a regime of zero transaction costs was also helpful since this meant that economists felt quite at home discussing it, remote from the real world though it may have been. It does not seem to have been noticed that the "theorem" applies to a world of positive transaction costs for all exchanges that are actually made, providing that the transaction costs are not significantly affected by the change in the legal position regarding liability, which will commonly be the case. Strangely enough, I believe the fact that the discussion was not concerned with the real world of positive transaction costs did not diminish but actually increased the attention given to my article. Another circumstance that led to much discussion in the literature was that I criticized Pigou's analysis (accepted by most economists). As a result many articles were written by economists defending Pigou (and themselves). Another, and quite separate, circumstance was that this article, by discussing the rationale of a property rights system and the effect of the law on the working of the economic system, extended the economic analysis of the law beyond its previous connection with antitrust policy.

The article greatly interested lawyers and economists in American law schools, spawned an immense literature, and led to the emergence of the new subject of "law and economics." All these quite special circumstances combined to make this article an immediate success. But it would be wrong to conclude that for the thesis of an article to gain acceptance it is necessary to have the support of a prestigious group or the stir of controversy or involve some similar circumstance. After all, "The Nature of the Firm," received at first with indifference, has by now had a very considerable influence on the thinking of many economists. Without the kind of factor that affected the reception of "The Problem of Social Cost," it just takes longer for a good idea to secure acceptance. As Edwin Cannan, the teacher of my teacher, Arnold Plant, said: "However lucky Error may be for a time, Truth keeps the book, and wins in the long run."[5]

Given the broad acceptance of my analysis in "The Nature of the Firm" and "The Problem of Social Cost," what is the task ahead? The Nobel Committee said that I had provided the blocks for the construction of a theory of the institutional structure. We now have to discover how they fit together so that we can construct it. I hope to assist in this work. But, as is obvious, in a few years my evolution will come to an end. However, other able scholars will continue their work, and the outlines of a comprehensive theory should begin to emerge in the near future. No doubt some of these scholars will visit you to present a lecture in this series and to tell you about their evolution.

Awarded Nobel Prize in 1991. Lecture presented April 12, 1994.

Date of Birth

December 29, 1910

Academic Degrees

B.Com. University of London, 1932

D.Sc. (Economics) University of London, 1951

Academic Affiliations

Assistant Lecturer, Dundee School of Economics and Commerce, 1932–1934.

Assistant Lecturer, University of Liverpool, 1934–1935

Assistant Lecturer, London School of Economics, 1935–1938

Lecturer, London School of Economics, 1938–1947

Reader, London School of Economics, 1947–1951

Professor of Economics, University of Buffalo, 1951–1958

Professor of Economics, University of Virginia, 1958–1964

Professor of Economics, University of Chicago Law School, 1964–1970

Clifton R. Musser Professor of Economics, University of Chicago Law School, 1964–1981

Distinguished Professor (visiting) of Law and Economics, University of Kansas, 1991

Clifton R. Musser Professor Emeritus of Economics, and Senior Fellow in Law and Economics, University of Chicago Law School, 1982–present

Selected Books

British Broadcasting: A Study in Monopoly, 1950

The Firm, the Market, and the Law, 1988

Essays on Economics and Economists, 1994

Douglass C. North

Ronald Coase was kind enough to send me the lecture he prepared for this series. He states right on the first page of his talk that "I came to realize where I was going only after I arrived." Not I. I knew where I was going from the day I decided to become an economist. I set out to understand what made economies rich or poor because I viewed that objective as being the essential prerequisite to improving their performance. The search for the Holy Grail of the ultimate source of economic performance has taken me on a long and certainly unanticipated journey, from Marxism to cognitive science, but it has been this persistent objective that has directed and shaped my scholarly career.

I was born in Cambridge, Massachusetts—not because my family had any connection with higher education, but because my father was a manager at the Metropolitan Life Insurance Company in a nearby town, and Cambridge was the nearest hospital in 1920. I was the youngest of three children, with a sister and a brother who were born before my father went off to Europe in World War I.

In the ensuing years we moved a number of times as a result of my father's business, first to Connecticut and then, when he became head of the Metropolitan's Canadian office, to Ottawa. Because my mother believed in education broadly construed, we traveled in Europe, and I went to school at the Lycée Jacquard in Lausanne, Switzerland, in 1929–30. I went to elementary school in Ottawa and then to a private secondary school. When we moved back to the United States in 1933, I went to private schools in New York City and on Long Island and then completed my high school education at The Choate School in Wallingford, Connecticut. While I was there I became deeply interested in photography, and indeed the most noteworthy event in my early life was winning first, third, fourth, and seventh prizes in an international photographic competition for college and high school students.

Our family life was certainly not intellectual. My father had not even completed high school when he started as an office boy working for the Metropolitan Life Insurance Company, and I am not sure that my mother completed high school. Nevertheless, she was an exciting person—intelligent, intellectually curious—and she played an important part in my intellectual development. My aunt and uncle were, and one of my aunts (Adelaide North) still is, a powerful influence. They introduced me to classical music and my aunt continues to be, to this day, a very special person in my life.

When it came time to go to college I had been accepted to Harvard when my father was offered the position of head of the Metropolitan Life Insurance Company office on the west coast, and we moved to San Francisco. Because I did not want to be that far from home, I decided to go instead to the University of California at Berkeley. While I was there my life was completely changed by my becoming a Marxist.

Marxism was attractive because it appeared to provide answers to the pressing questions of the time, including the Great Depression that we were in—answers missing from the pre-Keynesian economics that I was taught in 1939–40. I was opposed to World War II, and indeed on June 22, 1941, when Hitler invaded the Soviet Union, I suddenly found myself the lone supporter of peace since everybody else had, because of their communist beliefs, shifted over to become supporters of the war.

Because I was preoccupied with liberal student activities, my record at the University of California as an undergraduate was mediocre, to say the least. I had only slightly better than a "C" average, although I did have a triple major in political science, philosophy, and economics. I had hoped to go to law school, but the war started, and because of the strong feeling that I did not want to kill anybody, I joined the Merchant Marine when I graduated from Berkeley in May of 1942.

We had been to sea only a short time when the Captain called me up on the bridge and asked me if I could learn to navigate: most of the officers had only rudimentary educations, and we were on our way from San Francisco to Australia. I became navigator and enjoyed it very much. We made repeated trips from San Francisco to Australia, and then to the forward positions in New Guinea and the Solomon Islands.

What the years at sea did give me were three years of continuous reading, and it was in the course of reading that I became convinced that I should become an economist. The last year of the war I taught celo-navigation at the Maritime Service Officers' School in Alameda, California; I took up photography again and had a difficult decision as to whether to become a photographer or go into economics. In the summer of 1941 I had worked with Dorothea Lange, head of the photographic division of the Farm Security Administration, traveling with and photographing migrants through the Central Valley of California. Dorothea tried to persuade me to become a photographer. Her husband, Paul Taylor, who was in the economics department at the University of California, tried to persuade me to become an economist. He won.

I went to graduate school at the University of California at Berkeley—the only graduate school that would take me with my poor undergraduate record. My objective as a graduate student was to find out what made economies work the way they did or fail to work. Economic history appeared to be the best field for that objective. I cannot say that I learned much formal economics as a graduate student in Berkeley. My most influential professors were all outside the mainstream of orthodox economics—Robert Brady; Leo Rogin, a very influential teacher of history of economic thought; and M. M. Knight (Frank Knight's brother), who certainly was agnostic, to say the least, about theory, but who had a wonderful knowledge of the facts and background in economic history. He became my mentor and my thesis advisor at Berkeley. But while I learned by rote most of the theory I was supposed to know, I did not acquire a real understanding of theory.

It was not until I got my first job, at the University of Washington in Seattle, and began playing chess with Don Gordon, a brilliant young theorist, that I learned economic theory. In the three years of playing chess every day from noon to two, I may have beaten Don at chess, but he taught me economics; more important, he taught me how to reason like an economist, and that skill is still perhaps the most important tool that I have acquired.

I had written my dissertation on the history of life insurance in the United States and had had a Social Science Research Council Fellowship to go to the east coast and do the spade work. That turned out to be a very productive year. I not only sat in on Robert Merton's seminars in sociology at Columbia but also became involved in the Entrepreneurial Center of Arthur Cole at Harvard. The result was that Joseph Schumpeter, who had been an intellectual source of the Entrepreneurial School, had a strong influence upon me. My early work and publications centered around expanding on the analysis of life insurance in my dissertation and its relationship to investment banking.

I next turned to developing an analytical framework to look at regional economic growth and this led to my first article in the *Journal of Political Economy,* entitled "Location Theory and Regional Economic Growth." That work eventually led me to developing a staple theory of economic growth.

I was very fortunate that, at a meeting of the Economic History Association, I came to know Solomon Fabricant, who was then director of research at the National Bureau of Economic Research; and in 1956–57 I was invited to spend the year at the Bureau as a research associate. That was an enormously important year in my life. I not only became acquainted with most of the leading economists who passed through the Bureau but also spent one day a week at Johns Hopkins University in Baltimore with Simon Kuznets, whose wise council had a lasting influence on me. During the year at the NBER I did the empirical work that led to my early major quantitative study of the balance of payments of the United States from 1790 to 1860.

I married for the first time in 1944. During my graduate training my wife taught school, providing our major source of support. We had three sons, Douglass, Christopher, and Malcolm, born between 1951 and 1957. After the boys were in school my wife became a successful politician in the Washington State legislature.

Between my year at the National Bureau and 1966–67, when I went off to Geneva as a Ford Faculty Fellow, I did my major work in American economic history, which led to my first book, *The Economic Growth of the United States from 1790 to 1860.* It was a straightforward analysis of how markets work in the context of an export staple model of growth.

By this time (1960) there was a substantial stirring among young economic historians to try to transform the field from its descriptive, institutional character to make it an analytical, quantitative discipline. The year that I was at the NBER, that organization and the Economic History Association had the first joint quantitative program on the growth of the American economy, a conference that was held at Williamstown, Massachusetts, in the late spring of 1957. It was at this meeting that I presented my paper on the balance of payments of the United States from 1790 to 1860. This meeting was really the beginning of the new economic history, but the new approach to economic history really coalesced when Jon Hughes and Lance Davis, two former students of mine who had become faculty members at Purdue, called the first conference of economic historians interested in trying to develop and apply economic theory and quantitative methods to history. The first meeting was held at Purdue in February of 1960. This conference was highly successful and became an annual affair. The participants were a mixture of economic historians, theorists, and econometricians. They were no-holds-barred meetings in which the speaker frequently got mauled, but we knew we were reshaping the field of economic history, and that was exciting. The reception that we received amongst economists was certainly enthusiastic. Economics departments very quickly became interested in having new economic historians, or, as we came to call ourselves, cliometricians (Clio being the muse of history). Therefore, as I developed a graduate program jointly with my colleague, Morris David Morris, at the University of Washington we attracted some of the best students to do work in economic history, and during the 1960s and early 1970s the job market was very responsive, and our students were easily placed throughout the country.

In 1966–67 I decided that I should switch from American to European economic history, and therefore, when I received the above-mentioned grant to live in Geneva for a year, I decided to retool. Retooling turned out to change my scholarly life radically, since I quickly became convinced that the tools of neoclassical economic theory were not up to the task of explaining the kind of fundamental societal change that had characterized European economies from medieval times onward.

Neoclassical theory was concerned with the operation of markets and assumed the existence of the underlying conditions that were a prerequisite to the operation of markets. It had nothing to say about how markets evolved. Moreover it was a static theory, and we needed to have a theory that was dynamic and could explain the evolution of economies through time. We needed new tools, but they simply did not exist. It was in the long search for a framework that would provide new tools of analysis that my interest and concern with the new institutional economics evolved. As a graduate student I had read Thorstein Veblen and John R. Commons and been impressed by the insights they provided into the workings of economies, but they did not provide a theoretical framework. What we needed was a theoretical structure that we could use to explain and analyze economic history. The old institutional economics, because it failed to provide such a theoretical framework, never posed a serious alternative to neoclassical theory. Marxism was explicitly concerned with institutions, asked good questions, and had an explanation of long-run change, but there were too many flaws in the model. Making classes the unit of analysis and failing to incorporate population change as a key source of change were major shortcomings. The strengths of neoclassical theory were its uncompromising focus on scarcity and, hence, competition as the key to economics, its use of the individual as the unit of analysis, and the power of the economic way of reasoning. There had to be a way of melding the strengths of these diverse approaches into a theoretical structure. That is what I and others have set out to do in the new institutional economics.

Why focus on institutions? In a world of uncertainty they have been used by human beings in an attempt to structure human interaction. They are the rules of the game of a society and in consequence provide the framework of incentives that shape economic, political, and social organization. Institutions are composed of formal rules (laws, constitutions, rules), informal constraints (conventions, codes of conduct, norms of behavior), and the effectiveness of their enforcement. Enforcement is carried out by third parties (law enforcement, social ostracism), by second parties (retaliation), or by the first party (self-imposed codes of conduct). Institutions affect economic performance by determining, together with the technology employed, the transaction and transformation (production) costs that make up the total costs of production. Since there is an intimate connection between the institutions and technology employed, the efficiency of a market is directly shaped by the institutional framework.

My initial effort to incorporate institutions into historical economic analysis resulted in two books, one with Lance Davis, *Institutional*

Change and American Economic Growth, published in 1971, and the other with Robert Thomas, *The Rise of the Western World: A New Economic History,* published in 1973. Both were early attempts to develop some tools of institutional analysis and apply them to economic history. In the study with Lance Davis on American economic growth we attempted to spell out the way new institutions and organizations evolved in the context of American economic growth. In the study of Europe we made the formation of property rights the key to economic performance and explored the constrasting way they evolved in the Netherlands and England on the one hand and France and Spain on the other.

Both studies were still predicated on the assumptions of neoclassical economic theory. But there were too many loose ends that did not make sense—such as the notion that institutions were efficient (however defined). Perhaps more serious, it was not possible to explain long-run poor economic performance in a neoclassical framework. So I began to explore what was wrong. Individual beliefs were obviously important to the choices people make, and only the extreme myopia of economists prevented them from understanding that ideas, ideologies, and prejudices mattered. Once you recognize that, you are forced to examine the rationality postulate critically. The long road towards a new analytical framework involved (1) developing a view of institutions that would account for why institutions produced results that in the long run did not manage to produce economic growth, as well as (2) developing a model of political economy in order to be able to explain the underlying source of institutions. Finally, one had to come to grips with why people had the ideologies and ideas that determined the choices they made.

It was Ronald Coase who provided a critical link which began to structure the evolving framework. In "The Nature of the Firm" Coase forced us to think about the cost of economic organization. But whereas Coase was concerned with the transaction costs that determined the existence of firms, I was concerned with the transaction costs that determined overall economic performance. George Stigler had once remarked to me that he thought the efficiency of economic organization had probably been as important as technological change in historical development. I was convinced that he was right. Transaction costs provided the wedge to examine the costs of economic organization. Coase's other critical contribution, "The Problem of Social Cost," provided the link to connect neoclassical theory to institutional analysis. The message of that essay was that when transaction costs were positive, institutions mattered and shaped the resultant market structure. I was fortunate in having several colleagues at the University of Washington who early on took Coase's work seriously. Steven Cheung, a student of Armen Alchian at UCLA, came to Seattle after a post-doctoral fellowship at Chicago where he became acquainted with Coase. Cheung made a number of important contributions to transaction cost theory—in particular his emphasis on the costs of measurement of the multiple dimensions of a good or service or of the performance of agents as a critical source of transaction costs (since imperfect measurement resulted in imperfectly specified property rights). Yoram Barzel continued work that Cheung began (after Cheung left to go to the University of Hong Kong). I have learned a great deal from both of them, and their influence is apparent in my next book.

In *Structure and Change in Economic History* (1981) I abandoned the notion that institutions were efficient and attempted to explain why "inefficient" rules would tend to exist and be perpetuated. In that study I began to explore the transaction costs underlying different forms of economic organization in history and also to explore the way ideologies altered free-riding to influence political and economic decisionmaking. The theoretical chapters were followed by eight historical chapters that outlined a fundamental reinterpretation of economic history from the origins of agriculture in the eighth millennium B.C. to the twentieth century.

I was still dissatisfied with our understanding of the political process, and indeed searched for colleagues who were interested in developing political–economic models. Margaret Levi, a Marxist political scientist, and I had developed a political economy program but there was little interest in the subject among the faculty. This led me to leave the University of Washington in 1983 after 33 years and to move to Washington University in St. Louis, where there was an exciting group of young political scientists and economists who were attempting to develop new models of political economy. This proved to be a felicitous move. I created the Center in Political Economy, which continues to be a creative research center.

The central theoretical puzzle about politics was reflected in the diverse and conflicting perspectives that had evolved from the public choice theory that originated with Buchanan and Tullock's *The Calculus of Consent,* Mancur Olson's *The Logic of Collective Action,* and Anthony Downs's *An Economic Theory of Democracy*—three classics of the new public choice literature. Was the polity simply a leviathan to be contained as Buchanan and the Virginia school of public choice suggested? That perspective made the state little more than a giant theft machine. But how did that perspective square with the property rights argument that I had developed which made the political creation of secure and productive property rights the key to economic growth? The problem was hardly new. *The Federalist Papers* of Madison, Hamilton, and Jay were a brilliant exposition of many of the issues. In effect, you can't do with the state but you can't do without it. At a deeper level of analysis, Arrow's disturbing impossibility theorem had implications for the entire process of aggregating choices. In effect, one cannot achieve collectively rational choices by aggregating the individual choices of people with diverse values and preferences.

These issues are far from resolved and pose fundamental problems for polities and, therefore, for economic performance. In *Structure and Change* I had developed a neoclassical theory of the state which confronted the issue of why a ruler would ever produce inefficient property rights when efficient rights would increase aggregate income and hence the revenue of the ruler. In effect a competitive constraint (the threat of being replaced by competitors for the ruler) and a transaction cost constraint (efficient rules might have so much higher costs of tax collection that the ruler's revenue was decreased) were the sources of inefficient rules.

In "A Transaction Cost Theory of Politics" (*The Journal of Theoretical Politics* 1 [1991]), I developed a more general model of why political markets are inherently less efficient than economic markets; here I used the basic transaction cost framework I had developed to explore economic markets.

Transaction costs are the costs of measuring and enforcing agreements. In economic markets there are objective criteria (size, weight, color, etc.) to measure the physical dimensions of the goods and services exchanged and legal criteria to measure the property rights dimensions. Enforcement is carried out by the judicial system. Competition is a powerful force to reduce transaction costs but still economic markets are beset by high transaction costs. But political markets are far more prone to inefficiency. What is being exchanged are promises for votes; the voter has little incentive to be informed since the likelihood that his/her vote counts is infinitesimal; there is no comparable enforcement mechanism; and competition is very imperfect. The complexity of the issues (together with the lack of incentives of voters to be informed) leads to ideological stereotyping taking over. In effect the incentives for efficiency are diluted by the structure of political markets and the complexity of the issues.

The development of a political economic framework to explore long-run institutional change occupied me during all of the 1980s and led to the publication of *Institutions, Institutional Change, and Economic Performance* in 1990. In that study I explicitly attempted to evolve a theory of institutional change. The first step was to separate institutions from organizations. The former are the rules of the game but the latter are the players. That is, organizations are made up of groups of individuals with some objective function. They are firms, trade unions, cooperatives (economic organizations); political parties, legislatures, regulatory agencies (political organizations); churches, athletic associations, clubs (social organizations). Organizations and their entrepreneurs in the pursuit of their objectives (whether the firm maximizing profits or the political party trying to win an election, etc.) are the agent of change. The organizations themselves have come into existence because of the opportunities resulting from the incentives of the institutional framework. In the world of scarcity and competition that characterizes economies, they are in competition to survive. That competition will lead them to try to modify the institutional framework to improve their competitive position. The intensity of competition will determine the rate of change of institutions, but the direction of change will reflect the perceptions of the actors—the mental models that they possess that interpret the external environment for them.

I used this framework to examine the contrasting development of the Netherlands and Britain, where polities evolved that produced the property rights that underpin modern economic growth, and of Spain, where secular stagnation ensued from the polity.

In that book I began to puzzle seriously about the rationality postulate. It is clear that we need an explanation for why people make the choices they do; why ideologies such as communism or Muslim fundamentalism can shape the choices people make and direct the way economies evolve through long periods of time. One simply cannot get at ideologies without digging deeply into cognitive science in attempting to understand the way in which the mind acquires learning and makes choices. Since 1990 my research has been directed toward dealing with this issue.

Herbert Simon was the pioneer who attempted to persuade social scientists to examine the actor's subjective perception of the real world. Simon maintained that if both the knowledge and computational power of the decisionmaker are severely limited then we must distinguish the real world from the actor's perception if we are going to understand the choices that he/she makes. Moreover we must theorize about the reasoning processes that generated the actor's subjective representation. However Simon's emphasis was on bounded rationality—the limits on the computational power of the decisionmaker, whereas my concern with ideologies focused more on the information available to the actor and the imperfect feedback that the actor received as a result of the choices he/she made.

An understanding of how human learning occurs appears to be the most promising approach to the mental constructs that humans develop to explain and interpret the world around them. But the learning is not just a product of the experiences of the individual in his or her lifetime, it also includes the cumulative experiences of past generations embodied in culture. Collective learning, according to Hayek, consists of those experiences that have passed the slow test of time and are embodied in our language, institutions, technology, and ways of doing things. The accumulated stock of knowledge of past experiences is built into our learning and is the deep underlying source of path dependence—the powerful influence of the past on the present and future. Learning then is an incremental process filtered by the culture of a society that determines the perceived pay-offs, but there is no guarantee that the cumulative past experiences of a society will necessarily fit them to solve new problems. The learning process then appears to be a function of (1) the way in which a given belief system filters the information derived from experiences and (2) the different experiences confronting individuals and societies at different times.

This cognitive science/institutional approach to history offers the promise of making sense out of the economic past and the diverse performance of economies in the present. There is nothing automatic about evolving the conditions that will result in low-cost transacting in the impersonal markets that are essential to productive economies. Game theory characterizes the issue. Individuals usually will find it worthwhile cooperating with others in exchange when the play is repeated, when there is complete information about the other player's past performance, and when there are small numbers of players—in short the conditions that characterize small-scale societies with personalized exchange. Cooperation is difficult to sustain when the game is not repeated (or there is an end game), when information about the other players is lacking, and when there are large numbers of players—in short the conditions that characterize the interdependent world of impersonal exchange of modern productive economies. Creating the institutions that will alter the benefit-cost ratios in favor of cooperative solutions is the major issue of economic performance because it entails the creation of effective, that is productive, economic and political institutions. And given the inherent inefficiency of political markets and the key role that political institutions play in economic performance it is not surprising that economic performance through time has been less than satisfactory.

We still have a long way to go, but I believe that an understanding of how people make choices, under what conditions the rationality postulate is a useful tool, and how individuals make choices under conditions of uncertainty and ambiguity are fundamental issues that we must address in order to make further progress in the social sciences.

In 1972 I married again, to Elisabeth Case; she continues to be wife, companion, critic, and editor: a partner in the projects and programs that we undertake. It is as critic and editor that she has directly played an important part in my evolution as an economist. She has transformed my indifferent prose into good English, but more important, she has an unerring sense of when I have not thought out completely what I am trying to say and forces me to confront those ambiguities and confusions and clarify my thinking.

I would be remiss if I left the impression that my life has been totally occupied with scholarly research. My evolution as an economist has taken place within the larger context of a rich and varied life. True, economic research has been the fundamental focus of my life, but it has been intermingled with a variety of activities that have complemented that central preoccupation and enriched my life. I continue to be a photographer; I have enjoyed fishing and hunting with a close friend; and I have owned two ranches, first in northern California and then in the state of Washington. I learned to fly an airplane, and had my own airplane during the 1960s. I have always taken seriously good food and wine. In addition, music has continued to be an important part of my life.

My wife and I now live in the summers in northern Michigan in an environment which is wonderfully conducive to research, and where most of my work in the last fifteen years has been done. I work on research all morning. In the afternoons I hike with my dog, play tennis, or go swimming. In the evening, as we are only 16 miles from the Interlochen Music Camp, we listen to music as often as two or three nights a week. It is a wonderful place for that mixture of research and leisure which has made my life such a rich experience.

Awarded Nobel Prize in 1993. Lecture presented October 25, 1994.

Date of Birth

November 5, 1920

Academic Degrees

B.A.   University of California, Berkeley, 1942

Ph.D. University of California, Berkeley, 1952

Academic Affiliations

Acting Assistant Professor, University of Washington, 1950–1951

Assistant Professor, University of Washington, Seattle, 1951–1956

Associate Professor, University of Washington, Seattle, 1956–1960

Visiting Associate Professor, Stanford University, 1958

Professor of Economics, University of Washington, 1960–1983

Pitt Professor of American Institutions, Cambridge University, 1981–1982

Henry R. Luce Professor of Law and Liberty and Professor of Economics and of History, Washington University in St. Louis, 1983–present

Selected Books

The Economic Growth of the United States, 1790–1860, 1961

Growth and Welfare in the American Past: A New Economic History, 1966, 1983

Institutional Change and American Economic Growth, 1971 (with L. Davis)

The Rise of the Western World: A New Economic History, 1973 (with R. Thomas)

Structure and Change in Economic History, 1981

Institutions, Institutional Change, and Economic Performance, 1990

John C. Harsanyi

An Unusual Journey[1]

I was born May 29, 1920, in Budapest, Hungary. I attended the Lutheran Gymnasium in Budapest, one of the best high schools in Hungary, with such distinguished alumni as John von Neumann and Eugene Wigner. I was very happy at this school and received a superb education. In 1937, the year I graduated, I won the First Prize in Mathematics at the Hungary-wide annual competition for high school students. These mathematics competitions were a very important part of Hungarian high school education.

My parents owned a pharmacy, which provided us with a comfortable living. As I was their only child they wanted me to become a pharmacist, but my own preference had been to study philosophy and mathematics. When I actually had to decide my field of study, in 1937, I ended up choosing pharmacy, in accordance with my parents' wishes. I did so because Hitler was in power in Germany and his influence was steadily increasing in Hungary. As a pharmacy student, I would obtain a military deferment. Because I was of Jewish origin, I would otherwise have had to serve in a forced labor unit of the Hungarian army.

As a result of my choice to study pharmacy, I received a military deferment. But after the German army occupied Hungary in March 1944, I had to serve in a labor unit, from May to November 1944, when the Nazi authorities decided to deport my labor unit from Budapest to an Austrian concentration camp. I was lucky to escape from the railway station in Budapest, just before our train left for Austria. Most of my comrades eventually perished. I was far more fortunate. A Jesuit priest I had known provided me with refuge in the cellar of his monastery.

In 1946, following the war, I re-enrolled at the University of Budapest in order to obtain a Ph.D. in philosophy, with minors in sociology and psychology. I received credit for my prior studies in pharmacy, enabling me to get my Ph.D. in June of 1947, after writing a philosophy dissertation. From November 1947 to June 1948, I served as a junior faculty member at the University Institute of Sociology. It was at the Institute that I met Anne Klauber, a psychology student who later became my wife. Anne attended one of my courses. She was once late and I told her, "Young lady, you do not know that this class starts at 9 o'clock; it's 9: 15 now." She got very angry. But, as events unfolded, her anger eased and we became close.

Political pressure cut short my tenure at the Institute. It was not enough that I was an anti-Marxist. I also felt compelled to coin bad jokes at the expense of my Communist colleagues. They accepted this quite graciously at first, but over time they increasingly became annoyed with Anne and me. Eventually, the political situation no longer permitted them to employ an outspoken anti-Marxist, as I was, and in June of 1948 I had to resign from the Institute. Anne did get on with her studies, despite being continually harassed by her Communist classmates, who urged her to break up with me because of my political views. She did not do so. But the harassment made her realize, before I did, that Hungary was becoming a completely Stalinist country. The only sensible course of action was to leave Hungary.

We left Hungary, but not until April of 1950. The reason for the delay was that my father's pharmacy had been transferred to my name. My father had done so because he was ill, and wanted to make sure that I would eventually gain control of the pharmacy. If I were to leave Hungary, the pharmacy—now in my name—would be immediately confiscated by the Communist authorities. Therefore, we waited. Once we learned from reliable sources that pharmacies would be confiscated anyhow, within six weeks or so, it made sense to leave.

In order to leave, we needed to find a guide who, for good money, was willing to take us to Austria. We found a guide and left for Austria. This looked to be a relatively simple trip because our guide was a native of the border region of Hungary. It did not turn out that way. There is a lake near the border, which in the spring floods a large countryside. We brought some rubber boots. These were very good for walking, even in the very marshy terrain, except for the fact that they continually got stuck in the mud. Each of us had to pull them out by hand, which made us rather tired. This would not have been so big a problem had our guide not lost his way. He expected us to complete the trip over one night. Instead, it took three nights and the intervening two days to get there. We had enough food for 24 hours. After that time, we did not have enough food and had to drink muddy water to survive. But, eventually, we arrived at the border, crossing a little rivulet with his help.

At daybreak we confronted our next problem. We noticed that we were near to a highway, which we then climbed up. Much to our horror, we then saw that there was a Hungarian watchtower just behind us. It was not a perfect advantage that my wife had worn red clothes, very obviously visible from the Hungarian side. They could have shot at us, but nothing happened. We made our way to the first Austrian village, where the in-habitants spoke both German and Hungarian. They helped us get to a public bus, which took us to Vienna. The only problem was that the policemen, or *gendarmes* (the area was Russian occupied), had instruc-tions to hand over all persons looking like refugees to the Russian military authorities. Luckily, we saw no gendarmes when we arrived in Vienna, and we thought we were safe. Somebody then told us: "Do you know you are still in the Russian-occupied zone? If you go over to the other side, to the American zone, you will be okay." And so, that is what we did, and we were okay.

We wanted to go to Sydney, Australia, where Anne's parents had some friends who had previously emigrated from Hungary. We had to wait several months for our Australian immigration papers. When we got the permits, we traveled by ship to Sydney, along with Anne's parents, where we arrived the 30th of December 1950. Anne and I wanted to get married immediately but, since the New Year was near, all offices were closed. Anne and I had not married previously because her immigration papers were under her maiden name and, if she had married me, her name would have changed and the whole immigration procedure would have started anew. We returned to Sydney on January 2nd and went to the registration office where we could be married. Based on European customs, we expected that we would need to sign a form saying that we want to get married and then advertise this fact for two weeks or so. This would allow anybody so inclined to raise an objection to a marriage, for instance, because one of the persons was already married, because the man and woman were first cousins, or something similar. But when we requested to be married we were told: "Look, we are busy now, but come back in twenty minutes and then you can get married." And so we went back. It cost us something like two or three dollars, but we had enough money. I then realized that we spoke virtually no English and tried to communicate this concern. The registrar said, "Look, just repeat the words that I am telling you." I did not understand very much of what he said and Anne did not either. I told her that she had promised to make much better food for me than she usually did. So, we were married and everything was all right. Anne was not only my spouse, but she gave me unfailing emotional support. Her practical good sense always has been a very great help to me.

I was not an immediate success in Australia. My English was not very good and my Hungarian university degrees in pharmacy and philosophy were not recognized in Australia. It was clear that I would have to do factory work, which I did on and off for three years. Often I was unemployed because my manual skills were very deficient. I typically could not keep any factory job for more than a few days. Sometimes I would keep a job for a couple of weeks, but this was the exception. I would not have been able to survive during these periods of unemployment, except that Anne's parents, who were in their fifties, were staying with us. Anne was also working, so that the three of them could support me when I was unemployed. This was of course a great help to me.

At the same time as I was doing factory work during the day, I enrolled at the University of Sydney as an evening student. I did so as a student in economics. It would have been more natural for me to study sociology since in the last few months in Hungary I had studied sociology. But in the meantime I had become much more interested in economics—I loved the logical elegance of economic theory. Although the university did not recognize my degrees as such, I was awarded very generous credit for my Hungarian academic work. Instead of the usual four years required to get an economics degree in Australia, the university permitted me to complete only two years of course work and then write a master's thesis.

After receiving my M.A. degree in economics in late 1953, I applied for a position as Lecturer, not in Sydney, but at the University of Queensland in Brisbane, and I immediately got this position. The reason was twofold. First, I had an M.A. degree, while the other candidates had only B.A.s. The other reason was that British and American journals had accepted my papers and promised to publish them.

And so we did get to Brisbane. Living in Brisbane presented a couple of problems, although these were not serious. The first problem for us was that Anne's parents had come with us to Australia to live with us in the same city. Now we were living in another city. A second problem was that Brisbane, while a very nice city, has a hot and humid climate during the summer and the summer lasts for seven months. But we managed. Anne learned how to design women's frocks and became a frock designer for a small factory. Indeed, we made a good living combining her earnings with my academic salary.

We were in Brisbane from early 1954 until the middle of 1956, at which time I was awarded a Rockefeller Fellowship. The fellowship enabled Anne and myself to be Stanford students for two years. During that time I got a Ph.D. in Economics, with Ken Arrow being my dissertation supervisor. Following his advice, I spent much of my time at Stanford studying mathematics and statistics. Anne got an M.A. from Stanford in Child Psychology/Child Development. My student visa expired in 1958 and, whether we wanted to or not, we had to go back to Australia. Actually, we went back quite willingly because I knew with a Stanford Ph.D. I would get a very good job in Australia, which I did. I became what I call a Senior Fellow at the Australian National University in Canberra. This was a very prestigious and high-paying job that involved only research, which I preferred to teaching routine courses.

Although there were some quite good economists at the Australian National University, they had no interest whatsoever in game theory. Some did not even know what it was. I felt rather isolated and wrote to two of my American friends, Ken Arrow and Jim Tobin, two subsequent Nobel prize winners. I asked for their help in getting an American position. They recommended and helped me obtain an appointment at Wayne

State University in Detroit, and we moved back to America in 1961. In 1964, I moved to a position at the University of California at Berkeley, where I spent most of my career.

A Life of Research—From Nash to Selten

Let me now discuss my research. I begin by describing my research in Australia between our first arrival in Sydney in 1950 and our departure from Brisbane for Stanford in 1956. It was during that period that I started working on two subjects that have occupied me ever since.

One topic was utilitarian ethics, which I will discuss first, and the other was game theory. I published two papers in the *Journal of Political Economy*, one in 1953 ("Cardinal Utility in Welfare Economics and in the Theory of Risk-taking") and the other in 1955 ("Cardinal Welfare, Individualistic Ethics, and Interpersonal Comparisons of Utility"), where I argued that if you want to understand moral problems, you must distinguish between people's *personal preferences*, based on their personal interest, and their *moral preferences*, based on unbiased and impartial criteria (in other words, on moral criteria). Let me try to explain to you how personal preferences work. Suppose that you learn that a new mayor will take up duties in San Antonio. You tell your friend that you welcome the new mayor and think that it is a good thing that he has been elected. Now when your friend asks you why you prefer the new mayor to somebody else, you can give two different types of answers. One is that the new mayor is likely to introduce changes that will benefit you personally—for instance, your business situation will improve because of the changes the new mayor introduces. Well, in this case, you must say that your preferences are based on selfish or personal preferences, not on moral considerations.

The other answer you might give your friend is that you think the new mayor will do a lot of good for almost everyone in the city, independent of any direct impact his actions will have on you. Then you can say that your preferences are based on moral preferences or considerations. In my 1953 and 1955 papers, I argued that the main task of ethics is to understand the difference between people's personal preferences, which usually are not based on any altruistic considerations, and their moral preferences, which are based on moral or impartial criteria and not on self interest.

In order to develop a logical, mathematically precise theory of ethics you need some specific definition of what it means to be partial or impartial. I proposed that your preferences are impartial if you satisfy certain mathematical criteria. One such mathematical criterion would be that you are not influenced by your own personal position but are influenced by impartial considerations. One way to explain this is to say that we are considering a society which has *n* members; you can imagine that you rank these *n* members as the first, second, third, fourth, and so on to the end. The first person is in the best or most-favorable position, the second person is in the second-best position, and so forth. If you are really impartially motivated, then you have to make the choice as if you had the same probability, whatever the end, of being in any one of the social positions. For instance, suppose somebody asks you to choose between capitalism and socialism. Then you should make a choice as if you did not know which particular position you would be in. You are impartial if you do not know in advance whether you will be in a more favorable position under capitalism or in a more favorable position under socialism. Stated more precisely, in making your choice, it is assumed that you have the same probability of being in any one of the possible social positions.

And so it was these ideas that I eventually developed into a utilitarian theory of ethics and, more particularly, a rule utilitarian theory of ethics. As I have explained, this means that you develop an ethical theory based on moral rules that best serve the interest of all individual members of society and do it in an impartial way, without giving more weight to any individual's interest than to any other individual's interest.

Another important interest of mine was game theory. My interest was aroused by three brilliant articles of John Nash, one of the other two people with whom I was awarded the Nobel Prize. Nash published these articles in the period between 1950 and 1953. These influential papers were: "The Bargaining Problem" (*Econometrica*, 1950), "Noncooperative Games" (*Annals of Mathematics*, 1951), and "Two-Person Cooperative Games" (*Econometrica*, 1953).

I remember that when I had studied economics at the University of Sydney, I had been very disappointed to learn that classical economists did not provide a unique rational solution for the bargaining problem. In other words, suppose that you own a particular house and would like to sell it at a good price. Now suppose that you will not sell it for below $100,000—that is the minimum selling price you would ask. On the other hand, the person who most wants to buy your house will not pay more for it than $200,000. One would like to have a theory that can predict whether the eventual price would be closer to $100,000 or to $200,000, or what conditions determine whether it would be close to the lower limit or upper limit. Much to my disappointment, classical economic theory could not answer this seemingly simple question about price determination. I was very impressed to find that John Nash had a very clear mathematical answer to the question, and this answer was based on certain axioms that looked to me to be very plausible.

I also studied Nash's papers on bargaining very closely. The result was a paper that I published in 1956 in *Econometrica* ("Approaches to the Bargaining Problem Before and After the Theory of Games: A Critical Discussion of Zeuthen's, Hicks's, and Nash's Theories"). In this paper, I first of all found clear mathematical criteria for what determines whether the threats of two bargaining parties are really the best possible threats from their own points of view, thus providing a clear definition of optimal threat. I also showed that Nash's bargaining theory happened to be mathematically equivalent to a much earlier bargaining theory by the Danish economist Zeuthen, who published his theory in a 1930 book (*Problems of Monopoly and Economic Warfare*).

Another paper of mine ("A Bargaining Model for the Cooperative *n*-Person Game," 1959), also due to my study of Nash's work, addressed the so-called Shapley value, an important concept in game theory. This concept tells you how people are likely to divide a certain pie depending on how much each can make. But instead of having just two people to divide the pie, I looked at the more difficult question of how the shares of multiple parties, let's say ten people, might be determined. How the pie will be divided depends on how much money each coalition or possible combination of people can separately make. Thus, you want to know how much each player can make by himself, and how much players one and two together make, or five and six together make, how much each three person coalition can make, and so on. This is an interesting mathematical problem and Shapley found a good solution for it. But his theory was restricted to games in which people can transfer utility from one person to the other. He assumed that you could give five dollars to somebody else and he will be better off by five utility points, and if you give him ten dollars he will get ten units of utility. In other words, total utility does not increase or decrease when you transfer money from one to the other.

This was a very restrictive condition, but it was a great thing that he could devise a solution for the problem under these simplified conditions. I extended the Shapley value to games in which this simple condition does not hold, that is, without transferable utility. I also showed that the new generalized Shapley value was a generalization both of the original Shapley value and of Nash's bargaining solution for games in which threats, or so-called variable threats, play an important role. My paper united the two branches of game theory—the two-person "maximize the product of gains" solution of Zeuthen–Nash and the Shapley value solution for n-person games—within a coherent single model. Subsequent literature in the field then modified and extended my synthesis.

Now let me talk about another game theoretical problem that I tried to solve. Here the problem was to find a solution for games with incomplete information. Let me tell you what this involves. In classical game theory you always basically know what kind of opponent you have. You play, let's say, a tennis match against the other fellow and you know what his abilities are. The outcome of the match will be partly a matter of chance, along with other conditions such as skill and training. But your strategy is based on complete information about the type of player you face. Of course, the theorist does not know beforehand the strategies each player will use against the other, but he does know that once player 1 uses the third strategy and player 2 uses the fifth strategy, the outcome is determined and known. This is what classical game theory always assumed.

But there are important games where complete information is not the case. Let me digress for a moment. I first realized the importance of the incomplete information problem when I arrived in Berkeley as a young faculty member in 1964. A few weeks later I was approached by a representative from the government arms control agency. In those days everyone knew there was a big danger of atomic war between the U.S. and the Soviet Union, so both sides tried to overcome this problem by having arms control disarmament negotiations. The United States government set up a special agency for this purpose, called the Arms Control and Disarmament Agency; they hired about ten young game theorists to advise them how to make these discussions more fruitful and successful. We were asked to meet in Washington, D.C., about three times a year. In the meantime we worked on the disarmament problem. We would read our papers to each other and criticize each other. Then the unfortunate members of the arms control agency had to listen to us, too. I do not think our efforts had any practical effects on policy, but we did help advance the theory of games.

During this period I soon realized that there were some very fundamental reasons explaining why such information problems could not be easily overcome. The basic problem was that we did not know what kind of opponent we had. In normal games you know a lot about your opponents and therefore you know what to expect. But in the case of arms control negotiations we did not know whether our opponent was a Russian player who was basically a decent man and just wanted peaceful coexistence, or if our opponent was a Russian fellow who wanted only to gain time to attack the United States unexpectedly and get us into an atomic war. And, of course, in those scenarios, all sorts of intermediate possibilities are possible. Just what kind of Russian fellow we were meeting in the negotiations we could not tell in advance. Also, we did not know what the Russian capabilities were in developing new weapons. We usually assumed that the Russians would not invent very interesting new weapons in the near future, but we could not tell, and sometimes they actually did invent new things.

So, the whole problem was to find a mathematical model to represent games with incomplete information. The basic model is this: Let's assume there are, say, ten different types of possible Russian players and that the Americans can have eight different types. So, you have to develop such a mathematical model with ten different types for the Russians (types R1, R2, R3, up to R10) and eight different types for the Americans (types A1, A2, A3, up to A8). For example, type 1 of the Americans could meet type 5 of the Russians. We then form a model in which chance will decide which particular type of Russian will meet which particular type of American.

Once you define this clearly you can solve the problem. My work along these lines gave rise to a whole theory of games with incomplete information. I developed this theory in a long paper, which had to be published in three parts, in *Management Science*, because it was too long to publish in one issue ("Games with Incomplete Information Played by 'Bayesian' Players, I, II, III," 1967–1968). In these papers, I showed that any game with incomplete information can be transformed into a game with complete yet imperfect information. This was done as I have described, by this method of defining types for both players and asking what is the probability that a particular type of combination will come into being. I showed that once you use this model you can actually convert a game with incomplete information to a game with more complete information. Therefore the two are really equivalent, and it became possible to solve this problem with game-theoretic analysis.

After I published these papers it took some time, of course, for other game theorists to read the work and understand it. There was a lot of discussion, but by around 1975 the theory of games with incomplete information was increasingly used and after awhile completely transformed game theory. It was this particular work of mine, whose last piece was published in 1968, which twenty-six years later the Nobel Committee cited when they decided to award me the 1994 Nobel Prize in Economics.

As you know, I shared the 1994 Nobel Prize with John Nash and Reinhard Selten. Earlier in my essay, I spoke about the large impact that Nash's brilliant articles had in stimulating my early interests in game theory. Just as Nash greatly influenced my early work in game theory, I have had the privilege of working off and on with Reinhard Selten during much of my career. For example, early on we worked together for the Arms Control and Disarmament Agency, described previously, and subsequently worked closely together during Selten's visits to Berkeley and my visits to the University of Bielefeld. Following my retirement, Selten, with the assistance of H. W. Brock, edited the volume *Rational Interaction* (1992) in my honor. The last book I published, *A General Theory of Equilibrium Selection in Games*, published in 1988, was coauthored with Selten following many years of joint work. Receiving the Nobel Prize has not only been a great honor, but sharing it with John Nash and Reinhard Selten provides a particularly fitting set of bounds that spans my life as an economist.

Awarded Nobel Prize in 1994. Lecture presented March 5, 1997.

Dates of Birth and Death

May 29, 1920; August 9, 2000

Academic Degrees

Pharmacology, University of Budapest, 1944

Ph.D. Philosophy and Sociology, University of Budapest, 1947

M.A. Economics, University of Sydney, 1953

Ph.D. Economics, Stanford University, 1959

Academic Affiliations

University Assistant in Philosophy, University of Budapest, 1947–1948

Lecturer in Economics, University of Queensland, Brisbane, Australia, 1954–1956

Senior Fellow, Australian National University, 1959–1961

Professor of Economics, Wayne State University, 1961–1963

Visiting Professor of Economics and Business Administration, University of California, Berkeley, 1964

Professor of Economics and Business Administration, University of California, Berkeley, 1965–1990

Visiting Professor, University of Bielefeld, 1973–1974, 1978–1979

Professor of Economics and Business Administration, Emeritus, University of California, Berkeley, 1990–2000

Selected Books

Essays on Ethics, Social Behavior, and Scientific Explanation, 1976

Rational Behavior and Bargaining Equilibrium in Games and Social Situations, 1977

Papers in Game Theory, 1982

A General Theory of Equilibrium Selection in Games, 1988 (with R. Selten)

Myron S. Scholes

I was born in Timmins, Ontario, Canada, on July 1, 1941. My only brother, David, was born five years later. My father was born in New York City but moved to Toronto as a young man to live with his older brother. After graduation as a dentist and after a start as a teacher at the Eastman Clinic in Rochester, New York, that was cut short by the Great Depression, my father ventured to Timmins, a relatively prosperous gold-mining region in northern Ontario, to practice dentistry in 1930. This was targeted as a temporary move until the depression ended. His temporary move, however, lasted for twenty-five years. My mother had a longer journey to arrive in Canada. As a result of the many purges in Russia, as a two-year-old she had fled with her parents to Canada around 1908 and settled in South Porcupine, a very small town six miles south of Timmins.

As a young woman, my mother and her uncle established a successful chain of small department stores in and around Timmins. At its height, they employed over 1,000 employees in approximately ten stores.

In 1941, the year I was born, her uncle left by train for Toronto, 500 miles to the south, to formalize the legal relations among my mother and her family and her uncle and his family. Unfortunately, her uncle died on the train trip before any of the agreements could be formalized. The death of her uncle resulted in a family dispute, my first exposure to agency and contracting problems. Although it was not an equitable distribution, her uncle's sons-in-law claimed all of the stores registered in his name as their own, forcing my mother out of a large fraction of the business. This episode always fascinated me. After turning over the stores that happened to be in her name to others on her side of the family who worked in the business, she devoted her efforts to raising me and subsequently my brother while running the rest of the family business on the side.

I was always very proud of my mother's business accomplishments. It was quite an achievement in those days for a woman to run an organization, let alone one in northern Canada. As you might imagine she was a powerful woman, a family leader, and insightful in subjects pertaining to business and in dealing with others.

My father was a scholar, an extremely intelligent man, who was well read in many diverse subjects. When I was young, he seemed to know everything. He was respected for his work; his personality was the exact opposite of that of my mother's. He was a quiet, gentle, but firm man. To my parents, education, learning, thinking, and discussing issues were of prime importance. And, given my love of participating and learning, I thrived in this environment.

As you might imagine, Timmins was a small town. There were about 25,000 people in Timmins, then and today. The temperature fell to 40 below zero at times in the winter. The summers were short, maybe lasting from late June to early September. The town and region were famous for mining gold and silver. The town produced great hockey players. In more recent years, Timmins has become famous because of Shania Twain, the country and western singer. She was born there as well. I think that I am the only Nobel Prize winner. I was once asked to appear on a television program with Shania, but I turned the opportunity down. I suspected that her economics was as good as my singing.

Because I was outstripping the school system in Timmins, my parents sought a greater challenge for us. At the age of ten, I moved with my family to Hamilton, Ontario, thirty miles outside of Toronto. Thankfully it was much warmer in Hamilton than Timmins, but it still wasn't Florida. I had opted for Florida, but my father could not receive a license there without significant payoffs or a lengthy return to school.

Although I was a good student, I didn't really realize it until my first year of high school, when I was forced to work on my own at home for three months because I was sick with pneumonia. I still ended the year near the top of my class, as I did throughout my high school years. I attended public schools in both Timmins and Hamilton. In Ontario, at that time, your first year of college was also your last year of high school (that is, grade 13). I was class representative throughout my high school years and valedictorian of the senior class. I enjoyed school but did not take it too seriously. I would spend a considerable amount of time playing poker or chess with my classmates. I was even the trainer for the high school football team. Although I enjoyed puzzles and financial issues, I did not have a life's plan.

The educational system was excellent. In high school, I completed subjects in algebra, trigonometry, geometry, and calculus, as well as physics, chemistry, and biology. I scored extremely high in physics and the university in Hamilton solicited me to enter their engineering program.

Soon after we arrived in Hamilton, my life changed dramatically. My mother developed cancer. She died five years later, a few days after my sixteenth birthday. Another shock, but of much less import, befell me. I developed keratoconus, a condition in which scar tissue developed on each of my corneas and impaired my eyesight. It became difficult for me to read for extended periods of time. Because of this, I learned to think abstractly and to conceptualize the solution to problems. Out of necessity, I became a good listener—a quality appreciated by subsequent associates and students. Luckily, at age twenty-six, a successful cornea transplant greatly improved my vision in my right eye. I have had a subsequent cornea transplant in my left eye as well.

Through my parents, especially my mother, I became interested in economics and, in particular, finance. As I mentioned, my mother loved business and discussed stocks, world events, and finance in general whenever there was an opportunity to do so. Before she died, she suggested that I consider joining her brother in his book-publishing and promotion business. During my teenage years, I was always treasurer of my various clubs; I traded extensively among my friends; I gambled to understand probabilities and risks. I invested in the stock market while in high school and university through accounts set up first by my mother and then by my father. I was fascinated with the determinants of the level of stock prices. I spent long hours reading reports and books to glean the secrets of successful investing, but, alas, to no avail. The Holy Grail still awaits me.

I did mention that I loved physics. I loved solving complex problems. So I was torn between physics and economics. During the summer after my senior year of high school, however, I realized why I would not become a physicist. While working for my uncle's firm, I designed a puzzle for a magazine sold to teenage girls. I worked on this puzzle for weeks to make it interesting but difficult. When I presented it to the board and editorial committee of the magazine, no one understood what I had done. I decided then and there that I really enjoyed working with people, being involved in activities that were direct and not too abstract, removed or singular. I came to realize that I loved creating with others and working on problems that had real-world applications. For me, the most rewarding activities have always been conceptualizing difficult problems and then immersing myself in the details to test my theories.

Because of my mother's death, I decided to remain in Hamilton and attend McMaster University, a school close to my home, for my undergraduate studies. At that time, there were approximately 2,000 students attending McMaster University. Although the McMaster University entrance committee thought that I would concentrate in physics or engineering, I decided instead to concentrate on economics and the liberal arts. McMaster does have one other Nobel Prize winner, a physicist. There, I worked as a reporter and advertising manager of the school paper and yearbook and was a referee for the intramural football league, although I can't remember why, for my eyesight was not particularly good.

McMaster turned out to be a fortuitous choice. Because it was such a small school, Professor McIver, a University of Chicago graduate in economics, worked closely with me in my studies. He directed me to read and understand the work of many classical economists, including the more contemporary teachings of Milton Friedman and George Stigler, two subsequent Nobel Prize winners in economics. I was impressed with their writings.

Upon graduation in 1962, I was deciding between entering law school or graduate school in economics. After considerable thought, I decided to follow my mother's wishes and join my uncle in his publishing business on the condition that I complete my studies in a graduate program. Because of my enjoyment of economics and my planned return to business, I decided on business school, not law school. Although my family wanted me to apply to other schools, such as Harvard, I wanted to go only to the University of Chicago, where Stigler and Friedman were teaching and conducting research.

I had learned an important lesson, maybe at McMaster University. Intuitively, I knew that if I wanted to grow and achieve my potential, I should learn and work with those who were the best and who could bring out the best in me. That strategy has become a cornerstone of my career. I have always tried to go where the best were located. My thought at the time was that this would enable me to "steal" knowledge from them, but I subsequently realized that I had to contribute to the interchange of ideas to enable me to learn from others.

Chicago was a marvelous school for me. I did not know what awaited me on my arrival. During my first year at Chicago, I met a few classmates, who would become life-long friends, and from whom I have learned and continue to learn a tremendous amount over the years. In particular, Michael Jensen and Richard Roll, both in the Ph.D. program in finance, who have become world-renowned scholars in their own right and should also be awarded the Nobel Prize, added immeasurably to my understanding of economics and finance. Marshall Blum and Joel Stern were significant contributors to my learning and growth. I credit Jack Gould, who later became Dean of the Graduate School of Business, for helping me clarify many of the finer points of economic reasoning.

The summer of 1963, my first summer at Chicago, changed the direction of my life forever. During the first year at Chicago I had worked on a project for my uncle. I evaluated the possibility of buying a children's book company called Golden Books. My recommendation to buy what was then a wonderful franchise but a mismanaged company, was turned down for other than economic reasons. Once again I understood agency problems. As a result, I decided not to return to my uncle's company.

For that first summer, although I had never programmed before nor knew what a computer was, I secured a junior computer-programming position at Chicago through the kindness of Dean Robert Graves. On telling him that I knew nothing about computers or programming, he said that I did not have to worry: I was the "number seven" programmer and I would learn to program over the course of the summer by interacting with the other programmers.

I was the only one who showed up in the office. During my first few days on the job, several professors asked for computer-programming assistance on their research projects. I was able to fend them off by arguing that the senior programmers would soon be on scene to assist them, as I was only the "number-seven" programmer. The other programmers, however, never did show up.

By the third day, I could no longer fend off the aggressive professors seeking programming assistance. On confronting Dean Graves, he informed me that I, a novice, was the only "programmer" left. He pointed me in the direction of the computer facility some six blocks from the school, and I was on my way. I spent the next four and one-half months falling in love with computers and with the researchers that I met that summer. I must have been one of the first computer nerds; I worked all hours of the day and night. Computers were far more primitive in 1963. We had to program in native languages. But by the end of that summer, I was becoming a computer wizard, a skill that I would continue to develop over many years. If Chicago had had a computer science school, or if computer science had been a more developed field, I might have been tempted to become a computer scientist instead of an economist. Programming allowed me to conceptualize solutions to problems and then apply the solutions to demonstrate the actual results.

Another powerful force, however, had taken hold of me that summer: the love of economics and economic research. I was mesmerized by how the professors who were my computer clients created and addressed their own research projects. This was empowering. They enjoyed the process; they were absorbed by discovery. From time to time I ventured to ask them to explain their research, and occasionally I made suggestions on how to improve the research design. Lester Telser and Peter Pashigian were two of my clients. Merton Miller and Eugene Fama, two energetic and creative financial economics professors were clients as well. Merton Miller was awarded the Nobel Prize in economics in 1990, and Eugene Fama certainly deserves the award as well. At times, they were quite frustrated when I provided them with research output that they did not seek, but I thought that they would find interesting. They became my mentors, shaping my understanding of finance. And, fortunately, both became lifelong friends.

Either because of my scholastic qualities or because he did not want to lose me as a programmer, Merton Miller suggested that I enter the Ph.D. program. I did, and I came to love economics and its young new branch, which has come to be called financial economics. Chicago provided me with a wonderful learning environment. Miller and Fama were blazing ahead in financial economics. Stigler was leading the way in a new field of economics called "information economics." Friedman was fighting on in the macroeconomic front, persuading us that Keynesian economics was based on false economic rigidities.

I became interested in relative asset prices and the degree to which arbitrage prevented economic agents from earning abnormal profits in security markets. My province became risk and return. I concentrated my economics research during 1965–1978 on attempts to understand the trade-offs between risk and return in both frictionless and friction-filled economies. I made tremendous progress in this area.

My Ph.D. dissertation, for example, attempted to determine the shape of the demand curve for traded securities. Since, as I reasoned, risk and return characteristics were the features that distinguish one security from another, the extent of the market was far greater than that of the individual stock. It was new information that would cause a change in the price of the security, information that was signaled by the large sale by an informed investor. This was the first statement in finance of a rational expectations approach to understanding economic activity. That is, only new information could change the demand for securities, not whether an individual wanted to sell more or less of a particular security.

After formulating the theory, careful empirical tests provided evidence that the prices of securities change not because of a movement along a demand curve with increases in supply, but because of changes in the information set that affect valuations. Temporary supply/demand imbalances exist because of the time necessary for speculators to assess the importance of the new information, not the size of the sale itself. Even to this day, there is considerable confusion between attributing movement along a demand curve and changes in the positioning of the entire curve. For example, the effectiveness of "operation twist" during the 1960s, wherein the U.S. Treasury attempted to encourage long rates to fall in order to foster investment while retaining higher short-term rates, is only one of many examples along these lines.

In addition, I worked on measures of risk and the effect of differential risk on security returns in a paper with Merton Miller. I studied the relation between accounting and market-determined measures of risk in another paper with William Beaver and Paul Kettler.

After essentially finishing my Ph.D. dissertation in the fall of 1968, I became an assistant professor of finance at the Sloan School of Management at MIT. I had two job offers in 1968, one at MIT for $10,000 and one at the University of Texas at Austin for $17,500. I told MIT that $10,000 was too low a salary, and they increased it to $10,500. I went to MIT, but not for the pay. My professors wanted me to go to MIT for seasoning and to grow on my own. The next year, when MIT gave me a raise of only $250, I thought that I had failed as an MIT professor. But, the dean informed me that, on the contrary, the faculty was proud of my successes and that I had achieved one of the highest increases in salary that year. Given my scholarships at Chicago, I had made more per year after taxes as a graduate student at Chicago. I knew that MIT was going to be expensive. And again, relative, not absolute, pricing came to the fore.

Paul Cootner, Franco Modigliani, and Stewart Myers became my colleagues at the Sloan School. During my first year at Sloan I met Fischer Black, then a consultant working for Arthur D. Little in Cambridge. We hit it off immediately. We had many lengthy discussions about financial economics and research needs in the area. As a result of these discussions, we started to collaborate on many research projects. It was an extremely productive relationship for both of us. We would spend endless hours discussing financial economics, its models, how to test economic relations and the failings of economics to incorporate risk into economic models with sufficient prominence. In our minds, risk was a first-order consideration.

Although Paul Cootner unfortunately left the Sloan School in 1969, Robert Merton joined our group at that time. As you are aware, Robert Merton was my co-recipient of the Nobel Prize in 1997. Essentially, the senior faculty members in finance were not available to work with us; that is, Franco Modigliani was involved in large macro projects and Dan Holland was involved in macro tax policy, so the young assistant professors controlled the development of the financial economics teaching and research program at the Sloan school. We were on our own in both the research and teaching domains.

Stewart Myers greatly influenced my thinking in the area of corporate finance, and Franco Modigliani on macro and asset-pricing models. Robert Merton, Fischer Black, and I were interested in asset pricing and derivative pricing models. It was through many interactions that the three of us developed and extended the field of contingent-claims pricing. In my Nobel address I explained how we developed the Black–Scholes model and how Fischer Black and I used our understanding of risk, return, and arbitrage to define a new method to value risk and to price options. Although some have surmised a different approach, we developed the model from our economic intuition. We were confronted with an interesting economic problem, how to value options. We found the tools to solve it. We did not have a set of tools looking for a problem to address.

In 1973, soon after the Black–Scholes model was published, Texas Instruments (TI) marketed a calculator containing our formula. Traders on the options exchange such as the CBOE could use the calculator to calculate Black–Scholes model values given their inputs. I called TI and asked them whether they would provide us with royalties for using the model. They said no, the model was in the public domain. I asked if they would be willing to send me one of the calculators. They suggested that I buy one using my own nickel.

During my years at the Sloan school, I worked on testing the capital-asset pricing model with Fischer Black and Michael Jensen, and on developing the option-pricing technology with Fischer Black, while continuing to work with Merton Miller on several research projects. Fischer Black and I were interested in all aspects of finance but loved the capital-asset pricing model as a way to describe the trade-off between risk and return. It gave us the insights to figure out how to value options. An option is the right but not the obligation to acquire or sell an asset. It is the value of flexibility. The more uncertain the view on future outcomes, the more valuable the option.

I learned a tremendous amount through many hours of discussion with Paul Samuelson, Robert Solow, and many others at the economics table in the faculty club at MIT. Although I knew that I would miss working on a day-to-day basis with Robert Merton, I returned permanently in 1973 to the Graduate School of Business at the University of Chicago after a visiting year. Although Robert and I are no longer at the same institution, we have remained life-long friends and continue to discuss economic problems.

Fischer Black took his first position in academics as a professor at the University of Chicago in 1972. I wanted to return to Chicago and, in particular, work with Fischer Black, Gene Fama, and Merton Miller. It was an important period in the life of the school, and I had the opportunity to interact with many interesting colleagues. Although Robert Merton was successful in luring Fischer back to Boston in 1974, I resisted taking the offer to return as well and remained at Chicago.

During my Chicago years, I started to work on the effects of taxation on asset prices and incentives. For example, I studied the effects of the taxation of dividends on the prices of securities in three papers, one with Fischer Black and two others with Merton Miller. Merton and I studied the interaction of incentives and taxes in executive compensation. Robert Hamada and I addressed capital structure issues with taxation, and George Constantinides and I studied the effects of taxes on the optimal liquidation of assets.

I became heavily involved with the Center for Research in Security Prices at the University of Chicago during the 1973–1980 time frame. As director of the center, I led the development of large research data files containing daily security prices and related information on all New York and American Stock Exchange securities from 1962–1985 (now updated by others through the present), and merged these data with monthly data files back to 1926. This effort added immeasurably to the research output of colleagues around the world conducting research in financial economics. I believe that great empirical work leads to additional theory and new theory leads, in turn, to new empirical testing. With this in mind, Joe Williams and I wrote a paper on the estimation of risk parameters employing nonsynchronous data, the so-called "Scholes–Williams betas."

In 1981, I visited Stanford University and became a permanent faculty member of the Stanford Business School and the Stanford Law School in 1983. I believe to this day that re-potting oneself keeps the intellectual juices flowing. Staying put just became too comfortable for me. Even to this day, I love traveling and discussing new ideas with associates around the world.

The period at Stanford was a time of significant learning for me. My close colleagues in the business school included William Sharpe, James Van Horne, and a host of up-and-coming younger professors, most notably Jeremy Bulow, Anat Admati, Paul Pfleiderer, and Michael Gibbons. My close colleagues in the law school included Ronald Gilson and Kenneth Scott. With Jeremy Bulow, I wrote several papers on pension planning.

Most important, I was fortunate to work with and become a close friend of Mark Wolfson. We wrote several articles together on investment banking and incentives. We developed a new theory of tax planning under uncertainty and information asymmetry. Many of our published articles on these topics were rewritten and incorporated into our book, *Taxes and Business Strategy: A Planning Approach*, which was published in 1992.

In 1990 my interests shifted back to the role of derivatives in facilitating the financial intermediation process. I became a special consultant to Salomon Brothers, Inc., and continued on as a managing director and co-head of its fixed-income-derivative sales and trading group, while still conducting research and teaching at Stanford University.

My life as an economist was shaped by attempting to conceptualize and test real-world problems. My first consulting relation occurred in 1968 when I consulted with the management science department of Wells Fargo Bank on the efficacy of their security analyst system. I wrote a report suggesting that they abandon active management entirely and concentrate their efforts on evaluating risk and return, and how to create portfolios that would provide alternative risk and return tradeoffs.

John McQuown, head of the management science group at the bank, asked me to consult with them on such a project. Since Fischer Black wanted to leave Arthur D. Little at the time, he joined me on the project. We invented the concept of the *index fund*. Many of our research projects were funded under this research agenda. Although it took many years before index funds became mainstream, an entire industry was built on our efforts. John McQuown was correct in pushing this vision forward.

I enjoyed working with the Chicago Board Options market and with the clearing members to use the options-pricing technology to establish risk-management systems for the clearing-member firms. The clearing-member firms and the traders adopted the option-pricing technology to build the first quantitative-risk-management systems. They did so not because some regulator told them to do so for accounting or for some other purpose, but because they could offer more competitive prices on their products. Lowering their capital costs improved their competitive advantage; using models gave them an edge to set tighter spreads. The technology reduced transaction costs.

Absent a model, traders could neither price securities with embedded options with sufficient accuracy to compete against other traders with models, nor could they reduce the risks of their positions to employ their capital more efficiently at a low enough cost to compete with other traders. Although it is hard to prove, I do think that the success of the CBOE, the other exchanges, and the trillion dollar over-the-counter market in derivative products can be attributed to option-pricing models. Financial theory has spawned the development of an entirely new industry and changed how finance is practiced around the world. And, the risk-management technologies have become the backbone to risk-management systems now used in the banking community around the world.

In late 1993, I joined with several colleagues, many from the Salomon Brothers Group, to become a principal and co-founder of a firm called Long-Term Capital Management (LTCM). This experience has shaped my research interests in the last few years. In joining LTCM, I had hoped to further the application of financial technology to practice. My reason for joining Salomon Brothers and then LTCM was to achieve a deeper understanding of the evolution of financial institutions and markets and the forces shaping this evolution on a global basis. I felt that to achieve that deeper understanding, I needed to immerse myself in the markets. My research papers in the last few years have focused on the interaction and evolution of markets and financial institutions. I will return to that research program in a moment.

During 1997–1999 we have seen the movement of a financial crisis in the debt markets around the world. The Russian government default on their debt products in August of 1998 caused an increase in volatility and a flight to liquidity and to quality in markets around the world. The increase in volatility and the flight to liquidity around the world caused LTCM to experience an extraordinary reduction in its capital base in

August and then again in September of 1998. The August loss was attributable to the Russian crisis; the September loss was attributable to LTCM's own difficulties. The position sizes were too large and too concentrated to liquidate into a chaotic market. Correlations that had been low in the past became extremely high in all asset classes around the world as investors tried to reduce risks.

Some attribute this collapse to a failure of models, and, in particular, option-pricing models. In my opinion, this is false. First, option-pricing models were not used to determine the lion's share of LTCM's positions, and second, did not come into play in the risk-management system. The Salomon traders assumed that correlations would remain low enough to share capital among the positions. Instead, the correlations approached one as all positions lost money at the same time. The firm could not liquidate its illiquid positions into a chaotic market and its capital disappeared.

This reduction in capital culminated in a form of non-fault bankruptcy. A consortium of fourteen leading financial institutions, with outstanding claims against LTCM, infused new equity capital into the firm and took over its assets. The consortium hired the LTCM team to manage the portfolio under their direct supervision. The Federal Reserve coordinated this takeover. Although some called this a bailout, I have called it a coordinated liquidation to avoid the snails-pace processes of the bankruptcy courts, institutions that are not geared to handle a capital market crisis in an efficient manner.

The last few years have been terrific for me. I have been working on a book that models and explains why the prices of risk transfer and liquidity change in the market. I believe that understanding risk transfer and liquidity in modern financial markets in light of unanticipated changes in the opportunity set is an important and exciting research area. The book will be published by Princeton University Press.

Although I have not been teaching full time at Stanford, I have been giving lectures around the world to students, academics, and practitioners. This is enjoyable and lets me address much larger audiences efficiently. I will continue in this vein, for I enjoy it.

I have been working with former students and colleagues to build a hedge fund business, called Oak Hill Platinum Partners, an exciting and energizing enterprise. It allows us to marry theory with practice. As I stated earlier, I have always enjoyed the intersection of conceptualizing a problem with the testing and applying the results of the theory. Concepts to context and back to concepts is an important evolutionary process. Working with Chi-fu Huang, Ayman Hindy, T.S. Sung, and Lawrence Ng, my founding partners, has been rewarding, and we expect to build, work, learn, and develop new theories in the future.

Over the years, I have received honorary doctorate from three universities: University of Paris-Dauphine in 1989, McMaster University, my alma mater, in 1990, and Katholieke Universiteit Leuven in 1998.

I am fortunate to have two wonderful daughters, Anne and Sara, and a generous son-in-law, Anne's husband Seth. All of them continue to add tremendous joy to my life. My fortunes have also risen immeasurably, for I have found Jan. She completes my life. We were married in chaotic times on October 4, 1998. But, together we create order out of disorder. We enjoy each other's company and insights and plan to do so for many years to come. Her two sons by a first marriage, Peter and Mike, have become part of the family.

Although I do not have time for many hobbies, I do enjoy skiing and golf, two sports that allow me to be outdoors in both winter and summer. We have a ski home in the mountains outside of Salt Lake City, Utah.

I ski the race course from time to time. To do so, it is necessary to sign a release form. On seeing my name the attendant asked whether I was the Scholes of the Black–Scholes model. I asked him how he knew about the model. He replied that he was a 1995 Ph.D. in economics from MIT. I did not realize that the program had gone that far down hill since we left.

We span many related and unrelated disciplines in the evolving field of financial economics. I remember the tale of a friend, who graduated with a Ph.D. in physics, when applying for a position at a renowned investment-banking firm in their quantitative finance group, he was asked what he was studying and working on in his current position. He responded, "Black Holes." On mishearing "Black–Scholes," the questioner responded that "he was hired."

Awarded Nobel Prize in 1997. Lecture presented April 7, 1999.

Date of Birth

July 1, 1941

Academic Degrees

B.A.   McMaster University, 1962

M.B.A. University of Chicago, 1964

Ph.D.   University of Chicago, 1969

Academic Affiliations

Assistant and Associate Professor of Finance, Sloan School of Management, MIT, 1968–1973

Associate Professor, Graduate School of Business, University of Chicago, 1973–1976

Director, Center for Research in Security Prices, University of Chicago, 1976–1980

Professor, Graduate School of Business, University of Chicago, 1976–1983

Frank E. Buck Professor of Finance, Graduate School of Business, Stanford University, 1983–1996

Senior Research Fellow, Hoover Institution, Stanford University, 1985–1996

Frank E. Buck Professor of Finance, Emeritus, Graduate School of Business, Stanford University, 1996–present

Selected Books

Taxes and Business Strategy: A Planning Approach, 1992, 2001 (with M. Wolfson)

Gary S. Becker

It is my pleasure to be here and to participate in the Nobel economists lecture series, a series that has had the great modern figures in economics speak, people such as Friedman, Samuelson, and Buchanan, among others. I'm supposed to talk about my evolution as an economist and the forces that influenced me. I will take that as my charge. Yet it is a difficult assignment. It is hard to assess the forces that have had a major influence on one's research. What I can do is to talk a bit about my development as an economist. I will emphasize the many instances where I was extremely lucky to come into contact with people—giants in the field—who had a great influence on me. I will also discuss instances where I started down research paths that at the time seemed to be rather natural and appropriate extensions of microeconomics; I was not fully aware that these would develop into more comprehensive, path-breaking, and often controversial contributions to economics and social science. Following very brief remarks about my days growing up, I will turn my attention to my student days at Princeton, where I first became serious about economics.

I was born in Pottsville, Pennsylvania in 1930, but grew up in Brooklyn, New York, where our family moved when I was a young child. My father was a businessman and my mother was a housewife. My parents were very intelligent, I see in retrospect. I didn't always see that when I was growing up—they were not highly educated; neither one of them went beyond the eighth grade. My father, growing up in Montreal, Canada, left school because he was eager to make money, despite his mother's insistence that he remain in school. My mother's lack of schooling is not surprising since at that time most young girls were not expected to continue with their education. My parents did realize the value of a good education. They did not insist that we pursue higher education, although both my two sisters and my brother and I did so. We could tell growing up that there was an appreciation for education, in spite of the fact that there were not many books in our house and neither one of my parents read a great deal.

I was an excellent student, in general, at least to judge by grades, but up to the age of 16 I was not what I would call a serious student. I was more interested in sports than in academic subjects. I did the amount of work necessary to get good grades. I was not intellectually inclined in high school, at least initially. For some reason, I cannot precisely state what the forces were, but at about the age of sixteen my interests began to shift. I date them dramatically to when I voluntarily gave up on the high school handball team of which I was a member (I probably could have been the number one player), but instead chose to become a member of the math team. They met during the same period, and I had to choose one rather than the other. I went through a little bit of uncertainty, but finally chose the math team. I am glad I did so, because my subsequent academic interests were centered on mathematics and science.

What I liked about the math team was that we actually had competitions. This was in New York City, and there were competitions among schools in which we had to solve problems, two tough problems at a time, and solve them within an intense time frame, usually ten minutes to do both problems. And while there was a lot of pressure and tension, particularly when you did not know the answers, it was a fun and collegial process, with five members on each team. The math competitions had an important influence on me, first in seeing other students who were quite good, and second in proving to myself that our team could do well against Bronx Science and Stuyvesant and the other specialized high schools in science and mathematics.

My senior year in high school I became concerned about doing something for society. Here I was interested in math and science and then, all of a sudden, my interests began to shift as I became more socially conscious. Like most young people at the time, I considered myself a kind of a socialist and felt that I should move toward politics or history or some field where I could make more of a contribution to society. I had a really mixed view, continuing to be strongly interested in math, but no longer really wanting to become a mathematician.

A Princeton Undergraduate

I went to Princeton when I was seventeen and had this conflict going on—a strong interest in math but the desire to make a contribution to society. As freshmen we had to choose some electives and were required to take a course in the social sciences. And for some reason (I have no idea why) I chose to take the principles of economics. And for me this turned out to be a very good, or basically lucky, decision. As you will see, this was just one of several lucky decisions that came at various times. We used as our textbook an early edition of Paul Samuelson's *Economics: An Introductory Analysis.* It certainly has been one of the best-selling textbooks in economics, or in any other field. It is still in use. What I liked about this book was the rather brief section on microeconomics—how prices operate in a market system. It appealed to me because of its more mathematical discussion; basically microeconomics seemed to have a very compact mathematical foundation. Given my previous interest in math, microeconomics had a natural attractiveness for me, while at the same time it was dealing with social problems. I was less taken by Samuelson's extensive discussion of macroeconomics, which seemed to me to be rather vague and not fully satisfactory. I still feel that way about it, although there has been some real progress in that area.

I graduated from Princeton in three years, but during that period I read as many articles and books on economics that I could manage—probably the most influential being Stigler's *The Theory of Competitive Price,* as it was then called, and Hicks's *Value and Capital.* I remember reading Hicks one summer. When I saw one of my teachers in the fall and he asked what I was doing, I told him, "I read *Value and Capital* this summer, but I found it very hard." He said, "Don't worry about that, none of the faculty understand it either." So I felt they didn't understand it and I felt I didn't understand it either, but at least I was close to understanding it (or so I thought at the time). So that gave me a little confidence—maybe I could get someplace in economics.

The paper I wrote for my junior year thesis (required at Princeton) was on classical monetary theory. I criticized some analysis of Leontief and others that had been in the literature and debated at the time. Several faculty members said that I was correct in my criticism, and I think, in retrospect,

I was correct. Eventually I collaborated with a teacher, William Baumol; we published the analysis from my junior thesis, plus other material, in the *American Economic Review* in 1952. The paper was titled "The Classical Monetary Theory: The Outcome of the Discussion." My senior thesis was also published in the *American Economic Review* during 1952, in a paper titled "A Note on Multi-Country Trade."

So I was doing well in economics. During my senior year at Princeton, however, I was losing interest in economics and began to think that I should go into something else. Economics seemed excessively formal to me. I'm sure that cannot be true of anything you have been reading as students nowadays, but then that is how it seemed to me. Economics appeared incapable of helping me understand the issues in which I had an interest: inequality, class, race, prestige, and similar issues that were important for society. A sociology professor at Princeton suggested I look at Talcott Parsons's *Structure of Social Action*. Parsons, then the dominant figure in American sociology, started his career as an economist and believed that social theory included economics as a special case. I tried to read this book, but it contained an enormous quantity of jargon that did not lead anywhere, or at least anywhere that I could follow. I concluded that sociology was too hard, and returned, somewhat reluctantly, to economics. I remained unhappy—unhappy by what seemed to me a disconnect between what economists would talk about in textbooks and elsewhere and what I wanted to talk about.

I decided nevertheless to go on for a doctorate in economics. Adlai Stevenson once defined a graduate student as someone who didn't know when the party was over. Well, I wanted to continue in this party atmosphere, so I went for a doctorate. Most of the faculty wanted me to stay at Princeton, although I had already taken many graduate courses at Princeton; I felt, and some of my teachers agreed, that it would be better if I went someplace else. I was choosing between Harvard and Chicago and, for a variety of reasons, I decided to go to Chicago.

Chicago: The Early Years

From a professional point of view, the decision to go to Chicago was probably the most important decision I ever made. The atmosphere at

Chicago was enormously stimulating. Original work was going on in many different areas and by many economists there, most notably Milton Friedman. The Cowles Commission (which subsequently left) was very active in mathematical economics and econometrics.

Milton Friedman became the greatest influence on my development as an economist. Attending his graduate course in price theory was just exciting, and I would eagerly wait for that course to come twice a week. Some people would even ask my friends, "How can he be so excited about attending class?" A lot of the classes were boring, but that is nothing new for students. Friedman's class was different. Here I saw economics as a tool and not simply as a game played by clever academics, which is what had worried me most about economics. In Friedman's hands, economics was a powerful tool to understand a whole host of problems—in the class Friedman dealt with things such as birthrates, insurance and lotteries, personal and business responses to taxes, how labor markets functioned, and the effect of having unionized versus non-unionized markets. And, on and on, economics was used to understand business practices of all types. "Let's see," Friedman would have asked, "how can we understand what Microsoft is doing?" (had Microsoft existed at that time).

It was a great course that showed me what I thought was not possible. You can do economics and do it in a rigorous way and nevertheless talk about important problems. So my indebtedness to Milton Friedman, one of the greatest economists of the twentieth century, is unlimited.

There were other people in Chicago who were doing important, original work: Ted Schultz in human capital, Gregg Lewis in labor economics, Aaron Director in law and economics, L. J. Savage in statistics and probability. It was a wonderful intellectual environment, and as I developed within that environment, I no longer had this feeling that economics couldn't do it. Indeed I developed the Chicago chip-on-the-shoulder attitude that economics could unlock the mysteries of the real world. Right or wrong, it was a great feeling to have. Here I was being given this powerful tool and a belief that the mysteries of the social world could be unlocked if we applied this tool in some creative fashion. I began to believe this as a graduate student. I still believe that it is true.

I stayed at Chicago for six years, the first three as a graduate student. During the second year I was looking for a thesis topic and had already done some research on an economic approach to political democracy. My paper on this topic was almost published in the *Journal of Political Economy,* but one of my teachers, Frank Knight, was the referee, and he did not like it. I have kept his comments to this day. Knight was a great economist, but he looked at democracy with what I would characterize as a normative point of view. He defined democracy as government by discussion. I wanted to employ an approach to democracy that looked upon it as an institutional system operating in a particular way, for good or bad, which you could analyze using economic analysis. The approach I took in this paper was a very early work in what we now call public choice theory. The editor wanted to publish it in the *JPE,* but was persuaded not to by the referee. It eventually got published in 1956, in a shorter, toned-down version in the first issue of the *Journal of Law and Economics.*

I thought of developing this topic more broadly as one of my possible thesis subjects. But, finally, I hit on something in which I became more interested—an economic approach to the issue of discrimination against minorities, whether religious minorities, racial minorities, gender, or anything else. It was a topic that I had been interested in, of course, but never thought about systematically until I began to think in response to a question put to me by Friedman and Ted Schultz—how might we analyze the fact that there is discrimination in the economy? It occurred to me at the time, but again I am not sure exactly how, that we can associate with each person a taste for discrimination. This taste or prejudice would be measured based on how much income an employer is willing to forfeit in order to avoid hiring somebody who he didn't like from a group that he didn't like; or how much an employee is willing to forfeit to avoid working with a member of a group that he didn't like; or how much a consumer will pay to avoid a product that is served by or produced by a group that he didn't like. So my approach to discrimination was to look at the willingness to pay, or forfeit income, in order to exercise a prejudice. This is still the only right way that I can tell to look at discrimination in mortgage lending, searches for drugs in cars, and other issues that are of great contemporary interest right now. Once you took this approach, then you had to think about how to link the observed discrimination that we see in the marketplace to these personal preferences or prejudices.

To make the link between market discrimination (that is, market outcomes) and personal preferences for discrimination required that I provide a model and analysis. My Ph.D. thesis showed how the degree of market discrimination depended not only on the discriminatory preferences of employers, employees, and consumers but also on the degree of competition in product markets, production technologies, and many other economic variables.

As I was working on my dissertation, I was fortunate to get encouragement from my faculty advisors, but some members of the faculty were highly dubious whether this was an appropriate subject. Their attitude was: "What's a good economist doing working on discrimination?" They could not talk me out of this topic, however, so they insisted instead that a distinguished sociologist at Chicago, Everett Hughes, become a member of my thesis committee, just to make sure that I did not go off the deep end. I do not think Hughes was much interested in what I was doing. The nice part was that he did not object to anything I was doing either. I would go to see him once every nine months and he would say "okay" and that was it. That satisfied the faculty who were dubious whether this was a worthwhile project.

Prior to entering the academic job market, I went to Harvard to present some of my work and also to MIT to discuss this work with some people. I remember talking to a younger faculty member at MIT (a subsequent Nobel Prize winner who gave one of your lectures); he asked me what I was working on and I said "racial discrimination." He said, "I thought you were a neoclassical economist?" I said, "I *am* a neoclassical economist, but isn't this part of neoclassical economics?" But I could not convince him that discrimination was a legitimate subject for economists to work on.

And this was the general experience I had with my dissertation research on discrimination. Eventually a revised version was submitted to the University of Chicago Press. The Press received very negative reviews on my manuscript when it was sent out to readers. The editor did not want to publish it. The economics department finally "bribed" the press. You see, Chicago believes in the market system. So the department said we would put up part of the cost and would share any profits on the book. The press agreed to publish my book, but only because of that bribe.

It gave me great pleasure that about ten years after the Press published *The Economics of Discrimination,* the then editor of the press (who was also editor when my book came out) wrote an article, published in the *American Economic Review,* in which he admitted that my book was attracting sizeable interest. It was not selling a lot—but it was creating a great deal of interest.

The negative reaction to my work on discrimination, coupled with Frank Knight's hostility toward my article on democracy, made it clear to me that using economic analysis to discuss social and political issues was not going to be welcomed with open arms by most economists. I initially had expected economists to applaud attempts to widen the scope of their field. I was surprised that the main hostility toward my work, at least as it was explicitly stated, came from economists, not non-economists. I began to realize that my original view was naïve. All disciplines have a strong and probably justified degree of intellectual conservatism. You do not give up ideas and concepts you have held for a long time without a fight. It is necessary to fight to get new ideas accepted.

Even after I became aware of the extent of the hostility, I remained confident that the contribution of the economic approach to broader problems would eventually be recognized. This confidence in what I was doing helped me persist against sometimes considerable and vicious opposition. There were two reasons why I remained confident. First, it just seemed to me obvious that economics could contribute to these areas. Economics was not the whole story, it was not the final word on discrimination, but how could economists justify that prior to my book on discrimination, with two or three exceptions, there was virtually no work by economists on a topic as enormously important as discrimination in the marketplace? I mean, it's incredible! So it seemed obvious to me that there was a role here.

That was one factor. As important as this was, I do not think that this would have been sufficient to enable me to persist against continuing hostility. The other factor was that I was fortunate to have intellectually powerful people on my side. I gained strength from the support of senior economists I greatly respected. Support came from my teachers, like Milton Friedman and Gregg Lewis, George Stigler—who soon effectively became my teacher—and other friends I had met along the way such as Armen Alchian and Jack Hirshleifer.

In short, this was a period in which my research and intellectual discourse encountered an enormous amount of opposition. There was little demand to hire me from the major institutions. After three years as a graduate student, I accepted an assistant professorship at Chicago. And these six years, looking back on it now, were perhaps the most important and most exciting of my career. I formed the foundation of what I was going to do later on. And I was learning at a rapid rate as I absorbed so many new things that were coming from people at Chicago and from others who came through Chicago. Four of my teachers went on to win the Nobel Prize: Milton Friedman, Friedrich Hayek, who was then on the Committee for Social Thought (I attended his seminars), Tjalling Koopmans, and Ted Schultz. And in addition to that, the Chicago intellectual vitality had many others, some mentioned here, who did not win the Nobel Prize but have done very important work that has been continually recognized.

Chicago wanted me to continue there after my three-year term was up, but I wanted to leave, even though Chicago offered me more money and a good chance of getting tenure. I felt it was more important for me to leave the nest and go out on my own. I had protection at Chicago with the likes of Friedman, Schultz, and Lewis, among others, and that was great, but I wanted to see if I could make it on my own. I said in effect, "I appreciate the offer, but I really don't want to stay at Chicago." So I looked around, went on the job market, and as a lot of other students have experienced, I did not find a overwhelming demand for my services. Major universities, like Harvard, MIT, Berkeley, and Yale showed no interest in me and did not interview me at any of the meetings. This was probably because I was a Chicago graduate and Chicago at that time was an "outlaw" department in the profession. Its students were treated as suspect by representatives of most of the major institutions. It is not that extreme now.

I had only two interviews, with Johns Hopkins and Columbia. Hopkins decided not to make me an offer. So I considered all my choices and decided to choose among them and went to Columbia, which I was happy to do. I also was offered a position at the National Bureau of Economic

Research, which was then in New York City, so I could combine the two. I spent a dozen highly productive years at both institutions.

Columbia and the National Bureau of Economic Research

I started my work on human capital at Columbia and the National Bureau of Economic Research. When I came to the bureau, the then director, Solomon Fabricant, asked me what I would like to work on. From my work on discrimination, I had seen that there were enormous gaps in earnings between workers with different levels of education, among both blacks and whites. I knew the work Ted Schultz had been doing on human capital, which I found to be of considerable interest. So I told Fabricant that I would like to do a study on the rates of return to education and training. This would be a new departure for the bureau, but he said, "I will see what I can do." He got a small grant for me to work on education and earnings, which I began in 1957.

I soon realized that much more was needed in the human capital field than to calculate rates of return. There were no foundations for the theory of investment in human capital. My study was intended to be empirical, but I set about trying to sketch out a small set of foundations to give the work theoretical content. As I was sketching out some basic theory, I had no vision at all of what this would lead to. Once again, here is an example of the role of luck. As I delved into the theory and tried to develop a basic foundation for human capital investment, it looked to me that the theory could explain the way earnings rise with age (a concave age-earnings profile), the effect of education on the distribution of earnings, externalities of human capital, and many other issues that continue to this day to be discussed and debated. I was amazed and then greatly excited when I began to realize that this framework could integrate scores of observations and regularities in individual earnings, occupational differences in earnings, and employment.

In 1959, I made the first public presentation of some of my results at a session of the annual meetings of the American Economic Association. I presented a short paper that compared rates of return to schooling and returns on physical capital in the United States. And the discussants, to my amazement, were absolutely outraged. Once again, I continued to be surprised by what I should have anticipated. What was it that so outraged my discussants? In retrospect it seems silly. They were outraged that I was treating education as an economic activity, believing that this assumption somehow denigrated the cultural or non-economic aspects of education. I replied with some fervor and bluntness to my critics. It was one of the more heated sessions of the meeting. I was taken aback, but truth be told, I did not lose any confidence about what I was doing because their comments seemed so silly to me. I could not really believe that senior economists—I was 29 years old at the time—were making such dumb comments on my paper.

I continued working on the economics of human capital and in 1962 published an article on it. It was in fact well received. Then, in 1964, I published a book called *Human Capital: A Theoretical and Empirical Analysis, with Special Reference to Education*. The long subtitle is now forgotten—it is now called *Human Capital*. Actually, I debated a long time before I used the title *Human Capital* because I had been aware that people said that if you call it "capital" you are treating human beings as if they had no soul. Some people would make fun of it and call it "human cattle," suggesting that one is not treating humans as individuals. I knew that, and could have weaseled a little and called it "human resources," a phrase that was becoming common at the time. I decided to take the bull by the horns and title the book *Human Capital*, although it had this long subtitle to protect myself a little.

By the time I finished this research, I was indeed convinced that human capital was a crucial concept to understanding economic and social issues in many areas of life. Still, and this I will also confess, I was not prepared for the magnitude of its impact. Eventually, it would be referred to endlessly, and by that language—human capital—not only in academic writing but by politicians of both parties, journalists, even in ecclesiastical encyclicals. After a while some of the people who had resisted using this term began to think, "Well, look, if we call everything human capital and say we are investing in people, this can provide a good rationale for obtaining public monies." I remember the superintendent of the Chicago school system at that time, Benjamin Willis, inviting me to deliver an address to a meeting of superintendents. He told me, "I don't know why people dislike that word; it can be a great tool for us superintendents to get more money." So I think that this partly explains its success.

Everything is now called human capital, including some things that should not be so called.

The more fundamental reason why the term human capital has been so successful and has continued to grow rather than shrink in importance is that it integrates into one basically simple concept a lot of actions and behavior that affect the individual and economy. In essence, human capital analysis puts individuals at the center of attention in an economy, not machinery, plant and equipment, or other inanimate objects. It is people who move an economy, people who determine whether an economy is rich or poor; human capital is a major aspect of the productivity and well-being of people. And it is investment in human capital, by acquiring skills from one's parents, through going to school, or through training and knowledge in the workplace, that helps determine a person's and an economy's stock of human capital wealth. I think this explanation is the fundamental reason why the term human capital has proven appealing and durable. It integrates diverse aspects of human behavior, pushing people to the center of the economic stage, so to speak.

At the same time that I was doing research on human capital, I was also working on the economics of the family and the demand for children. I began this work by asking what determines how many children that families have. I gave my first paper on this topic in the late 1950s, around the same time that I presented my early work on education. At a conference on the economic analysis on fertility, I drew an analogy between the demand for children by parents and their demand for durable consumer goods. I used that language in my paper. Well, you can imagine the reaction from my audience—as soon as I used this language everyone started laughing. Well, not everyone. This was a mixed audience of economists and non-economists. One economist who was the discussant on my paper, a youngish economist at Harvard, was very negative about it, stating that this approach could not explain much about the demand for children. I had learned over time to expect a negative reaction from the audience. But, once again, I was a little surprised by just how much hostility (and this was verbally expressed in public comments) my work aroused among some eminent economists. And yet again, this was an instance in which I feel indebted to Milton Friedman. Friedman had been a participant at the conference and was attending my session. He got up and vigorously defended my paper during the discussion period. I felt, well, there are these fools on the one side criticizing me, but I have people like Friedman defending me. And that is all I needed. I had enormous respect for Friedman—I still do—so I thought, "Now look, if Friedman is defending my work, there must be something to what I am doing."

Another subject I was working on at this time was the theory of the allocation of time. As I worked on the economics of education, it soon became apparent, not only to me but to Schultz and others working in this area, that the major costs of going to school were generally the earnings students give up by not working full time. Even at private colleges and universities, where the tuition is high, the major cost is generally foregone earnings, or the opportunity cost of one's time. This seemed to me to be important, but apart from labor-leisure choice analysis used to understand labor supply, there was little formal role for the value of time or the allocation of time in microeconomic analysis. Once again, as I was working on one subject, I was led by the logic of the analysis into a different, albeit related, subject.

So I began at that time to try to generate a systematic analysis of time use. I eventually published an article called "The Theory of the Allocation of Time," (*Economic Journal,* 1965), which treated each household like a small-scale factory or enterprise that used time and goods to produce various commodities that they could not buy directly, like children, good health, a good meal, and things of that kind. Unlike the work on discrimination, human capital, and fertility, my work on time allocation was less controversial and more quickly and readily accepted within the economics profession.

As evident from the previous discussion, my time in New York was highly productive. At Columbia, Jacob Mincer and I jointly conducted a labor economics workshop that gained a large following among a new generation of labor economists. I greatly benefited from my colleagues at Columbia and the bureau; in addition to Mincer these included Victor Fuchs, Robert Willis, Finis Welch, and Sherwin Rosen. I had a remarkable group of students at Columbia, too numerous to mention here, that have gone on to make major contributions in the fields of human capital and labor economics, health, crime, and law and economics. So I was quite happy professionally at Columbia. I did not consider many other offers, partly because I did not get many. It made life easy.

In 1968 and 1969, student rebellions hit American universities. And there were few schools that were harder hit than Columbia. I was very disturbed by this, not so much by what the students were doing, but by the faculty's weakness and eventual unwillingness to stand up to disruptive and, in my opinion, intolerant student tactics. I was especially disappointed by the attitude of senior members of my department (not all, but most). They seemed to me to be weak and vacillating at a time when I thought there existed clear-cut and simple steps that could be taken to protect the intellectual integrity of the university.

I began to think of leaving Columbia at that time. The future to me looked dim, having lost a lot of confidence in my colleagues. I began to look around. I received an inquiry from the economics department at Harvard through an old friend of mine from undergraduate days, Otto Eckstein, who was a professor at Harvard. And he said: "Would I be interested in coming to Harvard? It would be a good change for me." I said I was interested, but then somebody else called me back and said Harvard had unanimously voted to give me a one-year visiting offer. On the spot I said, "I am not interested." To be unanimously voted a one-year visiting offer did not seem to me to be a display of great interest. Eckstein had been talking of my becoming a permanent member. It seemed obvious to me that a permanent offer had run into difficulty among some members of the department. So I turned the offer down. For years Chicago was the only major institution interested in me, and they again renewed their offer for me to come back. I told them, "I will come back for a one-year visit." I did what Harvard had asked me to do, but I knew that Chicago wanted me to stay for good.

Return to Chicago

Upon my return to Chicago, I found it to be at least as stimulating as when I was a graduate student. Friedman was still there in his prime, Stigler was doing very important work in industrial organization and political economy. They had Black, Fama, Miller, and Scholes working out rigorous approaches to finance and the evaluation of options. Coase,

Posner, Landes, Demsetz, and others were doing law and economics, building on the pioneering work of Aaron Director. My work on the economics of crime fit in well with their interests. We had Bob Fogel doing path-breaking work in economic history—slavery at first and then other topics. It was a magical place!

During my year there, following a lot of soul searching (because I did like my setup in New York), I decided to stay in Chicago and accepted an offer there. I thought that a permanent return to Chicago would help renew my energies, and it did. I developed a very close friendship with George Stigler, who became my best friend and collaborator on a number of projects. I learned a great deal from George over the years. Unfortunately he died in his prime. Although he was 80 at the time, his mind was still very active.

While I was at Chicago, I decided to continue my work on the family. I remember sitting in a hotel room in New York and thinking about the question of marriage—who marries whom? Now why I started thinking about this at that time, I do not know. True, my first wife had died and I was unmarried at the time, so perhaps that had something to do with it. As I thought about the question of who marries whom, it seemed to me that there is something we might think of as a marriage market. Not a market à la Li'l Abner on Sadie Hawkins Day, if any of you remember Al Capp's comic strip *Li'l Abner*. It's not literally a market with explicit buying and selling, but you can think of the matching of partners as operating like a market—people make their choices, they date, and so on. I worked out some rules that would determine who would marry whom, threw in a couple of "theorems," and submitted a paper to the *Journal of Political Economy*. The same distinguished economist that could not accept my discrimination work ended up as a referee (George Stigler was the editor and told me this). This referee hated the paper, saying, "What is Becker doing wasting his time working on these questions." Stigler disagreed. He told me that he liked the paper, to take account of the referee comments as best I could, and that they would publish the article, which they did. I then submitted a paper a couple of years later on the economics of divorce. Another very good economist wrote back and said they should not accept this paper. And Stigler again overrode the referee recommendation and, following revision, published my paper. Each of the papers turned out to have a good market, leading to a considerable body of subsequent research.

At about that time I decided that I should try to weave all this together into a book on the economics of the family. The book was to combine and integrate the topics of fertility, divorce, marriage, investment in children, and the evolution of the family over time. I even dealt with some nonhuman species. I worked very hard on this book for four or five years. I would wake up in the middle of the night, many nights, and work on it. It was very intense and, finally, in 1981, I published *A Treatise on the Family*. I was exhausted by that time, and it took me roughly two years to regain my mental energy. A comprehensive treatment of the family is inherently such a difficult problem, with so much history, so many cultures, and the like. I found it very difficult. And to this day the book remains controversial. When the Nobel Prize committee awarded me the prize in 1992, their news release stated, "Gary Becker's analysis has often been controversial and hence, at the outset, met with scepticism and even distrust." Nowhere has this characterization been truer than with my work on the family.

Time does not permit me to discuss much of my work in recent years. But I would be remiss if I did not mention my rewarding collaboration with Kevin M. Murphy, a former student and now a brilliant young colleague at Chicago. Building on earlier work on preferences and addiction in a paper I wrote with Stigler ("De Gustibus Non Est Disputandum," *American Economic Review* 1977) and a Chicago dissertation by Laurence Iannoccone, Murphy and I have written several articles on "rational addiction," among other topics.

Writing for a Popular Audience

Throughout my career, I had worked on topics closely related to public policy—education, crime, the family, discrimination, addiction, and politics, for example—yet I remained aloof from debates over public policy. I had never given advice to any political figures. Prior to 1985, I had never written one single word in the popular media, not a word, be it a newspaper, magazine, or the like. By 1985 I was 55, so I had gone through roughly 35 years of doing economic research, and not one single popular work. Nowadays, some economists hit 30 and begin writing op-ed pieces. I always felt it was a good division of labor on my part to concentrate on my research.

You can imagine then that it was a great surprise to me when in 1985 I received a telephone call from someone at *Business Week,* a magazine I had criticized a couple of years earlier because they misquoted me on something. Their representative said, "Would you be willing to write a regular column for the magazine—a one-page column every four weeks?" My initial reaction was to reject their proposal. But what I said was, "It is not something I have done, it would take me away from my research, but I will think it over and give you an answer." The response back was, "Oh good, I thought maybe you would turn us down on the spot."

So I went back and told my wife, Guity, and she said, "You should do it." She prevailed on me to try it for a while. She argued that the columns would help spread my ideas and might even have a small influence on public policy. And if I did not like doing it, I could always stop. Guity also promised that she would read my early drafts and provide comments. I am happy to say that she gave me good advice. And I might add at this point that I have been very fortunate for almost thirty years to be getting excellent advice and encouragement from her, both professional and personal. She has had an enormous influence on me.

So I got back to *Business Week* and said, "Okay, I am willing to write a column on a trial basis." They said, "Don't worry, we are looking upon it as a trial as well." And the contract sent to me stated that "either party can terminate the agreement with one month's notice." In academia we are used to tenure; there was no tenure here.

It was hard for me to learn how to write a popular column. The hardest part about writing is writing something short. I think it was Oscar Wilde who wrote to someone saying that he was sorry his letter was so long, but he did not have time to make it short. Writing short requires far more effort than writing long. I had to write roughly 800 words—one *Business Week* page comprising a certain number of *Business Week* lines—and to write in simple and nontechnical language.

And it was hard. But again, I was lucky. I do not know why they asked me, to tell the truth, but the experience has been great for me. It has taught me how to express economic ideas in a simple and nontechnical way. I will make the assertion that every single important economic idea can be stated simply. To develop an idea, you may have to use some apparatus to do it in a systematic way, of course, but you can state the essence of any idea simply. At least I have never heard one that could not be stated simply. And when people say that an idea is too complicated to state simply, it usually means they do not know how to state it simply, sometimes because they do not fully understand it.

Writing for a popular audience, I have addressed a wide range of topics. My interests in economics are broad and my column has resulted in my interests becoming even broader. I have written about baseball, the unfairness of the NCAA in not allowing student athletes to be paid, marriage contracts and religion, immigration, education, and the policies of different presidents or political candidates. Once again, this was one of several lucky events that ended up having a positive and important effect on me.

The Prize

The final thing I will discuss is the Nobel Prize. When I entered economics there was no Nobel Prize in economics; it is a recent award, having begun in 1969. There were two prizes awarded by the American Economic Association, the John Bates Clark medal for economists under the age of 40 (I was honored to receive this award in 1967) and the Francis Walker Prize for senior economists. The AEA abolished the latter once the Nobel Prize began.

By 1980 I began to be mentioned as a serious candidate for the Nobel Prize. I realized then that there were many older, highly deserving economists in the Nobel queue, mainly because the prize had not existed for very long. I realized that if I were ever to get the prize, and this was not assured, it would have to come later.

By the latter part of the 1980s, however, I felt pressure mounting on me because my name was so often mentioned as a leading candidate. A betting pool organized by some American economists had me listed as their favorite (i.e., the lowest odds person) for three or four years running before I got the prize. And so individuals and reporters had begun asking me with some regularity "When will you get the prize?" or, once the prize was announced each year, "Why didn't you get it this year?" Of course this bothered me.

I admit that I wanted to be awarded the prize, and for several reasons. Clearly the prestige and financial rewards were important. But there was another reason as well. I had a lot of students and others who had been pursuing research along the lines indicated by my work, often working outside the more narrow range of traditional economics topics. These economists were often given a tough time in the profession, and several had difficulty getting good jobs. One of my top students years ago, who worked on religion, generated almost no job market interest. Now he is considered a preeminent economist working in religion, perhaps the preeminent person in any field doing research on religion. But he had a difficult time getting a job. People would ask, "Religion, what kind of topic is that for an economist?" I wanted myself and others to get the validation that the Nobel Prize would provide—that the economic approach to human behavior is acceptable work and that we are doing real economics. Yet in 1992, my work continued to be controversial, especially in Western Europe, and I began to wonder whether I would ever receive the prize.

I thought there was no chance I would receive the prize in 1992. Economists from Chicago were among the three winners in 1990, and another Chicagoan, Ronald Coase, won in 1991. I concluded that the committee would never choose three Chicagoans in a row. In the fall of 1992, I had a terrible flu with a very high fever. Doctors wanted to put me in the hospital, but my wife resisted that move. For both these reasons, the last thing on my mind was the Nobel Prize. I had no idea when the announcement was coming. I had not been into school for a week and I was in bed at 5:30 on the morning of October 13, sleeping soundly for the first night in about a week. My wife, who had been up grading papers, answered the phone when it rang that morning, worried that it might interfere with my sleep. She was a bit nasty, she said to me later, but the caller said this was an important phone call for Professor Becker. My wife did not think it was the Nobel Prize, at least not for me. She went and woke me up and I kept saying, "I want to sleep, I haven't slept so well for a long time." "No, it's a call from Sweden," she said, and that was the magic word. A call from Sweden! I did not know that the prize was announced. But when I heard "a call from Sweden," I figured, "well, maybe" and picked up the phone. My wife subsequently said that she was sitting there as I was saying, "yes, yes" with no expression on my face, and she figured that they had called for my input on somebody else who was being considered. Finally, she hears me say "Thank you very much; tell the committee what a great honor it is that you have conferred on me." This of course was the call telling me I had been awarded the prize. The first thing Guity did was to let out a yell and the first thing I said was "I'm glad that monkey is off my back." We called our four children and then we took the phone off the receiver to have breakfast in some peace. Before 6:30 or so, the reporters, the *New York Times,* the university people, and so on, had found us.

So the long years of fighting attacks were largely over, although the official Nobel announcement called my work controversial. Still, they awarded me the prize. I did not realize at the time that there were some protests in Sweden about my getting the prize. Some Swedish feminist groups in particular complained about my receiving the award, charging that my work on the family was anti-feminist (I do not believe it is) and they had discussions about whether to picket my Nobel lecture. Perhaps that helped publicize the lecture—the hall was packed. People were standing all over the place, but they caused no disruptions, everything went very smoothly, and it was a great week.

The prize recognized my research in four broad areas: investments in human capital; behavior of the family (or household), including distribution of work and allocation of time in the family; crime and punishment; and discrimination in the markets for labor and goods. In private I was told that some members of the committee did not want to award me the prize. But because in the last couple of years I had been nominated the most often by the economists asked to identify potential recipients, the committee felt they had to give me the prize. Well, better than not. And so, it was a great week and a great period of recognition.

Some people have studied Nobel laureates and discovered that they did a whole lot less work after receiving the prize than before. I was aware of that work, done by several sociologists, and there is no doubt that there are many demands on your time as a result of getting the prize. I resolved to continue to do research and not change my life drastically. Since I have received the prize I have published three books. Two of the three books include new research; the other published book, *The Economics of Life,* is a collection of my *Business Week* columns. I hope that in my case the iron law of the negative effect of the Nobel Prize on productivity has been overcome.

To the best of my ability, I have tried to assess the factors that were most important in facilitating whatever accomplishments I have had. I have to give many thanks to my parents, my wife Guity, my children, my sisters, my brother, and certainly my teachers and colleagues. A series of lucky events over my life have put me into contact with enormously outstanding people and led me down paths whose rewards I could not have anticipated. I'm not suggesting that the Nobel Prize, or whatever is one's accomplishments in life, is simply a matter of luck. I am suggesting that success requires a number of fortuitous events to occur, many of which one cannot readily imagine, plan for, or determine. I suspect that there are a lot of equally able people out there, and it is only those who are particularly lucky or fortunate who end up receiving a Nobel Prize or some other noteworthy accomplishment. I have been fortunate.

Awarded Nobel Prize in 1992. Lecture presented April 13, 2000.

Date of Birth

December 2, 1930

Academic Degrees

B.A.   Princeton University, 1951

M.A. University of Chicago, 1953

Ph.D. University of Chicago, 1955

Academic Affiliations

Assistant Professor of Economics, University of Chicago, 1954–1957

Assistant Professor of Economics, Columbia University, 1957–1958

Associate Professor of Economics, Columbia University, 1958–1960

Professor of Economics, Columbia University, 1960–1968

Arthur Lehman Professor of Economics, Columbia University, 1968–1969

Ford Foundation Visiting Professor of Economics, University of Chicago, 1969–1970

University Professor of Economics, University of Chicago, 1970–1983

University Professor of Economics and Sociology, University of Chicago, 1983–present

Senior Research Fellow, Hoover Institute (Stanford), 1990–present

Selected Books

The Economics of Discrimination, 1957, 1971

Human Capital: A Theoretical and Empirical Analysis, with Special Reference to Education, 1964, 1993

The Economic Approach to Human Behavior, 1976

A Treatise on the Family, 1981, 1991

Accounting for Tastes, 1996

The Economics of Life, 1997 (with Guity Nashat Becker)

Social Economics: Market Behavior in a Social Environment, 2000 (with K. Murphy)

Robert E. Lucas, Jr.

1

Jane Templeton graduated in Seattle's Roosevelt High School's first class, in 1927. The Templetons lived right across 68th Street, in a house built the same year as the new high school. Jane enrolled as an art student at the University of Washington, hoping to become a fashion artist. But the art courses at the university were trivial—"tie-dyeing," she later dismissed them—and unrelated to the world she wanted to enter. She got the idea to study in New York, and she and two girl friends planned to rent an apartment and spend a year there. In 1930, when she was 20, Jane took the two-day trip to Chicago on the Northern Pacific and spent a few days visiting with her aunts Ruth and Mary. Then she was on to New York, beginning to enjoy the image she found she had back east, as a girl from the western edge of the country.

But the New York art school was a disappointment too: maybe schools were not where you learned design and the skills of a commercial artist. She picked up some work freelancing, looked around for a job, and—amazingly, in 1930—found one. She became the girl Friday for a fashion artist with the single name Leonard—LAY-o-nard—a recent immigrant from Austria, as far ahead of his American counterparts (I imagine) as were the physicists and psychiatrists who were also emigrating from central Europe around that time. He liked to talk to Jane about every aspect of the business: she was smart, talented, eager to learn, and fun to be around. Jane knew this was the real thing, and there were no more thoughts of school. But she was homesick and never considered staying longer than the year she and her friends had planned. She returned to

Seattle, and on the strength of the portfolio put together from her work for Leonard, got a job drawing newspaper ads for Best's Apparel.

All this and much more my brothers and sister and I learned from stories about our mother's New York adventure. We saw some of it firsthand during the war, when she resumed work to supplement our father's earnings in the Seattle shipyards. She would take the three of us, at ages 6, 4, and 3, all of us struggling to keep up with her clicking heels, on the half-mile walk to the bus and then on the long bus ride downtown, to the McDougal's store. There we would sit still while she handed over her drawings from last week, discussed her assignments for the week to come, and put the articles to be advertised into a shopping bag. On the return home, we received praise—if earned—for our successful venture into the world of adult work. At home, she took out a dress, shoes, and a belt from the shopping bag. She hung the dress up on a hanger near the drawing board, in the living room of the shabby house we rented during the war, and put the accessories in front of her, at the top of the board. She set out her paints—pure white, glossy black, elegant grays—and her tiny brushes, and as I watched there came into being on paper a confident and attractive woman, stylishly dressed in what I had seen as nothing more than an ordinary dress, limp on the hanger.

2

My own train trip east took place in September 1955, when I entered the University of Chicago as a scholarship student. Like my parents, I had graduated from Roosevelt High School, but I did not want to follow most of my classmates to the University of Washington. My mother chose to view my first year at Chicago as a temporary stay, as her year in New York had been. I may have seen it this way myself at first: my letters home made references to a possible transfer to the University of Washington, to study engineering. If so, it was not for long. I was homesick, for sure, and had doubts about my ability to succeed, but when my first quarter transcript showed a couple of A's—not just in calculus, where I could coast on my high school training, but in Humanities I, where everything was new—I knew I was at Chicago to stay.

This humanities course and several others I took over the next three years were part of the glorious Hutchins fourteen-year-long general-education courses that not long before had entitled a student to a Bachelor of Philosophy degree. By the time I got to Chicago, the Hutchins curriculum had been partially abandoned, and supplemented with enough conventional college courses to entitle you to a regular, four-year B.A. or B.S. in some specific field. But it was the Hutchins "great books" courses that were the real excitement for me, and except perhaps for the science majors, for most of us. It was these courses that gave us the sense of getting a distinctive education, of entering into a new world of culture and ideas, of becoming a new person.

Early in my first year, we were assigned to write a page or two on Brahms's *Variations on a Theme by Haydn*. A group of us checked out the LP from the library and sat around a dorm room, playing it over and over. My musical experience then consisted of Christmas carols and the top 40. What was the connection between Haydn's theme and all this music that Brahms claimed were variations? What could one *write* on such a topic? I'm sure I would not enjoy re-reading whatever it was that I handed in, but I can still hear Brahms's music in my head. I learned to listen to serious music with pleasure and was grateful for what Allan Bloom much later described as this improvement in my ability to care for my soul.

The only science course I took in college was Natural Sciences II—a biology course. We read a modern anatomy text and also selections from Darwin, Mendel, and others. I remember struggling over an incomprehensible paper on embryology by Spemann and Mangold and one by another German author called "The Continuity of the Germ Plasm" that had mysterious overtones.

But there was nothing spooky about Mendel's genetic theories. They were clear and made some kind of sense (though there was nothing molecular in our Nat Sci II readings); you could work out predictions that would surprise you, and these predictions matched interesting facts. We did a classroom experiment with fruit flies, focused on eyes, and pooled the results. Our assignment was to write up the results in a lab report and compare them to predictions from a Mendelian model. I had not enjoyed the lab work, but I liked writing the report and spent the better part of my weekend on it. It was the first time I can recall ever working out the predictions of a scientific theory from its basic principles and testing these predictions against experimental evidence.

On Sunday evening, my friend Mike Schilder returned to the dorm from a weekend that had clearly not been occupied with fruit flies. The report was due Monday, and he asked to copy mine. I agreed, in part just to get some reaction to a report that I was very pleased with. Mike came back in half an hour, and told me: "This is a good report, but you forgot about crossing over." "Crossing over" was a term introduced to us to describe a discrepancy between Mendelian theory and certain observations. No doubt there is some underlying biology behind it, but for us it was presented as just a fudge-factor, a label for our ignorance. I was entranced with Mendel's clean logic and did not want to see it cluttered up with seemingly arbitrary fudge-factors. "Crossing over is b—— s——," I told Mike.

In fact, though, there was a big discrepancy between the Mendelian prediction without crossing over and the proportions we observed in our classroom data, too big to pass over without comment. My report included a long section on experimental error, describing the chaotic scene that generated the data and arguing that errors could have been large enough to reconcile theory and fact. I handed it in as written. Mike, on the other hand, took my report as it stood, except that he replaced my experimental error section with a discussion of crossing over. His report came back with an A. Mine got a C−, with the instructor's comment: "This is a good report, but you forgot about crossing over."

I don't think there is anyone who knows me or my work as a mature scientist who would not recognize me in this story. The construction of theoretical models is our way to bring order to the way we think about the world, but the process necessarily involves ignoring some evidence or alternative theories—setting them aside. That can be hard to do—facts are facts—and sometimes my unconscious mind carries out the abstraction for me: I simply fail to *see* some of the data or some alternative theory. This failing can be costly and embarrassing to me, but I don't think it has any effect on the advance of knowledge. Others will see the blind spot (as Mike did with crossing over), keep what is good, and correct what is not.

3

The reality addressed by natural science always seemed to me someone else's province. In public school science was an unending and not very well organized list of things other people had discovered long ago. In college, I learned something about the process of scientific discovery, but what little I learned did not attract me as a career possibility. Introductory physics and chemistry were huge courses, designed to weed out pretenders, which I feared I would soon be discovered to be. More important, I think, was a sense that these areas were in good hands, that they would progress in pretty much the same way with my participation or without it.

What I liked thinking about were politics and social issues. My parents had become politically aware in the 1930s, and politics were always the leading topic of discussion in our house. My letters home, from undergraduate days through middle age, were full of politics and social commentary. I had read widely on these matters, and with this background, I got advanced placement in social science. It was not until my second year at Chicago that I could take Social Sciences III and the History of Western Civilization. I had never worked so hard or with as much enthusiasm as I did in these two courses.

When the time came to specialize, I wanted to prolong this excitement. By my second year I was fully socialized to Chicago's pristine intellectualism, and occupational considerations played no role in this decision. Since everything interesting seemed to begin with the Greeks, I majored in history, specializing in the history of ancient Greece and Rome and the European Middle Ages. I was drawn to the idea that economic forces were centrally important, but somehow never took an economics course. The general education courses from the Hutchins era paid no attention to economics. When I mentioned an interest in economics to my instructor in Social Sciences III, he suggested Heilbroner's *The Worldly Philosophers* and Galbraith's *American Capitalism,* books written for people who dislike economics and want their prejudice entertainingly humored. Neither book gives any clue to what economics is or what economists do.

I won a Woodrow Wilson Fellowship for graduate study in history, and was admitted at the University of California at Berkeley. The trip west was my honeymoon: Rita Cohen and I were married in New York in the summer of 1959. My weakness in languages—a classical historian needs five—discouraged me from pursuing my interests in ancient and medieval history. I took an English history seminar course—tweedy students imitating every mannerism of their tweedy professor—and courses in economic history from Carlo Cipolla and David Landes. For Landes, I wrote a bibliographical paper on nineteenth-century British business cycles—a topic I chose from Landes's list because it looked like the most theoretical, and so it was. I could see that without a better economics background I would always be on the fringe of a topic like this. I wanted to transfer into economics, but even with Landes's support the Berkeley economics department was not encouraging.

Rita and I were also homesick for Chicago. I talked the Social Sciences Division at Chicago into accepting me back as a graduate student. I talked the Woodrow Wilson Foundation into transferring my fellowship to Chicago. With the help of my brother Pete, who passed through Berkeley on his way to the Rose Bowl in Pasadena, we loaded a rented trailer and headed back to Chicago.

4

By the summer of 1960 my young wife was pregnant, I had lost my Woodrow Wilson Fellowship, and I had spent the better part of the year making up for the fact that I had had no economics as an undergraduate. But I had found a field that I loved and was good at, and I could hardly wait to start the regular first year graduate program with Milton Friedman and the rest of Chicago's faculty.

At the end of spring quarter, I had looked in the back of Kenneth Boulding's textbook and read Boulding's description of Paul Samuelson's *Foundations of Economic Analysis* as "the most important book in economics since the war." I had a summer to prepare for the beginning of graduate work in earnest, and there was no point in wasting the time on the second most important book. I got a copy from the library and all that summer, during lunch and coffee breaks from my research assistant job, I worked through Samuelson's first four chapters. When I got home each night, I wrote out what I had learned that day, line by line. It is impossible to invest this much in a single book unless you trust it, and though no one at Chicago had confirmed Boulding's recommendation for me, I immediately sensed that Samuelson was dealing with essential material in a way that was congenial to me.

Of course, I knew that Samuelson was regarded as a leading—perhaps *the* leading—economist in the world. I also knew that as an undergraduate at Chicago, he had taken Jacob Viner's graduate course along with Milton Friedman and George Stigler. In the preface, Samuelson says the book had "been conceived and written primarily in 1937," which is to say it was the product of Samuelson's early years of graduate school, at Harvard, when he was about the age I was then, in 1960. With this as background, the book's broad sweep and supremely confident tone was exhilarating. He patronizes the feared Viner: "As Professor Viner has pointed out with great insight . . . ," crediting Viner with understanding a mathematical point that Samuelson has just shown on the preceding page. He disagrees with Alfred Marshall—then the god of Chicago economics: "I have come to feel that Marshall's dictum that 'it seems doubtful whether anyone spends his time well in reading lengthy translations of economic doctrines into mathematics, that have not been made by himself' should be exactly reversed." He goes out of his way to quarrel with *our* feared teacher, Milton Friedman, by disagreeing with a point in Friedman's 1935 article on elasticities, and this after dismissing the whole idea of elasticities as unimportant "except possibly as mental exercises for beginning students!" Here is a graduate student in his 20s, reorganizing all of economics in four or five chapters, right before your eyes, and let Marshall, Hicks, Friedman, and everyone else get out of the way!

I could see that some of this style was just youthful brashness, and I imagine there are passages that Samuelson would say differently now. But what a waste it would have been if he had waited until his views had matured! The book would have lost the excitement of discovery that carries the reader forward and the patient instructions to the student on how economics is *done* that only an author who has only recently learned something for himself can provide effectively. Samuelson was the Julia Child of economics, somehow teaching you the basics and giving you the feeling of becoming an insider in a complex culture all at the same time.

I loved the *Foundations*. Like so many others in my cohort, I internalized its view that if I couldn't formulate a problem in economic theory mathematically, I didn't know what I was doing. I came to the position that mathematical analysis is not one of many ways of doing economic theory: it is the only way. Economic theory *is* mathematical analysis. Everything else is just pictures and talk.

5

Before the various University of Chicago libraries were consolidated in Regenstein Library, economics Ph.D. students studied in the business and economics library, on the top floor of what is now Stuart Hall. The room had been designed as the law library, and its Gothic arches and leaded glass windows lent a welcome seriousness to our efforts to gain some intellectual control over the vastness of economic knowledge. In this room, Neil Wallace set an issue of the *Review of Economics and Statistics* on the table in front of me: "Look at this." The issue contained a symposium on monetary policy, including the papers that had been presented along with commentary by assigned discussants. Neil had opened it to the opening paragraphs of Milton Friedman's comments on a paper by the Harvard economist Seymour Harris. I read the introduction, in which Friedman criticized Harris for mixing "prediction and prescription so thoroughly that it is difficult to tell when he is recording what is going to be done and when recommending what should be done." Section II then began,

The role of the economist in discussions of public policy seems to me to prescribe what should be done in the light of what can be done, politics aside, and not to predict what is "politically feasible" and then to recommend it. Accordingly, I shall not attempt a detailed criticism of Harris' comment.[1]

What excited me about this passage—and what I knew had excited Neil—was the confidence of Friedman's dismissal of Harris in this public, face-to-face interchange, and his own focus on what he saw as the economics of monetary policy without regard for how popular he or his analysis would be with his listeners. This focus and fearlessness was what we admired in Friedman's class: he was a moral example to us, just as Frank Knight had been for him and George Stigler.

Friedman rarely lectured. His class discussions were often structured as debates, with student opinions or newspaper quotes serving to introduce a problem and some loosely stated opinions about it. Then Friedman would lead us into a clear statement of the problem, considering alternative formulations as thoroughly as anyone in the class wanted to. Once formulated, the problem was quickly analyzed—usually diagrammatically—on the board. So we learned how to formulate a model, to think about and decide which features of a problem we could safely abstract from and which we needed to put at the center of the analysis. Here "model" is my term: it was not a term that Friedman liked or used. I think that for him talking about modeling would have detracted from the substantive seriousness of the inquiry we were engaged in, would divert us away from the attempt to discover "what can be done" into merely a mathematical exercise.

The quality of discussions in Friedman's classes was unique in my experience. He did not call on students by name, as I recall, permitting me and many other classmates to experience the intensity of engaging Friedman directly only vicariously. It was not dismissal that I feared—no graduate student would have been dismissed the way Harris had been—but the exposure of my confusion next to Friedman's quickness and clarity. He would engage a particular student in a dialogue, and once engaged no escape but assent was possible. Exit lines like "Well, I'll have to think about it" were no use: "Let's think about it now," Friedman would say. Friedman did not want to win the debate by convincing the rest of the class he was right, using the student as a foil—any experienced teacher can do that. He wanted the student he was engaged with to join him in thinking the problem through to the end, to be not merely exhausted but truly convinced. Of course, this meant that Friedman was completely exposed, too.

Students at Chicago, then as now, formed into study groups to prepare for the Core Exam that tested for knowledge of the entire first year curriculum. The Core questions were like the questions Friedman used in class: loose, notation-free statements of some economic question. Our job was to formulate the question sharply, focusing on essentials, and then answer it. Neil and I were in a study group of four or five, and we enforced the rule that everyone should prepare in advance. I still have the typed notes I prepared for these meetings. Looking at them again after all these years, I find little that I would change. The economics I learned from Friedman and Samuelson is a unified and manageable body of knowledge. It can be learned in a few months, and anyone who has mastered it can think about any problem in economics. I passed the Core Exam in winter quarter, 1961, less than a year after I had completed my first, remedial, undergraduate economics course.

6

My doctoral thesis was concerned with estimating the degree of capital-labor substitution in U.S. manufacturing. It was a part of a larger project that Arnold Harberger organized, involving many students, to calibrate a general equilibrium model he was using for tax analysis. The question involved capital, so a dynamic theory would seem to be called for, but I based my econometric work on a static marginal productivity condition that did not require either measuring capital or studying its determinants. These may have been econometric virtues, but they only postponed my entry into economic dynamics. I couldn't wait to finish my thesis and get on to something more interesting and ambitious.

The example I wanted to follow was the work of Dale Jorgenson, who was visiting at Chicago during my last year there. His study of the investment decision of the firm mixed theory, econometrics, and careful measurement in a way that I much admired (and still do). The modeling of firm and industry dynamics was at the top my agenda in 1963, when I became an assistant professor at the Graduate School of Industrial Administration (GSIA), the business school at Carnegie Tech.

Jorgenson had derived a formula for a firm's long-run capital-output ratio, but the theory did not explain why the adjustment to such a long-run target should be slow, as it appeared to be in the data. I modified the model by adding a penalty for rapid change—an adjustment cost—and used the calculus of variations to derive both the long-run target and the gradual approach to it from a single set of assumptions. I sent the paper to Dale, who directed me to an earlier paper by Eisner and Strotz that contained everything I had done. This was a setback, but somehow a stimulating one. I worked out a theory of firm-determined technological change, using the same variational methods. I generalized the Eisner–Strotz theory to many capital goods. It seemed there were enough unsolved problems in firm dynamics to support a lot of theorists.

Dick Schramm's GSIA thesis showed how to make a multiple capital good model operational econometrically. His model involved a lagged adjustment of price expectations to movements in actual prices. I remember a seminar presentation of Schramm's at which Jack Muth asked Dick why he had not assumed rational expectations. Of course, we all knew and admired Jack's paper "Rational Expectations and the Theory of Price Movements," but none of us knew how to exploit this idea econometrically. At that time, I thought of rational expectations as an elegant rationalization of the kind of lagged adjustment of expectations that Schramm assumed in his thesis, not as an alternate model. This was a half-truth that kept me from seeing the force of Jack's objections.

Schramm's thesis dealt with decisions of competitive firms, taking prices and expected future prices as given. So did the Eisner and Strotz paper, and my extensions of their work. Since these theories did not treat the determinants of prices, there was no internal inconsistency in the nonrational expectations they assumed. Serious inconsistency did emerge, though, when I made an entire Marshallian industry the unit of analysis, instead of the individual firm. In my "Adjustment Costs and the Theory of Supply," I took the industry demand function as a given, and solved for the time path of prices along with the paths of production and capital stock. I postulated "myopic" expectations—price expectations formed by simply extrapolating the current price into the future—and then deduced from this and other assumptions an equilibrium price path that was not constant but rather grew or declined in a predictable way. In such a model, you could *see* the profit opportunities that firms were passing up. Why couldn't they see these opportunities too? But if they did, the model couldn't be the right way to describe their behavior. Now I could go back to Muth's 1961 paper and see that this inconsistency was exactly his argument: In his words, "the marginal revenue product of economics" should be zero, or close to it. If your theory reveals profit opportunities, you have the wrong theory.

The context in which I came to this understanding was deterministic, so the assumption of rational expectations reduces to perfect foresight, using a terminology that I take from Buz Brock. Calculating a perfect foresight equilibrium for an industry, say, sounds as though it should involve solving a fixed point problem in a space of price paths: the actual path implies a forecast path, which in turn implies an actual path. This sounds hard, and it can be. But under competitive conditions, one can show that an industry over time will operate so as to maximize a discounted, consumer surplus integral—a problem that is mathematically no harder than the present value maximizing problem faced by a single firm. Who, exactly, is solving this planning problem? Adam Smith's "invisible hand," of course, not any actual person: but the mathematics of planning problems turned out to be just the right equipment needed to understand the decentralized interactions of a large number of producers. One can calculate equilibrium quantities over time using this fact and then read the equilibrium prices off the demand curve. I saw this in a particular context just by comparing the Euler necessary conditions for the equilibrium problem to those from the consumer surplus maximization problem. In fact, it is a consequence of one of the classic theorems of welfare economics.

In my first years at GSIA I worked furiously to pick up the mathematics of optimization over time—calculus of variations, the maximum principle of Pontryagin, Bellman's dynamic programming—and of the differential equations systems these optimization problems produced. I worked on applications of these methods to problems in economics and operations research. Theoretically minded economists of my cohort were doing the same thing all over the world. I was studying the dynamics of investment at the firm and industry level, as were many others. Still others were studying optimal growth of an economy, optimal accumulation of human capital, optimal advertising and R and D investment, and so on.

In 1966 I was invited to a workshop on economic dynamics, conducted in Chicago by Hirofumi Uzawa, that involved some of the best people in this group of younger theorists. Uzawa was a charismatic figure, an enormous influence on theoretically minded students, who had moved to Chicago from Stanford just after I had left. The seminars ran all day, through dinner, and into the evening. Discussions were noisy and intense, but friendly and constructive: I remember people going to the blackboard in the middle of a talk, to show how a speaker's argument had gone wrong and to try to help fix it.

Dave Cass spoke about work that he and Menahem Yaari were doing, trying to understand the logic of a model of an economy with an infinity of overlapping generations that Samuelson had published in 1958. This paper had not been on reading lists of mine, but I was immediately attracted by its simplicity and the role it had for money. This was the first model I had seen in which paper money had a useful role to perform and had a command over goods in equilibrium. This was exciting, and the following fall I began to use this setup in my graduate courses in macroeconomics.

The paper I had written for the Uzawa conference was never finished: I couldn't establish the mathematical result that was to be the paper's centerpiece. I proposed to Ed Prescott, a friend of mine from his student days at GSIA who was then on the faculty at Penn, that we work together on it. Even with Ed's help, the original problem proved intractable, but we found ourselves thinking together about the behavior of firms in a competitive industry that is subject to unpredictable demand shocks. Ed had used dynamic programming methods in his thesis, and introduced me to a paper by David Blackwell that worked out the underlying mathematics in a useful and beautiful way. We applied these methods to the problem of maximizing expected, discounted consumers' surplus in the industry. The solution takes the form of a Markov process or stochastic difference equation describing the evolution of capacity and production in response to recurring shocks to demand. Buz Brock and Leonard Mirman were thinking about optimal growth in similar terms at about the same time.

But then how can the solution to this maximum problem be related to a competitive equilibrium in which firms have rational expectations? Part of the answer lay in reformulating the rational expectations hypothesis in a way that did not require the linearity Muth had assumed in his analysis. The other part of the answer came from applying the competitive general equilibrium theory of Arrow, Debreu, and McKenzie, theory developed in the 1950s and gradually being extended to ever more general mathematical contexts. The potential of this body of theory for more applied work was, at that time, unrecognized. Prescott and I saw that it would be helpful to us, and plunged into a self-taught crash course. Putting the pieces together, we wrote "Investment under Uncertainty."

In 1963, I had thought of a competitive industry in terms of firms solving short- and long-run, deterministic profit-maximization problems, under the (false) belief that current prices would maintain their current values forever, and with the passage from one to the other and all the effects of unpredictable shocks tacked on as afterthoughts. Five years later, I thought of the same economics in terms of firms maximizing expected discounted present value, with rational expectations about the probability distributions of future prices, and with stochastic shocks and adjustment costs both fully integrated into the theory. From an objective point of view, this transformation can be viewed as a product of decades of research by many economists. From my subjective viewpoint, it was the most rapid, radical change of view I have ever experienced as an economist.

7

In those early years at GSIA, my closest friend was Leonard Rapping, a Chicago Ph.D. about two years ahead of me. As Leonard said in a 1982 interview,

I expect that we talked once or twice every day from '63 to '68. We talked about everything: about economics, about politics, about business school problems, just about everything. We would have coffee from about three until five. We were the two people who would always be at the afternoon coffee hours. Everyone else would be back at their offices.[2]

Maybe it was inevitable that we would do joint research, but it was surprising that this should turn out to be research in macroeconomics—a field in which neither of us had even taken a prelim. We got there by the back door, through labor economics: at Chicago, we had both studied with Gregg Lewis.

At that time, many people were regressing changes in nominal wages on the unemployment rate, a statistical relation known as a Phillips curve, interpreting the negative coefficient of unemployment as describing a trade-off: lower unemployment means higher wage inflation. People had just begun to consider what kind of economics might underly this statistical connection. Leonard and I started discussing supply and demand models of joint wage and employment determination, and tried these out in the classroom. We decided to formulate and test such a model more carefully. To get an aggregate time series of decent length, back then, one needed to go back to 1929, so our project turned into an attempt to understand wage and employment behavior through the depression and war years.

Like everyone else, we thought that the ultimate source of employment fluctuations in both these periods came mainly from the demand side:

fluctuations in spending on goods and services. But all the evidence we knew about indicated that labor supply was very inelastic. How could we get large employment swings out of demand shifts in such a setting? We used a device based on the old Keynesian idea of "money illusion": people in booms (like World War II) are willing to supply a lot of labor temporarily at the high money wage rates available then, without realizing that when they spend these dollars it will be at higher prices. Symmetrically, people in depressions temporarily pass up jobs at low money wages, not realizing that these low wages will buy a lot more goods than they would have two years earlier. This was the idea we used to reconcile an elastic short-run supply of labor with an inelastic long-run supply. I thought of my parents, both working throughout the war and saving most of what they made to build up a down payment for the house they bought when the war was over.

In our model, wages and employment levels were always in a kind of temporary equilibrium, and this equilibrium had the property that inflation would stimulate employment. What about *un*employment? We added a labor force participation equation that, combined with the rest of the model, gave us a Phillips curve.

Leonard and I did a careful job of working through the decision problems of households and firms in a world subject to these "illusions," and another careful job putting together a set of compatible time series. The econometric work came out well, and the ambitions of the project began to dawn on us. "Bob, we're going to be famous!" Leonard would say. It frightened me, and I managed to be out of town on the day that Leonard presented the paper to our colleagues at a GSIA seminar. We were both right. Albert Rees refereed the paper at the *JPE*: his outraged reaction was later published as a comment. But why outrage? Another economist, we heard, called the paper "fascist economics." Fascist! For writing down a labor supply curve and taking it seriously!

Before our paper was finished, Milton Friedman had used his presidential address to the American Economic Association to argue that in the long run, the unemployment rate would be independent of the inflation rate: there would be no Phillips-like trade-off between inflation and unemployment. Friedman's argument was theoretical, but his premises all seemed to Leonard and me to hold for our model. Yet our model *did* imply a long-run trade-off. Later, we came to see that this difference was due to our use of adaptive, rather than rational, expectations, but at the time we simply accepted it as an unresolved puzzle.

Edmund Phelps had been trying to use an equilibrium framework to think about unemployment and wage determination at about the same time, and he had reached the same theoretical conclusion that Friedman had. While making the rounds of the seminar circuit he had run across others engaged in the same kind of investigation he and Rapping and I were engaged in. He assembled these papers in a 1970 book, *Microeconomic Foundations of Employment and Inflation Theory*, now universally known simply as the "Phelps volume." This was the kind of fame that Leonard and I had dreamed of, and the book and the conference Ned organized around it gave us the first experience either of us had had of being at the forefront of an important research area.

In an early draft of the introduction to the volume, Phelps had written that ". . . perhaps Lucas and Rapping are 180 degrees to the truth," by which he meant that perhaps we should have emphasized income effects in our theory of employment fluctuations rather than the substitution effects we did emphasize. On a social occasion soon after the conference—when Leonard and I were still high—we joked about this remark. This shocked Elayne Rapping. She said, "All you two care about is being cited by a well-known economist, about being famous. It doesn't matter to you whether you are right or 180 degrees off." Elayne's remark stung, and she was certainly right that the source of our good mood that evening was the boost the conference had given to our ambitions. The desires for fame and truth are not inconsistent, though, and in fact we were laughing because we were so sure that Phelps's criticism could be dealt with. But this was not the occasion to try to explain income and substitution effects to Elayne, and anyway we knew that she was as pleased with our success as we were.

Not long after this occasion, Leonard and Elayne were swept up in the opposition to the war in Vietnam and moved far to the left, politically. Leonard lost interest in the kind of economics we had done together. When the *JPE* published Rees's comment on our paper, both of us signed the reply, but I had written it alone. Our friendship had been based on conversations that ranged much more broadly than our joint work, and we tried to maintain them, but without success. Soon after, Leonard moved to the University of Massachusetts, which was then becoming a center for radical economics.

8

By the end of the '60s, I was leading two lives as an economist. With Rapping, I was an empirical macroeconomist, estimating Phillips curves and aggregate labor supply functions. Working with Prescott, I had immersed myself in the mathematics of dynamic programming and general equilibrium theory and was applying these methods to construct tractable, genuinely dynamic models. In my graduate teaching, I was putting these elements together, using the overlapping generations models that I had learned about from Cass, to build models of monetary economies that would, I hoped, be helpful in addressing questions of macroeconomic policy.

At the Phelps volume conference, Ned Phelps had pushed one such question to the front of my thinking: if Rapping and I were right that monetary shocks affected people's willingness to supply labor by "fooling" them about their future options, then we needed to explain why everyone gets fooled in the same direction. Why isn't the worker who is over-optimistic about his job prospects offset by another who is too pessimistic? Phelps outlined an answer to this question in his essay in the volume, based on the idea that workers at any one location are short on information about what is happening elsewhere. When a worker sees a wage change, he thinks it is specific to his own market, not realizing that the same thing might be happening everywhere. I thought I could capture this effect with the kind of overlapping generations models I was using in class. I tried out one version in 1968. Further work led to "Expectations and the Neutrality of Money," submitted to the *American Economic Review* in 1970 and finally published in the *Journal of Economic Theory* in 1972.

The paper contained a careful and explicit construction of a theoretical example of an economy in which the motives, opportunities, and information of every economic actor was unambiguously spelled out. Expectations were rational. In this setting, as in Friedman's AEA address, there was no long-run trade-off between employment and inflation. Yet the model also implied the kind of correlations between employment and inflation that were then widely interpreted as hard evidence that such trade-offs did exist. I felt I understood for the first time both why Friedman and Phelps were right in arguing there was no long-run trade-off between unemployment and inflation and why econometric tests continued to reject this "natural rate" view.

Working out this example took me to the limit of my technical skills and beyond: it was not easy reading, nor had it been easy writing. It built closely on Rapping's and my view of the labor supply decision as well as on the formulation of rational expectations that Prescott and I had developed working on "Investment under Uncertainty." It is easy for me to see the influences of Phelps, Rapping, Prescott, and Cass in this paper, but the combination was new and striking: no one else was doing macroeconomics this way in 1970. The paper made my reputation.

9

My family and I spent the summer of 1970 in Seattle, driving our underpowered Plymouth Valiant into the headwind for days to get there. I had an office at the University of Washington. My ambition for the summer was to write a paper on Phillips curves for a conference to be held that fall at the Federal Reserve Board. I had been invited, I assumed, as a spokesman for the Friedman-Phelps position that there was no long run trade-off between unemployment and inflation. My plan was to translate what I had learned from writing "Expectations and the Neutrality of Money" into linear examples that would make it clear to a much wider readership why the standard tests for "long-run" effects—tests of the sort Rapping and I and dozens of others had used—were not informative about the Friedman–Phelps hypothesis. This paper became "Econometric Testing of the Natural Rate Hypothesis."

The stay in Seattle was a pleasure—I enjoyed being close to my Seattle family—but by the summer's end, I found I missed the more intense atmosphere of GSIA and was eager to get back to Pittsburgh. On my first day at the office Marty Geisel handed me a working paper by Tom Sargent, saying only, "I think you will be interested in this." Sargent's paper involved exactly the logic of the paper I had just completed (which of course Tom hadn't seen), applied to Irving Fisher's predicted relation between expected inflation and interest rates. Rational expectations connected expected inflation, which we cannot observe, to actual inflation rates, which we can, in just the right way to give Fisher's idea content. Sargent had based a test of Fisher's theory on this observation—the first econometric application of Muth's idea.

I gave my paper in Washington in the fall. It was the first time that many in attendance had heard of rational expectations. James Tobin gave it a generous review when he summed up the proceedings of the conference: it was clear that I had made my point. When my session ended, an economist of about my age whose work on Phillips curves I knew and respected came up to the podium and told me, "You just explained why everything I've done in the last few years is worthless." This shocked me: I was viewing myself as an underdog in the conference setting and was not prepared to assume this very different role. I protested, "Oh no, that wasn't what I said at all." He insisted, "Yes it was. It was exactly what you said. And you were right." I had not experienced anything like this before.

As Sargent's test of the Fisher hypothesis showed, the idea that rational expectations implied restrictions across equations was not special to Phillips curves. When Allan Meltzer and Karl Brunner asked me to give a paper on empirical Phillips curves for the first meeting of the Carnegie–Rochester Conference Series, I decided to try to illustrate this fact with a variety of econometric applications. The resulting paper, "Econometric Policy Evaluation: A Critique," explained in detail how rational expectations undermines the then-conventional uses of econometric models in simulating the effects of policy changes. This "Lucas critique," as it came to be known, is probably the most influential paper I have written.

My critical writing on the Keynesian macroeconometric models of the day showed that simulations of these models could not be expected to give accurate answers about the effects of changes in economic policy. Parallel work by Sargent, and Sargent and Neil Wallace, showed the same thing. These demonstrations effectively ended the role of these models in policy debates and eliminated the main intellectual basis for monetary and fiscal fine-tuning of the economy. We were certainly not the first economists who were skeptical of Keynesian econometric models—the whole monetarist tradition of Milton Friedman, Allan Meltzer, and Karl Brunner anticipated our conclusions—but Sargent and Wallace and I were critics from *within*. We were committed to the use of explicit models to evaluate policy changes; we knew the work we were criticizing in detail, and we could articulate the reasons for our skepticism in a way that those we criticized could see the arguments and respond usefully to them. Macroeconomic debate had changed course.

10

Not long after "Investment under Uncertainty" was finished, Ed Prescott returned to GSIA as a faculty member. I was working on monetary theory, a topic that Ed had never been much interested in. I was also thinking about unemployment, using a theoretical setting in which workers are distributed over a large number of distinct markets, and these markets are subject to persistent shocks to demand. If your market is hit with a bad shock, wages are likely to be low for a while. You are tempted to leave, to set out for brighter prospects elsewhere, but this will entail a spell of unemployment. The risks must be balanced and how this balancing comes out depends on what everyone else is doing. After some weeks of work, I felt I was very close to having a successful mathematical model of this situation, a theory of what Milton Friedman had called the "natural rate of unemployment."

But the pieces would not fall into place. I believed that my formulation had the economics of these interactions just right and that the problem was that I didn't know and couldn't invent the mathematics to work out the implications of the theory. Once again, I asked Ed to collaborate, and after I had taken him through the model, he agreed. This was late on a Friday afternoon, so we stopped working and went downstairs to the faculty–student TGIF.

After the party, walking home by myself through the Schenley Park golf course, thoughts of regret came over me. I had formulated, on my own, a great theoretical problem and had carried the analysis of that problem close to completion. Now I had shown the problem to Ed, who would surely see a quick resolution of the mathematical issues that I had been stuck on. He could write the paper by himself and since I had shown him no actual results, claim credit for himself. He might not even thank me for "helpful discussion" in his opening footnote! As soon as I got home I took out my typewriter and, in a kind of paranoid frenzy that lasted through the weekend, I wrote a draft of the entire paper: Introduction, Theorem 1, Theorem 2, and so on, right through to the end.

On Monday I felt foolish as soon as I saw Ed, but I handed him the draft anyway. Of course we soon discovered that most of the results stated in the draft were false and that we had no idea how to prove the theorems that were possibly true. How could it have been otherwise? If I had really known how to finish the paper I wouldn't have asked Ed to work with me! So we began work in earnest.

Some days, perhaps weeks, later I arrived at the office around 9 and found a note from Ed in my mailbox. The full text was as follows:

Bob,
This is the way labor markets work:
$$v(s, y, \lambda) = \max\{\lambda, R(s, y) + \min[\lambda, \beta \int v(s', y, \lambda) f(s', s)ds']\}.$$
Ed

Of course since our project was well underway, we had agreed on notation: s stood for the state of product demand at a particular location, y stood for the number of workers who were already at that location, $R(s, y)$ was the marginal product of labor implied by these two numbers, and $v(s, y)$ stood for the present value of earnings that one of these workers could obtain if he made his decision whether to stay at this location or leave optimally. Other features of the equation were as novel to me as they are (I imagine) to you.

The normal response to such a note, I suppose, would have been to go upstairs to Ed's office and ask for some kind of explanation. But theoretical economists are not normal, and we do not ask for words that "explain" what equations mean. We ask for equations that explain what words mean. Ed had provided an equation that claimed to explain how labor markets work. It was my job to understand it and to decide whether I agreed with this claim. This took me a while, but I saw that Ed had replaced an assumption of mine that workers who leave any one location hit on a new location at random—maybe a worse location than the one they had left—with the alternative assumption that searching workers were fully informed about options elsewhere and bee-lined for the best destination. Mathematically, this meant that a single parameter—Ed's λ—stood for two different things: the present value of earnings that all searching workers would have to expect in order to leave a location and the present value that a particular location would need to offer to receive new arrivals.

Mathematically, Ed's equation was a very familiar, comfortable object for me to analyze: once I convinced myself that it described some sensible economics, it took a few minutes to see that its properties could be established by standard methods and that these properties were interesting and reasonable. By lunchtime, I could see that I was to be a co-author of a very sharp paper, unlike anything anyone had seen before, a paper with a potential for helping us to think about important events.

If I had to pick a single day to represent what I like about a life of research, it would be this one. Ed's note captures exactly why I think we value mathematical modeling: it is a method to help us get to new levels of understanding the ways things work. No one could have written Ed's equation down at the beginning of an inquiry into the nature of unemployment: it is too far from earlier ways of thinking to be grasped in one step. The new understanding that this equation represents could be gained only through a trial-and-error process, involving formulating and analyzing explicit models. It is this struggle to capture behavior in tractable models that leads us deeper into the economics of market interactions and forms the progressive element in economic thought.

11

In October, 1978—leaf season—the Federal Reserve Bank of Boston sponsored a conference at the Bald Peak Colony Club in New Hampshire. Ed Prescott and I rented a car at Logan Airport and drove up together. Night fell before we reached the conference center and we got lost on country roads. We stopped for directions at a crossroads store, but after a few minutes of laconic "Nope, yep" New England conversation we realized that the two old men in the store were amusing themselves at our expense, conveying no information. We left in disgust and anger. The incident heightened my sense of entering foreign territory.

On the drive, neither Ed nor I discussed the papers we were to give at the conference. Ed had been reading Simon Kuznets's work and treated me to a review of Kuznets's main findings. I was grateful for the chance to learn something from this central figure in research on economic growth without actually having to read him. We talked about the kinds of theoretical models that might fit the regularities that Kuznets had documented. What better and more productive way to deal with anxieties about how one's work will be received than looking beyond to the next project?

When the conference began, the next day, it became clear that this was not the occasion for such anxieties. The attenders included representatives of the Keynesian establishment—including Paul Samuelson himself—and some "new classical" rebels. In my memory, the conference was a kind of triumph of the new classical views. My own paper was a reprise of Milton Friedman's 1948 paper, "A Monetary and Fiscal Framework for Economic Stability," emphasizing the support that recent research provided for Friedman's positions, with no pretense of new findings. I viewed it as my day to stand up and be counted as a Chicago economist. I later wrote to my parents:

The influence my work has had was astonishing to me. I was very nervous about my presentation, which was extremely negative on what most of this group is up to, yet people were lining up in the question period to take their turn to say how right I am.

The question period I referred to was chaotic, and I remember people calling for me to denounce work by John Taylor and Stan Fischer that, like some of my own work, attempted to account for real effects of monetary instability. I also preferred my approach, but I understood that this preference was not really defensible empirically. I said that on the basis of the evidence available now, I did not see how it was possible to distinguish between my views and Taylor's. Looking back on the occasion, an exciting one for me, I am pleased and a little surprised that I managed such a level-headed reply.

Though I did not see it at the time, the Bald Peak conference also marked the beginning of the end of my attempts to account for the business cycle in terms of monetary shocks. At that conference, Ed Prescott presented a model of his and Finn Kydland's that was a kind of mixture of Brock and Mirman's model of growth subject to stochastic technology shocks and my model of monetary shocks. When Ed presented his results, everyone could see they were important but the paper was so novel and complicated that no one could see exactly what they were. Later on, as they gained more experience through numerical simulations of their Bald Peak model, Kydland and Prescott found that the monetary shocks were just not pulling their weight: by removing all monetary aspects of the theory, they obtained a far simpler and more comprehensible structure that fit postwar U.S. time series data just as well as the original version. Besides introducing an important substantive refocusing of business cycle research, Kydland and Prescott introduced a new style of comparing theory to evidence that has had an enormous, beneficial effect on empirical work in the field.

12

By the time of the Bald Peak conference, I had moved from Carnegie Mellon to the University of Chicago. I was just over forty years old. The work that was later recognized by the Swedish Academy of Sciences was done. I had arrived at a research style that has continued over the years to lead me into new ways of seeing things.

In the more than twenty years since, I have continued to devote virtually all of my time to teaching and research. I have written on many subjects and participated in collaborations with Andy Atkeson, Esteban Rossi-Hansberg, and, especially, with Nancy Stokey, that have been as interesting and fruitful for me as those with Leonard Rapping and Ed Prescott. Perhaps at some later occasion I will review these years, too: I have enjoyed them, produced some work I am proud of, and accumulated enough memories for many more memoirs.

Awarded Nobel Prize in 1995. Lecture presented April 5, 2001.

Date of Birth

September 15, 1937

Academic Degrees

B.A.   University of Chicago, 1959

Ph.D. University of Chicago, 1964

Academic Affiliations

Lecturer, Department of Economics, University of Chicago, 1962–1963

Assistant Professor of Economics, Carnegie Institute of Technology, 1963–1967

Associate Professor of Economics, Carnegie Mellon University, 1967–1970

Professor of Economics, Carnegie Mellon University, 1970–1974

Ford Foundation Visiting Research Professor of Economics, University of Chicago, 1974–1975

Professor of Economics, University of Chicago, 1975–1980

Visiting Professor of Economics, Northwestern, 1981–1982

John Dewey Distinguished Service Professor of Economics, University of Chicago, 1980–present

Selected Books

Studies in Business-Cycle Theory, 1981

Models of Business Cycles, 1987

Recursive Methods in Economic Dynamics, 1989 (with N. Stokey and E. Prescott)

Lectures on Economic Growth, 2002

James J. Heckman

I write this essay with some trepidation. Most of the essays in this series are retrospectives rather than progress reports of scholars in mid-career. I am not ready to announce my retirement. I won the Nobel Prize at a relatively early age (56) and hope that I have many more years of active research ahead of me. I welcome the Nobel Prize as an award that opens doors for further growth and learning. So I write this essay in the spirit that past is prologue. I describe my evolution as an economist to this point (March 2003) and my current vision of how my future research will unfold.

My evolution as an economist was not direct. I drifted among academic fields before I settled on economics. Even after I decided to become an economist, I drifted among subfields of the discipline. Eventually I became a labor economist with a strong interest in empirical research, public policy, and the methodology of doing empirical research. If this essay meanders, so did my life.

I proceed in the following way. I present a few remarks on my early background that help to explain some of the motivations and choices throughout my career and how I came to address the problems I have worked on.

I then discuss my interactions with colleagues and students at two key environments: the place where I started as a professional economist, Columbia and the New York NBER in the early 1970s, and the place where I have spent the greatest amount of time: the University of Chicago from the mid '70s to the present. The practice of economics is a social activity greatly affected by the environment in which one works. Feedback, stimulation, and encouragement are central to this activity. I have been lucky to have had many brilliant and stimulating colleagues and students who have helped shape my approach to economics.

Early Influences

I was born in Chicago in 1944 near the University of Chicago, although neither parent was employed by it. Both of my parents were high school graduates. My father was a middle manager for the Armour meat-packing company, and my mother was a housewife. Both parents came from families with modest means. My father's high school degree was delayed several years by his having to drop out of school to work fulltime on his father's farm to support his family. My father's post–high school training was limited to a semester at the University of Oklahoma in the fall of 1929, an unpropitious time to start college, and night school training in accounting and management in the Executive Degree Program at the University of Chicago in the 1940s. Both my sister (who is four years older) and I received strong encouragement from our parents to get the college degrees that they lacked. There were books around our home, and my mother took us on frequent trips to museums, cultural events, and historical sites. The first institution of higher learning I ever saw was the University of Chicago, and my father always spoke with admiration about it. Thus began my relationship with an institution that has had a profound influence on my life.

My father fell victim to company politics and suffered various demotions and lateral transfers throughout his career. These transfers gave me a chance to visit many new places with very different social and cultural traditions. These involuntary transfers and demotions were a deep source of anxiety for my father. He urged me at an early age to enter a profession where I could develop an independent reputation and avoid the politics of the bureaucracy of middle managers that he had experienced. I took his message to heart and decided early on to enter a profession where I could make my own mark and be independent of the good will of any superior and where I would never have to be a company man.

My family on both sides is of southern origin. There is a Heckman family farmstead and gravesite in southwestern Virginia that survives to this day. The Heckmans of Virginia were an Old Baptist (Dunkard) family that migrated to North America in the 1740s from Germany to escape religious persecution. The family tradition was anchored in a strong form of fundamentalist Protestant Christianity in which I was raised. My father's father was a farmer-preacher. My mother's family also traces back to Virginia and had strong fundamentalist roots.

As a young child, I fervently embraced the faith of my parents and by age eight, I was a child minister giving sermons on Sunday evenings introduced by a motto taken from the New Testament, "A little child shall lead them." It was expected that when I became an adult, I would be a minister. The church in Western Springs, Illinois, where I preached, was the only pastorate held by the evangelist Billy Graham when he was a student at Wheaton College. After he started his famous crusades, he would occasionally visit his former church. As a child, I met him on several occasions, and he encouraged my calling.

My deep religious belief led me to read and study the Bible very closely. I committed vast passages of it to memory. I interacted with ministers to further my knowledge and even wrote a few tracts that were mimeographed and circulated. I attended religious camps and revival meetings and read with interest about the work of missionaries in exotic environments.

By my early teenage years, while living in Denver, Colorado, I began having doubts. The fundamentalist creed I was raised in and espoused took the Bible very literally. But I began to notice inconsistencies in the Bible, and as I read more broadly in science and philosophy, I came to question the literal interpretations of creation and other aspects of the fundamentalist Christianity with which I was raised. Matters came to a head in a high school term paper I wrote on the parallels between Zoroastrianism (which predated Christianity) and Christian teaching. I began to recognize the eclectic nature of Christian theology. A Zoroastrian origin for Christian traditions was not a welcome idea in the church I attended, nor was any departure from a strict and literal reading of scripture.

These intellectual doubts caused me at age fifteen to break with fundamentalist Christianity and abandon my plan to become a minister. This was not an easy decision for me because at the time my life was in the church and my parents had hopes for me to become a great evangelist.

I respected the sincerity of the beliefs held by my family and by members of my congregation, but I no longer shared them. My doubts were later reinforced by the virulent anti-Catholic rhetoric produced by many fundamentalist churches in the 1960 campaign of John F. Kennedy. The intolerance, bigotry and unwillingness of most of the elders in my church to discuss ideas left me deeply dissatisfied. I found that I was unable to accept authority qua authority, a trait that has characterized me ever since. At the same time, my break with the church isolated me from my family and friends. I learned to go it alone without much support at an early age. Having a deep faith and then abandoning it because of intellectual doubt was a wrenching experience. At the same time, I learned early to live off my own intellectual and emotional resources. My ability to go it alone, without the approval of others, has been a major asset to my career. I learned to stick to my guns irrespective of what others around me thought.

During this period, I applied and was encouraged to attend college at the University of Chicago in a special program for bored but high-achieving high school students. I was tempted to go to escape the awkward situation in which I found myself. However, family finances were poor and my parents thought me too young.

At about the same time I broke with fundamentalist Christianity and was considering enrolling at Chicago, a whole new world of ideas opened up to me thanks to the accidental introduction of Frank Oppenheimer into my life. Frank Oppenheimer was the brother of J. Robert Oppenheimer, the famous physicist and head of the Manhattan Project. Frank was an accomplished experimental physicist in his own right who had worked at Los Alamos during World War II and at the University of Minnesota afterward. Much later he gained fame for developing the Exploratorium—a major science teaching museum in San Francisco that has been emulated around the world. Frank Oppenheimer had been a member of the Communist Party, which raised questions about his brother's loyalty. It led to Frank's dismissal from the University of Minnesota during the height of the McCarthy era.

It was my good luck that the local superintendent of schools in Jefferson County, Colorado, invited Frank Oppenheimer to teach physics to a countywide class of selected students after he had spent five or so years ranching in rural Colorado. The offer of enrollment in his class convinced me to stay in high school to learn from him. That class and my exposure to him were truly life-transforming experiences. He was the first truly brilliant mind I had ever encountered. He introduced me to the life of the mind. Our class read everything he told us to read in science and other subjects. We rushed out to read the books and articles he casually mentioned while he conducted physics experiments with us. We learned to love the late quartets of Beethoven at his house, and we discussed the philosophy of science into the night. In the second year of his course, he introduced us to leading scientists such as George Gamow and Stanislaw Ulam, who came into our high school classroom to discuss cutting-edge science.

Oppenheimer transmitted a love of physics in his classroom evident today to any visitor to the Exploratorium. He showed us how theory explained facts. In a lab book I still own, I derived all the basic laws of Newtonian mechanics and tested them on a set of beautiful experiments designed in the post–Sputnik era to promote science literacy among American youth. The objective nature of physics and the ability of the laws of physics to predict empirical regularities was a splendid alternative to a religion and authority I no longer accepted. I became an enthusiastic protoscientist, amazed and gratified that theory worked so well in practice. The theory was beautiful. But it was the confirmation of theory, and the insistence that any physical law worthy of that name should conform to and predict physical reality, that were so pleasing. I remember a classroom discussion with Oppenheimer on Eugene Wigner's then recently written article, "The Unreasonable Effectiveness of Mathematics in Physical Science." The profound simplicity of the physical world and the ability of mathematics to predict it overwhelmed me. If I had any religion at that time, it was Deism. I was impressed by God the watchmaker. In my senior year in high school, I had decided to study physics at Cornell at the urging of Frank Oppenheimer. The possibilities of science seemed limitless.

But even then, I was interested in other things. My father's demotions and transfers took my family on a tour through the Border South and the West: St. Louis, Lexington (Kentucky), and Oklahoma City, ending up in Denver, Colorado, where I withdrew from organized religion and met Oppenheimer. In the first three towns, I saw firsthand the last vestiges of the Jim Crow system of racial discrimination. Its protocols and intrinsically demeaning effects on all participants fascinated me. Coming from Chicago, I had heard of racism (especially after the lynching of Emmett Till in 1955), but I had never witnessed it. My parents, while southern in origin, never uttered racist remarks. The Jim Crow system of social regulation intrigued me, and I became an avid follower of the activities of the civil rights movement that dismantled it through social activism. The late '50s and early '60s were times of great social change, and the politics of the era captivated me. When I was not doing science, I was reading history, philosophy, and politics. In the late 1950s, *Life* magazine, then a popular weekly, ran a series on the national purpose written by many distinguished Americans. I read every essay in the series and debated the contents of these essays with teachers and fellow students.

So despite my love of science, I also had a deep fascination with politics, social science, and history. In deciding where to go to college, Cornell or Stanford looked like good bets because they had strengths in history and social science, not just physics and mathematics. As fate would have it, I applied and got fellowship support from both schools. However, I also won a Boettcher Foundation scholarship. Boettcher scholarships were very generous. This gave me financial independence at an early age and allowed a graceful exit from an estranged relationship with my parents, thereby giving me independence at seventeen—something I valued greatly. The only stipulation for receiving the fellowship was that I had to attend a college in Colorado. That did not seem like a severe limitation at the time. I debated between the University of Colorado (where Oppenheimer had been hired in my senior year) and Colorado College, which by many accounts was the best school in the state.

College Days: A Drift to Economics

My choice of Colorado College was more eventful then I could have forecasted. After a few semesters, I found the physics there disappointing and gravitated toward math and just about everything else. The liberal arts environment let me try my hand at many things: anthropology, philosophy, English literature, political science, and economics. I edited the student paper, protested civil rights abuses, fought anti-Semitism, and anti-black restrictive policies by fraternities and took a trip through the segregated South with my Nigerian roommate, which led to some hair-raising encounters in Birmingham, Alabama, and Hattiesburg, Mississippi, which we wrote about in student newspapers. I also interacted with the organizers of the Freedom School, a libertarian organization near Colorado College where I learned about Friedrich Hayek, Frédéric Bastiat, Ayn Rand, and Milton Friedman. In my junior year, I took a readings class in economic growth from Ray Werner. It was my first serious introduction to economics. We read Ricardo, Smith, and Arthur Lewis, a future Nobel laureate and previous speaker in this series. The professor also loaned me his copy of Paul Samuelson's *Foundations of Economic Analysis* (which I still own) to read as an extra bonus.

Samuelson's *Foundations* had a major impact on me. It demonstrated to me that economics could be as rigorous and empirically relevant as physics. The theorem–proof format of the book appealed to my mathematical side. At the same time, it showed that economics had empirical content through the theory of revealed preference. I saw a counterpart in social science to the hard science I had first experienced in Oppenheimer's classroom.

Lewis's *Theory of Economic Growth* appealed to my liberal arts training. It synthesized economics, politics, history, and sociology into what appeared to me at the time to be a convincing theory of economic development. I could not put the book down. I read and reread it. Smith and Ricardo were also exciting, even if their language was more arcane. My junior year readings class led me to decide on economics as a career. It did not hurt that at the time the influence of economists was on the rise in the society at large, thanks to the apparent success of the 1962 Kennedy tax cut. Economics was perceived to be a science. It showed society how to control the business cycle. I entered the field in the era of "fine tuning," where the possibilities of prediction and control of the economy seemed endless. I could have my science and my social science too. The apparent scientific success of economics in controlling the macro economy led to the establishment of a Nobel Prize for the field in the late 1960s.

I graduated from college as a math major because I had taken so many math courses during my drift through college. However, I had decided to become an academic economist, studying economic development. The academic life, as I perceived it, being led by professors at Colorado College, was a life of the mind with interplay across fields. It seemed to me (and my parents) almost idyllic to be paid to discuss and research ideas. Tenure and publication would provide me with the autonomy and personal independence I craved. My first choice of graduate school was Princeton, which had Arthur Lewis plus a strong tradition in demography, which I saw as a handmaiden to development. It also had a strong tradition in mathematics. I also applied to Chicago at the urging of Ray Werner. I knew little about Chicago except that I had heard that Milton Friedman was good. I was familiar with some of his popular essays. I had also read his methodology of positive economics and enthusiastically supported his approach to testing theory with evidence. Swayed by his essay, a generous scholarship, and the urging of my undergraduate advisor, I chose Chicago. From childhood, I had respected the school. It didn't hurt that my wife could easily get a job teaching high school in a nearby suburb.

Graduate School

When I arrived at Chicago in 1965, I was overwhelmed by the large classes, impersonal atmosphere, the threats to physical safety in Hyde Park at that time and the race riots that plagued the city. Living near an encampment of National Guard troops during a race riot was an unforgettable experience. Despite my exposure to a few classics, my training in economics was weak compared to that of most of my fellow students, although my math skills were superior. As formal proofs were not encouraged in the program at that time, my math skills gave me no advantage whatsoever and may have handicapped me: I was always looking for formal statements of verbal and graphical propositions that I found vague and confusing. I took all of Milton Friedman's first-year classes and found them fascinating, albeit sometimes difficult to follow. He taught first-year students in monetary theory about natural rate theory before that term was widely known or used and before he made that term famous in his presidential address to the American Economics Association. To my amazement, I got high marks in his classes, and he was personally friendly to me. I also found Harry Johnson's classes on income distribution and capital theory interesting. He taught me two sector general equilibrium models and introduced me to Gary Becker's work on human capital, albeit in a cursory way. He also gave stimulating lectures on general topics in economics, which I admired greatly. He was surprisingly generous with his time.

I discussed my still-burning interest in the field of economic development with Harry Johnson, and to my surprise, he was very negative about the offerings at Chicago in development, and suggested that I go to Princeton to study with his friend and former Manchester colleague Arthur Lewis. In retrospect I think Johnson underrated the fundamental work of Chicagoans Ted Schultz and D. Gale Johnson on agriculture in development. However, at that time, I was not interested in agriculture and failed to appreciate its important role in development. I admired Lewis's book and its bold vision of the development process.

After consulting with Harry Johnson and with labor economist Albert Rees, who was then on his way from Chicago to Princeton, I decided to transfer to Princeton. The bucolic environment, small classes, and private tutorials at Princeton were much more to my liking and were more suited to my liberal arts background.

I also did not like the impersonality of Chicago or the cult of Friedman that characterized the graduate program at that time. Although I greatly valued my interactions with Friedman and found him brilliant, open, and stimulating, I did not like the uncritical, almost religious devotion to his ideas by many of my fellow students. The followers were much worse than the master and created a subculture imbued with a religious zeal reminiscent of the zeal of the groups I had recently rejected.

I also appreciated the wide array of courses in applied mathematics available at the time at Princeton. I concentrated on development and demography, and offered these as my principal fields. Lewis was friendly to me and encouraged my interest in development. Ansley Coale's courses in mathematical demography were fascinating to me although he was personally hostile to economics. My interactions with the Colombian polymath Alvaro Lopez at the office of Population Research were highly stimulating. I took a range of courses in probability theory, statistics, and game theory from first-rate people such as Willy Feller, John Tukey, and Albert Tucker. Courses in mathematical economics by Harold Kuhn were comprehensive and clear.

I immersed myself in development economics, finding Lewis to be brilliant and insightful but somewhat old fashioned even in his field as it was then being practiced. He was an intuitive economist at a time when development was becoming more formal. In addition, his theory was more speculative than I had imagined. Ironically, I discovered Schultz's work in Lewis's course, and I began to realize the importance of agriculture in development. I realized that Lewis's book, which had been a main motivation for me to enter economics, had serious limitations as an empirical description of the development process.

The new breed of development economists at Princeton treated the field as a branch of nonlinear and integer programming. While technically interesting, their vision of the field seemed sterile to me. I lost patience with results like "if you know the dual prices, you can solve the primal problem" because they begged the question of where the dual prices came from. For a while, demography intrigued me, and I came dangerously close to writing a Ph.D. thesis on the role of complex roots on the rate of convergence of populations governed by the classical Lotka integral equation of population. I came to my senses and realized that I would leave economics for good if I chose to work on that topic. So I began drifting again.

In retrospect, drifting was not so bad. It enabled me to acquire a large array of skills in economics and applied math, most of which proved useful. I have applied most of the skills I learned.

In my third year, I took a tutorial in labor economics from Al Rees. Rees was a hard-nosed, no-nonsense empirical economist with deep interest in public policy who was a direct descendant in a long lineage of first-rate Chicago empirical economists such as Paul Douglas, Henry Schultz, and H. Gregg Lewis. People sometimes forget that Chicago has a strong empirical tradition and think of the Chicago School as a body of scholars who embrace particular ideas about free markets. In fact, a central feature of the Chicago approach has been that it values careful empirical analysis and generally demands empirical justification for policy proposals.

Rees knew his price theory, but he rooted his research in data and encouraged students to take data very seriously. His vision of economics, like that of many Chicago economists of his generation, was that it is only of value if it is practically useful. He was an honest, open, friendly person who encouraged curiosity and imposed high standards on those around him. He had been helpful to me in making my decision to transfer to Princeton.

Rees introduced me to the exciting new field of neoclassical labor economics being pioneered by Gary Becker and Jacob Mincer at Columbia. Johnson's lectures at Chicago had briefly exposed me to some of this work, and I found it fascinating. Rees drew out the empirical implications of this work much more than Johnson had done. The economics of this new field was simple but the theory was empirically powerful. I read every article I could find by Becker, Mincer, and their students. Reading Jacob Mincer's famous article on the labor supply of married women for the first time was an exciting experience. Simple price theory applied to aggregate data reconciled a number of conflicting pieces of empirical evidence and explained how wage growth and household production could explain a major social phenomenon. The work combined basic economics with simple econometrics.

At about the same time, Al Rees also introduced me to the vast array of microdata sets on the labor market and the household that began to be produced on a wide scale in the 1960s. These data sets were a byproduct of the Kennedy–Johnson era. They were developed to evaluate its numerous programs, to monitor social life, and to assess the efficacy of alternative policies. At that time Rees was working on the first major social experiment to determine the impact of negative income taxes on labor supply. At his request, I even helped enroll some of the first participants in the experiment. The topic of the disincentive effects of welfare and taxation on labor supply attracted a lot of interest at that time, given the expanding size of the welfare state. Rees drew my attention to this debate. The empirical work on these topics largely ignored economics and used "simple" empirical methods that produced estimates difficult for me to interpret either as economic parameters or as answers to interesting policy counterfactuals.

I have closely followed the social experiment movement ever since those days. I am impressed by the blind enthusiasm the term "experiment" evokes and by the serious limitations of social experiments. The more carefully one looks at the product of social experiments, the less enthusiastic one can be about them. Human beings are purposeful in a way seed corn and laboratory rats are not. Economic policy design requires that analysts know more than the dose-response relationships produced by experiments. Years later I wrote on social experiments. What impressed me then was how little had been learned from the first wave of social experiments and how powerful and evocative the term "experiment" is to both popular and professional minds. The failed negative income tax experiments did little to prevent an uncritical embrace of social experimentation in the 1980s and 1990s.

Rees introduced me to theories rich in empirical content and to data on which it was possible to test them. During my tutorial with him, I decided to become a labor economist. There were many research opportunities to be exploited, and the possibilities for generalizing the theory seemed limitless. My goal was to make labor economics a rigorous branch of empirical science.

Although I greatly admired Mincer's article on female labor supply, I felt it did not go far enough in using the newly available data to test the theory of family labor supply. I saw an opportunity to apply the rigorous price theory of Samuelson's *Foundations* to the newly available cross section and panel data. My thesis developed a life-cycle model of family labor supply with wage growth induced by learning by doing. It was the first systematic test of the family theory of labor supply and the first model of labor supply with learning by doing as a determinant of wage growth.

My goals were to integrate labor supply with human capital theory and to test the theory of family labor supply using both aggregate and microdata. I was happy to be able to combine rigorous economic theory with microdata. I felt that the Becker–Mincer research program was wide open with lots of opportunities for theoretical and empirical work.

I shared my enthusiasm for this general research program with Orley Ashenfelter, who was two years ahead of me in the graduate program and who took a job at Princeton in my final year of residence there. Ashenfelter's enthusiasm for economics, data and life was infectious. We would discuss topics into the night. We shared a common vision about applying economic theory to empirical work in labor economics. We wrote several papers estimating Slutsky income and substitution effects in labor supply. He also acquainted me with Becker's *Economics of Discrimination* and shared with me his research ideas on explaining the time series of racial wage and employment patterns. Ashenfelter was the first to notice the improvement in black economic status after the passage of the 1964 Civil Rights Act. Yet his evidence, based as it was on aggregate data, was far from convincing. We discussed the economics of Jim Crow. I found these discussions to be very stimulating, given my personal observations of the Jim Crow South. They shaped some of my later research on government policy and racial wage differentials.

Together we wrote the first papers on the impact of a major federal government affirmative-action program on black employment. From this work, I learned the important lesson that racial employment and occupational advances in the 1960s were greatest in the South, a point I would build on and amplify in my later work.

My early interests were not at all motivated by econometric questions. Indeed my initial reaction to econometrics was negative. Princeton had a project on time series (spectral analysis) started by John von Neumann and continued by Oskar Morgenstern. Distinguished scholars such as Clive Granger and Michio Hatanaka were still around, although the project was winding down during my graduate student days. My experience with the new methods was not satisfactory. Although overtly nonparametric, choices of "windows" (or, in modern jargon, "bandwidths") and the like affected empirical conclusions in the short macro time series to which the new methods were applied. Most econometrics seemed very mechanical to me, and I had no interest in the big macro models of the day. I did not even take the econometrics field exam for the Ph.D.

The only work in econometrics that appealed to me was Richard Quandt's work on discrete choice and travel demand, which opened up an entire field that was enhanced and made fully rigorous by my co-laureate Daniel McFadden. I read Quandt's work with interest. Only after I left Princeton did I come to realize its relevance for my work on labor supply. I read a lot of statistics, however, because in my thesis research I faced an apparently unending array of new problems in using microdata that were not treated in any econometrics textbooks. I discussed many of these problems with the eminent statistician John Tukey, although his format was daunting. He would assemble a gallery of statistics graduate students to listen to our exchanges. Although I often disagreed with Tukey, I found his ideas interesting and helpful. I spent hours pouring over statistics journals and books at Princeton's Fine Hall to get some guidance on the empirical questions I faced in my daily work. I got little guidance from econometrics books except for the masterful textbook by Arthur Goldberger. Even Goldberger treated the topics I needed for my thesis in a cursory way.

Columbia University

I was hired at Columbia in 1970 as a labor economist and was excited by the opportunity to work firsthand with Gary Becker and Jacob Mincer. Becker left Columbia for Chicago shortly after I accepted the Columbia offer, so we were never colleagues there. My three years at Columbia were a major learning experience. At that time, the senior faculty was first rate and open minded. Daily lunches would produce intense discussions on wide ranging topics. I learned about capital theory, marginal cost pricing, Marxist economics, optimal control theory, and the economics of characteristics from my colleagues.

I faithfully attended the legendary Labor Workshop at Columbia. This workshop was founded by Gary Becker and Jacob Mincer and was the forum where so many important ideas in labor economics in the 1960s were first presented. Even though Becker had left, feelings about him were intense. Indeed, the first time I attended the workshop, I arrived late and sat down in an open chair at the head of the seminar table, just to the left of the speaker. When I sat down in that chair, I was told to take another chair. The one I had occupied was permanently reserved for Gary Becker even though he was now at Chicago.

Even without Becker, the workshop was remarkable. Mincer was an austere, often blunt, figure who demanded clarity and precision from all speakers. I learned something new from every seminar and learned even more from being the third reader on the dissertations of Becker–Mincer students, many of whom went on to become leading labor economists.

The rules of the seminar were clear—simple price theory, simple econometrics, simple empirical work. Becker visited Columbia for several thesis defenses. I found interactions with him stimulating and informative.

In my second year at Columbia, I was invited to join the NBER in New York; the bureau supported my research. Victor Fuchs was the guiding organizational force who generously supported young scholars such as myself, although he was more than a little wary of my technical interests. There was an active labor group comprised of Jacob Mincer, Finis Welch, Bob Willis, Jim Smith, and a host of distinguished visitors who made the place an exciting venue.

The younger people in the group all attended the Labor Workshop at Columbia, but there were separate informal workshops at the NBER and intellectual free-for-alls that were profoundly stimulating. NBER was a complement to the more austere environment of the Labor Workshop—a place to relax with ideas in an informal setting. Discussions were intense. One workshop I participated in started at 1:30 P.M. and concluded at midnight.

Finis Welch was the intellectual leader of the group of young economists at NBER. Gifted with a deep economic intuition and a powerful sense of the data, he made provocative suggestions on my work and that of many others. He was the ideal leader for a young research group of empirical economists. Active, engaged, and encouraging, he taught me a lot and offered both intellectual and financial support.

My most intense interactions at NBER were with Robert Willis. By separate routes, we had independently discovered the importance of accounting for heterogeneity across people in understanding patterns found in microeconomic data. Working together and apart, we later developed panel data models for fertility, earnings, and labor force dynamics. Anyone who looks at microdata cannot help but be impressed by heterogeneity among agents. R. G. D. Allen and Arthur Bowley had already documented this phenomenon in the analyses of budget data in the 1930s, but the new flood of microdata, and especially panel data, forced this point home.

The econometrics of the time, developed as it was for representative agent models, ignored individual heterogeneity, although there were dissenting voices such as those of Marc Nerlove, Arnold Zellner, and Zvi Griliches. The whole approach to heterogeneity and unobservables in econometrics in this period was typified in a famous 1960 paper by

Hendrik Houthakker on addilog utility functions. Turning to the data, after developing his model, he wrote,

I adorn the equation with an error term.

That phrase pretty much summarized the dichotomy between the model and the sources of error typical of the econometrics of the day. In my work on labor supply, I had become aware of the importance of accounting for unobservables in developing econometric estimators of economic parameters. The sources of error and the way unobservables entered agent decisions mattered greatly. Yet they were barely discussed in any econometrics text.

An Accidental Econometrician

At the end of my first year at Columbia, the chair of the department, Kelvin Lancaster, approached me to teach graduate econometrics because the resident econometrician was leaving and no one else in the department knew anything about econometrics. I took this as an occasion to teach myself Henri Theil's then-new *Principles of Econometrics*. His was a breakthrough book that introduced basic asymptotic theory into econometrics. Teaching this course enabled me to break into graduate teaching.

I was lucky to be given this challenge because it forced me once and for all to confront the existing literature in econometrics to see if it was helpful for the problems I was working on. I deepened my understanding of the available tools but found that they did not solve my problems. In the course of my work on labor supply, I had encountered a whole host of empirical problems that seemed rather mundane but which, on reflection, had no easy answers.

The prototypical problem was the missing wage problem. In my thesis I faced the recurring problem of having missing wages for about half the women whose labor supply I was seeking to determine. Moreover the missing wages were associated with women not working (zero hours of work).

Three problems were conjoined: (1) What values to assign the missing wages? (2) What labor supply function(s) described the work–no work decision and the hours-of-work decision for workers? Could the various dimensions of labor supply be reconciled in a common framework?

(3) How could heterogeneity and measurement error be accounted for in a common framework?

These problems were very much in the air. Mincer's seminal article on female labor supply answered question (2) under strong implicit assumptions that time was intertemporally perfectly substitutable. Notes by H. Gregg Lewis and Yoram Ben-Porath treated the work–no work decision as a corner solution for each period. Mincer, my Columbia senior colleague, strongly rejected this approach.

Some relevant econometrics was around, too. James Tobin's "Tobit" model (the term was coined by Goldberger) showed how to estimate models with truncated dependent variables, but surprisingly, in light of his eminence as an economic theorist, he offered no *economic* interpretation of his statistical model. In a paper written in 1972 and published in 1974, I wrote down an econometric model that addressed all three questions. I used the reservation wage ("virtual price" or "shadow wage") derived from consumer preferences to unify the different dimensions of labor supply in a common economic framework. I specified the unobservables in market wage and reservation wages to generate a consistently specified labor supply function. Using this setup I could interpret all previous approaches to the estimation of different types of labor supply functions as special cases of this model. I was able to show which empirical specifications estimated economically interpretable parameters (Hicks–Slutsky income and substitution effects), which ones did not, and how they approximated the desired parameters. I was fortunate that Reuben Gronau, who was visiting the NBER and working on related issues, let me try out my models at his blackboard. He made many constructive comments at that crucial time in my thinking. I followed up this work with a life cycle version also published in 1974 in which I explicitly outlined a method for estimating preference heterogeneity in the marginal rate of substitution between goods and leisure. I developed a framework for estimating the effect of taxes on labor supply and for measuring exact welfare gains and losses from taxation and public policy.

These two papers let me answer nagging questions that had bothered me since I had begun to work on labor supply. I viewed them as contributions to labor economics and to the economics of shadow prices and rationing. I could now consistently account for the error specification of my empirical models and do Samuelson-like revealed preference on real data. The asymptotic theory needed to justify the model was not to be found in Theil or in the published literature. Fortunately, Takeshi Amemiya of Stanford had just written a fundamental paper on the asymptotics of nonlinear models, which I could adapt to my framework. Work on "limited dependent variables" was in its infancy in econometrics, and work on general models with joint discrete-continuous random variables was unknown in econometrics before I wrote the paper. I became aware of the work of McFadden on discrete choice only after completing this work. In fact it was not until a 1974 conference at Berkeley organized by McFadden that I became aware of the emerging wide-scale interest in discrete choice and limited dependent variables models. McFadden proved to be a steady source of stimulation and support after that conference. I organized a follow-up conference in Chicago in 1975 and collected the papers from the two conferences into a special issue of the now-defunct *Annals of Economic and Social Measurement*. That publication established the new field of discrete choice and limited dependent variables.

The framework I developed in these early papers has proven to be useful to many economists. Indeed it has become common coin. It has been used to estimate the demand price for new goods (read "virtual price" in place of "virtual" or "shadow" wage), the purchase of durables and the effects of taxes and other social programs on labor supply, among other applications. It also provided a rigorous framework for analyzing causal effects of policies.

While still working at Columbia, I began to develop a general framework for organizing discrete, continuous, and joint discrete-continuous variables in a common framework. I realized that my method for using economic theory to produce counterfactual missing wages was more generally applicable. In early 1973, I wrote a paper called "Dummy Endogenous Variables" that spelled out a general framework for modeling interrelated discrete and continuous choice models. It handled the simultaneous probit, Tobit, and other frameworks, and it unified many strands of the literature using the notion of an "index function" (a term I coined) representing latent variables (like shadow prices). I also developed a simple estimator for these models that has subsequently been widely used (the "inverse Mills ratio" method).

I circulated unpublished versions of this paper and discussed it freely with students and colleagues. While I received considerable credit for this work, and various versions of it were published in good places, I was slow in getting it to print. Some of this work did not appear until as late as 1979.

Leaving Columbia

I developed my latent variable framework and an entire agenda based on it during three crucial years in New York. I found my colleagues at Columbia and NBER very stimulating. At the same time, my work was very "econometric" in the context of the Labor Workshop and violated its implicit rules of play, which emphasized simple ideas and often ruled out considerations of simultancity or reverse causality in explaining data.

Columbia had many diverse groups in economics. There was a strong Marxist or radical economics group that had grown up in the wake of the 1968 riots. A steady stream of Marxist scholars came through, and Luigi Pasenetti was a frequent visitor. For me the high point of this activity came when Joan Robinson visited for a month, wearing a North Korean commissar's uniform. I had high hopes for her visit because I had admired her early work. I moderated a debate between her and Abba Lerner on the impossibility of capitalism based on the inability to form simple aggregates of capital. I found her position absurd. She was unwilling to listen to any objection. I found the entire reswitching debate sterile on both sides and was amazed that it had attracted the attention of good minds.

As a junior faculty member, I was asked to be on the dissertation committees of Becker–Mincer students as well as on the dissertation committees of Marxists. Two dissertations impressed me with the difficulties of resolving conflicts between these warring factions. Two students ran the same wage regression. Both found that mother's education raised wages. The Marxist interpreted this as showing the power of networks and family influence to affect the child's placement in the labor market. The human capital student claimed that this evidence showed that mothers invested in child human capital. Although I was inclined to take the latter view, I was more than willing to grant that a simple regression could not settle the matter. When I asked each student to read the work of the other, and to present more cogent identification arguments to discriminate between these interpretations, I got angry phone calls from their chairs.

Human capital theory for me is too elastic and inclusive. In many forms, it verges on tautology. Too many models of the pricing of labor services and the production of skills can explain the same least-squares wage equation. Sharper models are needed that use additional information. At Columbia, I began a line of work that continues to this day that goes behind the celebrated Mincer wage equation to explain investment, labor supply, and wage growth using explicit models of optimization based on a common set of technology and preference parameters. The optimal control theory and nonlinear econometric methods used to formulate and estimate these models were not welcome by either faction at Columbia.

In early 1973, I was pleased to be invited to speak at Chicago in Becker's workshop and to discover that Chicago was proposing to make me a job offer as a labor economist and as an econometrician. Both Gary Becker and Marc Nerlove were very supportive of my work, and I respected both greatly. When the offer came, I accepted it. The main group at the New York NBER was moving to Palo Alto so that important source of stimulation was leaving. I felt that Chicago was a bigger stage, with a higher level of intellectual activity. I had flirted with Chicago all my life. I had tried it once but was not ready for it at that time. I now felt ready and was eager to learn from it.

Chicago in the 1970s

The Department of Economics that I joined in 1973 was a cauldron of intellectual activity. The pantheon of economists in residence was impressive. In the department I joined, there were at least five future Nobel laureates in economics (Lucas arrived two years later), and the business school and law school had at least two more. Unquestionably, Milton Friedman was the dominant mind, but there was a wide range of talent in the environment. Chicago at that time emphasized price theory. If anything, it was weak in formal mathematical modeling. However, even that gap was being closed by William A. Brock and José Scheinkman.

The entire department seemed to embrace Friedman's methodology of positive economics. Indeed, carved onto the facade of the social science building (1929) was Lord Kelvin's motto:

When you cannot measure, your knowledge is meager and unsatisfactory. (Lord Kelvin, 1889)

This motto seemed to embody the ethos of the department. No theory was worthwhile unless it survived a reality check. A rigorous empirical test was preferred. In that department, it didn't take a theory to beat another theory; it took a fact. Having a "clean" model was never enough; it had to explain real-world phenomena. The contingent of empirical economists in residence was strong. At that time, Becker conducted empirical tests of his theories. Ted Schultz and D. Gale Johnson promoted empirical studies in agriculture and development. H. Gregg Lewis was a renowned taskmaster in labor economics who in the words of Zvi Griliches (who preceded me at Chicago and left before I came) "kept everybody empirically honest."

The workshop system was the heart of Chicago in the 1970s. Founded by D. Gale Johnson, it was perfected by Milton Friedman. There were as many as three workshops a day. People came to these workshops having read the speaker's paper, and discussions were intense. A high premium was placed on verbal quickness, and some workshops, most notably George Stigler's, seemed to delight in humiliating speakers with verbal insults. I remember one day when my former Columbia colleague Ned Phelps came to Stigler's workshop to present a paper on the then-taboo subject of altruism in economics. The response was a torrent of invective that went on for one and a half hours. The image that came to my mind during that workshop was that of Russian Prime Minister Nikita Khrushchev pounding his shoe on the table at the U.N. in 1960.

Friedman's workshop set a very high standard. All participants read the paper being presented in advance of the seminar, and discussions were of the form "any questions on line two of paragraph three?" He was very quick and intimidating. I later learned that students presenting papers would deliberately put errors in their papers so that they could answer questions motivated by them quickly and thus appear to be very intelligent. Becker's workshop was less exacting, but it allowed one to learn Becker's views.

Whereas Friedman explored a paper using the author's framework, Becker would force the speaker to recast his paper into a Beckerian framework.

In my early years, I immersed myself in this system, going to as many as two workshops per day. It was a marvelous learning experience that would be supplemented by pre-workshop lunches and post-workshop dinners. Another form of learning was reading scores of Ph.D. theses, a practice suggested to me by Harry Johnson.

These workshops had a collective mind. One person would make a suggestion that would spark another suggestion that would make the discussion vastly better than any one person could conduct. I have presented many workshops at Chicago. Knowing that a paper will be closely and publicly scrutinized induces the author to sharpen his argument. After all, one of the credos of Chicago is that a person is "only as good as his latest paper." So one's local reputation is at stake when one gives a paper. The workshop inevitably leads to improvements in the paper if only because it forces the author to recast his thoughts to respond to the perspectives of others. I have learned that grudging acceptance of a paper at Chicago means that the paper will be a hit everywhere else.

The intellectual honesty fostered by the workshop system makes Chicago an impersonal environment compared to many other academic economic environments that more closely resemble country clubs. Chicago is not a place for the faint-hearted or the weak. It can be very demanding on even the best people. At the same time, it fosters excellence in many dimensions, albeit at the cost of some personal stress. The Chicago system de-emphasizes networking and cronyism and emphasizes intellectual honesty and candor.

The Chicago department that I joined believed in the power of simple economic models to explain the economy and the power of incentives in motivating behavior. At that time, the dominant Keynesian view did not recognize incentives and the Chicago position was quite distinctive. It is fair to say that in the past thirty years the Chicago view has prevailed.

Chicago also had an aversion to the technocratic vision of economic policy making then favored by many leading schools. Rather than endorsing the concept that a brilliant elite should make policy for the masses, Chicago believed in the innate common sense of the common man if an argument were presented clearly. There was the belief that anything really important could be conveyed in a simple, effective manner. Friedman's steady stream of clearly written *Newsweek* policy columns was the best demonstration of this approach to public policy. People should be educated to make informed choices, not managed by technocrats who know more than they do.

In retrospect, the array of first-rate work done at Chicago in the early 1970s was astounding. George Stigler was busy developing the political economy of regulation. Robert Fogel was completing his work on slavery. Becker was developing models of marriage, divorce, social interactions, and parental altruism. Ted Schultz, in his 70s, was vigorously working on development and agriculture. D. Gale Johnson was active in serious policy analysis of world agriculture, despite undertaking heavy administrative burdens at the university and in the community at large. William Brock and José Scheinkman were extending the formal theory of economic growth. Harry Johnson had become ill and was much less in evidence than I had hoped. Nonetheless his influence on students in trade and development was felt. H. Gregg Lewis, who was slow to publish, was engaged in constructing market equilibrium evaluations of the impact of unionism and regulation on the economy. Arnold Harberger was actively engaged in developing cost-benefit analysis and in introducing market reforms into the Chilean economy. In the business school, Arnold Zellner and Hans Theil, while often in conflict, were producing volumes of interesting econometric research (Marc Nerlove left before I arrived, and Zvi Griliches was long gone). Myron Scholes, Fischer Black, Gene Fama, and Merton Miller were making pathbreaking advances in finance.

The vitality of the entire enterprise invigorated me. Ideas were abundant, and new discoveries were being made every day. I could test out my ideas on colleagues all of the time, and this made research rewarding and easy to do. Exchange benefited everyone.

I do not want to suggest that Chicago was nirvana. The Chicago School had brilliant minds, and engaging with them was often exhilarating. Yet even brilliant minds have their weaknesses. A great weakness of many bright people is their frequent inability to distinguish between agreement with their personal views and genuine intelligence and creativity. A second-tier group of people at Chicago, selected more for their agreeability than their creativity or originality, left much to be desired. Often rabidly political, they were careless with data and careless with theory. However, they concurred with the masters and were valued as disciples or co-religionists to spread the truth. They were the downside of the place.

George Stigler once wrote that economics was a conservative field because it emphasized the cost of social policy. Yet, there is nothing intrinsic in economic thinking that should lead one to ignore the benefits of public policy either. No serious empirical economist who looks at the facts can be conservative all of the time. There was a conservative undercurrent that tended to shade empirical evidence and analysis among the believers who invariably found all government interventions harmful. However, among most of the intellectual leaders, politics played no role in day-to-day economic analysis or discussions.

Dynamics, Counterfactuals, Selection Bias, and Missing Data

Chicago in the 1970s was an ideal environment for me to conduct research. One-on-one interactions and seminars improved my thinking on any project I undertook. I had developed an agenda in my first three years at Columbia, and I expanded on it and generalized it in my early years at Chicago.

Although I have had many brilliant colleagues, and I have benefited greatly from them, it is to the students of Chicago that I owe my greatest debt. Top students at Chicago are brilliant and hard working. Early on in their careers, they get caught up in the intensity of the place. They are deeply curious and willing to learn. Interacting with them on their work has taught me a lot. For years I have run a kind of apprenticeship system in which students do empirical work, applied econometrics, and theory under my close supervision. Students participating in this system have been very helpful sounding boards for my ideas over the years, and many have been coauthors on papers on which they have been full partners. I am proud that many first rate Chicago students now prominent in the profession coauthored their first publications with me. They were and are a major stimulus to my own work. They helped me extend the research program I had brought with me from Columbia.

Stepping back from the particular details of the labor supply problem I had been working on, I realized in the mid-1970s that I had developed a new framework for addressing the problem of missing data when the data were missing nonrandomly. Statisticians who had previously addressed the problem of missing data assumed that they were missing at random, but the economics of the problem suggested that in many contexts (e.g., the wages of women) data were missing in a selective way. Using the economics of the problem joined with distributional assumptions provided a general answer to this problem. This work attracted a lot of attention when it was published. One reason for its success was that I developed a simple estimator that was easily applied to many problems. I also developed a general framework that unified a variety of scattered special cases. I developed a class of simple, easily applied estimators based on what is now known as the "control function" principle (the term was coined in my papers with Richard Robb). The initial reception of these models by economists and statisticians was very enthusiastic. Only much later would the statisticians develop "parallel" analyses of selectively missing data, based on these ideas, and ignore the earlier work by economists.

I applied these models to areas outside of labor supply to show their generality. Building on a paper by my Columbia and Chicago colleague Bill Landes on the economics of fair employment laws, I analyzed the effect of accounting for the endogeneity of laws in estimating the impacts of legislation. Happily, Landes's results held up. I also examined the effect of selectively greater withdrawal of black males from the work force on the growth in black (relative to white) wage rates. Accounting for dropouts greatly reduces the measured wage gains of blacks. The process of selective withdrawal has, if anything, accelerated since I did this work, and recent analyses (for example, by Amitabh Chandra) demonstrate the even greater relevance of this issue.

At about this time H. Gregg Lewis, one of the pioneers of modern labor economics, asked me to teach his graduate course on labor demand. This was a daunting task: his class was legendary; he was in residence; and I was required to teach his classic 1963 book, *Unionism and Relative Wage Rates.* That book is not a model of clarity, but its first chapter introduced me to the problem of constructing and measuring counterfactual states. I locked myself in my apartment for about two weeks as I tried to make sense of the book. The effort was worth it. Most people read the later chapters, where

Lewis reanalyzed earlier empirical studies of unionism conducted under his guidance. This is a valuable exercise. However, the first chapter was the most interesting to me because in it he considered the definition of various unionism "effects" in a market equilibrium setting. It also became clear to me while reading his work that my framework could be used to address the problem of constructing and estimating counterfactuals (e.g., what would a union member have earned if he or she were a nonunion member), and in fact I addressed this problem with George Neumann in a paper written in 1976. Any good answer to this problem should also take into account the extent of unionism because it affected the pricing of labor services, but we did not take the required step in our paper.

With a long gestation period (twenty-five years), Lewis's book influenced my work with Lance Lochner and Christopher Taber on the general equilibrium evaluation of social programs. The immediate effect the book had on my research was that it led me to think about the issue of defining and estimating policy counterfactuals, albeit initially in a partial equilibrium setting. This led to my work on evaluating educational reforms and job training programs.

I continued my research, begun in New York, on the dynamics of the life cycle. I developed and estimated dynamic models of human capital accumulation and labor supply. I formulated a dynamic panel version of the latent variable index models that I had developed for cross sectional data. I applied these models to the dynamics of female labor supply to address the implicit assumption of perfect substitution of time over time in the Mincer model. His model implied a Bernoulli process (a random flipping of a coin each period where the odds were determined by lifetime wages and income). My framework nested the Bernoulli assumption as part of a more general stochastic process. Empirical work with Robert Willis and later work on my own demonstrated the untenability of the assumption and the importance of accounting for temporally persistent unobservables in explaining labor force dynamics. Willis applied this framework to the analysis of earnings dynamics in an important paper with Lee Lillard.

The empirical evidence on persistent heterogeneity in earnings, labor supply, and fertility forced me to confront the difficult problem of accounting for unobservables in nonlinear frameworks. A dynamic extension of my earlier cross section model developed such a framework but the economics was implicit. More explicit economic models were developed in the early 1980s with first-rate graduate students Tom MaCurdy and Chris Flinn, who went on to distinguished academic careers. In this work, we integrated economic models and panel data, accounting for heterogeneity. Everywhere we looked, we found heterogeneity, and those who followed us have found the same. It is a feature of employment and unemployment durations, labor force participation, preferences toward leisure (as I discovered in my 1974 papers), and in many other areas of economic life.

My work on labor force and earnings dynamics attracted considerable attention. I was invited to a 1977 SSRC conference on longitudinal data methods in the social sciences and became aware of a vast body of very good work in mathematical sociology on longitudinal methods. I met James Coleman, an eminent sociologist, who I knew socially but not professionally, and Burt Singer, a polymath applied mathematician.

In an effort to understand the literature in sociology, I taught a joint course on panel data analysis with Coleman and learned a lot from it. I also developed a life-long intellectual and personal relationship with him, frequently attending the mathematical sociology workshop. I also began to collaborate with Burt Singer, who taught me a lot of new mathematics and statistics. We wrote a series of papers on heterogeneity and dynamic sampling plans.

At this point in my career (in the late 1970s and early 1980s), I had multiple lines of research going simultaneously. I was deeply engrossed in the mathematics and statistics of heterogeneity. I was also engaged in building structural dynamic models and estimating them on data.

With the usual gestation period, the methods I had developed began to be applied by many scholars to a wide array of problems. The practitioners wanted simple methods to solve hard problems. This led to universal application of normal distributions in settings where normality was not appropriate. It led to some bizarre empirical estimates: union wage "effects" of 350%; labor supply estimates by Jerry Hausman where consumption was an inferior good, and so forth. In a 1986 book, far below the quality of his earlier book, H. Gregg Lewis (then at Duke) denounced the application of selection methods to the study of unionism, because "they didn't work." What he really meant is that they did not produce numbers that accorded with his priors, which were based on least-squares estimates.

There were many responses to the perceived sensitivity of selection estimators to normality. Some tried more general non-normal distributions that nested the normal model. Many began to reject the approach entirely. My own approach was to develop a nonparametric approach that was more robust.

Burt Singer and I were working together on unobservables in duration models. We developed an identification strategy and estimator for the distribution of unobservables that has wide applicability outside of duration analysis. We showed that we could identify the parametric portion of models while being robust with respect to distributions of unobservables. The method is widely applied, but it is not directly tied to the original selection framework.

In 1980, I developed a simple nonparametric alternative to the parametric normal selection estimator based on polynomials in the probability of selection, but surprisingly, at that time, it attracted little attention. In subsequent work in 1985 and 1986 with Richard Robb and in 1990 with Bo Honore, I developed a systematic investigation of semiparametric identification in economic selection models. This work has had a lot of influence, and in work with Pedro Carneiro and Lars Hansen published in 2003, I have extended the basic setup to a variety of dynamic and cross-sectional settings, recently completing work on the identification of distributions of counterfactuals under much more general conditions. In related work with Ed Vytlacil, we developed robust, easily applied, nonparametric instrumental variable approaches to the selection models. This work built on my 1998 *Econometrica* paper with Hideko Ichimura, Jeff Smith, and Petra Todd.

This area continues to be a research frontier as I write. But the original concerns of the applied economists have not been fully met. Nonparametric identification analyses are important. They determine whether or not *in principle* it is possible to identify key parameters without imposing arbitrary distributional assumptions. We now know that selection models (and closely related auction models) are nonparametrically identified under very general conditions.

Estimation is another matter. High dimensional nonparametric estimation is not feasible in the sample sizes available to most economists. Choices of "auxiliary" parameters (smoothing parameters, penalty functions, and bandwidths) matter greatly. This is a lesson learned forty years ago in spectral analysis that is being relearned in the applications of nonparametric econometrics today. With the sample sizes available to most economists, general nonparametric methods for models with many explanation variables are often not useful, except for very low dimensional models.

The Conditional Nature of Causal Knowledge

In the mid-1980s, in the course of my research with Richard Robb on the nonparametric identification of selection models and causal models, I was invited to an interdisciplinary conference on inference from self-selected samples. Robb and I presented a paper before an audience that consisted largely of statisticians. Our discussant was none other than John Tukey, the distinguished statistician with whom I had interacted in graduate school.

Robb and I welcomed the opportunity to present our work before a distinguished group of statisticians. We discussed the fundamental identification problem that arises from self selection when evaluating the impact of "treatment" on outcomes. How can one separate true treatment effects from preexisting differences among treatment and comparison group members? We used as an example the evaluation of job training programs, but our message was more general. We presented the fundamental causal model that economists have been using since the work of Trygve Haavelmo in the 1940s, and we showed how alternative assumptions about agent program participation rules, outcome equations, distributions of unobservables and access to different types of data solved the problem of causal inference.

We were stunned by the overwhelming negative reaction to our paper and especially to our main point about the conditional nature of causal knowledge. We made what we thought was the obvious point that in the absence of an idealized experiment, answers to causal questions required assumptions. We sought to identify the minimal assumptions and trade-offs among these assumptions. We demonstrated the value of making implicit assumptions explicit. We showed the value of economic models of choice in selecting a particular set of identifying assumptions. We were not happy with this intrinsic ambiguity in causal models, but we felt it was necessary to be intellectually honest about it. In later work, I have developed this theme in a number of contexts.

The response to our paper took many forms. Some statisticians with proprietary interests wanted to claim that explicit models of counterfactuals were not first developed in econometrics, although the recent influential work by Judea Pearl recognizes the priority of econometrics in developing casual models. Others sought to deny the problem entirely. Tukey wrote a condescending review of our paper, which we rebutted. As a result of this episode, I realized the great value of the economic approach to causal modeling. Economists have theories that produce the set of admissible counterfactuals. The statisticians have only vague appeals to "closest worlds" without any precise definition of what "close" means. Economists can use economic theory to settle which particular selection of treatment model is appropriate. Statisticians typically assumed random assignment or random assignment conditional on observables, i.e., the method of matching.

One of the many estimators Robb and I discussed was the standard method of instrumental variables. This was rejected at that occasion as being useless, but was later "invented" and popularized in statistics by one of the statisticians present.

The conditional nature of causal knowledge was disturbing to this group, and to many others. I learned the hard way that most people deny this basic point and prefer to gloss over it with implicit assumptions. "Let sleeping dogs lie" is a more popular approach to solving identification problems. Making people aware of the difficulty of reaching simple conclusions from analyses of widely used samples and estimators is not a popular activity.

At its very heart, any causal conclusion rests on maintained assumptions. My quest for an objective economics was thwarted by my understanding of the identification problem. Econometrics and statistics could only go so far. However, there was more information that could be used, but it was not in the form of precise probability distributions or selection rules.

Toward a More General Approach to Identification

While I was working on the econometric aspects of the identification problem in general treatment and selection models, I was also engaged in investigating the sources of the economic progress of black Americans. My interest in the status of black Americans began in my early years in the border South and later trips to Alabama and Mississippi. A trip to the same locations after passage of the 1964 Civil Rights Act revealed how dramatically the Jim Crow system had been dismantled. Using aggregate time series data, Ashenfelter had demonstrated that the post–1964 Civil Rights Act era showed greater progress than before. The data were fragile. An update of his study by Freeman showed stronger effects. However, that study was still highly aggregated.

Ashenfelter and I had analyzed firm level panel data on the progress of blacks, 1966–1970. We established that government contractors covered by an affirmative action program were more likely to integrate and to upgrade their black work force. The most dramatic effects were in the South.

All of this suggested that government policy had improved the status of black Americans. This view ran counter to the prevailing Chicago view that it was improvements in basic economic forces: (1) schooling, (2) schooling quality, and (3) migration that promoted black economic progress and not some law. My work with Richard Butler showed that a substantial part of the wage growth of blacks was illusory and was due to selective withdrawal of low-wage black labor from the work force, which induced apparent wage growth in the aggregate that was not experienced by anyone. This work was well received at Chicago and elsewhere, and its empirical importance in accounting for aggregate distributions is now well established. But this work did not foreclose other explanations for black economic progress.

Around 1978, I became aware of a unique data set from South Carolina collected to enforce a 1915 law forbidding employment of blacks as operatives in textile mills, then the largest industrial employers in the state. The data were annual observations by county for about 60 years. Casual inspection of the data revealed a huge breakthrough in black employment in the post-1964 era when textile companies were targeted by government affirmative action policies.

There were numerous competing explanations: (1) tight labor markets in the 1960s due to the Vietnam War, (2) entry of higher wage nontextile industry into the state, (3) tough foreign competition from abroad that made discrimination more costly, and (4) improvements in the educational quality of the black population. I was convinced that these competing explanations were more plausible than the government activity hypothesis. Indeed, such a conclusion was congenial with the Chicago view that government policy is ineffective or harmful. For more than 10 years, and with three graduate students, I tried to establish this case. But, after employing a variety of methods, and drawing on context and historical accounts as well as various statistical adjustments, I was forced to admit that there is no plausible alternative explanation for the breakthrough in black economic progress other than government pressure. Using all of the data, including the contextual evidence, I crafted a powerful case for the effectiveness of law in the 1960s and early 1970s. Laws directed against southern discrimination had their greatest effect in the South. John Donohue and I synthesized this evidence, and a variety of supporting pieces in a 1991 article. We showed that the law worked with minimal enforcement precisely because it allowed employers to break informal community norms and respond to competition by hiring black workers.

This work is widely cited by scholars of discrimination and civil rights. It is ignored, to this day, by many conservative economists who cling to the "basic economic forces" interpretation of the evidence, despite the fact that many of the "basic economic forces" were caused by government policy and that the rapid response of firms in hiring black labor once informal sanctions were broken demonstrates the power of self-interest in markets.

The larger lesson I took from this research was that one had to use all of the available information to analyze causal questions. The available information does not necessarily come in the form of sampling distributions from government surveys or bounds on the ranges of random variables. Knowing the problem being studied and its context, which in this case meant reading the relevant history and newspapers, reading court and legislative records, using the relevant theory, and looking at all of the available data, were essential in reaching any causal conclusion. There is no algorithm to crank out convincing evidence, although econometrics textbooks are often written as if there were. This lesson forever impressed on me the limitations of standard econometrics, the even greater limitations of the universal context-free nostrums for finding causal relationships offered up by statisticians, and the need to understand the relevant economic models and contextual information in establishing causal relationships.

Chicago after the 1970s

In this essay, I dwell on Chicago in the 1970s because that department was so distinguished and had the greatest impact on my intellectual development. Chicago renews itself. First-rate people attract other first-rate people to work with them. The Chicago department is a living demonstration of this maxim. I have learned greatly from the successors to the Chicago School I encountered in 1973 and hope to learn much more from them. Their intensity, curiosity, creativity, and intellectual honesty stimulate me and keep me honest and down to earth.

Among all of the arrivals after 1980, Lars Hansen, more than anyone else, best embodies the virtues of the place. I have learned much from him, as has the rest of the profession. I am grateful for incisive discussions with him on a wide array of topics in economics.

My Approach to Economics

Economics is useful only if it helps to explain the economy and solve practical problems. It produces wise policy advice when it is anchored in data and potentially dangerous advice when it is not. If rigorous empirical testing were required of economic models, many fewer papers would be written, the subject would become boring to many current practitioners, and the scientific reputation of the field would rise. There would be fewer fads and more lasting contributions. The criterion of success would be to understand phenomena rather than to maximize citation indices. In the words of John Maynard Keynes,

If economists could manage to get themselves thought of as humble, competent people, on a level with dentists, that would be splendid! (Keynes, 1931)[1]

This vision of economics does not sanction an atheoretical, purely empirical field. Solutions to practical problems and interpretations of real phenomena require formal models to define questions and produce answers to them. Tool building is an essential activity. Adam Smith built new tools when he described the British economy of his day; so did David Ricardo and Alfred Marshall. Much of the creative and lasting work in economics of the past century was research that fashioned new models to explain real phenomena. Economic and social reality is complex. Digesting and understanding it is a major source of new ideas in economics and econometrics.

An alternative approach to economics is to build "clean" models that improve upon earlier models but that do not make contact with any phenomena. In place of testability and empirical content, in this approach, models are evaluated by their cleverness, by the power of the methods used and their distance between assumptions and conclusions in developing the theory. This is an internally motivated vision of economics as a branch of applied mathematics. But mathematics and science are not the same thing, although mathematics is essential to the execution of good economic science.

My work on labor supply, schooling, affirmative action, labor force dynamics, evaluating job training programs, the sources of improvement in black economic status, on the pricing of labor services and the formation of skills over the life cycle, and more recently, my studies of regulation and deregulation in Europe and Latin America have all had a very practical focus. Yet at the same time, they have led to new theory and new econometrics that are required to address these problems adequately. These questions, carefully addressed, pose formidable challenges to standard theory and econometrics. Good answers to these questions require good theory and econometrics. It is unfortunate that many economists now equate public policy analysis with careless once-over-lightly analysis suitable for journalism but not for science. Careful public policy analysis requires good science.

Anchoring my own research in serious empirical analysis has protected me from the fads that plague the profession and has given me the autonomy and independence I have always craved, albeit at the cost of sometimes appearing to be stodgy. There will always be a market for good answers to important social questions. This is my way of following my father's advice of being independent and developing an independent reputation and my way of avoiding appeals to authority in any form—whether mathematical or divine—that motivated my early break with organized religion.

Awarded Nobel Prize in 2000. Lecture presented March 19, 2003.

Date of Birth

April 19, 1944

Academic Degrees

B.A.   Colorado College, 1965

M.A.   Princeton University, 1968

Ph.D.   Princeton University, 1971

Academic Affiliations

Instructor, Assistant Professor of Economics, Columbia University, 1970–1972

Associate Professor of Economics, Columbia University, 1972–1974

Associate Professor of Economics, University of Chicago, 1974–1977

Professor of Economics, University of Chicago, 1977–1984

Irving Fisher Visiting Professor of Economics, Yale University, 1984

Henry Schultz Professor of Economics, University of Chicago, 1985–1994

A. Whitney Griswold Professor of Economics, Yale University, 1988–1990 (on leave from Chicago)

Henry Schultz Distinguished Service Professor of Economics, University of Chicago, 1994–present

Selected Books

Longitudinal Analysis of Labor Market Data, 1985 (ed. with B. Singer)

Handbook of Econometrics, Vol. 5, 2001 (ed. with E. Leamer)

Inequality in America: What Role for Human Capital?, 2003 (with A. Krueger)

Law and Employment: Lessons from Latin America and the Caribbean, 2004 (with C. Pagés)

Lessons from the Laureates: An Afterword

A goal of the Nobel Economists Lecture Series at Trinity University has been to enhance our understanding of the link between biography, and most especially autobiography, and the development of modern economic thought. Each of the eighteen lectures, organized around the theme "My Evolution as an Economist," provides source material for this endeavor.

The purpose of this afterword is twofold. The first section identifies common themes, as well as some disparate views, expressed in the lectures. The laureates identify several common themes in describing their development as economists. Among these are the importance of real-world events and a desire for relevance, the critical influence of teachers and scholars during the laureates' formative years, the necessity of scholarly interaction and a lively intellectual environment, and the role of luck or happenstance in their lives. Most but not all of the laureates view their research program as having been largely unplanned, evolving via the marketplace for ideas and taking form as a coherent body of thought only after the fact. There are exceptions, however. In summarizing these themes, we rely heavily on the words of the laureates, taken from their Trinity University lectures.

The second section assesses the difficult question of whether or not biography is important for understanding the development of modern economic thought. Ultimately, we cannot provide a definitive answer to this question. One can neither observe nor simulate in any methodical fashion the appropriate counterfactual—how economic thought would have developed absent these individuals and their particular life histories. Even if one could do so, one would face the nontrivial task of determining what constitutes an important or a minor impact on economic thought. Inability to answer this question in a definitive way, however, does not imply that we should ignore it. These eighteen essays provide ample source material for reasoned speculation on the importance of biography in the evolution of economic thought.

Common Themes and Disparate Voices

Few individuals begin life expecting or desiring to be an economist. This same generalization holds true among Nobel economists. The laureates came to economics based on the influence of particular teachers or scholars, because of the intellectual challenge and rigor of economics, or because economics was perceived as being relevant for real-world issues. Several of the laureates cite their favorable reaction following exposure to formal economics. Three examples follow:

Rare is the child, I suspect, who wants to grow up to be an economist, or a professor. . . . Cutting my teeth on *The General Theory,* I was hooked on economics. Like many other economists of my vintage, I was attracted to the field for two reasons. One was that economic theory is a fascinating intellectual challenge, on the order of mathematics or chess. I liked analytics and logical argument. . . . The other reason was the obvious relevance of economics to understanding and perhaps overcoming the Great Depression and all the frightening political developments associated with it throughout the world. . . . Thanks to Keynes, economics offered me the best of both worlds. (James Tobin)

In the first semester of my sophomore year I took required courses in accounting and microeconomics. The former was, in reality, bookkeeping—and mindless bookkeeping at that. I loathed it. But microeconomics had everything: rigor, relevance, structure, and logic. I found its allure irresistible. The next semester I changed my major to economics and never turned back.

Thus my first stroke of luck. I sometimes break out in a cold sweat thinking about what might have happened had I taken a modern accounting course and an institutional economics course. (William Sharpe)

My choice of Colorado College was more eventful then I could have forecasted. . . . In my junior year, I took a readings class in economic growth from Ray Werner. . . . We read Ricardo, Smith, and Arthur Lewis. . . . The professor also gave me his copy of Samuelson's *Foundations of Economic Analysis* (which I still own) to read as an extra bonus. Samuelson's *Foundations* had a major impact on me. It demonstrated to me that economics could be as rigorous and empirically relevant as physics. . . . At the same time, it showed that economics had empirical content through the theory of revealed preference. I saw a counterpart in social science to the hard science I had experienced in Oppenheimer's classroom. Lewis's *Theory of Economic Growth* appealed to my liberal arts training. . . . This junior year readings class led me to decide on economics as a career. . . . I could have my science and my social science, too. (James Heckman)

For at least some, economics appears to be chosen because alternatives paths are closed or unappealing:

I gather that the sponsors of this set of lectures hope to see how one's thinking is tied to one's environment. I am not a very good example. I began by showing you that I became an economist when I really wanted to be an engineer, became a university teacher because there was nothing else for me to do, and became an applied economist because that was my mentor's subject. The next phase of this story continues in the same vein. I am not complaining; fate has been kinder to me than to most other persons. I am merely recording what happened. (W. Arthur Lewis)

I was not an immediate success in Australia. My English was not very good and my Hungarian university degrees in pharmacy and philosophy were not recognized in Australia. It was clear that I would have to do factory work, which I did on and off for three years. Often I was unemployed because my manual skills were very deficient. I typically could not keep any factory job for more than a few days. Sometimes I would keep a job for a couple of weeks, but this was the exception. . . . I enrolled at the University of Sydney as an evening student. I did so as a student in economics. . . . I loved the logical elegance of economic theory. (John Harsanyi)

The desire for relevance is an important theme in the lectures. As indicated in the earlier quote from James Tobin, for the older generation of Nobel laureates it was the Great Depression that triggered interest in economics. Tobin, as well as other laureates, make this point forcefully:

Keynes's uprising against encrusted error was an appealing crusade for youth. The truth would make us free, and fully employed too. . . . Economic knowledge advances when striking real-world events and issues pose puzzles we have to try to understand and resolve. (James Tobin)

Yes, 1932 was a great time to be born as an economist. The sleeping beauty of political economy was waiting for the enlivening kiss of new methods, new paradigms, new hired hands, and new problems. Science is a parasite: the greater the patient population the better the advance in physiology and pathology; and out of pathology arises therapy. The year 1932 was the trough of the Great Depression, and from its rotten soil was belatedly begot the new subject that today we call macroeconomics. (Paul Samuelson)

Soon there will be no more active economists who remember the 1930s clearly. The generation of economists that was moved to study economics by the feeling that we desperately needed to understand the depression will soon have retired.

Most of today's younger and middle-aged macroeconomists think of "the business cycle" as a low-variance, moderately autocorrelated, stationary, stochastic process taking place around a generally satisfactory trend. That is an altogether different frame of mind from the one with which I grew up in the profession. (Robert Solow)

Although the Great Depression is long past, the desire for relevance, in particular with respect to social issues, remains important among more recent Nobel laureates. Gary Becker is one example:

During my senior year at Princeton, however, I was losing interest in economics and began to think that I should go into something else. Economics seemed excessively formal to me. . . . Economics appeared incapable of helping me understand the issues in which I had an interest: inequality, class, race, prestige, and similar issues that were important for society. . . . I remained unhappy—unhappy by what seemed to me a disconnect between what economists would talk about in textbooks and elsewhere and what I wanted to talk about. . . . [At Chicago] Milton Friedman became the greatest influence of any individual on my development as an economist. Attending his graduate course in price theory was just exciting, and I would eagerly wait for that course to come twice a week. . . . Here I saw economics as a tool and not simply as a game played by clever academics . . . It . . . showed me what I thought was not possible. You can do economics and do it in a rigorous way and nevertheless talk about important problems. (Gary Becker)

The above quote from Gary Becker shows how Milton Friedman opened his eyes about the relevance of economics. Most who were students at Chicago mention the charismatic importance of Friedman in their lives. Personality matters. But none of the Nobel laureates, even Friedman, is more renowned for their personality than for their scientific work. Becker is far from alone in recognizing the influence of a great teacher or particular individual. Myron Scholes and James Buchanan are among the others:

McMaster turned out to be a fortuitous choice. Because it was such a small school, Professor McIver, a University of Chicago graduate in economics, worked closely with me in my studies. He directed me to read and understand the work of many classic economists, including the more contemporary teachings of Milton Friedman and George Stigler. . . . Because of my enjoyment of economics and my planned return to business, I decided on business school, not law school. Although my family wanted me apply to other schools, such as Harvard, I wanted to go only to the University of Chicago, where Stigler and Friedman were teaching and conducting research. (Myron Scholes)

I am not a "natural economist" as some of my colleagues are, and I did not "evolve" into an economist. Instead I sprang full blown upon intellectual conversion, after I "saw the light." . . . I was indeed converted by Frank Knight, but he almost single-mindedly conveyed the message that there exists no god whose pronouncements deserve elevation to the sacrosanct, whether god within or without the scientific academy. Everything, everyone, anywhere, anytime—all is open to challenge and criticism. There is a moral obligation to reach one's own conclusions, even if this sometimes means exposing the prophet whom you have elevated to intellectual guruship. (James Buchanan)

James Tobin emphasizes the important role played by his graduate school professors, but suggests that much of this learning occurred outside the classroom:

I see in retrospect that our professors left most of our education to us. They expected us to teach ourselves and learn from each other, and we did. They treated us as adult partners in scholarly endeavor, not as apprentices. I am afraid our graduate programs today try too hard to convey a definite and vast body of material and to test how well students master what we know. (James Tobin)

Nearly all the laureates identify a particular work environment, usually but not always a university economics department, as a critical factor in their evolution as an economist. Stigler, Klein, and Sharpe are particularly emphatic on this point:

So to understand the conditions under which modern work in economics has emerged, one must look at the conditions of training and work of the modern scholar. Those conditions are no substitute for creativity, but they have become an indispensable condition for creativity to be exercised. . . . There is good reason for believing that economics is a social science in quite another sense from the indisputable one that it concerns itself with mankind in social relationships. It appears also to be a social science in the literal sense that it is a science in which it is difficult to do creative work if one is not in a congenial intellectual environment. (George Stigler)

A truly exceptional group of people was assembled in Chicago during the late 1940s. I doubt that such a group could ever be put together again in economics. From our closely knit group, four Nobel laureates have emerged, and two others came from the next bunching of Cowles researchers—partly at Chicago and partly at Yale. We worked as a team and focused on a single problem—to put together an econometric model of the American economy (a second attempt after Tinbergen's of the 1930s)—using the best of statistical theory, economic theory, and available data. After about four or five years of intensive research built up around this theme, the team dispersed to new openings in academic life. (Lawrence Klein)

The Rand [Corporation] of 1956 was a truly unique organization. . . . Employees were free to work any hours they chose, within wide limits. Office doors were open, intellectual discussions on the most wide-ranging topics were de rigueur, and everyone was expected to spend one day per week on research of strictly personal interest.

Those were heady days. Some of the key work in systems analysis, operations research, computer science, and applied economics was being done at Rand. One of our first computers was designed by John von Neumann. George Dantzig was working on linear programming. Some of the most illustrious academics served as consultants. Everyone was on a first-name basis. If ever there was a place for one interested in practical theory, the Rand Corporation in the 1950s was it. (William Sharpe)

A common theme in the laureates' lectures is the role of luck. Emphasis on the role of luck no doubt stems in part from the general tone of humility expressed in many of the lectures. Obviously, a combination of brilliance and hard work is a necessary, albeit not sufficient, condition for being awarded a Nobel prize. The laureates often use the term "luck" to mean the unpredictability or unplanned path through which their career evolved. Each can readily imagine some alternative turn taken early in life that would have set them on an altogether different path. Friedman and Becker make this fact explicit:

I have been enormously impressed by the role that pure chance plays in determining our life history. . . . As I recalled my own experience and development, I was impressed by the series of lucky accidents that determined the road I traveled. (Milton Friedman)

I soon realized much more was needed. . . . There were no foundations for the theory of investment in human capital. . . . I set about trying to sketch out a small set of foundations to give the work theoretical content. . . . I had no vision at all of what this would lead to. Once again, here is an example of the role of luck. . . . I was amazed and then greatly excited when I began to realize that this framework could integrate scores of observations and regularities in individual earnings, occupational differences in earnings, and employment. (Gary Becker)

One area where there is not a consensus among the laureates is how research programs are developed. The quote above from Gary Becker shows that he had little idea what eventually would develop from his early forays into human capital theory. Many of the laureates likewise insist that their research was not part of any grand design or vision, but rather evolved within the highly competitive market for ideas. Coase, Buchanan, and Samuelson are exemplars:

If his words are interpreted to mean that I started with a relatively simple theory and gradually, purposefully added building blocks until I had accumulated all that were needed to construct a theory of the institutional structure, it would give a misleading view of the development of my ideas. I never had a clear goal until quite recently. I came to realize where I had been going only after I arrived. The emergence of my ideas at each stage was not part of some grand scheme. In the end I found myself with a collection of blocks which, by some miracle, fit together to form, not a complete theory, but, as Lars Werin indicated, the foundation for such a theory. (Ronald Coase)

I recognize of course that my own research-publication record may be interpreted as the output of a methodological and normative individualist whose underlying purpose has always been to further philosophical support for individual liberty. In subjective recall, however, this motivational thrust has never informed my conscious work effort. I have throughout my career and with only a few exceptions sought to clarify ambiguities and confusions and clear up neglected pockets of analysis in the received arguments of fellow economists, social scientists, and philosophers. To the extent that conscious motivation has entered these efforts, it has always been the sheer enjoyment of working out ideas, of creating the reality that is reflected finally in the finished manuscript. (James Buchanan)

Repeatedly I have denied the great-man or great-work notion of science. Every drop helps, the old farmer said, as he spat into the pond. One does the best one can on the most pressing problem that presents. And, if after you have done so, your next moves are down a trajectory of diminishing returns, then still it is optimal to follow the rule of doing the best that there is to do. Besides, at any time a Schumpeterian innovation or Darwinian mutation may occur to you, plucking the violin string of increasing return. . . . Scientists are as avaricious and competitive as Smithian businessmen. The coin they seek is not apples, nuts, and yachts; nor is it the coin itself, or power as that term is ordinarily used. Scholars seek fame. The fame they seek . . . is fame with their peers—the other scientists whom they respect and whose respect they strive for. (Paul Samuelson)

North, Modigliani, and Tobin are three laureates who describe a more methodical course. One knew where he was headed early on, one attempted to run counter to whatever was currently in fashion, and one states that he consciously aimed for the big problem of his day.

I knew where I was going from the day I decided to become an economist. I set out to understand what made economies rich or poor because I viewed that objective as being the essential prerequisite to improving their performance. The search for the Holy Grail of the ultimate source of economic performance has taken me on a long and certainly unanticipated journey, from Marxism to cognitive science, but it has been this persistent objective that has directed and shaped my scholarly career. (Douglass North)

As I contemplate my contributions, I find one unifying thread: a propensity to swim against the current by challenging the self-evident orthodoxies of the moment, be it that the classics are altogether outdated, or that the rich must save a larger fraction of their income than the poor, or that debt financing is cheaper because the interest rate on high-quality debt is lower than the return on equity.
   I would love to be able to continue to play that role. But I don't want to think too much about where I am going. I just like to let things come and be ready to jump in where there is excitement. (Franco Modigliani)

The most important decisions a scholar makes are what problems to work on. Choosing them just by looking for gaps in the literature is often not very productive and at worst divorces the literature itself from problems that provide more important and productive lines of inquiry. The best economists have taken their subjects from the world around them. (James Tobin)

Important breakthroughs in economics do not occur in a vacuum. Some of the major developments in economics are likely to have occurred in much the same fashion absent the contribution of a particular economist. Other contributions are more distinct—very much shaping the future path of economic literature in that area. These alternative possibilities are evident in the following quotes:

Multiple discoveries are in fact very common in science. . . . Developments in related fields with different motivation help one to understand a difficult problem better. Since these developments are public knowledge, many scholars can take advantage of them. It is pleasant to the ego to be first or among the first with a new discovery. However, in this case at least, the evidence is clear that the development of general equilibrium theory would have gone on quite as it did without me. (Kenneth Arrow)

Further work led to "Expectations and the Neutrality of Money," . . . finally published in the *Journal of Economic Theory* in 1972.

The paper contained a careful and explicit construction of a theoretical example of an economy in which the motives, opportunities, and information of every economic actor was unambiguously spelled out. Expectations were rational. In this setting, as in Friedman's AEA address, there was no long run trade-off between employment and inflation. Yet the model also implied the kind of correlations between employment and inflation that were then widely interpreted as hard evidence that such trade-offs did exist. I felt I understood for the first time both why Friedman and Phelps were right in arguing there was no long run trade-off between unemployment and inflation and why econometric tests continued to reject this "natural rate" view.

Working out this example took me to the limit of my technical skills and beyond: It was not easy reading, nor had it been easy writing. . . . It is easy for me to see the influences of Phelps, Rapping, Prescott, and Cass in this paper, but the combination was new and striking: no one else was doing macroeconomics this way in 1970. The paper made my reputation. (Robert Lucas)

The "lessons from the laureates" identified in this section provide considerable insight into the intellectual process through which ideas in economics, and no doubt in other disciplines, develop and evolve. One cannot come away from these lectures without an appreciation for the critical role of teachers, the intellectual environment, the search for rigor and relevance, and happenstance in the evolution of modern economic thought. Contained within these "lessons" is at least the suggestion that biography matters. It is to this topic that we turn.

Does Biography Matter? Lessons from the Laureates

Do the autobiographies presented at Trinity University over the twenty-year period that began in 1984 reveal anything of scientific significance? Would our understanding of the laureates' path-breaking achievements be incomplete absent these stories of their intellectual journeys, as told in their own words?

The phrase "as told in their own words" is significant. For in the Trinity lecture series each author was the living subject, each providing an "oral history" of his own "evolution as an economist." Of necessity, time constraints forced the scholars to present their glimpses into the past in a much-abbreviated form. What they chose to reveal and not reveal was of their own choosing. But in the case of autobiographical data the voice and image of the living subject is before us in a way not possible in biographies written by others. There is a sense of immediacy in these personal histories that typically will not be found in more impersonal narratives of their lives. It is likely that the more influential of these economists will inspire biographies composed by others long after these subjects have passed from the scene. Absent direct contact with these laureates, they will not capture the uniquely idiosyncratic perspective that only autobiography can provide. For that reason future biographers might find the Trinity lectures providing invaluable insights for their work.

When the senior editor organized the lecture series in 1984, he stated that the larger purpose was to provide important source material for a theory of scientific discovery. Twenty years later it is fair to ask whether the rationale has been in any significant sense justified. Do these autobiographical accounts reveal a connection between the economist's life and his intellectual achievements?

Certainly the lectures make obvious some links between one's environment and subsequent intellectual development. The traumatic impact of the Great Depression led several future laureates to identify economics as their intellectual discipline of choice. But this evidence for the role of biography hardly suffices. After all, the most casual observation would lead one to expect that experience affects choices. Does the study of the lives of the laureates do nothing more than confirm what everybody knows? Or can we say something about the extent to which the very substance of their contributions is a reflection of the individual lives they have led?

This last question is complex and can be answered only through the careful study of the autobiographies themselves. In that way, we become observer-participants in the lives of the speakers, focusing not only on what they explicitly reveal, but also for any inconsistencies and self-deceptions in their narratives. But in doing so the authors of this afterword must assume the role of biographers themselves, as distinct from the autobiographer/subjects of the lecture series. Autobiography is, of course, a subset of biography. But it forms a crucial part of the archive from which biographical data are drawn. The autobiographies provide valuable material from which we, as biographer/editors, try to reach a deeper understanding of the connection between the lives led and the path-breaking work achieved. If we can accomplish this task the larger purpose of the lecture series will have been realized.

In the introduction to this volume we asserted that "these autobiographical essays reveal psychological truths, perhaps hidden from the subjects themselves, that an especially perceptive reader will discern." The autobiographical elements give us some tantalizing glimpses into the imaginative and creative minds of these scholars, insights that only autobiography could provide. Below we provide three examples.

The link between autobiography and subsequent intellectual development is made explicit in James Heckman's essay. As Heckman recounts his childhood,

My father fell victim to company politics and suffered various demotions and lateral transfers throughout his career. . . . He urged me at an early age to enter a profession where I could develop an independent reputation and avoid the politics of the bureaucracy of middle managers that he had experienced. I took his message to heart and decided early on to enter a profession where I could make my own mark independent of the good will of any superior and where I would never have to be a company man (James Heckman)

His father's career also took his family to towns in the border South and West, where "I saw firsthand the last vestiges of the Jim Crow system of racial discrimination. Its protocols and intrinsically demeaning effects on all participants fascinated me."

Also critical for Heckman was his early faith, being raised in a tradition of fundamentalist Protestant Christianity. "As a young child, I fervently embraced the faith of my parents and by age eight, I was a child minister giving sermons on Sunday evenings introduced by a motto taken from the New Testament, 'A little child shall lead them.' It was expected that when I became an adult, I would be a minister. . . . My deep religious belief led me to read and study the Bible. I committed vast passages to memory." But Heckman's deep faith did not survive:

By my early teenage years . . . I began having doubts. . . . I began to notice inconsistencies in the Bible, and as I read more broadly in science and philosophy, I came to question the literal interpretations of creation and aspects of the fundamentalist Christianity with which I was raised. . . . The intolerance, bigotry, and unwillingness of most of the elders in my church to discuss ideas left me deeply dissatisfied. I found that I was unable to accept authority qua authority, a trait that has characterized me ever since. . . . At the same time, I learned early to live off my own intellectual and emotional resources. (James Heckman)

Heckman ends his essay by summarizing his approach to economics:

Economics is useful only if it helps to explain the economy and solve practical problems. It produces wise policy advice when it is anchored in data and potentially dangerous advice when it is not. . . . Good answers to these questions require good theory and econometrics. . . . Anchoring my own research in serious empirical analysis has protected me from the fads that plague the profession and has given me the autonomy and independence I have always craved. . . . This is my way of following my father's advice of being independent and developing an independent reputation, and my way of avoiding appeals to authority in any form— whether mathematical or divine—that motivated my early break with organized religion.

For Heckman, the lessons of his childhood experience not only made the choice of economics and empirical inquiry irresistible, but also helped frame his personal and intellectual approach to his career within economics.

Intriguing glimpses into these private realms can be illustrated as well by the example of Robert Lucas, although here the link is not made explicit for the reader. Lucas begins his memoir with a reminiscence of his mother, who worked as a commercial artist drawing newspaper ads for a clothing store. He tells us that she took him and his two siblings (at ages 6, 4, and 3) to an apparel shop in downtown Seattle where she received the items that were to be advertised by the store the following week. His recollection of this early childhood experience is told in vivid detail:

She would take the three of us . . . all of us struggling to keep up with her clicking heels, on the half mile walk to the bus and then on the long bus ride downtown, to the McDougal's store. There we would sit still while she handed over her drawings from last week, and discussed her assignments for the week to come, and put the articles to be advertised into a shopping bag. . . . At home, she took out a dress, shoes, and a belt from the shopping bag. She hung the dress up on a hanger near the drawing board, in the living room of the shabby house we rented during the war, and put the accessories in front of her, at the top of the board. She set out her paints—pure white, glossy black, elegant grays—and her tiny brushes, and as I watched there came into being on paper a confident and attractive woman, stylishly dressed in what I had seen as nothing more than an ordinary dress, limp on the hanger. (Robert Lucas)

Lucas's creative work for which he is admired by his peers and which earned him his Nobel is his construction of ingenious theoretical models of the economy that brought a refocusing of the way economists think about the world. In his own words he gives his opinion of why he values mathematical modeling: "It is a method to get to new levels of understanding the way things work. . . . It is this struggle to capture behavior in tractable models that leads us deeper into the economics of market transactions and forms the progressive element in economic thought" Just as the ordinary dress on the hanger was transformed into a stylishly dressed woman at the artistic hands of his mother, so too would his own model building bring us to new levels of viewing and understanding the welter of confusing data that make up the macroeconomy. Lucas's choice of subject matter to open his lecture is surely a way of leading his audience into a significant area of his being. We are allowed to see him as the observant little boy who had watched with astonishment as his mother skillfully used paints and tiny brushes to transform something ordinary and mundane into something beautiful.

What are we to make of this unexpected story? Surely this: long before Lucas had a conscious interest in economics, he had cultivated an eye for bringing new ways of seeing the evidence before him. This tale of innocence and wisdom was surely a crucial episode in his life. The story offers grounds for conjecture about the value of autobiographical details in bringing us to understand at least some part of the creative process.

A final example linking autobiography and one's intellectual approach is that of Milton Friedman. But here, we attempt to draw a perhaps unconscious link that the author has not drawn. Friedman made it respectable for economists to question the efficacy of Keynesian policy; he resurrected the quantity theory of money and placed it on a secure footing; and he championed the private market economy at a time when intellectuals who did so were often subjected to ostracism in respectable academic circles. Few would doubt that we are all richer for his having become an economist. But why did he enter graduate school in economics? Initially Friedman had planned to choose mathematics because he liked the subject. But the Great Depression was underway and Friedman was intrigued by what he called "the great paradox of great need on the one hand and unused resources on the other." Moreover, making the decision process more difficult, he had offers of financial aid from two universities, one for the study of mathematics at Brown; the other to study economics at Chicago. The final decision came down almost to the toss of a coin. Economics and the puzzle of the Great Depression won out. In his autobiographical lecture he attempts to explain his choice. To do so he quotes Robert Frost's famous poem, "The Road Less Traveled."

Two roads diverged in a yellow wood,
And sorry I could not travel both
I took the one less traveled by.
And that has made all the difference.

And yet, reference to the Frost poem does not seem appropriate in his case. During the Great Depression, when Friedman entered college, economics was not the road "less traveled by." To the contrary, it was among the most popular of majors. He said he chose economics because of its relevance to the issues of the day, as with so many others of his generation. But this leaves us with a mystery. What is the relevance of Robert Frost's poem? Why did he quote it?

Perhaps the choice of the poem reveals something about Friedman that was hidden from him when he quoted its words. Even if entering economics during the Great Depression was not really taking the road less traveled, nevertheless Friedman's subsequent career persistently took him along untrampled pathways *within economics*. Was this a conscious decision? For in his attempt to answer questions posed by the depression, Friedman stood apart and almost alone. He rejected the Keynesian solutions that the overwhelming majority of the profession had come to accept. Friedman has lived long enough to see many of his ideas become the consensus view of a younger generation of economists. Because he was different, he attracted attention; his persuasive powers, style, and charisma did the rest. For Friedman, the road "less traveled" indeed "made all the difference."

In the end, the case for biography is a strong one. To believe that biography is *essential* for understanding economics and the evolution of economic ideas, however, admittedly requires a leap of faith. We simply are unable to meaningfully compare the current state of economic science to what might have existed under some reasonable counterfactual. That being said, the eighteen lectures in this volume provide strong evidence that biography matters. We have seen how the most important developments in modern economics did not spring out of the air randomly, but were intimately related to the laureates' backgrounds, intellectual environments, interactions with teachers and colleagues, their desire for relevance and rigor, and competition in the marketplace for ideas. For individual laureates, the road traveled was sometimes the result of happenstance and sometimes not. Following the laureates on their intellectual journeys not only makes for fascinating reading, but also has greatly enriched our understanding of the development of contemporary economic thought.

Notes

Introduction

1. For an authoritative discussion of the history, purpose, and qualifications for the Nobel Prize in Economics by one of the members of the Prize Committee, see Assar Lindbeck, "The Prize in Economic Science in Memory of Alfred Nobel," *Journal of Economic Literature* 23 (March 1985): 37–56.

2. See William Breit, "Biography and the Making of Economic Worlds," *Southern Economic Journal* 53 (April 1987): 823–833.

Klein

1. *The Brookings Quarterly Econometric Model of the United States,* eds. J. Duesenberry, G. Fromm, L. Klein, and E. Kuh (Chicago: Rand McNally, 1965); *The Brookings Model: Some Further Results,* eds. J. Duesenberry, G. Fromm, L. Klein, and E. Kuh (Chicago: Rand McNally, 1969); *The Brookings Model: Perspectives and Recent Developments,* eds. G. Fromm and L. Klein (Amsterdam: North-Holland, 1975).

2. Irma and Frank Adelman, "The Dynamic Properties of the Klein-Goldberger Model," *Econometrica* 27 (October 1959): 596–625; H. Wagner, "A Monte Carlo Study of Estimates of Simultaneous Linear Structural Equations," *Econometrica* 26 (January 1958): 117–133.

3. The evolution of project LINK is spelled out in three volumes and updated by some descriptive articles. See R. J. Ball, *The International Linkage of National Economic Models,* J. Waelbroeck, *The Models of Project LINK,* J. Sawyer, *Modelling the International Transmission Mechanism* (Amsterdam: North-Holland, 1973, 1976, 1979); B. G. Hickman and L. R. Klein, "A Decade of Research by Project LINK," *ITEMS,* Social Science Research Council, N.Y. (December 1979); 49–56; L. R. Klein, Peter Pauly, and Pascal Volsin, "The World Economy—A Global Model," *Perspectives in Computing* 2 (May 1982): 4–17.

Stigler

1. "The Adoption of the Marginal Utility Theory," reprinted in G. J. Stigler, *The Economist as Preacher* (Chicago: University of Chicago Press, 1982): 72–85.

Buchanan

1. James M. Buchanan, "The Qualities of a Natural Economist," in Charles Rowley, ed., *Democracy and Public Choice* (New York: Blackwell, 1987): 9–19.

2. James M. Buchanan, "Better Than Plowing," *Banca Nazionale del Lavoro Quarterly Review* 159 (December 1986): 359–375.

3. For an extended discussion of Knight's ambiguity in this respect, see my paper, "The Economizing Element in Knight's Ethical Critique of Capitalist Order," *Ethics* 98 (October 1987): 61–75.

4. For a discussion of two kinds of socialism in this setting, see the title essay in my book, *Liberty, Market, and State: Political Economy in the 1980s* (New York: New York University Press, 1985).

5. James M. Buchanan, "The Public Choice Perspective," *Economia delle scelte publiche* 1 (January 1983): 7–15.

6. Cecil G. Phipps, "Friedman's 'Welfare' Effects," *Journal of Political Economy* LX (August 1952): 332–334.

7. Milton Friedman, "A Reply," *Journal of Political Economy* LX (August 1952): 334–336.

8. James M. Buchanan and Robert D. Tollison, "A Theory of Truth in Autobiography," *Kyklos* 39 (Fasc. 4, 1986): 507–517.

9. Frank H. Knight, "Fallacies in the Interpretation of Social Cost," *Quarterly Journal of Economics* XXXVIII (1924): 582–606. Reprinted in *The Ethics of Competition* (London: Allen and Unwin, 1935): 217–236.

Sharpe

1. William F. Sharpe, *Investments* (Englewood Cliffs, NJ: Prentice-Hall, 1978).

2. William F. Sharpe, *Investments,* 3d ed. (Englewood Cliffs, NJ: Prentice-Hall, 1985).

3. William F. Sharpe and Cathryn M. Cootner, eds., *Financial Economics: Essays in Honor of Paul Cootner* (Englewood Cliffs, NJ: Prentice-Hall, 1982).

4. Peter L. Bernstein, *Capital Ideas: The Improbable Origins of Modern Wall Street* (New York: The Free Press, 1992).

Coase

1. Virginia Woolf, *Mr. Bennett and Mrs. Brown* (London: Hogarth Press, 1928), pp. 4–5.

2. Frank H. Knight, *Freedom and Reform* (New York: Harper, 1947), p. 244.

3. R. H. Coase, "The Federal Communications Commission," *Journal of Law and Economics* II (October 1959): 27.

4. R. H. Coase, "The Problem of Social Cost," *Journal of Law and Economics* III (October 1960): 18–19; and *The Firm, the Market, and the Law* (Chicago: University of Chicago Press, 1988), pp. 118–119.

5. Edwin Cannan, *A History of the Theories of Production and Distribution in English Political Economy from 1776 to 1848* (London: Staples Press, 1893), p. 392.

North

The author would like to thank Alexandra Benham and Elisabeth Case for editing this essay.

Harsanyi

1. The Harsanyi lecture is based on transcripts of his talk given at Trinity University. The opening section of his talk extends the brief *Autobiography* that was provided to the Nobel Foundation.

Lucas

1. Reprinted in Milton Friedman, *Essays in Positive Economics* (Chicago: University of Chicago Press, 1953).

2. Arjo Klamer, *Conversations with Economists* (Savage, MD: Rowman and Littlefield, 1983), p.223.

Heckman

I wish to thank Pedro Carneiro, Barry Hirsch, Derek Neal, Greg Orlowski and Lynne Pettler Heckman for helpful comments on this essay. References to the papers mentioned in this lecture, as well as to my other research are available at my Web site: <http://lily.src.uchicago.edu/>.

1. John Maynard Keynes, *Essays in Persuasion* (1931), in *The Collected Writings of John Maynard Keynes*, Vol. 9 (London: Macmillan, 1972), p.332.